ONE WEEK LOAN

D1493312

COPYRIGHT LAW IN THE DIGITAL SOCIETY

Multimedia technology is a key component of the Digital Society. This book comprehensively examines the extent to which copyright and database right protect multimedia works. It does so from the perspective of UK law, but with due attention being paid to EU law, international treaties and comparative developments in other jurisdictions, such as Australia and the US. The central argument of the book is that the copyright and database right regimes are, for the most part, flexible enough to meet the challenges presented by multimedia. As a result, it is neither necessary nor desirable to introduce separate copyright protection or *sui generis* protection for multimedia works.

This important and original new work will be essential reading for any lawyer engaged in advising on IP matters relating to the new media industries, and scholars and students working in intellectual property and computer law.

Copyright Law in the Digital Society

The Challenges of Multimedia

Tanya Aplin

School of Law
King's College London

·HART·
PUBLISHING
OXFORD – PORTLAND OREGON
2005

Hart Publishing
Oxford and Portland, Oregon

Published in North America (US and Canada) by
Hart Publishing
c/o International Specialized Book Services
920 NE 58th Avenue, Suite 300
Portland, OR 97213-3786
USA
Tel: +1-503-287-3093 or toll-free: (1) 800-944-6190
Fax: +1 503 280 8832
E-mail: orders@isbs.com
Web Site: www.isbs.com

Hart Publishing, Salter's Boatyard, Folly Bridge,
Abingdon Road, Oxford OX1 4LB
Telephone: +44 (0)1865 245533 or Fax: +44 (0)1865 794882
e-mail: mail@hartpub.co.uk
WEBSITE: http//www.hartpub.co.uk

British Library Cataloguing in Publication Data
Data Available
ISBN-13: 978–1–84113–356–0 (hardback)
ISBN-10: 1–84113–356–6 (hardback)

Typeset by Hope Services (Abingdon) Ltd
Printed and bound in Great Britain by
TJ International Ltd
Padstow, Cornwall

For my parents, Frank and Sue

PREFACE

Multimedia[1] occurs at the intersection of other, wider technological transformations produced by digital, software and networking technologies. At a time when it is common to doubt the ability of copyright law to embrace recent technological developments, it is worthwhile investigating whether it has responded to this particular instance of technological change. The debate concerning the challenges that multimedia presents for copyright law is ongoing. With a few exceptions, a comprehensive and rigorous analysis of the legal issues has not emerged.[2] This book contributes a thorough examination of the protection of multimedia in the UK.

This book is divided into six chapters. The first two chapters deal with the important preliminary issues of defining multimedia and justifications for its protection. Chapter 1 considers the different understandings of multimedia in the technical and legal literature and draws out a working definition. Chapter 2 argues that some theoretical support (based mainly on an economic rationale) exists for protecting multimedia. In the subsequent three chapters, a detailed analysis of UK copyright law and its application to multimedia is undertaken. Chapter 3 considers whether multimedia may fall within existing copyright subject matter and the *sui generis* database regime. Chapters 4 and 5 investigate whether the scope of protection offered by copyright and database right is adequate, from the perspective of exclusive rights and exceptions, respectively. In the light of the preceding analysis, chapter 6 examines at length the need for reform. It argues that the copyright and database right regimes are, on the whole, flexible enough to accommodate multimedia works. Further, that substantial reform, along the lines of a new multimedia category or *sui generis* multimedia right, is unnecessary and undesirable. Some reform of UK copyright law is, however, warranted. Specifically, the category of film work should be replaced by an audiovisual work category. If this reform proves unpalatable to lawmakers then the protection given to film works should, at the very least, extend to preventing unauthorised non-literal reproduction.

---

[1] The concept of 'multimedia' is explored at length in chapter 1.

[2] See I Stamatoudi, *Copyright and Multimedia Works: A Comparative Analysis* (CUP, Cambridge 2002) and to a lesser extent, Julian Rodriguez Pardo, *Copyright and Multimedia* (Kluwer, The Hague, 2003).

This book is a development of my doctoral research. Along the way, I have been fortunate to receive significant financial support from several sources: the Rhodes Trust, IMAGO Multimedia Centre and Baker & McKenzie, London. I have also been greatly assisted by colleagues and library staff at Murdoch University, University of Oxford, University of Cambridge and King's College London, to whom I am indebted. In particular, I would like to thank Professor Michael Blakeney and Professor Fiona Macmillan for encouraging and facilitating my doctoral research in this area. Thanks also to Professor Colin Tapper for his excellent supervision and to my examiners, Professor William R Cornish and Dr Michael Spence, for their constructive comments which enabled me to refine and strengthen my arguments. Special thanks must go to Professor Lionel Bently, Mr David Bausor, Dr Jennifer Davis, Dr Kirsten Campbell, and Ms Estelle Derclaye for reading draft sections of my manuscript and offering insightful comments. Last, but not least, warmest thanks to my family and friends for their abiding generosity and support.

CONTENTS

TABLE OF CASES

United States

TABLE OF LEGISLATION

TABLE OF TREATIES AND CONVENTIONS

1

Understanding Multimedia

If there is a term or phrase that has appeared in more diverse publications than any other over the last few years, it must be multimedia. The number of definitions for it are as numerous as the number of companies that are working on it.[1]

Multimedia is probably one of the most overused terms of the early 1990s.[2]

The term 'multimedia' is amorphous.[3]

Introduction

This book is concerned with the implications of multimedia for copyright law. The immediate question is therefore: what is multimedia? Defining multimedia is not a straightforward task. Pardo suggests that it is 'the relative youthfulness of the concept [of multimedia] . . . that hinder[s] the formulation of a clear-cut definition'.[4] One could also blame the imprecision around meaning on the fact that 'multimedia' became a 'buzz' word during the last decade of the 20th century (along with terms such as 'cyberspace', 'information society', 'digital technology' and 'e-commerce') and thus was liberally and loosely used in technical, popular and legal writing. Although a definition of 'multimedia' has not yet solidified, certain key understandings have emerged in recent years. For example, it could be said that 'multimedia' has been used in three main senses: to describe hardware, commercial enterprises, or products and applications. In the first sense, 'multimedia' is simply being used to describe hardware (such as a sound card, sound driver, speakers, CD-Rom drive, screen display) which has the capacity to show or play different media, such as graphics and sound.[5] As far as commercial enterprises go, Pardo explains that: '[multimedia is] used to describe the commercial enterprises

---

[1] S Heath, *Multimedia and Communications Technology*, 2nd edn (Focal Press, Oxford, 1999) 1.

[2] F Fluckiger, *Understanding Networked Multimedia: Applications and Technology* (Prentice Hall, London, 1995) 3.

[3] M Scott and S Talbott, 'Interactive Multimedia: What is it, Why is it Important and What Does One Need to Know about It?' [1993] 8 *EIPR* 284.

[4] JR Pardo, *Copyright and Multimedia* (Kluwer, The Hague, 2003) 5.

[5] See generally J Tranter, *Linux Multimedia Guide* (O'Reilly, Sebastopol, CA, 1996).

that diversified their investments among different types of media, moving away from their focus on only one segment of the market and expanding their activities to different areas of this business.'[6] An example of this would be the conglomerate, AOL Time Warner, which resulted from the merger of AOL and Time Warner, and whose businesses include 'interactive services, cable systems, filmed entertainment, television networks and publishing.'[7] Finally, multimedia applications or products are works which are a digitised combination of diverse media with which a user can interact. It is 'multimedia' in this third sense which poses the greatest challenge for copyright law and which dominates most of the literature. It will be in this sense that the term 'multimedia' is used this book.

To arrive at a working definition of 'multimedia' this chapter begins with a brief survey of how technical commentators view multimedia in order to provide an industry-based understanding of this technology. It then goes on to consider how multimedia has been portrayed in the legal literature.

Technical View

The broadest understanding of 'multimedia' probably comes from Heath, who defines it as 'the use or presentation of data in two or more forms'.[8] According to this definition, a wide range of communication forms would qualify as multimedia, including television programmes, films,[9] plays and encyclopaedias. However, most technical commentators depict multimedia in a more limited sense, describing it typically as a *digital, computerised combination* of *multiple media* available in either *off-line* or *on-line* form with which users can *interact.*

Considerable support exists for the view that, in order to qualify as multimedia, the multiple, diverse inputs that are combined together must be *digital* and *computerised.*[10] For example, Fluckiger[11] describes multimedia as 'the field concerned

---

   [6] Pardo (2003) p 6.

   [7] See 'Overview' on official website http://www.aoltimewarner.com/.

   [8] Heath (1999) p 1.

   [9] According to J Monaco, *How to Read a Film: Movies, Media, Multimedia,* 3rd edn (OUP, Oxford, 2000) 534: 'Artists have been combining text, images, and sounds since the invention of movies. Edison was the first multimedia artist, and film is the first multimedium.'

   [10] See *The Hutchinson Dictionary of Computing, Multimedia and the Internet,* 3rd edn (Helicon, Oxford, 1999) 190 (hereinafter: 'Hutchinson Dictionary'); F Botto, *Dictionary of Multimedia and Internet Applications: a Guide for Developers and Users* (Wiley, Chicester, 1999) 220–21; N Chapman and J Chapman, *Digital Multimedia* (Wiley, Chicester, 2000); B Cotton and R Oliver, *The Cyberspace Lexicon: An Illustrated Dictionary of Terms from Multimedia to Virtual Reality* (Phaidon Press, London, 1994) 121; RA Earnshaw and JA Vince (eds), *Multimedia Systems and Applications* (Academic, London, 1995) 104; Fluckiger (1995) p 5; DD Peck, *Pocket Guide to Multimedia* (Delmar Publishers, New York, 1999) 3; F Steinmetz and K Nahrstedt, *Multimedia: Computing, Communications and Applications* (Prentice Hall, Upper Saddle River, NJ, 1995) 15–16; Tranter (1996) pp 3–4.

   [11] Fluckiger (1995) p 5.

with the *computer-controlled integration* of text, graphics, still and moving images, animation, sounds, and any other medium where every type of information can be represented, stored, transmitted, and processed *digitally*' (emphasis supplied). In the *Hutchinson Dictionary* multimedia is defined as:

> [A] computerized method of presenting information by combining audio and video components using text, sound, and graphics (still, animated, and video sequences) . . . Multimedia applications emphasize interactivity between the computer and the user.[12]

The digital quality of the combination refers simply to the fact that each input is encoded in (a common) binary notation. Such encoding allows diverse inputs, including text, still images, moving images, graphics, music and other sounds, to be combined together into the same (digital) format. Although the different types of information are represented in a common, binary notation and thus rendered capable of being integrated onto the same digital storage device, each type of information may be dealt with *independently* from the others, which is not the case with analogue technology.[13] The computerised nature of the combination flows directly from the digital nature of the inputs since digital data can only be processed with the aid of a computer processor.

The digital and computerised combination that forms the basis of multimedia appears to have additional quantitative and qualitative characteristics. Quantitatively speaking, multimedia logically has to include the combination of *two or more* different types of media. Further, a large combination of media can be envisaged, since sizeable amounts of digitised information can be stored with the aid of data compression techniques.[14] Qualitatively speaking, Steinmetz and Nahrstedt suggest that the requisite two or more media must include *both* discrete and continuous media in order to understand multimedia in more than just a quantitative sense and to differentiate it from systems that existed prior to the notion of multimedia being used in a computer environment.[15] Generally speaking, discrete media means space-based media, while continuous media refers to time-based media.[16] Fluckiger also agrees that multimedia should include both types of media, arguing that, '[t]he term multimedia when used by the profession usually implies that at least one of text, graphics, or image—what we shall later call discrete media—is associated with either audio or motion video information—what we shall call later continuous media.'[17] Similarly, Tranter maintains

[12] *Hutchinson Dictionary*, 190.

[13] Fluckiger (1995) p 9 and Steinmetz and Nahrstedt (1995) pp 15–16.

[14] N Negroponte, *Being Digital* (Hodder & Stoughton, London, 1995) 15–17.

[15] Steinmetz and Nahrstedt (1995) pp 14–15. At 15 they state: 'one should talk about multimedia only when both continuous and discrete media are utilized. A text processing program with incorporated images is therefore not a multimedia application.'

[16] Fluckiger (1995) p 7. See Steinmetz and Nahrstedt (1995) pp 13–14, for a more detailed understanding.

[17] Fluckiger (1995) p 7.

that multimedia will often include continuous media, such as sound and moving images.[18]

Interactivity is viewed as another crucial feature of multimedia, although most commentators see it as a typical, as opposed to mandatory, feature.[19] The scope of interactivity is heavily influenced by the underlying software used in the multimedia work and 'the amount of control offered is strictly limited within parameters established by the multimedia producer'.[20] Interactivity also appears to be understood as involving typically non-linear user interaction,[21] but the technical literature does not elaborate much else on the requisite level of interactivity. The interactive quality of multimedia has been the subject of more discussion amongst legal commentators.

According to most technical commentators, multimedia is not limited to a particular distribution form,[22] but may be available in stand-alone (or off-line) form and networked (or on-line) form. The former refers to 'stand-alone applications which make use of no extra resources than those present on the local system to provide the multimedia services',[23] whereas the latter refers to multimedia that is accessed or offered at a distance.[24] In the past, multimedia has often been distributed in tangible media, such as Compact Disc-Read Only Memory (CD-Rom), Compact Disc Interactive (CD-I), and Digital Versatile Disc-Read Only Memory (DVD-Rom). However, it is increasingly being distributed across networks, with the Internet being the most significant network at present.[25] The trend towards on-line distribution of multimedia is explicable because it 'offers possibilities which are not available offline. In particular, it enables the delivery of (almost) live multimedia content, which in turn makes possible novel applications such as video conferencing and broadcast multimedia.'[26]

However, so long as domestic Internet connections remain slow (because of low bandwidth), then off-line distribution of multimedia will continue to have market value.[27] Since multimedia may be distributed in off-line and on-line forms, this

[18] Tranter (1996) p 3.

[19] Botto (1999) pp 220–22; Chapman and Chapman (2000) pp 13, 15; Fluckiger (1995) pp 8–9; B Hansen, *The Dictionary of Multimedia: Terms and Acronyms* (Fitzroy Dearborn, Chicago, 1999) 205; *Hutchinson Dictionary*, 190: 'Multimedia applications emphasize interactivity between the computer and the user.' See also Tranter (1996); Steinmetz and Nahrstedt (1995); and Earnshaw and Vince (1995), who do not discuss interactivity as a key element. *Cf* Cotton and Oliver (1994) p 121, who regard multimedia as synonymous with interactive multimedia and Negroponte (1995) p 70: 'Interaction is implicit in all multimedia.'

[20] Chapman and Chapman (2000) p 13.

[21] Eg, see Monaco (2000) p 535.

[22] *Cf* Cotton and Oliver (1994) p 121, who argue that interactive multimedia primarily embraces CD-Rom or videodisc based programmes, ie, tangible forms of multimedia.

[23] Fluckiger (1995) p 9.

[24] Fluckiger (1995) p 10.

[25] Botto (1999) p 221; Chapman and Chapman (2000) pp 6–7.

[26] Chapman and Chapman (2000) p 7.

[27] Chapman and Chapman (2000) pp 6–7.

means that potentially a vast array of applications could qualify as multimedia, including interactive cable TV, websites, video games, databases, and stand-alone booths.

The concepts of hypertext, hypermedia and virtual reality are terms which are often mentioned in connection with multimedia. They need to be understood in order to place multimedia in its wider context.

Hypertext refers to 'a document that contains traditional text as well as links to other parts of the document, or other documents.'[28] More specifically, Cotton and Oliver describe hypertext as 'software that enables the user to read texts linked in a variety of linear and non-linear ways, and to create new links between words or passages of text.'[29]

Closely related to hypertext is the notion of hypermedia,[30] which is essentially the application of hypertext to diverse media.[31] The *Hutchinson Dictionary* defines hypermedia as:

> . . . [a] system that uses links to lead users to related graphics, audio, animation, or video files in the same way that hypertext systems link related pieces of text. The World Wide Web is an example of a hypermedia system . . .[32]

Cotton and Oliver provide a more general description of hypermedia as:

> [A]n entirely new kind of media experience born from the marriage of TV and computer technologies. Its raw ingredients are images, sounds, text, animation and video, which can be brought together in any combination. It is a medium that offers 'random access'; it has no physical beginning, middle or end. It is this combination of random access with multiple media that opens up such exciting possibilities for radically new ways to communicate ideas, information and entertainment.[33]

This description highlights the issue of overlap between hypermedia and multimedia. However, Cotton and Oliver appear to regard multimedia as distinct from hypermedia,[34] since they define 'multimedia' as:

> . . . [a] generic term for 'multimedia computing' or 'interactive multimedia': the use of a wide variety of media within a computer interface or hypermedia programme.[35]

---

[28] Tranter (1996) p 41.

[29] Cotton and Oliver (1992) p 148. Note that the *Hutchinson Dictionary* defines hypertext as including linking text *and* pictures.

[30] A term apparently coined by Ted Nelson, according to Cotton and Oliver (1992) p 35.

[31] Note, however, that J Nielsen, *HyperText and HyperMedia* (Academic Press Profession, Cambridge, MA, 1993) prefers to use 'hypertext' in lieu of 'hypermedia'.

[32] *Hutchinson Dictionary*, 142. See also Tranter (1996) p 42 who describes hypermedia as 'hypertext that includes multimedia information such as sound, graphics and video.'

[33] Cotton and Oliver (1992) p 8.

[34] Cotton and Oliver (1994) p 121. See generally B Cotton and R Oliver, *Understanding Hypermedia: from Multimedia to Virtual Reality* (Phaidon Press, London, 1992).

[35] Cotton and Oliver (1992) p 149.

Further, Cotton and Oliver see multimedia as restricted to tangible distribution forms.

Botto also distinguishes between multimedia and hypermedia. However, Botto draws his distinction differently from Cotton and Oliver since he describes hypermedia as 'an extension of the hypertext concept where text is combined with images'.[36] Botto's notion of hypermedia focuses on the combination of text and images only (as opposed to all forms of media). Where his notion of hypermedia coincides with that of Cotton and Oliver's is that it requires that hypermedia is presented or accessed in a non-linear fashion.[37] Botto's understanding of hypermedia is narrower than most because it is restricted to text and images.

Earnshaw and Vince also describe hypermedia as distinct from multimedia because it is:

> . . . a comprehensive multimedia system that also has hyperlinks between its 'pages' . . . A hypermedia system is a hypertext system that incorporates a significant number of distinct media types. We prefer the term hypermedia because the term 'multimedia' does not connote hypertext functionally.[38]

Finally, Nielsen stresses that multimedia and hypermedia are not interchangeable concepts and that multimedia is not inherently hypertextual in nature. Rather, it is only when multimedia allows users 'interactively [to] take control of a set of dynamic links' that it will have a hypertextual quality.[39]

It seems that the line between hypermedia and multimedia is drawn differently according to different commentators. Earnshaw and Vince, along with Nielsen, see multimedia as a combination of media types but without hypertext functionality (or least not as an essential element). Cotton and Oliver see multimedia as an example of hypermedia, but restricted to tangible distribution forms. Botto sees multimedia as the hypertext concept applied to *all* forms of media, and yet according to other definitions his understanding would be labelled hypermedia. There is thus some evident confusion in the literature about the nature of the differences between hypermedia and multimedia.[40]

Virtual reality is also mentioned in connection with multimedia. However, virtual reality appears to be more readily distinguishable from multimedia than is hypermedia. The *Hutchinson Dictionary* defines 'virtual reality' in terms of its hardware as:

> . . . [an] advanced form of computer simulation, in which a participant has the illusion of being part of an artificial environment. The participant views the environment through two tiny television screens (one for each eye) built into a visor. Sensors detect

[36] Botto (1999) p 147.
[37] Botto (1999) pp 147–48. See also Cotton and Oliver (1994) p 98.
[38] Earnshaw and Vince (1995) p 81.
[39] Nielsen (1993) p 10.
[40] For Hansen (1999) p 205, however, multimedia is equated to hypermedia.

movements of the participant's head or body, causing the apparent viewing position to change. Gloves (datagloves) fitted with sensors may be worn, which allow the participant seemingly to pick up and move objects in the environment.[41]

Cotton and Oliver prefer to describe virtual reality in terms of its functionalities:

> The simulation of reality through realtime 3d animation, position tracking and stereo audio and video techniques. By immersing the user within a computer generated, simulated environment, VR systems introduce an entirely new way of interacting with multimedia information.[42]

Finally, Monaco's description of virtual reality demonstrates how the concept may be understood in both narrow and broad senses:

> In its narrowest commercial sense, virtual reality intends to apply digital technology to computer games and entertainment to increase the apparent reality of the experience by making it both more verisimilitudinous and more fully interactive.
>
> At one extreme lies 'fully immersive' virtual reality, which attempts a full range of sensory impression, including three-dimensional video, full-range audio and touch. At the other end of the scale we find basic, yet elegant, applications that simply allow us to control our point of view of standard images.[43]

In having a continuum of sophistication, multimedia is similar to virtual reality. The fact that multimedia encompasses a range of works, from off-line to on-line, from unsophisticated to sophisticated, exacerbates some of the legal difficulties posed by this technology. However, there seems to be a clear point of distinction between virtual reality and multimedia, namely that the aim of virtual reality is to create a verisimilar environment.[44]

This brief review of the technical literature highlights that multimedia is accepted as a technological phenomenon and that its characteristics are generally agreed upon. At the same time, it exposes the fact that multimedia is fairly loosely defined and its relationship with other technological concepts (particularly hypermedia) is inadequately explained.

Legal View

There is a significant body of literature concerning the legal implications of multimedia. This literature reveals a reasonably uniform understanding of the

---

[41] *Hutchinson Dictionary*, 283.

[42] Cotton and Oliver (1992) p 151.

[43] Monaco (2000) p 544.

[44] N Fawcett, *Multimedia* (Hodder & Stoughton, Berkshire, 1994) 8 explains that '[i]n its simplest form VR is the creation of a virtual world with which we, the users, can interact' and that virtual reality is closely linked to multimedia.

characteristics of multimedia.[45] Most legal commentators agree that multimedia is a *computerised combination,* in *digital* form, of at *least two or more different media* (such as text, sound, still images, moving images, and graphics).[46] Some commentators suggest that the combination will contain a large quantity of diverse media, mainly because large amounts of digital data can be stored with the aid of data compression techniques.[47] Finally, commentators generally agree that an essential characteristic of multimedia is that it is *interactive,*[48] and that it may come in *off-line* form (such as CD-Rom, CD-I or special purpose location based

---

[45] Although some commentators leave the reader to supply her own understanding of multimedia to the text: eg, JM Conley and K Bemelmans, 'Intellectual Property Implications of Multimedia Products: A Case Study' (1997) 6 *Information and Communications Technology Law* 3; P Kamina, *Film Copyright in the European Union* (CUP, Cambridge, 2002) discussing multimedia at 79 and 92; A Latreille, 'The Legal Classification of Multimedia Creations in French Copyright Law' in I Stamatoudi and P Torremans (eds), *Copyright in the New Digital Environment* (Sweet & Maxwell, London, 2000) 45–74; and YF Lim, 'Multimedia: Authorisers of Copyright Infringement?' (1994) *J L & Inf Sc* 306. Pardo (2003) pp 6–8, points to three possible definitions of 'multimedia', but manages to arrive at workable and defensible definition.

[46] J Choe, 'Interactive Multimedia: A New Technology Tests the Limits of Copyright Law' (1994) 46 *Rutgers L Rev* 929, 931; F Daun, 'The Content Shop: Toward an Economic Legal Structure for Clearing and Licensing Multimedia Content' (1996) 30 *Loyola of Los Angeles L Rev* 215, 216; J Davies, 'The Developing Law of Multimedia' (1994) 10 *Computer Law & Practice* 6; J Douglas, 'Too Hot to Handle? Copyright Protection of Multimedia' (1997) 8 *AIPJ* 96; A Fitzgerald and C Cifuentes, 'Copyright Protection for Digital Multimedia Works' [1999] *Ent L Rev* 23; M Gilligan, 'The Multimedia Maze—an Illustration of the Legal Rights in Multimedia Products' (1997) 2 *Communications Law* 49; J Goldberg, 'Now that the Future has Arrived, Maybe the Law should Take a Look: Multimedia Technology and its Interaction with the Fair Use Doctrine' (1995) 44 *American University L Rev* 919, 921; M Henry, *Publishing and Multimedia Law* (Butterworths, London, 1994), ch 19; S Jones, 'Multimedia and the Superhighway: Exploring the Rights Minefield' (1996) 1 *Communications Law* 28; R Kreile and J Becker, 'Multimedia und die Praxis der Lizenzierung von Urheberrrechten' [1996] *GRUR Int* 677, 689; P Leonard, 'Beyond the Future—Multimedia and the Law' (1994) 7 *Australian Intellectual Property Law Bulletin* 105; U Loewenheim, 'Multimedia and the European Copyright Law' (1996) 27 *IIC* 41; HJ Meeker, 'Multimedia and Copyright' (1994) 20 *Rutgers Computer and Technology Law Journal* 375; Pardo (2003) p 10; C Saez, 'Enforcing Copyright in the Age of Multimedia' (1995) 21 *Rutgers Computer and Technology Law Journal* 351; Scott and Talbott (1993); I Stamatoudi, *Copyright and Multimedia Works: A Comparative Analysis* (CUP, Cambridge, 2002) pp 19–20; I Stamatoudi, 'To What Extent are Multimedia Products Databases?' in I Stamatoudi and P Torremans (eds), *Copyright in the New Digital Environment* (Sweet & Maxwell, London, 2000) 19, at 21–22; RD Sprague, 'Multimedia: the Convergence of New Technologies and Traditional Copyright Issues' (1994) 71 *Denv U L Rev* 635; G Wei, 'Multimedia and Intellectual and Industrial Property Rights in Singapore' (1995) 3 *Int J of L & Information Technology* 214.

[47] Daun (1996) p 224 (referring to the volume of content); J Jonkers and W Wanrooij, 'Music, Copyright and New Techniques Seen From The Perspective Of Collecting Societies' in W Roos and J Seignette, (eds), *Multimedia Deals In The Music Industry* (Apeldoorn, MAKLU, 1996), 131–41; Stamatoudi (2002) pp 23, 24.

[48] Choe (1994) p 933; Daun (1996) p 216; Davies (1994); Douglas (1997); Fitzgerald and Cifuentes (1999); Goldberg (1995) pp 927–928; Kreile and Becker (1996) p 689; Leonard (1994); Jones (1996) p 28; Pardo (2003) p 10; G Pedde, 'Multimedia Works under Italian Copyright Law and Contractual Practice' [1988] 2 *Ent L R* 39, 42; M Radcliffe, 'Legal Issues in New Media: Multimedia for Publishers' in D Campbell and S Cotter (eds), *International Intellectual Property Law: New Developments* (Wiley, Chicester, 1995) 181, 182; Saez (1995); Sprague (1994); Stamatoudi (2002) pp 20–21, 24–26; Stamatoudi (2000) p 21; Wei (1995). *Cf* Loewenheim (1996) p 42 who maintains that interactivity is a typical, as opposed to mandatory, feature of multimedia.

machines) or *on-line* form (such as computer networks like the Internet, inter-active television, or video on demand).[49]

Multimedia is portrayed in the legal literature in a manner similar to that in the technical literature, with two main exceptions. First, there is no suggestion in the legal literature of a qualitative requirement for the combination of diverse media (ie, a combination of discrete *and* continuous media). Second, there is a greater discussion of interactivity and hence wider divergence in views concerning what interactivity entails.

This next section will explore the notion of interactivity that emerges from the legal literature. For some, interactivity is depicted as the opposite of passive use. For example, Radcliffe comments that, 'multimedia works tend to be interactive instead of passive, unlike traditional copyrightable works such as books and films, which are passive and are not changed by the action of the "viewer"'.[50] When Radcliffe uses the word 'passive', he does not seem to be suggesting that the user is an empty vessel into which communications are poured without intellectual processing, but rather he refers to the inability of the user to affect or alter the communication that is being received.[51]

Commentators also describe interactivity in terms of a user's ability to interact with the content in a *non-linear* manner.[52] According to Goldberg, non-linearity is the potential for a user to '*choose* to go from A to B, or to C, or from B to A and then to D, or to A1, or to Z23' and consequently 'each person who uses multi-media will rarely use it in the same way as another.'[53] The non-linear quality of multimedia is also contrasted with the linear nature of other works, such as film. Pedde comments that:

[49] Choe (1994) p 931 (stating that multimedia CD-Roms are the most popular distribution form, but anticipating that in the future multimedia would also be in on-line form); Davies (1994); Douglas (1997); Fitzgerald and Cifuentes (1999); Gilligan (1997) p 49; Goldberg (1995) p 927; Henry (1994); Leonard (1994); Loewenheim (1996); Meeker (1994); Pedde (1988) p 39; Saez (1995); M Sherwood-Edwards and J Dickens, 'Legal Developments in Multimedia in 1994' in E Barendt, (ed), *Yearbook of Media and Entertainment Law 1995* (Clarendon Press, Oxford, 1995) 457 (noting the shift in meaning of multimedia from mainly off-line media to also include on-line distribution); Sprague (1994); Stamatoudi (2002) pp 16, 22; Wei (1995). *Cf* Daun (1996) p 223 who suggests that most multimedia is disk-based, a not uncommon view at the time, but now it appears that the on-line format will proba-bly triumph because of better bandwidth and the increased flexibility given by this distribution form.

[50] Radcliffe (1995) p 182.

[51] Eg, Sprague (1994) p 637 in discussing interactivity, states that '[t]he recipient can control the manner in which the information is delivered, change the order and method in which it is presented, and alter the final product.'

[52] D Bainbridge, *Intellectual Property,* 5th edn, (Longman, Harlow, 2002) 235; Daun (1996) p 216; Douglas (1997) pp 97–99; Goldberg (1995) p 928; Leonard (1994) p 106; Pedde (1988) p 42; Pep (1995) p 146.

[53] Goldberg (1995) p 928 (emphasis original). See also Radcliffe (1995) p 182 who states that 'many multimedia works can be revised and re-ordered by the viewer, whereas traditional copyrightable works have a fixed order'.

the multimedia work diverts from the character of the film work in many respects, for example due to multimedia's non-linear structure ... While there is no doubt that a multimedia work is largely comprised of images, these are not reproduced linearly like film frames but rather—in an interactive context—they assign the design of the sequence to the ultimate user of the work.[54]

For Douglas, multimedia must include some non-linearity. However, she argues that there is a wide spectrum of non-linear interaction since:

> At its simplest, a multimedia product may require a user to select a linear sequence from a number of pre-defined options arranged in a non-linear fashion. The user may then be required to select from a further set of options. A more interactive product may allow the user to move or vary objects in the presentation to produce information or trigger different events. The most interactive multimedia product will require a user to participate actively in every step of the presentation, creating her or his own experience, such as by determining how a plot develops by unravelling certain clues.[55] (Footnotes omitted)

On the other hand, Stamatoudi seeks to restrict multimedia to works that feature *substantial* interactivity.[56] Stamatoudi's definition is important because it underpins her argument for a new copyright category of multimedia. Further, she is one of the few commentators to analyse copyright protection of multimedia in any detail. However, her definition is not one which is adopted in this book. In an article published in 2000, Stamatoudi elaborates upon the interactive quality of multimedia in the following terms:

> They [multimedia works] allow users to interact with the information they carry, not simply by giving simple instructions to the machine or by choosing a limited number of available pathways, *but also by manipulating and interfering with the materials contained in them to such an extent that they can morph and blur them.* The outcome of such an activity should not immediately or necessarily be recognisable as one of the elements initially included in the work. That should not necessarily mean that the user should engage himself in the activities of morphing and blurring, *but the potential for such manipulation should be there. In other words, a substantial degree of interactivity should exist.*[57] (Emphasis supplied)

Stamatoudi then goes on to distinguish between unsophisticated and sophisticated forms of multimedia, or, to use her words, first generation and second generation multimedia products, based on whether or not the work features substantial interactivity:

> [In] [p]rimitive forms of multimedia products ... authors may interact with the work but not to a substantial degree. *They may only make simple choices amongst the limited*

---

[54] Pedde (1988) p 42.
[55] Douglas (1997) pp 97–99.
[56] Stamatoudi (2002) pp 19–21, 26; Stamatoudi (2000) pp 21, 22.
[57] Stamatoudi (2000) p 21.

number of options provided by the producer of the work, which in their turn can only give rise to a predefined sequence of images, (eg certain types of video games), or which can affect only the selection or arrangement of the substance of those elements, (eg an electronic encyclopaedia such as Microsoft Encarta). These works (which can be referred to as the first generation of multimedia products) would fall foul of the definition of multimedia works as it is set out in this article.[58] (Emphasis supplied)

Stamatoudi only addresses second generation multimedia products in her 2000 article because she claims that first generation multimedia products can be likened to conventional and existing copyright works, such as films or databases, and thus are adequately protected by existing copyright legislation.[59]

Subsequently, in her monograph *Copyright and Multimedia Works*, Stamatoudi maintains the first generation/second generation distinction. She focuses her analysis on second generation products. This is apparent from the following passage:

> It should be noted that the degree of interactivity is capable of introducing differences in quality between the various multimedia products found on the market. Multimedia works with a primitive form of interactivity (such as electronic encyclopaedias or interactive databases) can still be adequately protected by the existing copyright legislation. This is the *first generation* of multimedia products. However, multimedia works with an advanced level of interactivity (and a sufficient degree of integration of their various elements) constitute the *second generation* of multimedia products. In this book we will primarily focus on the second generation of multimedia products.[60]

It is apparent that Stamatoudi's primary justification for concentrating on second generation multimedia products remains the same, namely, that existing copyright legislation already adequately protects first generation multimedia products.

Unlike Stamatoudi's work, this book does not limit its scope to 'second generation' or sophisticated multimedia works. Instead it addresses multimedia works that range across the spectrum of interactivity for three main reasons. First, it is important to examine (rather than assert) whether or not low-level interactive multimedia is in fact adequately protected by existing copyright law. Second, it is difficult clearly to distinguish between first and second generation multimedia, as is apparent from Stamatoudi's own lack of precision around this distinction. Finally, the bulk of the literature does not favour Stamatoudi's characterisation of multimedia.

The difficulty of distinguishing between first and second generation multimedia requires further elaboration. What does Stamatoudi actually mean when she uses the phrase 'substantial interactivity', which is for her the crux of second generation multimedia products? She stresses this feature as a key difference between

---

[58] Above, at 22.
[59] Above.
[60] Stamatoudi (2002) p 21. (Emphasis original).

multimedia and conventional media. She describes interactivity as occurring when:

> Computer technology allows the user to interact with the information contained in a multimedia work by selecting the pathways that will eventually lead him to the bits of information that will serve his particular needs. He is also offered *the freedom to organise this information as he wishes by manipulating its arrangement, re-arrangement, selection, combination, input or outputs on his screen.*[61] (Emphasis supplied)

More specifically, Stamatoudi refers to the additional potential to manipulate and interfere with the contents 'to such an extent that they [the user] can morph and blur them.'[62] In other words:

> the user must be provided with *the ability to morph* (digitally blur and alter images beyond recognition) *and sample* (sample and blur any kind of works to an unlimited degree). *In other words he must be able to initiate newly created works using existing material.*[63] (Emphasis supplied)

Substantial interactivity apparently means the capacity to morph and sample, thereby creating new material from the material which is contained in the multimedia work. Although Stamatoudi gives examples of first generation multimedia products, namely, electronic encyclopaedias, interactive databases and video games, she does not give examples of second generation multimedia products. Further, according to Stamatoudi's own description of substantial interactivity, it would be possible to characterise some first generation products, such as a video game, as second generation. For example, the video game 'MTV Sports: Snowboarding' gives users the option of taking existing components—half-pipes, mountains, rails—and combining them together in order to build a new course.[64] This sort of interactivity can be considered as creating a new work (ie, a new course) from existing material. We can conclude that insufficient guidance is given as to what qualifies as 'substantially interactive' multimedia. In turn this uncertainty makes the first generation/second generation distinction problematic.

The final reason for not restricting multimedia to works with substantial interactivity (in the sense discussed above) is that there is little support in the literature for this approach. Stamatoudi relies mainly on Choe for the requirement of substantial interactivity. Choe classifies interactivity into five levels, progressing from 'no interactivity' to 'manual interactivity', to 'limited interactivity', to 'true and versatile interactivity' and culminating in 'full interactivity'.[65] Stamatoudi states

---

[61] Above, at 25.
[62] Stamatoudi (2000) p 21.
[63] Stamatoudi (2002) p 26.
[64] See MTV Sports: Snowboarding for Sony PlayStation 1, released 31 December 1999. The feature which allows users to build a new course is 'Create a Park'. See http://uk.playstation.com/games/gamesinfo04_game.jhtml?localeTitleId=1009466&linktype=SSL for details.
[65] Choe (1994) pp 934–35. She relies on one technical text for this classification: Choe (1994), n 16.

that '[m]ultimedia products are thought necessarily to be able to provide the fourth or fifth level of interactivity'.[66] Choe illustrates the top level of interactivity ('full interactivity') with the following example:

> a program might allow a user to retrieve several clips from music videos, the corresponding sound recordings, and a written textual background of the musical period. *The user could record these works, then alter and add changes to the underlying music, video or text. The user might even be able to digitally blur and fuse images or sounds, a process called 'morphing', which could result in unrecognizable images or sounds.* The resulting work would be, in effect, a new piece of music, video and text, based on the underlying works.[67] (Emphasis supplied)

Stamatoudi's notion of substantial interactivity corresponds to Choe's notion of 'full interactivity'. However, it is interesting to note that Choe does *not* confine multimedia to any particular level of interactivity, but instead envisages multimedia across the full range of interactivity.[68] There is minimal support (including in the technical literature) for restricting interactivity to substantial interactivity.[69] More usually, commentators view interactivity as involving a *spectrum* of non-linearity and *potentially* (but not necessarily) the ability to create new material from existing material.[70] This is the approach that will be adopted in this text.

We need to conclude by briefly considering how hypertext, hypermedia, and virtual reality have been portrayed by legal commentators, to see whether or not there is any discord with the technical understandings described in the previous section. Stamatoudi proffers the following layperson's description of 'hypertext' which corresponds to the technical definitions discussed in the previous section:

> Hypertext is an underlying structure in multimedia design. It is an 'interlinkedness' between different elements of information which allows the users to follow pathways in order to access that information, in the order in which they wish to do so. 'Hypertext' makes this non-sequential approach to information possible by offering the very connections needed to jump instantly to other locations in a database or at any other site where one finds related information of interest.

In terms of hypermedia, Stamatoudi describes it as the 'multimedia version' of hypertext where the 'information elements may be text, sound, images or a combination of the three'.[71] Similarly, Pardo describes hypermedia as the combination

---

[66] Stamatoudi (2002) p 26.
[67] Choe (1994) pp 976–77.
[68] See above.
[69] Jones (1996) p 28; Pardo (2003) p 10: multimedia has 'a larger or lesser degree of interactivity'.
[70] Eg, see Davies (1994) p 6: 'Multimedia is, in essence, a combination of text, still images, sounds and film/video through which a user can browse using a number of different approaches . . . The key element of multimedia works is the ability to step through interrelated information at the user's whim, *possibly also modifying that information or combining samples together.*' (emphasis supplied) See also Kreile and Becker (1996) p 689, where interactivity is described as the user influencing the contents or the sequence of events.
[71] Stamatoudi (2002) p 15.

of multimedia and hypertext, whereby 'the structuring of a multimedia work through a hypertextual or branched system to retrieve information whose elements are linked to each other.'[72] What exactly distinguishes multimedia from hypermedia is not made clear.

Finally, in respect of virtual reality, some commentators take the view that this amounts to an advanced form of multimedia.[73] For example, Stamatoudi argues:

> One form of distribution of multimedia is virtual reality. *Virtual reality is a 3–D multimedia product or service.* It is a way of enabling users to interact in real time with a computer-simulated environment by entering this environment with their own human senses by means of special equipment, ie, gloves, helmets, glasses, etc. A computer is used to map their body and senses directly into the digital world. *Virtual reality, though still at a primitive stage, presents the most advanced form of multimedia applications and is used in entertainment, health and science.*[74] (Emphasis supplied)

By contrast, Dasios[75] sees multimedia as distinct from virtual reality. He describes virtual reality as 'based on a marriage of technologies that allows users to immerse themselves totally and to interact in a computer-generated three-dimensional virtual environment (sometimes referred to as "cyberspace").'[76] Multimedia, on the other hand, is 'the marriage of existing media forms such as video, photography, animation, music, sound and text into a completely new medium of expression', and he cites Microsoft's *Encarta* as an example.[77] The main difference between multimedia and virtual reality seems to be that the multimedia combines old media forms in new ways, whereas virtual reality 'is about creating something completely new'.[78] Once again, we can observe some confusion in the legal literature about the relationship of multimedia to other technological concepts.

Conclusion

The above discussion of technical and legal understandings of multimedia has shown that generally the key features of multimedia can be agreed upon. The two main uncertainties are whether multimedia must feature at least one discrete media and one continuous media (the qualitative requirement), and whether substantial interactivity is essential. For the reasons already expressed, substantial

---

[72] Pardo (2003) p 10.
[73] Stamatoudi (2002) p 14; Choe (1995) p 943; Daun (1996) p 221.
[74] Stamatoudi (2002) p 14.
[75] NJ Dasios, 'Virtual Environments: Protecting Virtual Works under Copyright' [1995] *IPJ* 105.
[76] Above, at 109–10.
[77] Above, at 112, n 18.
[78] Citing Sandra Morris in K Pimental, *Virtual Reality: Through the New Looking Glass* (Windcrest/McGraw-Hill, New York, 1993) at 10: see Dasios (1995) p 112, n 18.

interactivity should not be considered as an essential element of multimedia. However, the qualitative requirement should be adopted because it is supported by some of the technical literature[79] and also because it provides a means of distinguishing multimedia from hypermedia. Taking into account the various issues discussed in the above review of technical and legal literature, the best working definition of 'multimedia', 'multimedia work' and 'multimedia product'[80] should be:

> A computerised combination of multiple digital media, including at least one discrete media, such as text, graphics or still images, and one continuous media, such as sound, animation or moving images, where a user may interact with that digital information in varying degrees. It can be distributed in either stand-alone (off-line) media, such as CD-Rom or DVD-Rom, or via communication networks, such as the Internet (ie on-line).

Having established a suitable working definition of multimedia, we turn to address the important question of *why* multimedia should be protected by copyright or related rights.

---

[79] And by one legal commentator: see F Koch, 'Software—Urhebrrechtsschutz für Multimedia—Anwendungen' [1995] *GRUR* 459, 459 and n 1 adopting Steinmetz's definition.

[80] Thus far, the term 'multimedia' has been used as a noun. However, for largely stylistic reasons, the term will be employed as an adjective and the compound terms 'multimedia work' and 'multimedia product' will be used interchangeably with the term 'multimedia'.

2

Justifications for Protecting Multimedia Works

Introduction

This chapter seeks to answer the important question concerning *why* we should grant intellectual property protection, in the form of copyright or related rights, to multimedia works? Few commentators have tackled this question in any substantive way. Most have simply pointed to the multimedia work as representing a 'new' type of work, which either does not fit comfortably within existing categories of copyright subject matter, or whose protection is 'inadequate' under the existing copyright regime, as justification for introducing a separate category of protection.[1] The related questions of whether existing legal categories properly accommodate multimedia works and whether such works are adequately protected is examined in detail in this book. However, while these contentions are true to a certain extent they do not, in themselves, explain the underlying imperatives for reform.

Examining the justifications for protecting a new type of work is an important exercise.[2] It is more pressing in the digital context because of fears concerning a

---

[1] Eg, the Copyright Law Review Committee (CLRC) recommends copyright protection of multimedia works on the basis that existing protection is inadequate: see Aust Copyright Law Review Committee, *Simplification of the Copyright Act 1968, Part 2: Categorisation of Subject Matter and Exclusive Rights and Other Issues* (AGD, Canberra, 1999) (CLRC Report: Part 2), paras 7.05–7.17. J Choe, 'Interactive Multimedia: A New Technology Tests the Limits of Copyright Law' (1994) 46 *Rutgers L Rev* 929, 996, argues for a subject matter category of 'multimedia works' because of 'interactive multimedia's unique feature of digital data storage that combines and blurs distinctions between the rigid section 102(a) subject matter categories of the [US] Copyright Act' and so 'an interactive multimedia work will be protectable as one work'. See also J Douglas, 'Too Hot to Handle? Copyright Protection of Multimedia' [1997] 8 *AIPJ* 96, 105; MJ O'Connor, 'Squeezing into Traditional Frames: Intellectual Property Law in the Shadow of the Information Society' (1998) 12 *IPJ* 285, 317; and G Wei, 'Multimedia and Intellectual and Industrial Property Rights in Singapore' (1995) 3 *Intl J of L & Information Technology* 214, 244–45.

[2] Indeed, some commentators argue that the burden of justifying intellectual property rights rests firmly on those who desire them and not on those who wish to use intellectual products: see E C Hettinger, 'Justifying Intellectual Property' (1989) 18 *Philosophy & Public Affairs* 31; and

'copyright grab'.[3] Several scholars[4] have argued that the development of digital technology and the Internet has been met by an unbridled expansion of copyright protection, where the interests of authors and owners have been automatically privileged over those of users. For example, Halbert, in relation to the United States, argues that 'the narrative Congress and policymakers endorse is one where copyright is uncritically extended to the information age and seen as the only legitimate tool for providing meaningful information on the Internet.'[5]

The concern of commentators such as Halbert is that the precious balance between private rights and public interest is being undermined and may ultimately be lost.[6] A flourishing public domain[7] is seen as vital for the possibilities of political and cultural speech[8] and for creative expression generally.[9] Academics such as Lessig, Litman, Vaidhyanathan and Boyle argue in favour of recalibrating the 'balance' in copyright law.[10] They also argue that further extensions of copyright law should not be introduced on the basis of faith alone—whether that faith is in economic justifications, or that the legislative process will reflect the public interest, or in the notion of 'authorship'. Instead, any extensions need to be scrutinised carefully in order to see whether they are warranted. Given the growing scepticism about whether increased copyright protection is a good thing, this chapter analyses whether protection of multimedia works is desirable and ultimately argues that it is.

Stamatoudi[11] argues strenuously for the introduction of a new copyright category of 'multimedia work', along with *sui generis* protection of multimedia

J Waldron, 'From Authors to Copiers: Individual Rights and Social Values in Intellectual Property' (1993) 68 *Chicago-Kent L Rev* 841.

[3] This phrase appears to have been first coined by Pamela Samuelson in her article, P Samuelson, 'The Copyright Grab' Issue 4.01 *Wired Magazine* January 1996.

[4] Notably D J Halbert, *Intellectual Property in the Information Age: The Politics of Expanding Ownership Rights* (Quorum Books, Westport, Conneticut, 1999); L Lessig, *The Future of Ideas: the Fate of the Commons in a Connected World* (Random House, New York, 2001); J Litman, *Digital Copyright* (Prometheus, New York, 2001); S Vaidhyanathan, *Copyrights and Copywrongs: the Rise of Intellectual Property and How it Threatens Creativity* (NYU Press, New York, 2001).

[5] Halbert (1999) p 27.

[6] See especially Lessig (2001).

[7] It is important to note that what constitutes the public domain is itself contentious: see J Boyle, 'The Second Enclosure Movement And The Construction Of The Public Domain' (2003) 66 *L & Contemporary Problems* 33, 58–62.

[8] See R Coombe, 'Authorial Cartographies: Mapping Proprietary Borders in a Less-Than-Brave-New World' (1996) 48 *Stanford L Rev* 1357; Halbert (1999); Vaidhyanathan (2001).

[9] Lessig (2001).

[10] Lessig (2001) pp 249–59, proposes the most far reaching reforms; Litman (2001) ch 12, suggests that copyright law be reformed in line with the public's perception of what constitutes a fair and sensible copyright, namely to provide owners with a right of commercial exploitation; Vaidhyanathan (2001) argues more generally for 'thin', leaky copyright protection, as does J Boyle, *Shamans, Software and Spleens: Law and the Construction of the Information Society* (Harvard University Press, Cambridge, MA, 1996).

[11] I Stamatoudi, *Copyright and Multimedia Works* (CUP, Cambridge, 2002).

works. In doing so, she relies on *both* economic[12] and natural rights[13] rationales to support protection for multimedia works. The fact that she does this is not unusual, since the cumulative use of different justifications is often seen in debates concerning the extension of protection.[14] Given that Stamatoudi argues for reform at a European level, it might also be that she wishes to engage with justifications associated with both common law and civil law traditions.[15] The following discussion will examine the applicability of economic and natural rights rationales to multimedia works in recognition of the fact that attempts to reform copyright law are usually considered within the framework of these theories.[16]

Economic Rationale

Stamatoudi argues that a multimedia work reflects a value greater than the sum of its individual parts.[17] The 'additional value' derives from having a combination of information that is interactive and integrated, and this is insufficiently protected by existing categories.[18] Accordingly, she argues that:

> The additional value they present remains unprotected and, in a climate of digital ease of copying at a fraction of the original investment costs, the market is unable to correct this failure through its own mechanisms. The result of this is an absence of an optimum level

[12] See generally, S Breyer, 'The Uneasy Case for Copyright: a Study of Copyright in Books, Photocopies, and Computer Programs' (1970) 84 *Harvard L Rev* 281; W M Landes and R A Posner, 'An Economic Analysis of Copyright Law' (1989) 18 *J of Legal Studies* 325; P Geller, 'Must Copyright be for Ever Caught between Marketplace and Authorship Norms?' in B Sherman and A Strowel, (eds), *Of Authors and Origins* (Clarendon Press, Oxford, 1994) 159–201; H M Spector, 'An Outline of a Theory Justifying Intellectual and Industrial Property Rights' (1989) 11 *EIPR* 270; A C Yen, 'The Interdisciplinary Future of Copyright Theory' in M Woodmansee and P Jaszi, (eds), *The Construction of Authorship* (Duke University Press, Durham, NC, 1994) 159–73.

[13] See generally, Breyer (1970); P Drahos, *A Philosophy of Intellectual Property* (Aldershot: Dartmouth, 1996); Geller (1994); Spector (1989); M Spence, 'Justifying Copyright' in D McClean and K Schubert, (eds), *Dear Images: Art, Copyright and Culture* (Ridinghouse, Manchester, 2002) 389.

[14] L Bently and B Sherman, *Intellectual Property Law,* 2nd edn, (OUP, Oxford, 2004) 37.

[15] Common law jurisdictions, such as the UK and the US, are typically aligned with economic or utilitarian justifications and civil law jurisdictions, such as France and Germany, with natural law justifications: see Geller (1994) p 159. However, commentators have argued that this classification is an oversimplification and misleading: see, for example, J Ginsburg, 'A Tale of Two Copyrights: Literary Property in Revolutionary France and America' in B Sherman and A Strowel, (eds), *Of Authors and Origins* (Clarendon Press, Oxford, 1994) 131; and P Goldstein, *International Copyright: Principles, Law and Practice* (OUP, Oxford, 2001) 7.

[16] Both Spence (2002) pp 402–3; and Bently & Sherman (2004) pp 36–37, comment that, as a matter of political and reform tactics, debates concerning reform of the law revolve around such theories of protection, even if the theories do not necessarily explain the principles of copyright law.

[17] See also M Turner, 'Do the Old Legal Categories Fit the New Multimedia Products? a Multimedia CD-Rom as a Film' [1995] *EIPR* 107, who also states that this is analogous to film works.

[18] See also Douglas (1997) p 105. *Cf* M Salokannel, *Ownership of Rights in Audiovisual Productions: a Comparative Study* (Kluwer, London, 1997) 89.

of protection and therefore an absence of an incentive for the creation of new high-quality multimedia products since the creators cannot recoup their efforts nor the entrepreneurs their investment.[19]

Stamatoudi outlines here the basic economic justification for protecting multimedia works. In the absence of an exclusive right, and because of the 'public good' characteristics of multimedia works as intangible creations, third parties can simply copy multimedia works instead of purchasing them from the author (the 'free rider' problem). As a result of the 'free rider' problem, the market price of multimedia works will eventually be bid down to the marginal cost of copying. Ultimately, the effect is that works will not be produced in the first place because the author will be unable to recoup the costs of creating the work. If authors cease to produce multimedia works, overall social welfare will be harmed. In order to ensure sufficient incentives for authors to produce works which will promote social welfare, authors should acquire a limited monopoly over their works.[20]

A multimedia work has value *beyond* the value of its individual components. Specifically, this extra value flows from having diverse inputs brought together in one work with which a user can interact. This value is separate from and additional to the individual elements reflected in the work. The notion that the 'whole is greater than the sum of its parts' can also be seen in other types of works, such as databases and films. With databases, the value comes from being able to access a range of comprehensive information from a central source. With film, the value flows from having various creative elements brought together in a visual narrative form. Given that multimedia works are themselves valuable,[21] we can argue that society is enriched if such works are created. It is therefore important to facilitate their creation.[22]

---

[19] Stamatoudi (2002) p 195.

[20] See Landes and Posner (1989) p 326; Yen (1994) p 161; J Boyle, 'Cruel, Mean, or Lavish? Economic Analysis, Price Discrimination and Digital Intellectual Property' (2000) 53 *Vanderbilt Law Review* 2007, 2012.

[21] See also Stamatoudi (2002) p 195.

[22] Indeed, the European Union maintains a continuing interest in promoting the development of multimedia works. See 96/339/EC Council Decision of 20 May 1996 adopting a multiannual Community programme to stimulate the development of a European multimedia content industry and to encourage the use of multimedia content in the emerging information society (INFO 2000) (OJ L 129 30 May 1996) which established the INFO2000 programme, under which multimedia rights clearance projects were initiated. For details of the outcomes of these projects see *Multimedia Rights Clearance Systems: Report on Project Final Reviews* (January 2001), available at http://www.cordis.lu/econtent/mmrcs/home.html. Multimedia rights clearance projects are now being pursued under the eContent programme: see 2001/48/EC Council Decision of 22 December 2000 adopting a multiannual Community programme to stimulate the development and use of European digital content on the global networks and to promote linguistic diversity in the information society (OJ L 014 18 January 2001), Annex I, para 3.2. For up-to-date details of this programme see http://www.cordis.lu/econtent/. In addition, the 'Multimedia Content and Tools: Key Action 3' (KA3) of the Information Society Technologies Programme has been 'created to manage research projects aimed at fostering and stimulating these all-important technologies of the future' and forms part of the Information Society Directorate-General of the European Commission: see http://www.cordis.lu/ist/ka3/home.html for

However, would authors produce multimedia works in the absence of monetary incentives? Some academics[23] have suggested that market incentives do not necessarily explain what motivates authors to create.[24] Lacey, in particular, points to a variety of non-monetary incentives that may prompt an author to create, including: personal satisfaction; recognition by one's peers; promotional concerns; or the desire to persuade an audience of a point of view.[25] In the context of multimedia works, it seems reasonable to suggest that at least some authors create multimedia works for nothing more than personal satisfaction or in the context of an academic exercise. What of those multimedia works that are commercialised? Would these works be commercially funded and distributed if it were not for financial incentives? Geller notes that the lack of solid evidence that *authors* create on the basis of market incentives is usually hidden by collapsing incentives for authors and publishers into one set of incentives for creating and communicating a work.[26] This tendency is noticeable in the analysis of Landes and Posner. They assume that there is the cost of creating the work (the cost of expression), as well as the cost of producing the work (which increases with the number of copies produced), and they treat these two types of costs (incurred by authors and publishers respectively) under the rubric of 'author' or 'creator'.[27] They conclude that a work will be created only if expected revenues, less the cost of producing the work, exceed the cost of expression.

Taking into account the interests of the 'publisher' of multimedia works (ie, the multimedia *producer*) the economic justification regains some of its initial force, because it seems unlikely that multimedia producers would support the creation and distribution of such works if they believed their financial interests were insufficiently protected. Are the financial interests of producers endangered? To answer this question, we need to consider the possibility of using practical obstacles or contractual arrangements as alternative means of limiting copying that would protect the producer's investment.

details. Finally, promoting multimedia works is also part of a wider concerning for promoting audiovisual works: see 2000/821/EC Corrigendum to Council Decision of 20 December 2000 on the implementation of a programme to encourage the development, distribution and promotion of European audiovisual works (MEDIA Plus Development, Distribution and Promotion)(2001–2005) (OJ L 336 30 December 2000), (OJ L 013 17 January 2001), recital 8.

[23] LJ Lacey, 'Of Bread and Roses and Copyright' [1989] *Duke L J* 1532. Geller (1994) pp 174–75; P Geller, 'Copyright History and Future: What's Culture Got to Do With It?' (2000) 47 *J Copyright Soc'y USA* 209, 258: 'Unfortunately, simplistic economic arguments for copyright blithely ignore the incommensurability of the great variety of motives for creators, assimilating them all to the narrower range of profit seeking incentives for media enterprises.'

[24] See also Spence (2002) p 390, who argues that there is much which copyright protects that would be produced and disseminated even without the incentive effects of the copyright regime.

[25] Lacey (1989) p 1574. Hettinger (1989) pp 47–51 argues that we should explore the possibility of alternative incentives (other than property rights) for the production of intellectual products—ones that will stimulate production, but not also restrict the use and availability of intellectual products.

[26] Geller (1994) p 175.

[27] Landes and Posner (1989) pp 326–27. See also Z Chafee, 'Reflections on the Law of Copyright: I' (1945) 45 *Columbia L Rev* 503, 510–11, who suggests providing incentives to authors and publishers.

Landes and Posner identify two important *practical* obstacles to copying: 1) that the copy is of inferior quality and thus an imperfect substitute for the original, and 2) the natural lead time of the original publisher.[28] Neither of these obstacles is particularly applicable to multimedia works. Multimedia works are digital products, and so copies will also be in digital form. In the absence of technological protection mechanisms, it will be relatively swift and effortless to copy a multimedia work to obtain a near-perfect (if not perfect) substitute for the original.[29]

The use of technological protection measures[30] to regulate who may access a multimedia work or how many copies may be made of it is a practical obstacle which has the potential to extend a producer's lead time sufficiently to protect the producer's investment. However, protracted lead time will depend upon the efficacy of the technological protection measure adopted, and experience shows that many types of protection measures are vulnerable to circumvention.[31] For example, Content Scramble System (CSS)[32] sought to prevent persons from playing DVDs other than on machines that had been licensed to decrypt CSS-encrypted content, but it was eventually circumvented by the program DeCSS which allowed the playing of DVDs on operating systems other than Windows and Macintosh.[33] Further, efforts by the Secure Digital Music Initiative (SDMI) to 'develop open technology specifications that protect the playing, storing, and distributing of digital music such that a new market for digital music may emerge'[34] have been stalled by a lack of consensus on the appropriate technologies to adopt.[35] In terms of lead time, it is at best uncertain whether multimedia producers will be able to rely on technological means to protect their investment.

Would it be possible for multimedia producers to rely instead on *contractual terms* to protect their investment? Landes and Posner propose the option of licensing a work on condition that the licensee does not make copies of it or disclose it to others in a way that would enable them to makes copies.[36] They acknowledge

---

[28] Landes and Posner (1989) pp 329–30.

[29] This point is made more generally by Landes and Posner (1989) p 330, when speaking of modern technology.

[30] For a pithy description of the type of technological protection measures that are available see P Akester, 'Survey of Technological Measures for Protection of Copyright' (2001) 12 *Entertainment L Rev* 36.

[31] K Dam, 'Self Help in the Digital Jungle' in R Dreyfuss, DL Zimmerman and H First, (eds), *Expanding the Boundaries of Intellectual Property: Innovation Policy for the Knowledge Society* (OUP, Oxford, 2001) 103, 110–12.

[32] Discussed in Lessig (2001) pp 187–90.

[33] See also the Serial Copy Management System (SCMS): Akester (2001) p 37.

[34] See http://www/sdmi.org/index.htm.

[35] See http://www.sdmi.org/index.htm and Litman (2001) pp 155–56. According to D Balaban, 'The Battle of the Music Industry: The Distribution of Audio and Video Works via the Internet, Music and More' (2001) 12 *Fordham Intellectual Property, Media & Entertainment L J* 235, 261–62, there was considerable debate about whether the protection technologies developed by SDMI were in fact secure.

[36] Landes and Posner (1989) p 330.

that this solution may not be feasible where widespread distribution is sought.[37] However, the ability to enter into 'shrink-wrap'[38] or 'click-wrap' licenses[39] arguably facilitates the mass licensing that would be required for global distribution of multimedia works.[40] Nonetheless, it would be costly to enforce such contractual licences and they would remain ineffective vis-à-vis third parties.[41]

Is the claim of under-production of multimedia works resulting from inadequate protection supported by any empirical evidence? There is a lack of direct evidence about the extent to which intellectual property rights stimulate the creation of intangible works,[42] and this includes multimedia works. However, statistics indicate that multimedia works are important for the European economy.[43] This is supported by statistics for the software industry generally, which can be cited in connection with multimedia works, because the software industry produces multimedia works in the form of entertainment software (ie, video games). For example, the UK is cited as being the third largest developer of computer games, with a global market share of 15.3%.[44] This market has 'generated £1.6bn of value for the UK in 2001 from retail, distribution and publishing margins, development advances and royalties.'[45] The Western European software industry

---

[37] Above.

[38] This refers to standard-form contractual terms that are bundled with software products and which are visible to the purchaser at the time of purchase, or shortly thereafter: see L Guibault, *Copyright Limitations and Contracts* (Kluwer, The Hague, 2002) 200–1.

[39] This refers to electronic standard-form contractual terms, where the user is asked to indicate their assent by clicking on an 'I agree' button: see Guilbault (2002) pp 203–4.

[40] Guibault (2002) p 204, cautions that the validity of shrink-wrap and click-wrap licences is uncertain, both in US and Europe. However, Andrew Murray is more sanguine about the validity of click-wrap licences in the UK: see A D Murray, 'Entering into Contracts Electronically: The Real WWW' in L Edwards and C Waelde, (eds), *Law and the Internet: A Framework for Electronic Commerce* (Hart Publishing, Oxford, 2000) 17–35. In J Ginsburg, 'Copyright Without Walls? Speculations on Literary Property in the Library of the Future' (1993) 42 *Representations* 53, 63, the author suggests that, by using access technologies to control and enforce licensing, 'no functional difference may exist between a contract and a property right.'

[41] See also Stamatoudi (2002) p 195. On the privity point, see RP Merges, 'The End of Friction? Property Rights and Contract in the "Newtonian" World of On-Line Commerce' (1997) 12(1) *Berkeley Technology L J* at http://www.law.berkeley.edu/journals/btlj/articles/vol12.html who argues that the privity requirement could be dispensed with in 'cyberspace'.

[42] Geller (1994) pp 174–75; S Ricketson, 'New Wine into Old Bottles: Technological Change and Intellectual Property Rights' (1992) 10(1) *Prometheus* 53, 58. The Commission on Intellectual Property Rights in their Report, *Integrating Intellectual Property Rights and Development Policy* (2002) 5 and 20–24, comment that much of the economic evidence relating to the impact of intellectual property rights, particularly in relation to developing countries, is inconclusive and contested.

[43] Stamatoudi (2002) p 4.

[44] DTI, *From Exuberant Youth to Sustainable maturity: Competitiveness analysis of the UK Games Software Sector* (2002) available at: www.dti.gov.uk/cii/services/contentindustry/computer_games_leisure_software.shtml (DTI Report), p18.

[45] DTI Report, p 19.

is also predicted to grow significantly from 56.7 billion euros (in 2000) to 109.3 billion euros (in 2005).[46] Finally, it is estimated that piracy has cost the European software industry 3.4 billion euros (in 2000),[47] the US software industry 2.6 billion US dollars (in 2000)[48] and 6.5 billion US dollars (in 2003)[49] and the worldwide software industry 28.8 billion US dollars (in 2003) in lost revenue.[50]

The above statistics have limited usefulness because they provide an incomplete picture of the market trends involving *multimedia works*. To the extent that inferences regarding multimedia works can be drawn from statistics concerning software, they suggest a healthy software industry exists in the UK and the EC. It can reasonably be inferred that this is in some way attributable to the existence of copyright protection for computer programs.[51] However, this amounts to fairly weak evidence that protection is necessary for multimedia works. Although it has been repeatedly suggested that rampant piracy has a strong disincentive effect on software developers,[52] there is little evidence to support this claim. Even if it is true, it relates more to the effectiveness of copyright enforcement, as opposed to the existence or non-existence of protection. It seems reasonable to conclude that the economic rationale for protection of multimedia works is not supported by empirical evidence.

Is this lack of empirical evidence fatal to an economic argument favouring intellectual property protection of multimedia works? No, for several reasons: first, protection has been extended to other types of subject matter (such as computer programs) without evidence showing under production;[53] second, as a *theoretical* justification, the economic rationale does not require empirical evidence in support (although this type of evidence can only serve to bolster the theoretical claims); and finally, those commentators who criticise the lack of empirical

---

[46] Business Software Alliance, *The Thriving European Software Industry*, available at http://global.bsa.org/usa/policyres/admin/2002–04–17.108.pdf, p 1.

[47] Above, at 5.

[48] In terms of entertainment software, the Entertainment Software Association state that worldwide piracy is estimated to have cost the US industry in excess of $US 3 billion in 2001: see http://www.theesa.com/piracy.html.

[49] Business Software Alliance, 'First Annual BSA and IDC Global Software Piracy Study' July 2004, p 9, available at http://www.bsa.org/globalstudy/

[50] Above.

[51] See Directive 91/250/EEC on the legal protection of computer programs, [1991] OJ L122/42 ('Software Directive').

[52] Business Software Alliance, *The Thriving European Software Industry*, available at http://global.bsa.org/usa/policyres/admin/2002–04–17.108.pdf, p 5.

[53] C Tapper, *Computer Law*, 4th edn, (Longman, London, 1989) 32, comments that 'the validity of the economic case for copyright protection [of software] is very difficult to demonstrate.' At 32–33, he observes that the US software industry experienced rapid growth even though the US Copyright Office only accepted programs for registration on a provisional basis.

evidence usually do so in the context of criticising the way in which economic theory *structures* copyright law, rather than seeing it as fatal to the existence of copyright protection.[54]

On balance, the better view is that multimedia works *should* be protected in order to provide incentives for their creation and dissemination. At the same time, it is important to recognise the criticisms of how the economic justification informs the *structure* of copyright law. According to the economic rationale, copyright protection is granted because it induces creative activity. However, the exclusive rights granted by copyright produce corresponding losses in the form of decreased access to works (because each owner is able to charge a monopoly price[55] in respect of their work) and increased creation costs for future works.[56] Landes and Posner argue that the principal legal doctrines of copyright law therefore 'must, at least approximately, maximize the benefits from creating additional works minus both the losses from limiting access and the costs of administering copyright protection'.[57] It is a difficult task to ensure that across the *spectrum* of copyright subject matter the 'deadweight' losses are outweighed by the benefits of monopoly rights.[58] It is also a project which conflicts with the aim of producing clear, uniform and easily applicable principles.[59] In fleshing out the substance of copyright, the principles may only roughly mirror the economic basis for protection.[60]

The use of an economic analysis of copyright law to justify the narrow construction, or even elimination, of exceptions to infringement is more problematic. An example of this trend is in relation to the US doctrine of 'fair use'. It has been argued by some that the doctrine of 'fair use' exists to correct market failures, such as when high transaction costs or an irrational refusal on the part of the owner to grant a licence prevents an otherwise desirable bargain regarding

---

[54] See Breyer (1970); Lessig (2001); and Vaidhyathan (2001). See also E W Kitch, 'Elementary and Persistent Errors in the Economic Analysis of Intellectual Property' (2000) 53 *Vanderbilt Law Review* 1727, 1740 who criticises the literature on intellectual property rights as tending to see the policy issue as one of the existence/non-existence of the intellectual property right, as opposed to 'considering the full range of features that can be varied by the law in order to affect the operation of the right.'

[55] Cf Kitch (2000) pp 1729–38 who criticises the persistent assumption in the literature that an intellectual property right confers an economic monopoly, which he argues arises from 'an underlying confusion about the meaning of the term "monopoly"', p 1735. Kitch believes that whether an IPR is a monopoly is an empirical question and that there needs to be a better explanation of why a monopoly analysis is used.

[56] Yen (1994); Landes and Posner (1989) p 332.

[57] Landes and Posner (1989) p 326.

[58] Spence (2002) p 390.

[59] Chafee (1945) sets out six ideals of copyright law. At 514–15 he notes that ideal 6, 'The legal rules should be convenient to handle' clashes with ideal 4, 'protection should not go substantially beyond the purposes of protection'.

[60] To put it another way, the economic argument does not tell us '*how much* protection would suffice for [minimizing free-riding] . . . nor when *too much* protection would stifle cultural feedback' (emphasis original). See Geller (2000) p 260.

copyright use.[61] Consequently, the principles guiding 'fair use' ought to reflect its character as a means of correcting market failures, or should reflect the overall utilitarian purpose of copyright law,[62] and other *non-market* or *non-economic* considerations, such as 'fairness' or 'public policy', should not enter into the equation.[63] There is also the related view that if the function of 'fair use' exceptions is to correct market failures, then where other means can be relied upon to correct them, (for example, through the use of technological and/or contractual measures) the scope of the exception should be reduced.[64] For some academics, the consequence of this logic is the expansion of copyright protection and the erosion of exceptions and limitations in favour of technologically controlled and enforced licensing. These consequences are seen as alarming, since they suggest that 'perfect control' of a copyright work is the ideal situation, without proper regard to balancing protection against the public interest in allowing access.[65]

As discussed above, economic analysis can affect the structure of copyright law. Importantly, these concerns do not undermine the argument that extending copyright or *sui generis* protection to multimedia works will encourage authors and producers to create such works. Rather, they suggest that it is crucial to strike an appropriate balance in determining the scope of protection for multimedia works. In seeking to preserve an appropriate balance, it may be better to adopt a loose utilitarian analysis rather than a strict economic one.[66]

---

[61] WJ Gordon, 'Fair Use as Market Failure: A Structural and Economic Analysis of the *Betamax* Case and its Predecessors' (1982) 82 *Columbia L Rev* 1600; Landes and Posner (1989) pp 357–58.

[62] PN Leval, 'Toward a Fair Use Standard' (1990) 103 *Harvard L Rev* 1105, adopts a slightly different approach to Gordon's in that he argues that 'fair use' and its principles must remain true to the utilitarian purpose of providing incentives to create, as opposed to arguing that 'fair use' is a substitute for the market when it fails.

[63] L Weinreb, 'Fair's Fair: A Comment on the Fair Use Doctrine' (1990) 103 *Harvard L Rev* 1137.

[64] See Guilbault (2002) pp 85–86:

the digital networked environment has both the potential to significantly reduce the transaction costs that exist in the analogue world between rights owners and users and to increase the excludable character of protected works. As a result of these technological changes, a number of commentators and courts have suggested that the scope of fair use in the digital environment should be narrowed wherever new technologies or licensing mechanisms enable markets to form.

See also Guilbault (2002) n 318; and P Goldstein, *Copyright's Highway: From Gutenberg to the Celestial Jukebox*, Revised edn, (Stanford Law and Politics, Stanford, 2003) 202–3, 207.

[65] Lessig (2001), ch 11 and 249–50; Vaidhyanathan (2001) pp 158–59.

[66] The utilitarian approach is used by commentators such as Lessig (2001); Litman (2001); Vaidhyanathan (2001); and Boyle (1996).

Natural Law Rationale

Stamatoudi also favours protecting multimedia works because they are 'original creations of the mind.'[67] This bare statement can be linked to two key natural law justifications, namely, the *personality* theory and the *labour* theory.[68]

1. Personality Theory

The writings of Kant and Hegel[69] are often associated with different versions of the personality theory.[70] With a Kantian based personality theory, the crucial idea is that a work is not a commodity, but principally an expression or embodiment of the author's personality. To enable an author to control her personality, she must therefore be able to control her work.[71] Applying this logic to a multimedia work, it can be argued that this type of work also embodies the personality of its author (or more likely authors, but more on this later) and so should be able to be controlled by the author.

Hegel's writing on property is also said to support a personality theory of intellectual property.[72] In the *Philosophy of Right*, Hegel is concerned with the concept of a will and its progression from an abstract state to one where it 'has located itself in the context of the state and world history.'[73] The task of the will is to achieve absolute freedom. Freedom is posited by Hegel in the sense of a realised state of being of the agent, as opposed to the classical liberal notion of freedom from external restraint.[74] The task of the will occurs in several stages, and 'personality' is linked to the first stage of the will's struggle to manifest itself.[75] For Hegel,

---

[67] Stamatoudi (2002) p 208. See also A Christie, 'A Proposal for Simplifying United Kingdom Copyright Law' [2001] *EIPR* 26, 30. Turner (1995) p 107, also suggests that the producer of a multimedia work has 'undoubtedly' exercised his creativity in producing the work. Sterling is also of the opinion that insofar as there is a creative contribution in the selection, arrangement and presentation as a whole of the mediagraphic work, this should be protected: Sterling (1998) para 6.77. Mediagraphic work is Sterling's idiosyncratic description for a multimedia work: see paras 6.16 and 6.52.

[68] This is the taxonomy used by J Hughes, 'The Philosophy of Intellectual Property' (1988) 77 *Georgetown L J* 287.

[69] G Hegel, TM Knox, (tr), *Philosophy of Right* (OUP, Oxford, 1967).

[70] For Kant, see S Strömholm, 'Droit Moral—The International and Comparative Scene from a Scandinavian Viewpoint' (1983) 14 *IIC* 1; Drahos (1996) pp 80–81; and Geller (1994) pp 168–69. For Hegel, see MJ Radin, 'Property and Personhood' (1982) 34 *Stanford L Rev* 957; Hughes (1988); Drahos (1996) ch 4. Note that Spence (2002) p 399 argues that the personality theory has been wrongly attributed to Kant and Hegel and that a Hegelian-based theory is one of personal autonomy.

[71] Strömholm (1983) pp 11–15; Spence (2002) p 399.

[72] What follows is a sketch of Hegel's theory of property—it is discussed more comprehensively in Drahos (1996), ch 4; Radin (1982); and Hughes (1988).

[73] Drahos (1996) p 75.

[74] Drahos (1996) p 75; Hughes (1988) pp 331–32.

[75] Drahos (1996) p 76.

'[p]ersonality is the first, still wholly abstract, determination of the absolute and infinite will.'[76] Personality has to achieve a concrete existence. This is where property becomes relevant, since it allows the external world to be appropriated,[77] there being an 'absolute right' to the appropriation of things.[78] As Hughes explains, '[a]cting upon things is an initial step in the ongoing struggle for self-actualization. Socially mandated property rights do not trigger this self-actualization; they are only a means to protect the individual's initial attempt to take command of the world.'[79] According to Hegel, property rights facilitate the will's attempt to appropriate the external world in order to actualise itself.

Hegel's theory of property has been described by Radin[80] as an 'occupancy theory'. Radin suggests that in order to sustain the property relationship the owner's will has to remain in the object.[81] It is possible for the will to be actively withdrawn, and this provides the basis for the alienability of property.[82] Hegel does not take a limited view of the 'things' into which personality may be invested. Thus 'things' can include 'mental aptitudes, erudition, artistic skill and inventions' which can be legally possessed once they are externalised.[83]

Both the Kantian and Hegelian personality theories have been the subject of critique. An obvious difficulty is what is meant by 'personality'.[84] Spence suggests that 'personality' may differ from the concept of reputation in defamation law (which focuses on how others perceive a person) and instead mean self-presentation, including self-expression (in other words, how the author wants to present herself).[85]

Even if we can agree on the nature of 'personality', whether personality *can in fact be discerned* in an author's work may be doubted.[86] Geller argues that author's personalities 'rarely permeate, or even identifiably mark, their works. If some authors leave personal imprints, they do so most often on singularly creative

---

[76] Hegel (1967), para 41.

[77] See Hegel (1967), paras 45 and 46. See also Drahos (1996) p 77; Radin (1982) pp 972–73; Hughes (1988) pp 332–33.

[78] Hegel (1967), para 44. See also Radin (1982) p 973.

[79] Hughes (1988) p 333. Spence (2002) at 400 also provides a helpful elucidation of the role of property: 'property helps individuals to develop as autonomous persons by carving out an area over which they can exercise their will. It does this by enabling them to make choices about taking, possessing, using and alienating things in the external world.'

[80] Radin (1982) p 974. See also Hughes (1988) p 334.

[81] Hegel (1967) para 51: 'Since property is the embodiment of personality, my inward idea and will that something is to be mine is not enough to make it my property; to secure this end occupancy is requisite.'

[82] Hughes (1988) pp 334–35.

[83] Hegel (1967) para 43: 'Attainments, eruditions, talents, and so forth, are, of course, owned by free mind and are something internal and not external to it, but even so, by expressing them it may embody them in something external and alienate them . . .'

[84] Spence (2002) p 399.

[85] Above. Geller (1994) p 178 also talks of an author's 'self-expression'.

[86] Spence (2002) p 399; Hughes (1988) pp 340–43.

works, not all across the spectrum of works.'[87] Consequently, Geller challenges the assumption that copyright is needed to protect the autonomy of an author's purported self expression.[88] Hughes shares the view that some works are better suited to displaying an author's personality than others. He argues that poems, stories, novels, musical works, sculpture, paintings, and prints are 'clearly receptacles for personality',[89] whereas computer software and other technological categories of intellectual property (such as patents, microchip masks and engineering trade secrets) are not generally regarded 'as manifesting the personality of an individual, but rather as manifesting a raw, almost generic insight.'[90] Hughes does not consider that certain categories of works are incapable of manifesting personality, but rather that economic, efficiency and physical considerations constrain the range of expression and '[a]t some point, these constraints on a particular form of intellectual property may be too great to permit meaningful expressions of personality.'[91]

At first glance, it appears that multimedia works will rarely manifest an author's personality because they are highly *technological* works[92] (being heavily dependent on software[93]) and are also constrained by economic considerations. However, there is arguably considerable scope for programmers to *express* themselves in software.[94] There remains much scope for artistic skill to be applied in conceiving the overall multimedia work, creating its visual layout, and in designing the various inputs (such as graphics, icons, video clips or music) that comprise the work. It seems therefore unreasonable to characterise multimedia works as a category of work incapable of featuring expressions of personality. This conclusion is reinforced by the fact that other types of works, which also reflect an intersection of technological, economic and artistic considerations, are protected by copyright law. For example, in the case of films, we see that '[f]ilm-making is characterized by a precarious interdependence between technological possibilities, economic

---

[87] Geller (1994) p 178. At 180 Geller explains that some authors may be at pains to leave no trace of personal involvement and he gives the examples of Duchamp's Ready-mades and Warhol's paintings of soup-cans.

[88] Geller (1994) p 181.

[89] Hughes (1988) p 340.

[90] Above, at 341.

[91] Above at 343. Hughes' approach of distinguishing 'personality-rich' categories of works from 'personality-bare' has been criticised by Drahos (1996) p 80, who argues that it 'interprets personality as some sort of essence which in varying degrees is "poured" into objects.'

[92] T Dreier, 'Authorship and New Technologies from the Viewpoint of Civil Law Tradition' (1995) 26 *IIC* 989, 995 comments that the more technical the resulting digital work is in character, and the more a machine is used in the creation of the work, the less will the final outcome reflect the creator's personality.

[93] Software is critical to the determining the functions of a multimedia work, along with its visual user interface through which the user operates the work.

[94] Hughes (1988) p 342. See also AL Clapes, P Lynch and MR Steinberg, 'Silicon Epics And Binary Bards: Determining The Proper Scope Of Copyright Protection For Computer Programs' (1987) 34 *UCLA L Rev* 1493.

constraints, and artistic creation:'[95] yet copyright law, particularly in *droit d'auteur* countries, recognises films as authorial (as opposed to entrepreneurial) works.[96] At the same time, it is interesting to note that not every person who contributes (creatively or otherwise) to the making of a film necessarily will be considered an author of such a work.[97] If multimedia works are recognised as works capable of manifesting personality, this gives rise to the issue of who is to be classed as the (legal) author/s of the work.

The *collaborative* nature of multimedia works also poses a problem for justifying their protection under the personality theory. Where multiple creators are responsible for bringing a work into existence (which is often the case with multimedia works) it may be difficult to discern each individual's self-expression. The individual contributions may have become merged to such an extent that they are no longer distinguishable from one another. The tendency for this to occur probably increases as the number of authors involved in the creative process increases. Even if it can be assumed that each contributor's personality *is* identifiable in the collaborative work, it should follow that copyright law principles would accommodate multiple authorship. However, the principle of 'joint authorship' in copyright law is fairly restrictive.[98] Many commentators have

---

[95] M Salokannel, 'Film Authorship in the Changing Audio-Visual Environment' in B Sherman and A Strowel, (eds), *Of Authors and Origins* (Clarendon Press, Oxford, 1994) 57–77 at 60.

[96] This is illustrated by the fact that *droit d'auteur* countries generally recognise the director as an author and also grant moral rights to authors of films: see, eg, Art L 113–7 and Art L 121–1, French Intellectual Property Code 1992 ('French Code'); and Arts 11–14, German Law on Copyright and Neighbouring Rights 1965 ('German Law'). *Cf* the US which does not grant authorship in motion pictures to directors, but rather to film producers and does not grant moral rights in films: see s 106A, United States Copyright Act 1976 ('USC'). This was the position under UK law until recently. The UK now represents a hybrid position. Since the enactment of the Copyright Designs and Patents Act 1988 (UK) (CDPA) it has granted moral rights solely to the director of a film (ss 77, 80, 84, CDPA). Further, as a consequence of implementation of the Directive 93/83/EEC harmonising the term of protection of copyright and related rights [1993] OJ L290/9 ('Term Directive'), for films made after 1 July 1994, the principal director is classified as a co-author of a film, along with the producer (s 9(2)(ab), CDPA). For details of the history of film copyright in the UK see P Kamina, *Film Copyright in the European Union* (CUP, Cambridge, 2002) chs 2 and 4.

[97] Salokannel (1994) pp 71–76. For a detailed discussion of authorship of films in the UK and other EC countries see Kamina (2002) pp 130–61.

[98] For example, in the UK, s 10 CDPA defines a 'work of joint authorship' to mean 'a work produced by the collaboration of two or more authors in which the contribution of each author is not distinct from that of the other author or authors.' There must be a significant contribution of the right kind (*Brighton v Jones* [2004] EMLR 26, 521–22); a common design that unites the authors but *not* an intention of joint authorship; and the respective contributions must be merged to form an integrated whole (*Beckingham v Hodgens* [2004] ECDR 6, 59, Parker LJ). In the US, a 'joint work' is defined in s 101 USC as 'a work prepared by two or more authors with the intention that their contributions be merged into inseparable or interdependent parts of a unitary whole.' The contribution must be sufficiently original and there must be an intention of joint authorship (*Childress v Taylor* 945 F 2d 500 (2nd Cir, 1991), 506–8). In addition, the contributions may be either inseparable or interdependent. P Jaszi, 'On the Author Effect: Contemporary Copyright and Collective Creativity' in M Woodmansee and P Jaszi, (eds), *The Construction of Authorship: Textual Appropriation in Law and Literature* (Duke University

argued that the notion of authorship is heavily tied to the notion of the Romantic author.[99] It is suggested that the personality theory is heavily tied to individualistic notions,[100] and so tends to support copyright law principles that are similarly 'individualistic' in nature. However, it does not follow that multimedia works should be automatically disqualified from copyright protection. Rather, this suggests that if multimedia works are recognised as works manifesting personality, this may cause difficulties in terms of the definition of authorship. This certainly has been the case in respect of another type of collaborative work, namely film,[101] where different jurisdictions have produced a variety of solutions to the question of film authorship.[102] The complex issue of authorship of multimedia works will be explored in more detail in chapter 3.

The final criticism of the personality theory is that it provides little guidance about *how much* control an author should be given over their self-expression.[103] As Spence explains, 'against the claim that control over a creator's work is essential to the protection of her personal autonomy, must be set the claim that the grant of such control is a limitation of the autonomy of those who would seek to use the work without her permission.'[104]

How then to reconcile competing personal autonomies? In the context of Hegelian based personality theory as applied to property generally (and not intellectual property), Radin has tried to address this difficulty by distinguishing between fungible and personal property, where personal property increases self-actualization and fungible property does not.[105] Her approach is to say that where property is fungible to person X, then it should be denied to X if it would in fact

Press, Durham, NC, 1994) 29 suggests at 51–52 that US copyright law treats joint authorship as a 'deviant form' of individual authorship. For a similar view see Halbert (1999) p 123.

In France, Art L 113–2 of the French Code defines a collaborative work as 'a work in the creation of which more than one natural person has participated.' A collaborative work must be the result of creativity and a concerted effort conducted in common by a number of authors (*Le Brun v Braesheather*, Cass civ 1, (1995) 164 RIDA 305).

In Germany, Article 8(1) of the German Law defines joint authorship as where 'several persons have created a work jointly and their respective contributions cannot be separately exploited.' Thus, co-authors must contribute in common and 'the court has to determine that the contributions of the several co-authors are inseparable when concretely exploited, rather than analyze how these contributions relate inside the work in abstract.' (M B Nimmer and P E Geller, *International copyright law and practice* (Looseleaf, Matther Bender, New York) para 4[1][a] Germany).

[99] Eg, see K Aoki, '(Intellectual) Property and Sovereignty: Notes Toward a Cultural Geography of Authorship' (1996) 48 *Stanford L Rev* 1293; Boyle (1996), ch 6; and M Woodmansee, 'On the Author Effect: Recovering Collectivity' in M Woodmansee and P Jaszi, (eds), *The Construction of Authorship: Textual Appropriation in Law and Literature* (Duke University Press, Durham, NC, 1994) 15–28.

[100] See Radin (1982) pp 964–65, 971.

[101] Salokannel (1994) p 70. Kamina (2002) p 131 notes that for audiovisual works, 'the question of copyright entitlement has proved to be one of the most complex and controversial in copyright law.'

[102] See Kamina (2002) pp 138–61 for details of approaches in different EC Member States.

[103] Spence (2002) p 402.

[104] Spence (2002) pp 401–2. See also Waldron (1993) p 877.

[105] Radin (1982) pp 989–91.

deny personal (ie, self-actualizing) property to Y. Hughes has criticised the usefulness of Radin's fungible/personal dichotomy on the basis that it still raises the question of how to distinguish 'personal' property from 'fungible' property—whether it is to be decided entirely on a subjective basis or according to artificial constraints.[106]

The problem of reconciling competing autonomies, or competing self-expressions, is a serious one. It affects the balance between authors and users in copyright law, as well as the balance drawn between authors and owners in terms of the interrelationship between moral rights and economic rights. It is beyond the scope of this work to suggest the conceptual tools for striking the appropriate balance. Rather, it is sufficient to recognise that the personality theory offers limited support for protecting multimedia works. Assuming personality is discernible in such works, this will give rise to complications in respect of authorship rules.

2. Labour Theory

Locke's labour theory of *property* has been utilised by commentators to provide a justification for intellectual property. Drahos suggests that this extension of Locke's theory may be an attempt to lend the totemic status of Locke to justify intellectual property.[107] Spector suggests that Locke's theory is applied to intangible property because the extension 'does not appear to be far-fetched.'[108] The key tenets of Locke's theory[109] are encapsulated in the following passage from chapter V, 'Of Property' from *The Second Treatise of Government*:

> [E]very Man has a *Property* in his own *Person*. This no Body has any Right to but himself. The *Labour* of his Body, and the *Work* of his hands, we may say, are properly his. Whatsoever then he removes of out of the State that Nature hath provided, and left it in, he hath mixed his *Labour* with, and joyned to it something that is his own, and thereby makes it his *Property*[110] (emphasis original).

Central to Locke's theory is the notion that every person has property in their own person, and therefore their own labour, and so a person may appropriate objects by mixing their own labour with something from the commons.[111] Locke imposes two provisos, namely, that a property right to the object to which labour is mixed

---

[106] Hughes (1988) pp 336–37.

[107] Drahos (1996) pp 41, 48.

[108] Spector (1989) p 271.

[109] A more detailed discussion is found in Drahos (1996) pp 41–47; and Hughes (1988) pp 297–300.

[110] See Locke, Laslett (ed), *Two Treatises of Government* (CUP, Cambridge, 1988) 287–88.

[111] Note that Drahos (1996) pp 44–47 argues that the 'commons' could be interpreted as referring to either a positive or negative commons—the former being a commons which belongs jointly to all members of the community and the latter being a commons which belongs to no one, parts of which may be appropriated.

only arises 'where there is enough, and as good left in common for others', and that a person cannot remove that from the commons which they will waste (or will not be able to use to advantage). These provisos have been described as the 'sufficiency' and 'spoilage' limitations.[112]

Labour is the key concept in Locke's justification for property.[113] Drahos argues that 'Locke suggests that property rights are a just reward for the industrious . . . [and] also argues that the labour of individuals adds value to a product and confers a general social benefit.'[114] The former 'reward' reasoning tends to support a moral justification,[115] whilst the latter 'social value' reasoning seems to support a utilitarian justification. Hughes presents two alternative interpretations of the role of labour in Locke's theory: the first is the 'avoidance' view of labour, and the second is the 'labour-desert' theory. The first 'avoidance' theory sees labour as an activity which is in itself unpleasant. Hughes explains that this can give rise to either a moral or utilitarian imperative: either '*the unpleasantness of labor should be rewarded with property*' or 'the unpleasantness of labour should be rewarded with property *because people must be motivated to perform labor.*'[116] The second 'labour-desert' theory characterises labour as an activity which 'creates *social* value, and it is this production of social value that "deserves" reward, not the labor that produced it.'[117] Hughes notes that this theory is often understood as an instrumentalist argument, but points out that it may also be treated as a normative proposition since 'people *should* be rewarded for how much value they add to other people's lives, regardless of whether they are motivated by such rewards.'[118] We may conclude that a Lockean labour theory is capable of supporting either a moral or utilitarian justification for intellectual property. For the purposes of this discussion, we are concerned only with the moral rationale.

Applying Locke's theory of property to intangible property, it can be said that every person has property in their *intellectual labour* and that whenever a person mixes their intellectual labour with something from the commons (such as ideas or theories) they thereby make it their property.[119] However, difficulties arise when one attempts to map a justification of *intellectual property* according to a labour theory.

---

[112] Drahos (1996) p 49. Hettinger (1989) p 34 explains the sufficiency proviso as: 'As long as one does not worsen another's position by appropriating an object, no objection can be raised to owning that with which one mixes one's labor' and the spoilage proviso as, 'one must not take more than one can use' because that would be wasteful.

[113] Drahos (1996) p 48 writes: 'Generally speaking, people who use Locke's theory tend to concentrate on labour and the mixing metaphor.'

[114] Drahos (1996) p 44.

[115] See also Hettinger (1989) pp 40–41.

[116] Hughes (1988) p 303 (emphasis original).

[117] Above, at 305.

[118] Above, at 306.

[119] Spector (1989) p 271 argues that the notion of 'body' clearly embraces the 'mind' and 'labour' must extend to 'intellectual labour', since no labour is purely physical.

Probably the most serious difficulty relates to the role of *labour* as a justification for property rights. Several objections may be raised to such a justification. First, it is arguable whether the labour of an individual in fact gives rise to an intellectual product. Drahos suggests that abstract objects may actually arise from an external source (like god) where individuals are passive recipients of ideas or inventions.[120] However, Drahos' objection rests on the controversial premise that a metaphysical entity is responsible for intellectual creations.[121] A less controversial objection discussed by Hettinger is that 'intellectual products result from the labor of many people besides the latest contributor'.[122] In other words, it is not clear that the total value of an intellectual product is entirely attributable to the labour of an individual,[123] since 'intellectual products are fundamentally social products.'[124] Moreover, Hettinger argues that it is problematic to maintain that a labourer, by virtue of their labour, has a natural right to the market value of an abstract object, since market value is a socially created phenomenon.[125] A further objection is why labour should entitle an individual to ownership over the *whole* work when a person's labour may only explain the *added value* of the intellectual product and not its entire value.[126] Indeed, it has been suggested that it may be more appropriate for the labourer to lose their labour rather than obtain property rights in the resultant product.[127] Finally, labour is an imprecise tool for designating the boundaries of intangible objects.[128]

Some of the above difficulties regarding labour are apparent when it comes to multimedia works. In particular, the collaborative and derivative nature of multimedia works poses a problem in terms of justifying their protection according to

[120] Drahos (1996) p 50. Hettinger (1989) p 37, n 19 also touches on this argument, where he states that whether ideas are discovered or created affects the persuasiveness of the labour argument for intellectual property, with the discovery of an intellectual product being far less persuasive than creating one.

[121] Drahos (1996) p 50, acknowledges that this is a controversial premise.

[122] Hettinger (1989) p 39.

[123] Hettinger (1989) p 37 gives the example of the wheel and argues that 'the entire human value of which is not appropriately attributable to its original inventor.'

[124] Hettinger (1989) p 38. Brennan (1993) p 692 comments that,

> It is no accident that the stories used to support the classical theory [eg, Locke's] are pastoral and agrarian. The image is of an unskilled farmer collecting apples from a tree or plowing a field. In such a world, there is no meaningful joint production combining contributions from many persons to make goods and service. There is no ambiguity in deciding who is responsible for a particular piece of property being created.

[125] Hettinger (1989) pp 38–39. See also Drahos (1996) p 52. At most, it seems that labour gives the labourer a *prima facie* right to possess and personally use the intellectual product for her own benefit: Hettinger (1989) pp 39–40.

[126] Hettinger (1989) p 37; and Spector (1989) p 272.

[127] Spence (2002) p 401 argues that this might be appropriate where an abstract work is the product of inspiration rather than labour; see also Hettinger (1989) p 37.

[128] Hettinger (1989) p 37; Drahos (1996) pp 51–52. Both commentators discuss Robert Nozick's example of pouring a can of tomato juice into the ocean and then asking whether property rights ought to inhere in the ocean or the person should simply lose the tomato juice.

a labour theory. By their very nature, multimedia works are derivative since they involve an interactive *combination* of various inputs. These inputs are often (but not always) pre-existing, and are thus attributable to the labour of individuals other than the multimedia creator. Further, as discussed above, multimedia works are frequently collaborative in nature. Similar to film works, they involve contributions from a wide array of persons rather than from a single individual. According to a labour justification, it would be necessary to recognise the labour of these various contributors when it comes to authorship rules. However, recognising the labour of numerous individuals in relation to the one abstract object may undermine the claim that property rights in that object are crucial to a person's autonomy. Brennan argues that 'joint property cannot be defended easily as an extension of the self, without straining the intrinsic values of integrity and autonomy that justify the granting the right in the first place.'[129]

Finally, multimedia works highlight the inadequacy of labour as a means of designating the abstract object in which property rights inhere. In the case of multimedia works, it is unclear what should be the scope of protection. Should it extend only to the selection and arrangement of the contents, or to the aggregate contents, or to the possible manipulation of the contents that the underlying software permits? No clear answer is provided by a labour analysis.

In terms of whether labour should be rewarded with property rights, it can be queried whether property rights are an appropriate form of reward.[130] According to Hettinger, '[t]he mistake is to conflate the created object which makes a person deserving of a reward with what that reward should be.' He cites other examples of possible rewards, including 'fees, awards, acknowledgment, gratitude, praise, security, power, status, and public financial support.'[131] Hettinger suggests that various factors influence whether property rights are an appropriate reward. For example, he argues that the value of the property rights should at least be proportionate to the effort expended by the labourer in producing the intellectual product. Further, if the person laboured with no desire or expectation of property rights, then it is not fitting to reward the person with such rights. Finally, he argues that there may be certain types of intellectual products (such as abstract theories) where it is never fitting to grant property rights.[132]

Waldron raises another objection to a Lockean based theory by challenging the premise that we have property in our person. Waldron here relies on postmodern theory and its concomitant critique of the notion of the 'author' as the creative genius or subject.[133] He argues that it is possible to view an author or an individ-

---

129 T Brennan, 'Copyright, Property, and the Right to Deny' (1993) 69 *Chicago-Kent L Rev* 677, 692.
130 Spence (2002) p 399; Hettinger (1989) p 41.
131 Hettinger (1989) p 41.
132 Hettinger (1989) pp 40–43.
133 For a classic postmodern critique of the 'author' see M Foucault, 'What is an Author?' in P Rainbow, (ed), *The Foucault Reader* (Penguin, London, 1991) 101–20.

ual as itself a cultural product. In this formulation, it becomes much harder to speak of every man having property in his own person.[134]

Some commentators are also of the view that property rights in intellectual products may run counter to the Lockean provisos concerning 'sufficiency' and 'spoilage'. For example, Drahos argues that even if we assume an infinite stock of abstract objects, it may be that there are conditions of shortage created by the state of cultural and scientific knowledge or human capabilities.[135] Further, he argues that ideas may be capable of spoilage insofar as technological improvements could be confined to certain periods and may become obsolete over time.[136] By contrast, Hettinger believes that copyright is unlikely to be contrary to the sufficiency proviso since (unlike patent law) it does not preclude a person using copyright expression that is independently created (rather than copied). In terms of the spoilage proviso, Hettinger argues that the non-exclusive (or non-rivalrous) quality of intellectual products means that there will always be some degree of waste.[137]

As discussed above, there are difficulties in justifying intellectual property rights on the basis of a labour theory. Multimedia works epitomise some of these difficulties because of their highly derivative and collaborative nature. However, of the two natural law justifications that have been discussed, it is the personality based theory that is the more compelling.

Conclusion

The above analysis has shown that *some* theoretical support exists for the protection of multimedia works. This support exists mainly on the basis of an economic rationale and to a lesser extent according to a natural law rationale. Given this is the case, it seems legitimate to investigate whether or not existing copyright law in the UK, and also at EC and international levels, is adequate to protect multimedia works. To the extent that it is inadequate then what is the appropriate solution? Determining the appropriate solution will be influenced by how much of a 'gap' there is in protection and we will once again have to return to the issue of justifications and assess their consistency with the possible solutions. However, before this can be done it is necessary to undertake a close inspection of UK copyright law and its ability to protect multimedia works.

---

[134] Waldron (1993) p 880. Waldron does not believe that this criticism affects the economic justification.

[135] Drahos (1996) p 51.

[136] Drahos (1996) p 51.

[137] Hettinger (1989) pp 44–45.

3

Subsistence of Copyright in Multimedia Works

Introduction

Copyright protection of multimedia works can be considered at two levels. First, at the level of the individual elements that comprise the multimedia work, or secondly at the level of the multimedia work in its entirety. This chapter is solely concerned with whether a multimedia work taken as an *entire* product is capable of protection under the Copyright Designs and Patents Act 1988 ('CDPA').[1] This issue has both practical and conceptual significance. In practical terms, the market for multimedia works is continually expanding and there is a need to be clear as to the intellectual property rights that may be assigned or licensed in relation to these works.[2] From a conceptual perspective, it is important to explore whether multimedia works are challenging the notions of copyright subject matter.[3]

---

[1] For an analysis under French law see: A Latreille, 'The Legal Classification of Multimedia Creations in French Copyright Law' in I Stamatoudi and P Torremans, (eds), *Copyright in the New Digital Environment* (Sweet & Maxwell, London, 2000) 45–74; and P-Y Gautier, '"Multimedia" Works in French Law' (1994) 160 *RIDA* 90. For a brief, general analysis see M Salokannel, *Ownership of rights in audiovisual productions: a comparative study* (London, The Hague: Kluwer, 1997) pp 313–328 and for a detailed, comparative law analysis see I Stamatoudi, *Copyright and Multimedia Works: A Comparative Analysis* (CUP, Cambridge, 2002).

[2] This has a direct bearing on licensing of multimedia works. Licensing difficulties created by multimedia works are discussed in: F Daun, 'The Content Shop: toward an Economic Legal Structure for Clearing and Licensing Multimedia Content' (1996) 30 *Loyola of Los Angeles L Rev* 215; J Fitzgerald, 'Licensing Content for Multimedia' [1998] *Copyright World* 23; Latreille (2000) pp 58–73; A Monotti, 'University Copyright in the Digital Age: Balancing and Exploiting Rights in Computer Programs, Web-Based Materials, Databases and Multimedia in Australian Universities' [2002] *EIPR* 251; H Sakkers, 'Licensing and Exploiting Rights in Multimedia Products' (1995) 11 *Computer Law & Security Report* 244; S Talbott, 'Content and Licensing Issues in Multimedia Agreements' (1995) 11 *Computer Law & Security Report* 250.

[3] For 'virtual reality' works under Canadian copyright law, see NJ Dasios, 'Virtual Environments: Protecting Virtual Works under Copyright' [1995] 9 *IPJ* 105.

There are eight[4] types of work in which copyright may subsist under the CDPA: original literary, dramatic, musical or artistic works; sound recordings, films, broadcasts; and the typographical arrangement of published editions.[5] Unlike most other jurisdictions, such as the United States,[6] France[7] and Germany,[8] the eight categories constitute an *exhaustive* list of protected subject matter.[9] For copyright to subsist in works, they must fall within the respective definitions of one or more of these types of works.[10] In the case of literary, dramatic, musical and artistic works, they must also be original.[11] The meaning of originality has been developed by case law. Originality requires that the work has not been copied, that it originates with the author,[12] and that it reflects sufficient labour, skill and/or judgment.[13] For databases, originality requires that the selection or arrangement of the contents be the 'author's own intellectual creation'.[14] Sound recordings, films, published editions and broadcasts are not required to be original in nature. However, copyright will not subsist in sound recordings, films and published editions if they are (or to the extent that they are) a copy taken from a previous sound recording, film or typographical arrangement of a published edition.[15] In the case of broadcasts, copyright does not subsist if the broadcast infringes (or to the extent that it infringes) the copyright in another broadcast.[16]

Literary, dramatic and musical works are also subject to a fixation requirement because they must be recorded in writing or otherwise.[17] 'Writing' includes any form of notation or code, regardless of the method by which, or medium in or on which it is recorded.[18] The recording may be in print form or intangible binary

---

[4] Until recently, there were nine categories of works, the ninth being cable programmes. This category was deleted as a result of The Copyright and Related Rights Regulations 2003 SI 2498 ('Copyright Regulations'), reg 5, which came into force on 31 October 2003.

[5] S 1(1), Copyright Designs and Patents Act 1988 (UK) ('CDPA').

[6] S 102(a) of the US Copyright Act 1976 ('USC'), states that copyright may subsist in 'original works of authorship' and gives a non-exhaustive list of categories of work.

[7] French Intellectual Property Code 1992 ('French Code'), Art L112–1 protects 'works of the mind' and Art L112–2 contains a non-exhaustive list of such works.

[8] German Law on Copyright and Neighbouring Rights 1965 ('German Law'), Art 1 protects literary, scientific and artistic works and Art 2(1) defines such works in a non-exhaustive manner.

[9] This has been criticised by A Christie, 'A Proposal for Simplifying United Kingdom Copyright Law' [2001] *EIPR* 26. The same approach is reflected in the Australian Copyright Act 1968 (Cth).

[10] For literary, dramatic and musical works, see s 3; for artistic works see s 4; for sound recordings see s 5A; films s 5B; broadcasts, s 6; and published editions s 8. For an example of subject matter that fell outside the definition of 'artistic work' see *Creation Records v News Group Newspapers* [1997] EMLR 444.

[11] S 1(1)(a), CDPA.

[12] *University of London Press v University Tutorial Press* [1916] 2 Ch 601.

[13] *Walter v Lane* [1900] AC 359; *Cramp v Smythson* [1944] AC 329; *Ladbroke (Football) Ltd v William Hill (Football) Ltd* [1964] 1 WLR 273; *Express Newspapers v News (UK)* [1991] FSR 36.

[14] S 3A, CDPA.

[15] See s 5A(2) for sound recordings; s 5B(4) for films; and s 8(2) for published editions.

[16] See s 6(6) for broadcasts.

[17] S 3(2), CDPA.

[18] S 178, CDPA.

form. With regard to other works, such as sound recordings, films, and published editions, fixation is implicit in the definitions of these works. Artistic works are not subject to an express requirement of fixation, but some cases suggest that fixation is a necessary feature of an artistic work.[19] Broadcasts are not required to be fixed or recorded in material form.

The CDPA also sets out certain qualification requirements which are directed at establishing a sufficient connection with the UK. Qualification may occur via authorship, place of first publication or (in the case of broadcasts) the place of first transmission.[20] Finally, even if the requirements of subject matter, fixation, originality, and qualification are met, it is still possible for copyright protection to be refused on the grounds of public policy.[21]

This chapter examines whether copyright or the database right can subsist in an entire multimedia work, either as a computer program, compilation, copyright database, *sui generis* database, film, dramatic work or broadcast. As such, it looks at whether multimedia works fall within the definitions and understandings of these categories of work. This chapter also considers the consequences of classifying multimedia works under each of these categories, in terms of authorship, ownership, and duration.

1. Computer Program

The underlying computer program in a multimedia product is responsible for how the various inputs are *presented* to the user such as through aesthetically pleasing screen displays or screen icons. More importantly, the computer program determines how the user may *interact* with or *navigate* through those inputs. For example, through 'user friendly' menu hierarchies, toolbars or search commands, or through options that permit a user to manipulate the inputs, such as by allowing a user to create a subset of inputs of interest to the user. This crucial feature of multimedia works is the *user interface*[22] and it is determined by the underlying computer program.

---

[19] See *Creation Records v News Group Newspapers* [1997] EMLR 444, 450; *Merchandising Corporation of America v Harpbond* [1983] FSR 32, 46 per Lawton LJ (with whom Brightman LJ and Oliver LJ agreed).

[20] For details, refer to ss 154–56, CDPA.

[21] *Glyn v Weston Film Feature* [1916] 1 Ch 261, 269–70 (Younger J); *Attorney General v Guardian (No 2)* [1990] 1 AC 109, 275–76 (Lord Griffiths) and 294 (Lord Jauncey).

[22] A distinction will be made between user interface and non-user interface features. Christie and Fong describe user interface features as being either visual (eg, display sequences, screen displays and layouts, icons) or non-visual (eg, functional sequences, operations, options, prompts, menu hierarchies, key assignments and macro commands). They are distinct from non-user interface features, which are those features that make programs internally compatible (eg, file formats, constants and formulae): see A Christie and K Fong, 'Copyright Protection for Non-Code Elements of Software' [1996] 7 *Journal of Law & Information Science* 149; see also S Lai, *The Copyright Protection of Computer Software in the United Kingdom* (Hart Publishing, Oxford, 2000) 211–13.

Copyright subsists in original literary works.[23] A 'literary work' is defined to include a computer program.[24] However, there is no definition of computer program in the CDPA.[25] This is in marked contrast to other common law jurisdictions, such as Australia and the United States, where section 10(1) of the Australian Copyright Act 1968 (Cth) and section 101 of the US Copyright Act 1976 define a 'computer program' as:

> a set of statements or instructions to be used directly or indirectly in a computer in order to bring about a certain result.[26]

In the absence of a statutory definition of 'computer program',[27] UK courts have not had to examine in detail what constitutes a computer program. By contrast, in Australia, the High Court has considered whether individual word commands, a collection of word commands or macro commands constitute a 'set of instructions' and thus a computer program.[28] The conclusion reached by the High Court was that they did not.[29] In the few reported UK decisions on copyright protection of computer programs, the issue has been mainly one of infringement, rather than

---

[23] S 1(1)(a), CDPA.

[24] S 3(1)(b), CDPA. The definition of 'literary work' also includes preparatory design material for a computer program: s 3(1)(c), CDPA. Computer programs were expressly incorporated into legislation, namely, Copyright Act 1956 (UK), by the Copyright (Computer Software) Amendment Act 1985. Prior to this legislation, courts in the UK seemed willing enough to protect computer programs as literary works: see *Gates v Swift* [1982] RPC 339; *Sega Enterprises v Richards* [1983] FSR 73; *Thrustcode Ltd v WW Computing Ltd* [1983] FSR 502. Copyright protection of computer programs as 'literary works' is now mandated by international copyright law: see Article 4 of WIPO Copyright Treaty 1996 ('WCT') and Article 10(1) of the Agreement on Trade Related Aspects of Intellectual Property Rights 1994 ('TRIPs Agreement'). At a European level, protection of computer programs is required by Directive 91/250/EEC on the legal protection of computer programs OJ L122 17/5/91, pp 42–46 ('Software Directive'), Article 1.

[25] H Laddie, *et al, The Modern Law of Copyright and Designs,* 3rd edn, (Butterworths, London, 2000) para 34.19 suggest that an industry definition would be used by the courts, along the following lines: 'a series of instructions capable of being fed into a computer system, by typing in at a keyboard or in any other way, and, when so entered, of controlling its operation in a desired manner'.

[26] This definition was introduced into the Australian Copyright Act 1968 (Cth) by the Copyright Amendment (Digital Agenda) Act 2000 ('DAA'), schedule 1, item 7. It replaced an earlier, more cumbersome definition. In doing so, it was consistent with a recommendation in Aust Copyright Law Review Committee, *Final Report on Computer Software Protection* (AGD, Canberra, 1995) ('Software Report') paras 6.20–6.22.

[27] The Software Directive is also silent on the definition of a computer program. The Commission is not in favour of inserting a definition of 'computer program' into the Software Directive since it feels that any advantage of certainty and accuracy would be outweighed by the risk of the definition becoming outdated by developments in technology: see *Commission Staff Working Paper on the review of the EC legal framework in the field of copyright and related rights* Brussels, 19 July 2004 SEC (2004) 995 ('Working Paper') para 2.2.1.1.

[28] See *Data Access Corporation v Powerflex Services Pty Ltd* (1999) 202 CLR 1, although note that the High Court of Australia was considering the previous definition of 'computer program' in section 10(1) prior to the DAA amendments. Both definitions refer to a 'set of instructions'.

[29] *Data Access Corporation v Powerflex Services Pty Ltd* (1999) 202 CLR 1, 26–27, 29, 35–36 (Gleeson CJ, McHugh, Gummow and Hayne JJ). The same conclusion was reached in the recent UK decision *Navitaire Inc v Easyjet Airline Co* [2005] ECDR 17 ('*Navitaire*').

the subsistence of copyright. Nonetheless, UK courts have made some comments about what constitutes a computer program and these will be considered.

John Richardson Computers Ltd v Flanders ('*Flanders*')[30] involved a claim of infringement in a program that enabled pharmacists to label drugs and maintain an inventory of drugs stocked. The plaintiff's program was designed to run on BBC computers and was written in assembly code. The defendant, who had been previously employed by the plaintiff as its chief programmer, had written a rival program in source code to operate on IBM computers. The plaintiff conceded that no substantial part of the code of its program had been copied, but claimed that the defendant had copied the general scheme of the plaintiff's program, including the idiosyncratic details of certain routines.[31]

The ratio of this case concerned the substantial copying of the non-literal elements of the program and is discussed in the next chapter. However, Ferris J commented on what constitutes a computer program, when observing that a screen display is a product of a program and 'not itself the literary work which is entitled to copyright protection'.[32] He further explained that this conclusion did not preclude the possibility that a screen display (or visual user interface element) may attract 'separate copyright protection as an artistic work in the form of a photograph, or as a film, or as being a reproduction of an artistic work in the form of a drawing'.[33] Thus, *Flanders* highlights that whilst visual user interface features will not be protected as a computer program, they may be protected in their own right as separate works. This view has found support elsewhere.[34]

IBCOS Computers Ltd v Barclays Mercantile Highland Finance Ltd ('*IBCOS*')[35] was another instance of a former employee (and shareholder) of the plaintiff writing a competing software package. The plaintiff's software was an accounting package tailored to transactions in agricultural machinery. It consisted of a complex suite of individual programs, routines and subroutines. The suite contained 335 program files, 171 record layout files and 46 screen layout files, which interacted and functioned as a whole. In order to lure customers away from using the plaintiff's package, the defendant wrote file transfer programs that would allow data compatibility between the two programs. The plaintiff alleged that the defendant's software package, including its file transfer programs, infringed the copyright in their software package.

---

[30] *John Richardson Computers Ltd v Flanders* [1993] FSR 497 ('*Flanders*').

[31] *Flanders*, 519.

[32] *Flanders*, 527.

[33] *Flanders*, 527. See also *Navitaire*, paras 97–98.

[34] In its Software Report, para 9.33, the Australian Copyright Law Review Committee ('CLRC') recommended that protection of computer programs should not extend to non-literal aspects, such as screen displays, but these non-literal aspects should be protected in their own right. See also K Garnett, J James and G Davies, (eds), *Copinger and Skone James on Copyright*, 14th edn, (Sweet & Maxwell, London, 1999)('Copinger') vol 1, para 3–20.

[35] *IBCOS Computers Ltd v Barclays Mercantile Highland Finance Ltd* [1994] FSR 265 ('*IBCOS*').

Jacob J held that not only did copyright subsist in the individual programs within the software package,[36] but the whole suite of programs could be classified as a copyright work, namely, a compilation.[37] However, Jacob J did not regard design features of the software package as forming part of the copyright compilation. This was because the design features reflected minimal originality, such that copying them would be the copying of a general idea and not the expression.[38]

The limited UK case law that exists indicates that copyright in a computer program does not extend to visual user interface features, such as screen displays. Further, it seems that the data embedded with the program generally will not be classified as part of the computer program.[39] However, the lack of definition of 'computer program' can sometimes make the boundary between computer programs and data difficult to identify.[40] Thus, the category of computer program offers inadequate protection for multimedia works that incorporate visual user interface features and a vast range of multiple inputs (ie, data). As the next chapter will demonstrate, non-visual user interface features and the structure of a program fare somewhat better in terms of protection when considered at the infringement stage. Even so, the fact that visual user interface features and data have questionable protection makes this category problematic from the point of view of protecting multimedia works.

2. Compilations and Copyright Databases

As a result of the implementation of the Directive 96/9/EC on the legal protection of databases ('Database Directive')[41] via the Copyright and Rights in Databases Regulations 1997 ('Database Regulations'),[42] a 'database' is a type of literary work within the CDPA, along with 'tables or compilations *other than databases*'.[43]

---

[36] *IBCOS*, 289, 293.

[37] *IBCOS*, 289–90.

[38] *IBCOS*, 305.

[39] Laddie, *et al* (2000) para 34.24.

[40] See D Bainbridge, *Software Copyright Law*, 4th edn (Butterworths, London, 1999) 183: 'With modern programming techniques and software development tools it is, however, not always an easy task to distinguish between database and program. Some databases contain executable instructions. A database file may include forms and reports with associated macros and queries, all contained within the same computer file.' According to Copinger (1999) para 3–20 this difficulty is accentuated by programming techniques such as object-oriented programming. See also C Rees and S Chalton (eds), *Database Law* (Jordans, Bristol, 1998) 29. V Bouganim, *The Legal Protection of Databases: From Copyright to Dataright* (University of London, unpublished PhD thesis, 1999) 67 suggests that where data is intended to control the flow, processing, manipulation and presentation of objects held in computer storage, it would form part of the computer program. But when data is the object to be processed, manipulated or presented it does not constitute part of the computer program.

[41] OJ L77 27/3/96, pp 20–28.

[42] SI 1997/3032. These came into force on 1 January 1998.

[43] S 3(1), CDPA.

(a) Meaning of Table or Compilation

Neither 'table' nor 'compilation' is defined in the CDPA. However, it is clear that these works will fall outside the definition of 'database' in section 3A.[44] From the point of view of protecting multimedia works as 'tables' or 'compilations', it is necessary to consider whether a 'table' or 'compilation' may be *electronic* and the sorts of material that may comprise them.

It is useful first to examine the UK's international obligations in this area. The Berne Convention for the protection of literary and artistic works 1886 ('Berne Convention'), Article 2(5)[45] mandates copyright protection for 'collections of literary or artistic works such as encyclopaedias and anthologies which, by reason of the selection or arrangement of their contents, constitute intellectual creations'. According to Ricketson, Article 2(5) allows collections (or compilations—the words are interchangeable) of a *diversity* of subject matter. Since Article 2(5) refers to 'literary and artistic works', the collection must be of subject matter capable of attracting copyright protection. It does not impose any obligations to protect collections of non-copyright material, such as telephone directories, but leaves this as a matter for national legislation.[46] Further, Article 2(5) does not appear to require protection for electronic collections. This may be contrasted with the Agreement on Trade Related Aspects of Intellectual Property Rights 1994 ('TRIPs Agreement'), Article 10(2), which requires copyright protection for 'compilations of data or other material, *whether in machine readable or other form*, which by reason of the selection or arrangement of their contents constitute intellectual creations' (emphasis supplied). Article 5 of the WIPO Copyright Treaty 1996 ('WCT') is to the same effect. Unlike Article 2(5) of the Berne Convention, Article 10(2) of the TRIPs Agreement and Article 5 of WCT clearly envisage that *electronic compilations of non-copyright material* should be protected.

Under UK copyright law, it appears that a 'table' or 'compilation' may be in *electronic* form,[47] since section 3 of the CDPA states that literary works must be *recorded in writing* and 'writing' is defined in sufficiently broad terms to include binary notation.[48]

However, the material which may comprise a table or compilation is restricted. A collection of dramatic or musical works cannot qualify as a compilation because

---

[44] E Derclaye, 'Do Sections 3 and 3A of the CDPA Violate the Database Directive? A Closer Look at the Definition of a Database in the UK and its Compatibility with European Law' [2002] *EIPR* 466.

[45] Compilations have been protected since the Berlin Act of the Berne Convention: see S Ricketson, *The Berne Convention for the Protection of Literary and Artistic Works: 1886–1986* (Kluwer, London, 1987), 299.

[46] Ricketson (1987) p 303.

[47] This also is the case under Australian copyright law—see *Data Access Corporation v Powerflex Services Pty Ltd* (1999) 202 CLR 1 (HCA)—the Huffman compression table. The Explanatory Memorandum to the Copyright Amendment Act 1984 (Cth) clearly envisaged that the amendment to the definition of 'literary work' in respect of compilations would serve to protect databases (para 26).

[48] See s 178, CDPA.

the definition of 'literary work' in section 3(1) expressly excludes dramatic and musical works. Further, because tables and compilations are categorised as *literary works*, collections of artistic works are probably excluded from being compilations.[49] To expand, a literary work must be 'written, spoken or sung' and whilst 'writing' is defined to include 'any form of notation or code, whether by hand or otherwise' (and 'written' shall be construed accordingly), it is difficult to see how artistic works could be characterised as being in 'notation or code'.[50] The same may be said for sound recordings and films.[51] Whilst it seems possible to protect compilations that are only partly 'written', there is uncertainty over the minimal level of literary material that would be required.[52]

Given tables or compilations may only comprise certain material, this means that potentially large amounts of a multimedia work may be excluded from protection as a compilation.[53] This seriously undermines the ability of this sub-category of 'literary work' to protect multimedia works.[54] Such a limited notion of 'compilation' in the CDPA can be criticised since, logically speaking, *any type* of copyright work should be able to form part of a compilation:

> There is no justification for denying subsistence of copyright to one type of compilation, for making its subsistence depend on the extent of 'literary' content in the work or for denying protection to compilation skills expended on non-literary material when the nature of the skills which are being recognised and protected apply equally to any type of compilation.[55]

Moreover, it seems contrary to the UK's international obligations, discussed earlier, to exclude certain copyright works from the scope of 'compilation' in section 3, CDPA.[56]

The recent amendments to the CDPA to include 'databases' as a literary work appear to alleviate to some extent the difficulties identified above.[57] We now turn to examine the definition of 'database' within the CDPA.

---

[49] See A Monotti, 'The Extent of Copyright Protection for Compilations of Artistic Works' [1993] 5 *EIPR* 156, 161; Stamatoudi (2002) p 76. *Cf* Copinger (1999) para 3–14. See also *Football Association Premier League Ltd v Panini UK Ltd* [2004] FSR 1, 13–14, per Mummery LJ, who comments obiter that an album collection of artistic works (in the form of stickers) is a literary work in the form of a 'compilation'.

[50] See Monotti (1993) p 161, 'The definition of "writing" is inclusive, but most paintings, drawings and photographs are unlikely to be within the normal meaning of this term.'

[51] Stamatoudi (2002) pp 85–86 explains that a multimedia work comprising diverse inputs will not satisfy the requirements of a literary work simply because it is in digital form.

[52] See Monotti (1993) p 160.

[53] See also Stamatoudi (2002) p 87 who argues that multimedia works, to be protected as compilations, would have to mainly comprise literary works; and Monotti (2002) pp 252–53.

[54] P Leonard, 'Beyond the Future—Multimedia and the Law' (1994) 7 *Australian Intellectual Property Law Bulletin* 105, 110; Stamatoudi (2002) p 87.

[55] Monotti (1993) p 160.

[56] Under Berne Convention for the Protection of Literary and Artistic Works 1886 ('Berne Convention'), Art 2(5); TRIPs Agreement, Art 10(2); and WCT, Art 5.

[57] See also Stamatoudi (2002) p 78; and L Bently and B Sherman, *Intellectual Property Law*, 2nd edn, (OUP, Oxford, 2004) 64–65.

(b) Definition of Database

Section 3A(1) defines 'database' as:

> 3A. –(1) . . . a collection of independent works, data or other materials which—
>
> are arranged in a systematic or methodical way, and
> are individually accessible by electronic or other means.[58]

The definition in section 3A implements verbatim Article 1(2) of the Database Directive. The fact the definition refers to 'independent works, data or other materials' suggests that a wide range of material may comprise a database.[59] This is confirmed by recital 17 of the Database Directive which states that databases include 'literary, artistic, musical or other collections of works or collections of other material such as texts, sounds, images, numbers, facts, and data'.[60] However, a 'database' is classed as a literary work, which suggests that a database is subject to the same restrictions discussed above in relation to compilations. Accordingly, it is arguable that UK implementation of this aspect of the Database Directive is incomplete.[61] The better view is that the amendments effected by the Database Regulations should be construed (as far as possible) in line with the Directive[62] so that the broad definition of database contained in (separate) section 3A can be given its full effect.[63]

Since the definition of 'database' refers to the contents being individually accessible by 'electronic or other means', it is clear that both electronic and non-electronic (or hard copy) databases are included. In the original and amended proposals of the Database Directive the definition was initially restricted to electronic databases. This was because the Database Directive was originally targeted at the problems surrounding electronic data. However, in the Directive as adopted the distinction between electronic and non-electronic databases was removed. The Council, in its Common Position, indicated that this approach was simpler to

[58] Added by Copyright and Rights in Databases Regulations 1997, SI 1997/3032 ('Database Regulations'), regs 4 and 6.

[59] According to MJ Davison, *The Legal Protection of Databases* (CUP, Cambridge, 2003) 73 'works' probably refers to individual copyright works; whereas 'data' are 'facts, especially numerical facts' and 'other materials' probably refers to information generally.

[60] Note, however, that compilations of several recordings of musical performances on a CD do not fall within the scope of the Directive, due to lack of originality under copyright or lack of substantial investment under the database right. Note also that Stamatoudi (2002) p 89 n 6, states that 3D objects are excluded according to the Explanatory Memorandum COM (93) 464 final SYN 393 at 41. E Derclaye, 'What is a Database? A Critical Analysis of the Definition of a Database in the European Database Directive and Suggestions for an International Definition' (2002b) 5 *J of World Intellectual Property* 981, 998–1003 argues persuasively that the definition of 'database' does not extend to collections of tangible objects. *Cf* Davison (2003) p 73 who believes that a library or gallery may be a 'database'.

[61] Davison (2003) p 145; Rees and Chalton (1998) p 49.

[62] Bainbridge (1999) p 186.

[63] Stamatoudi (2002) pp 77–78.

apply. Further, it was inappropriate for the same database to enjoy different standards of protection, based on whether it was distributed in electronic or non-electronic form. Finally, this approach was consistent with the TRIPs Agreement and the (then incipient) WCT.[64]

Although section 3A implements verbatim Article 1(2) of the Database Directive, Article 1(3), which states that the Directive 'shall not apply to computer programs used in the making or operation of databases accessible by electronic means', is not directly reflected in the Database Regulations. Nevertheless, it seems that computer programs will *not* amount to a 'database' within the CDPA because section 3(1) draws a distinction between computer programs and databases, and the legislation should be construed in conformity with the Directive. However, there is a more general concern about whether it is *possible* to distinguish a computer program from a database[65] especially when there is no definition of computer program in the CDPA[66] and the recitals to the Database Directive indicate that thesauruses and indexation systems may nevertheless form part of a database.[67] Davison identifies another tension between computer programs and databases when he points out that the broad definition of 'database' allows protection for data stored *within* a computer program and crucial to the program's operation,[68] as happened in *Mars UK Ltd v Teknowledge Ltd* ('*Mars*').[69] In *Mars*, data concerning the dimensions and other qualities of coins was stored on the EEPROM (electronically erasable programmable read-only memory) devices. This data was crucial to the operation of the computer program, because it allowed it successfully to discriminate between legitimate and illegitimate coins. The defendants conceded that their reproduction of the data in the EEPROMs was an infringement of the claimant's database right. Davison is critical of such data being protected as a database. He argues that it is inappropriate to protect data within computer programs in this manner, because 'the recitals suggest that there is no intention to increase or alter the existing protection provided by copyright to computer programs or parts of them.'[70] Further, he argues that data in a computer program is only there to help the program function, and not to instruct or inform a person, yet the purpose of the Database Directive as reflected in the recitals is apparently 'to improve investment in the generation and processing of information and modern information

---

[64] See the Statement of the Council's Reasons in Common Position (EC) No 20/95 adopted by the Council on 10 July 1995 (C 288/14) at p 24. See also Davison (2003) pp 54, 62–63, 66.

[65] Bainbridge (1999) p 183; Davison (2003) pp 74–75.

[66] Rees and Chalton (1998) p 29.

[67] Directive 96/9/EC on the legal protection of databases OJ L77 27/3/96, pp 20–28 ('Database Directive'), recital 20, states that protection under this Directive 'may also apply to the material necessary for the operation or consultation of certain databases such as thesaurus and indexation systems.' See also Bainbridge (1999) p 187, who regards these elements as non-literal elements of a database.

[68] See also Bently and Sherman (2004) p 64.

[69] *Mars UK Ltd v Teknowledge Ltd* [2000] ECDR 99 ('*Mars*').

[70] Davison (2003) p 71.

storage and processing systems.'[71] It seems that even if the CDPA, mirroring the Database Directive, distinguishes protection of databases from that of computer programs, there remains some confusion about how to draw this distinction.

To qualify as a database there must be a collection of '*independent* works, data or other materials' (emphasis supplied). Some guidance to the meaning of independence is provided by recital 17 of the Database Directive, which states that 'a recording or an audio visual, cinematographic, literary or musical work as such does not fall within the scope of this Directive'.[72] For some multimedia works, the 'independence' requirement may prove to be an obstacle to protection. Beutler considers that:[73]

> The question arises whether the elements of multimedia products can be said to be independent of each other, contrary to the elements of films. The answer, clearly, has to be positive in the case of, for example, a multimedia encyclopaedia or a multimedia catalogue, both bringing together a huge number of different materials which, broadly speaking, interrelate but do not depend on each other.
>
> But what about the vast number of complex multimedia games which, besides the fact that they are interactively accessible, for viewers, are comparable to films? Are not the elements interrelated in such a way that it would be difficult to qualify them as 'independent'? Are not the complicated graphics and the underlying software dependent on one another?[73]

According to Beutler, interrelated works can be either independent of, or dependent upon, each other, but there is a correlation between the degree of interrelatedness between works and the likelihood of them being dependent on one another.

The qualification 'independent' creates uncertainty as to the kinds of works that can comprise a database. The *Shorter Oxford English Dictionary* defines the word to include the following meanings: 'not depending upon the authority of another; not in a position of subordination; not subject to external control or rule; self governing or free'; or 'not contingent on or conditioned by anything else; not depending on the existence or action of others, or of each other'; or in mathematics, 'not depending on another for its value'.[74] The dictionary definition is useful for understanding the meaning of 'independent' in section 3A(1) of CDPA. However, it is not determinative of its interpretation, because the term must be viewed in its legislative context.

A means of unravelling the meaning of 'independent' in this context is to make a distinction between physical and conceptual independence. Physically 'indepen-

---

[71] Davison (2003) p 71 (footnote omitted).

[72] See also Rees and Chalton (1998) p 50.

[73] S Beutler, 'The Protection of Multimedia Products through the European Community's Directive on the Legal Protection of Databases' [1996] 8 *Ent L R* 317, 324.

[74] *The Shorter Oxford English Dictionary on Historical Principles*, 3rd edn (Clarendon Press, Oxford, 1991) ('SOED') vol 1, p 1054.

dent' might refer to the physical separateness of a work. However, this is probably not the meaning of 'independent' in section 3A(1), since it would be either stating the obvious or inapplicable.

'Independent', for the purposes of section 3A(1), is more likely to relate to conceptual or logical independence. A work will be conceptually independent where it is capable of having the same meaning both inside and outside the collection, as opposed to relying on the surrounding context for its meaning.[75] This interpretation does not consider whether or not the work has a different value or worth depending on its context. In other words, it ignores whether the work has an 'added value' as part of the database.[76] Rather, it is intended only to focus on the consistency of meaning ascribed to an element.[77]

The above interpretation finds support in the ruling of the European Court of Justice (ECJ) in *Fixtures Marketing Ltd v Organismos prognostikon agonon podosfairou AE ('OPAP')*.[78] This case involved football fixture lists produced by the Football Association Premier League Ltd and the Football League Ltd in England and the Scottish Football League in Scotland. The fixture lists were exploited by Football Fixtures Ltd within the UK and outside the UK by Fixtures Marketing Ltd. Fixtures Marketing complained that OPAP repeatedly extracted a substantial number of fixtures and placed them on its websites to facilitate betting activities, thereby distributing and making them available to the Greek public. The Single-Judge Court of First Instance, Athens stayed proceedings and referred three questions to the ECJ. Questions 1 and 2 sought preliminary rulings on the definition of database and whether or not the football fixture lists enjoyed protection as databases.[79] In discussing the requirement of 'independence' within Article 1(2), Advocate General Stix-Hackl had opined:

---

[75] This interpretation is similar to Beutler (1996) p 324, except that he expresses the issue in terms of the degree of inter-relatedness between elements. See also Derclaye (2002) p 469: '"independent" means that an element makes sense by itself: its meaning does not depend on another element, another piece of information.' She gives the example of stock market information being the type of information that is not independent since it relies on the surrounding information in order to make sense.

[76] See also Stamatoudi (2002) p 90 who argues that a work, data or other material can be independent and yet have an enhanced value because it forms part of a database.

[77] Cf Laddie, *et al*, (2000) para 30.19 who argue that: 'To be independent the works data or other materials should be capable of being, or intended to be, appreciated or useful in isolation.' As such, chapters in a literary work or scenes from a dramatic would be excluded, but encyclopaedias and other reference texts would satisfy the test.

[78] C–444/02, *Fixtures Marketing Ltd v Organismos Prognostikon Agnon Podosfairou (OPAP)* C–444/02 (Grand Chamber, 9 November 2004) ('*OPAP* (ECJ)').

[79] Question 1: 'What is the definition of database and what is the scope of the Directive 96/9/EC and in particular Article 7 thereof which concerns the *sui generis* right?'; and question 2: 'In the light of the definition of the scope of the directive, do lists of football fixtures enjoy protection as databases over which there is a *sui generis* right in favour of the maker and under what conditions?' See *OPAP* (ECJ) para 10.

That criterion should be understood as meaning that the data or materials must not be linked or *must at least be capable of being separate without losing their informative content,* which is why sound or pictures from a film are not covered. One possible approach to interpretation is to focus not only on the mutual independence of the materials from one another but on their *independence within a collection.*[80] (Emphasis supplied)

The ECJ took a similar view to the Advocate General, in holding that 'independent' materials refers to materials 'which are separable from one another without their informative, literary, artistic, musical or other value being affected.'[81] The ECJ indicated that football fixture lists contain 'independent' materials because the date and time of fixtures, along with the identity of the two teams playing, had 'autonomous informative value.'[82] The view taken by the ECJ is consistent with the interpretation of 'independent' argued for above, namely, that it means conceptual independence, such that works, data or materials are capable of having the same meaning both inside and outside the collection.

Two examples will assist in illustrating the notion of 'conceptually independent'. In a multimedia encyclopaedia the elements contained within it have the same meaning whether they are grouped together with other works or are viewed as separate items. An entry on 'solar eclipses' makes sense as a separate work and as part of the collective work. It may well be that there is an additional value in having that work in a reference form, but the meaning remains the same regardless of the different form. This may be compared with a multimedia video game, such as Virtua Cop, which has a simple plot of two police officers investigating and chasing a criminal organisation.[83] An aspect of this game, such as the graphical representation of the protagonist, may have a different meaning depending on the context. While the graphic might have a meaning as a single graphic when it exists outside the game, its meaning is significantly altered and enhanced by being placed within the context of the entire game.[84]

---

[80] C–444/02, *Fixtures Marketing Ltd v Organismos Prognostikon Agnon Podosfairou (OPAP),* Opinion of the Advocate General delivered on 8 June 2004 ('*OPAP* (Opinion)') para 39.

[81] *OPAP* (ECJ) para 29.

[82] *OPAP* (ECJ) para 33. At para 34 the ECJ remarks: 'Although it is true that the interest of a football league lies in the overall result of the various matches in that league, the fact remains that the data concerning the date, the time and the identity of the teams in a particular match have an independent value in that they provide interested third parties with relevant information.'

[83] This was the video game in *Galaxy Electronics Pty Ltd v Sega Enterprises Ltd* (1997) 37 IPR 462 ('*Galaxy Electronics*'). A series of computer generated images resembling, more or less, a traditional movie film, was presented together with sound effects, music and simple dialogue. There were three scenarios in the game that unfolded only if the players gave the correct responses to all of the cues. When the players gave incorrect responses several variations resulted so that, within certain limits, different events were shown on the screen each time the game was played. For a more detailed description of the game see *Galaxy Electronics,* 464–65 (Wilcox J, delivering the leading judgment).

[84] This approach is similar to that of Rees and Chalton (1998) p 27: 'The requirement of independence was apparently to exclude from the definition works which comprise elements of content capable of standing alone as works in their own right and of being accessed, read or used independently of one another, but which in reality form part of the compiled complete work.'

A consequence of interpreting the requirement of 'independent' to mean 'conceptually independent' is that multimedia video games will be excluded. Similarly, intermediate multimedia works, which combine reference qualities with the use of moving user interfaces,[85] will have trouble demonstrating that the works they include are independent. Reference-type multimedia works will have no difficulty in satisfying the requirement of 'independent' works, data or other materials.

The second (and least problematic) requirement of the definition in section 3A(1) of the CDPA is that the collection is 'arranged in a systematic or methodical way'. The *Shorter Oxford English Dictionary* defines 'arrange' as 'to place in some order, dispose'.[86] What is required is *systematic or methodical ordering* of the contents. With contents stored in electronic form, ordering can occur in a physical *and* conceptual way (or, rather, one can distinguish between physical and conceptual ordering whereas this merges in the case of hard copy works). The physical ordering relates to how the information is stored for the purposes of interaction with the computer program. By contrast, conceptual ordering refers to how the material is presented to its user.[87] Recital 21 of the Database Directive makes it clear that 'it is not necessary for those materials to have been physically stored in an organized manner'.[88] This means that 'arranged in a systematic or methodical way' should be understood to refer to the *conceptual arrangement* (or *presentation*) of contents to the user. Support for this view is apparent from the following statement of the ECJ in *OPAP*:

> While it is not necessary for the systematic or methodical arrangement to be physically apparent, according to the 21st recital, that condition implies that the collection should be contained in a fixed base, of some sort, and *include technical means* such as electronic, electromagnetic or electro-optical processes, in the terms of the 13th recital of the preamble to the directive, *or other means, such as an index, a table of contents, or a particular plan or method of classification, to allow the retrieval of any independent material* contained within it. (Emphasis supplied)[89]

In *OPAP*, the ECJ held that the conditions of systematic and methodical arrangement and individual accessibility of the constituent materials were met by the arrangement of the data according to 'dates, times and names of teams in those various football matches'.[90] As such, the fixture list constituted a database.

---

[85] Eg, Australia, Department of Communications and the Arts, *Real Wild Child: Australian Rock Music and Culture 1950s–90s*, 1998, Multimedia CD Rom ('Real Wild Child CD-Rom').

[86] SOED, 106.

[87] WL Austin, 'A Thoughtful and Practical Analysis of Database Protection under Copyright Law and a Critique of Sui Generis Protection' [1998] 3 *Journal of Technology, Law & Policy* at http://journal.law.ufl.edu/~techlaw/3–1/austin.html, paras 32, 33 and 37.

[88] In *OPAP* (Opinion), Advocate General Stix-Hackl opined, at para 40, that recital 21 'serves to exclude random accumulations of data and ensure that only planned collections of data are covered, that is to say, data organised to specific criteria.'

[89] *OPAP* (ECJ) para 30.

[90] *OPAP* (ECJ) para 35.

Thus, it appears that the requirement of 'systematic or methodical arrangement' will be relatively easy to satisfy, provided the collection is not haphazard in nature.[91] The types of collections that have qualified as databases include telephone directories,[92] football fixture lists,[93] news websites[94] and trade directories.[95] From these cases, and the ruling in *OPAP*, it can be inferred that alphabetical, chronological or subject arrangement will suffice.

The requirement that 'works, data or other materials' be 'individually accessible by electronic or other means' is the final and perhaps the most perplexing aspect of the definition of 'database'.[96] The *Shorter Oxford English Dictionary* defines 'individually' as 'in an individual or distinctive manner; as single persons or things; each by each, one by one; opposite to collectively'[97] and 'accessible' as 'capable of being entered or reached'.[98] Following the dictionary definition, a literal interpretation of 'individually accessible' probably requires that (independent) works, data or other materials are *separately retrievable*. Although support exists for this literal interpretation,[99] it is problematic since it would exclude a number of hard copy databases that are archetypal examples of databases.[100] A hard copy telephone directory is an archetypal database,[101] and yet the independent data (ie, names and telephone numbers) within a telephone directory are *not*

---

[91] See also Derclaye (2002) pp 468–69; L Kaye, 'The Proposed EU Directive For the Legal Protection Of Databases: A Cornerstone Of The Information Society' [1995] *EIPR* 583; Laddie, *et al*, (2000) paras 30.21–30.22; Stamatoudi (2002) p 93.

[92] *Unauthorised Reproduction of Telephone Directories on CD-Rom* [2002] ECDR 3 (BGH).

[93] *OPAP* (ECJ) para 36.

[94] *Sa Prline v Sa Communication & Sales and Sal News Investment* [2002] ECDR 2 (financial news website); *Danske Dagblades Forening (DDF) v Newsbooster* [2003] ECDR 5 (selection of news articles on a website).

[95] *Societe Tigest Sarl v Societe Reed Expositions France* [2002] ECC 29 (directory of trade exhibitors) ('Societe Tigest'); *British Horseracing Board Ltd v William Hill Organization Ltd* [2002] ECDR 4 (CA) (horse racing industry database).

[96] Derclaye (2002) p 469 describes this requirement as 'quite obscure' in its meaning. According to M Powell, 'The European Union's Database Directive: an International Antidote to the Side Effects of *Feist*?' (1997) 20 *Fordham International Law Journal* 1215, 1229, this requirement will operate to limit the range of works and materials covered by the Database Directive.

[97] SOED, 1059.

[98] SOED, 11.

[99] See Stamatoudi (2002) pp 99–102 who argues that materials which are conjunctively retrieved or integrated cannot satisfy this part of the definition, unless they are also individually accessible. See also Derclaye (2002) p 469 suggesting that it means that elements cannot be 'tied-in' but must be separately retrieved.

[100] Note that the definition in s 3A(2) CDPA emphasises that works, data or other materials may be individually accessible by non-electronic means, thus including hard copy databases within its ambit: see also recital 14, Database Directive.

[101] Several major cases concerning databases have been about the protection of telephone directories: see *Feist Publications Inc v Rural Telephone Service Co* (1991) 499 US 340; *Tele-Direct (Publications) Inc v American Business Information Inc* 154 DLR (4th) 328 (1997); *Unauthorised Reproduction of Telephone Directories on CD-Rom* [2002] ECDR 3; *Desktop Marketing Systems Pty Ltd v Telstra Corporation Ltd* [2002] FCAFC 112.

separately retrievable, since they are listed alongside one another.[102] The same may be said for a trade catalogue or football fixture list. With these sorts of collections, data may be separately *viewed* insofar as it is visually distinct from other data. However, the data cannot be separately accessed or retrieved. One way of reconciling the literal interpretation of 'individual accessibility' with the types of works that are usually considered to be databases, is to argue that 'individual accessibility' has a different meaning depending on whether the database is electronic or non-electronic (ie, hard copy). This is an inappropriate approach, because it runs contrary to the intention underlying the Database Directive not to discriminate between hard copy and electronic databases.

A more sensible approach to the requirement of 'individual accessibility' is to consider it in tandem with the requirement that works are arranged systematically or methodically.[103] The ECJ in *OPAP* seemed to take this approach, in reaching the conclusion that '[t]he arrangement, in the form of a fixture list, of the dates, times and names of teams in those various football matches meets the conditions as to systematic or methodical arrangement and individual accessibility of the constituent materials of that collection.'[104] Thus, it is argued that 'individual accessibility' means that the collection must be in a *searchable form* and that the materials within can be *viewed distinctly*, as opposed to being separately retrievable ('purposive interpretation'). A work will be 'individually accessible' if it is possible to search for the work (whether that is by keyword, alphabetical arrangement or otherwise) and perceive it, even if the work is accessed alongside other material.[105]

If the literal interpretation of individual accessibility is adopted, then multimedia video games will not fall within the definition of 'database' in the CDPA. The elements that make up a multimedia game cannot be separately retrieved because the player (or user) triggers certain predetermined sequences to unfold. The sequence that unfolds does depend on the player's skill to a certain degree, but is largely predetermined by the underlying computer program. A player's ability to see a particular feature of the game depends on contingencies: those of the player's skill in reaching the requisite level and the response of the computer program to the player's actions at that moment.[106] Multimedia works that integrate their

---

[102] The same may be argued for electronic telephone directories, such as www.yell.co.uk and www.whitepages.com.au, where a search for particular data can produce the data sought, alongside other data that is a near match. Where this happens the data may be viewed distinctly, but it is not, strictly speaking, correct to say that it has been separately retrieved.

[103] Cf Bouganim (1999) p 55 who argues that the requirement of individually accessible appears closely related to the requirement of 'independent' and, as such, is redundant.

[104] *OPAP* (ECJ) para 35.

[105] In support, see Laddie, *et al*, (2000) para 30.24 who argues that in order to satisfy the requirement of 'individually accessible' it is not necessary to completely exclude the other contents of the database from view. To follow such an interpretation would impose too strict a requirement and would exclude many paper databases.

[106] Note that multimedia games may still be protected as either a 'computer program' or 'film'.

constituent inputs may face similar difficulties to multimedia video games. If sound, text, and visual elements are combined so that they are presented *simultaneously*, then it will not be possible to show that they are separately retrievable.

If the purposive interpretation of individual accessibility is adopted, then multimedia video games will continue to fall outside the definition of 'database' since the materials within will not be searchable. However, multimedia works which present their constituent inputs in an integrated manner[107] (but which are not video games) should fall within the definition of 'database' provided they have a search function. Reference-type multimedia works should have no difficulty in showing that their constituent inputs are individually accessible according to a purposive interpretation.

(c) The Test of Originality

Both compilations and databases must be original[108] literary works in order to qualify for copyright protection.[109] Section 3A(2) of the CDPA[110] explicitly sets out the test of originality for databases.[111] It states:

3A

. . .

(2) For the purposes of this Part a literary work consisting of *a database is original* if, and only if, by reason of the *selection or arrangement* of the contents of the database it constitutes the *author's own intellectual creation.* (Emphasis supplied)

Compilations other than databases appear to remain subject to the traditional test of sufficient 'labour, skill and judgment'.[112] An important question is whether these two tests, of 'labour, skill and judgement' and an 'author's own intellectual creation', reflect different standards of originality. If they do, this will lead to a class

---

[107] See, for example, Australia, Department of Communications and the Arts, *Moorditj—Australian Indigenous Cultural Expressions*, 1998, Multimedia CD-Rom ('Moorditj CD-Rom').

[108] For comparative analyses of originality see D Gervais, '*Feist* Goes Global: a Comparative Analysis of the Notion of Originality in Copyright Law' (2002) 49 *J Copyright Soc'y USA* 949; and G Wei, 'Telephone Directories and Databases: The Policy at the Helm of Copyright Law and a Tale of Two Cities' [2004] *IPQ* 316.

[109] Ss 1(1)(a); 3(1)(a) and (d), CDPA.

[110] s 3A(2), CDPA, inserted by the Database Regulations, implements Article 3(1) of Database Directive. But see GWG Karnell, 'European Originality: A Copyright Chimera' in J Kabel and G Mom, (eds), *Intellectual Property and Information Law: Essays in Honour of Herman Cohen Jehoram* (Kluwer, The Hague, 1998) 201–9 who doubts the success of this harmonization of originality.

[111] Which is the first time the originality test has been explicated in the UK statute: S Lai, 'Database Protection in the United Kingdom: the New Deal and its Effects on Software Protection' [1998] 1 *EIPR* 32.

[112] *Macmillan & Co Ltd v Cooper* (1923) 1B IPR 204, 209 (Lord Atkinson); *Cramp v Smythson* [1944] AC 329, 340 (Lord Porter); *Ladbroke (Football) Ltd v William Hill (Football) Ltd* [1964] 1 WLR 273, 277 (Lord Reid) and 282 (Lord Evershed); *Express Newspapers v Liverpool Daily Post* [1985] 1 WLR 1089, 1093.

of compilations (which are not databases) that are protected in the UK according to a *different* standard of originality. This appears contrary to the Database Directive, which seeks to harmonise copyright law protection of all compilations.[113] In terms of multimedia works, this may mean that they are more easily protected as non-database compilations than as databases.

The UK test of 'labour, skill and judgment' has been equated to the 'sweat of the brow' (or 'industrious collection') doctrine.[114] This doctrine defines a compilation as original where there has been sufficient expenditure of labour or expense *in collecting the information recorded in the compilation*, without requiring any creativity or skill.[115] This doctrine is most commonly associated with US copyright jurisprudence[116] prior to the Supreme Court decision in *Feist Publications Inc v Rural Telephone Service Co* ('*Feist*').[117] However, it is doubtful whether the UK test of 'labour, skill and judgment' is in fact tantamount to the 'industrious collection' doctrine.[118] The main arguments for equating these tests were articulated by the Full Federal Court of Australia in *Desktop Marketing Systems Pty Ltd v Telstra Corporation Ltd* ('*Desktop*').[119] In this case, a telephone company, Telstra, had produced white pages and yellow pages telephone directories for areas within Australia. Desktop Marketing Systems had produced three CD-Rom products which contained white and yellow pages listings data that had been extracted from Telstra's directories. Desktop had copied the primary data for its CD-Rom products from Telstra's directories, verified it, and to a limited extent had added to it. Telstra claimed that Desktop's products infringed copyright in their directories which were protected as original literary works.[120] In its defence, Desktop claimed that Telstra's products were not original works because they lacked sufficient skill

---

[113] Derclaye (2002) p 474; Lai (1998) p 33. Given the broad definition of 'database' in s 3A, CDPA, there are unlikely to be many 'compilations other than databases' and so this may not be a major problem.

[114] D Gervais, 'The Compatibility of the Skill and Labour Originality Standard with the Berne Convention and the TRIPS Agreement' [2004] *EIPR* 75 argues that the traditional UK test of skill and labour is probably the result of not having a tort of misappropriation. Further, that the test is incompatible with the UK's international obligations under the Berne Convention and the TRIPs Agreement. Ricketson (1987) supports this latter point at para 16.15 where he argues that common law countries, in protecting works that result from the investment of time, labour and money, depart from the spirit of 'intellectual creation', which is a requirement implicit in the notion of literary and artistic work. However, the Berne Convention mandates minimum standards of protection and does not preclude Berne Union members from using a lower standard of originality. Further, Ricketson (1987) at para 16.15 points out that no guidance was provided on what constituted 'intellectual creation'. Thus, it is argued that a 'skill and labour' test is not contrary to international obligations, as set out in the Berne Convention and the TRIPS Agreement.

[115] *Desktop Marketing Systems Pty Ltd v Telstra Corporation Ltd* [2002] FCAFC 112 ('*Desktop*') para 160 (Lindgren J) para 409 (Sackville J). See also Lai (1998) 32–33.

[116] See for example, *Jeweler's Circular Pub Co v Keystone Pub Co* 281 F 83(1922).

[117] *Feist Publications Inc v Rural Telephone Service Co* (1991) 499 US 340 ('*Feist*').

[118] Cf Bently and Sherman (2004) pp 99–100.

[119] *Desktop Marketing Systems Pty Ltd v Telstra Corporation Ltd* [2002] FCAFC 112.

[120] Pursuant to ss 32 and 10(1) of the Australian Copyright Act 1968 (Cth).

in their selection or arrangement of data. They also argued that their CD-Rom products were not substantially similar to Telstra's directories because their products contained additional information and the data was presented differently, ie within separate records as opposed to within columns on a page. Finkelstein J at first instance in the Federal Court[121] held that Australian copyright law, which relied heavily on UK authorities (pre-Database Directive), *did* protect compilations that were a result of 'industrious collection' and found that Desktop had reproduced a substantial part of Telstra's directories.[122]

The Full Federal Court of Australia[123] upheld Finkelstein J's decision on appeal.[124] Lindgren and Sackville JJ each delivered judgments (with which Black CJ agreed) in which they comprehensively reviewed UK case law on protection of compilations both before and after the Copyright Act 1911 (UK), along with the relevant Australian authorities. This led Lindgren J to conclude that:

> Decisively for the present case, there is no principle that the labour and expense of collecting, verifying, recording and assembling (albeit routinely) data to be compiled are irrelevant to, or are incapable of themselves establishing, origination, and therefore originality; on the contrary, the authorities strongly suggest that labour of that kind may do so.[125]

Sackville J arrived at a similar conclusion (albeit stated more positively) that:

> the course of authority in the United Kingdom and Australia recognises that originality in a factual compilation may lie in the labour and expense involved in collecting the information recorded in the work, as distinct from the 'creative' exercise of skill or judgment, or the application of intellectual effort.[126]

The conclusion reached by Lindgren J and Sackville J is underpinned by two main arguments. First, support for the industrious collection doctrine may be drawn from several judicial statements of the originality test that referred to 'skill *or* labour'. In other words, the use of the word 'or' in these statements was disjunctive, so expenditures of labour or expense *alone* could form the basis for satisfying the originality threshold.[127] Second, there were numerous cases in which compilations had been protected that reflected substantial labour or expense, but which did *not* demonstrate skill or judgment.[128]

---

[121] *Telstra Corporation Ltd v Desktop Marketing Systems Pty Ltd* [2001] FCA 612 ('*Telstra*').

[122] For comment: see T Aplin, 'When are Compilations Original? *Telstra Corporation v Desktop Marketing Systems Pty Ltd*' [2001] *EIPR* 543.

[123] For comment, see S Strasser, 'Industrious Effort is Enough' [2002] *EIPR* 599.

[124] Special leave to appeal to the High Court of Australia was refused see *Desktop Marketing Systems Pty Ltd v Telstra Corporation Ltd* M85/2002(20 June 2003).

[125] *Desktop*, para 160 (Lindgren J).

[126] *Desktop*, paras 407 and 409 (Sackville J).

[127] *Desktop*, paras 364–73 (Sackville J).

[128] *Desktop*, para 160 (Lindgren J).

The reason why it is doubtful that the UK test of 'labour, skill and judgment' is tantamount to the US 'sweat of the brow' doctrine is that, post Copyright Act 1911 (UK), courts generally have not used the terminology of 'sweat of the brow'.[129] However, Upjohn J in *Football League v Littlewoods* commented *obiter* that, 'a great deal of painstaking hard work with complete accuracy' in the preparation of a chronological football fixture list would satisfy the originality threshold.[130] Whereas US courts have readily described originality in terms of 'sweat of the brow'[131] or 'industrious collection',[132] UK (and Australian) courts have preferred the compound test of 'labour, skill and judgment' (or a permutation of this test). Although 'or' has sometimes replaced 'and' in the test 'labour, skill and judgment', it does not seem that the phrase should be read disjunctively, since judges have been lax in switching between formulations.[133] However, it must be acknowledged that there have been cases in which compilations that have displayed marginal skill in their selection or arrangement but which have involved considerable labour or expense have been protected.[134] Moreover, courts have been prepared to consider skill and effort applied in collecting, gathering, or calculating data for a compilation, in addition to that which may be expended in the selection or arrangement of data.[135]

Does the UK test of 'labour, skill and judgment' differ from the 'author's own intellectual creation' requirement? It is widely assumed that it does,[136] but the criterion has yet to be explored by UK courts,[137] with the exception of Laddie J in

---

[129] See also Davison (2003) pp 14, 143.

[130] *Football League v Littlewoods* [1959] Ch 637, 656. Similarly, there is rarely express reference to 'sweat of the brow' or 'industrious collection' in Australian cases post Copyright Act 1912 (Cth), except for *Australian Consolidated Press Ltd v Morgan* (1964) 112 CLR 483 at 487 (Barwick CJ) and in the recent *Desktop* decision. Note that UK cases pre Copyright Act 1911 (UK) did refer to 'labour and expense': *Matthewson v Stockdale* (1806) 12 Ves 270; 33 ER 103; *Kelly v Morris* (1866) 1 Eq 697; *Morris v Ashbee* (1868) 7 Eq 34; *Jarrold v Houlston* (1857) 3 K & J 707; 69 ER *1294*; *Collis v Cater, Stoffell and Fortt Ltd* (1898) 78 LT (NS) 613.

[131] *Feist*, 353, 359.

[132] *Jeweler's Circular Pub Co v Keystone Pub Co* 281 F 83(1922), 88.

[133] In support of this view see *Tele Direct (Publications) Inc v American Business Information Inc* 154 DLR (4th) 328, paras 29 and 30 (Décary JA delivering the judgment of the Federal Court of Appeal). For example, see *Cramp v Smythson* [1944] AC 329, per Lord Porter at 340 'work, labour and skill' and at 341, 'knowledge, labour, judgement or literary skill'. See also *Macmillan & Co Ltd v Cooper* (1923) 1B IPR 204, per Lord Atkinson at 209, 'labour, skill and capital' and at 212–13 'knowledge, labour, judgment, or literary skill or taste' and at 231, 'knowledge, literary skill and taste, labour and sound judgment'.

[134] For example, see *British Broadcasting Company v Wireless League Gazette Publishing Company* [1926] Ch 433; *Purefoy Engineering Co Ltd v Sykes Boxall & Co Ltd* (1955) 72 RPC 89; *Football League v Littlewoods* [1959] Ch 637, 656.

[135] *Ladbroke (Football) Ltd v William Hill (Football) Ltd* [1964] 1 WLR 273; *Football League v Littlewoods* [1959] Ch 637; *Autospin (Oil Seals) Ltd v Beehive Spinning (A Firm)* [1995] RPC 683.

[136] Bently and Sherman (2004) pp 102–3; WR Cornish and D Llewelyn, *Intellectual Property: Patents, Copyright Trade Marks and Allied Rights*, 5th edn (Sweet & Maxwell, London, 2003) para 19–37; Laddie, *et al* (2000) paras 30.26–30.27; Lai (1998) pp 32–33.

[137] This is despite the fact that it is also relevant to computer programs and photographs. Bainbridge (1999) p 192, argues that the criterion reflects that the work must have originated from the author and that, for a database, it is not 'commonplace in terms of the selection and arrangement of its contents'.

British Horseracing v William Hill,[138] who commented *obiter* that 'there must be a quantitative baseline of originality before protection is acquired'.[139] Recital 19 of the Database Directive was said to support this view.[140] The relevant part of the Directive states:

> as a rule, the compilation of several recordings of musical performances on a CD does not come within the scope of this Directive . . . because, as a compilation, it does not meet the conditions for copyright protection.

One view is that the criterion is akin to the civil law standard of originality, such as the German test of 'personal intellectual creation'[141] or the French test of 'author's imprint of their personality'.[142] According to the German standard, official telephone directories did not constitute personal intellectual creations (and therefore were not protected) because the data was presented in a customary alphabetical manner and expediency dictated the geographical breakdown of subscribers.[143] Similarly, in the Netherlands, radio, and television programme listings were held not to bear the personal stamp of their creator.[144] However, because few civil law countries have incorporated the criterion of 'author's own intellectual creation' into their law[145] it cannot be assumed that courts in member states are giving substance to the EU criterion in interpreting originality.[146] Assuming that courts are giving effect to the EU criterion, it seems that mundane works, such as directories or other listings, will no longer be protected under UK copyright law.[147]

Alternatively, it has been suggested[148] that the 'author's own intellectual creation' is synonymous with the standard set out in *Feist*. In this landmark decision, the US Supreme Court unequivocally repudiated the 'sweat of the brow' test of originality and substituted in its place a test of 'independent creation' plus a 'minimal level of creativity'.[149] However, the Court emphasised that the creativity

---

[138]   *British Horseracing Board v William Hill* [2001] CMLR 12 ('BHB (ChD)').

[139]   *BHB* (ChD) para 28.

[140]   *BHB* (ChD) para 28.

[141]   See German Law, Art 2(2).

[142]   M B Nimmer and P E Geller, *International copyright law and practice* (Looseleaf, Matther Bender, New York), 'France', para 2[1][b][iii].

[143]   *Unauthorised Reproduction of Telephone Directories on CD-Rom* [2002] ECDR 3 (Bundesgerichtshof) paras 19 and 20.

[144]   *NV Holdingmaatschappig De Telegraaf v Nederlandse Omroep Stichting (NOS)* [2002] ECDR 8 (Ct of Appeal of The Hague, Netherlands).

[145]   Although Germany has done so in relation to software: see Art 69(a)(3), German Law.

[146]   See GWG Karnell, 'European Originality: a Copyright Chimera' in J Kabel and G Mom, (eds), *Intellectual Property and Information Law: Essays in Honour of Herman Cohen Jehoram* (Kluwer, The Hague, 1998) 201–9.

[147]   Laddie, *et al*, (2000) para 30.27.

[148]   JAL Sterling, *World Copyright Law*, 2nd edn, (Sweet & Maxwell, London, 2003) 309.

[149]   *Feist*, 345, 347 and 358–59. R Versteeg, 'Sparks in the Tinderbox: *Feist*, "Creativity" and the Legislative History of the 1976 Copyright Act' (1995) 56 *U of Pittsburgh L Rev* 549 argues that the Supreme Court's decision is contrary to the legislative history of the US Copyright Act 1976 and is highly critical of the test of 'independent creation' plus 'minimal level of creativity'.

requirement is extremely modest. 'To be sure, the requisite level of creativity is extremely low; even a slight amount will suffice. The vast majority of works make the grade quite easily, as they possess some creative spark, 'no matter how crude, humble or obvious', it might be.'[150]

Cases subsequent to *Feist* have affirmed the principle that minimal creativity will boost a compilation over the originality hurdle.[151] Whether minimal creativity has been expended appears to turn on whether there is an entirely typical selection or arrangement of materials according to the type of work involved. If it is entirely typical then the tendency is for courts to decide that insufficient creativity has been applied.[152] The *Feist* criterion has not always been applied consistently in subsequent US cases,[153] and it has not been followed in other common law jurisdictions.[154] Ginsburg has argued that, since *only* the creative selection or

---

[150] *Feist*, 345.

[151] *Bellsouth Advertising & Publishing Corp v Donnelly Info Publishing Inc* 999 F 2d 1436(11th Cir, 1993), 1441; *Key Publications, Inc v Chinatown Today Publishing Enterprises* 945 F 2d (2nd Cir, 1991); *Skinder-Strauss Associates v Massachusetts Continuing Legal Education* 914 F Supp 665 (D Mass, 1995); *Hyperlaw v West Publishing Co* 158 F 3d 693, 48 USPQ 2d (BNA) 1545 (2nd Cir, 1998); and *Bender v West Publishing Co* 158 F 3d 674, 48 USPQ 2d (BNA) 1545 (2nd Cir, 1998).

[152] See *Bellsouth* (yellow pages directory); *Skinder-Strauss* (directory of attorneys); and *West Publishing* (case reports) cases.

[153] *Cf Key Publications* with *Bellsouth Publishing*.

[154] See *Desktop* where the Full Federal Court of Australia refused to follow *Feist*. See also *CCH Canadian Ltd v Law Society of Upper Canada* [2004] 236 DLR (4th) 395; [2004] 1 SCR 339 ('*CCH*') where the Supreme Court of Canada chose a test of originality between the extremes of 'sweat of the brow'/'industriousness' and *Feist*. 'Sweat of the brow' was said to derive from cases such as *University of London Press v University Tutorial Press* and require that a work originates from an author and is not a mere copy of a work, whereas a *Feist* standard requires that a work be creative to be original (para 15). Maclachlin CJ (delivering the judgment of the court) concluded 'that the correct position falls between these extremes. . . . What is required to attract copyright protection in the expression of an idea is an exercise of skill and judgment.' (para 16) The originality test is further explained:

> By skill, I mean the use of one's knowledge, developed aptitude or practised ability in producing the work. By judgment, I mean the use of one's capacity for discernment or ability to form an opinion or evaluation by comparing different possible options in producing the work. This exercise of skill and judgment will necessarily involve intellectual effort. The exercise of skill and judgment required to produce the work must not be so trivial that it could be characterized as a purely mechanical exercise (para 16).

The court explained its reasons for adopting this standard:

> The 'sweat of the brow' approach to originality is too low a standard. It shifts the balance of copyright protection too far in favour of the owner's rights, and fails to allow copyright to protect the public's interest in maximizing the production and dissemination of intellectual works. On the other hand, the creativity standard of originality is too high. A creativity standard implies that something must be novel or non-obvious—concepts more properly associated with patent law than copyright law. By way of contrast, a standard requiring the exercise of skill and judgment in the production of a work avoids these difficulties and provides a workable and appropriate standard for copyright protection that is consistent with the policy objectives of the Copyright Act (para 24).

Cf Tele-Direct (Publications) Inc v American Business Information Inc 154 DLR (4th) 328(1997) paras 34–37, where Décary JA in the Federal Court of Appeal appears to suggest that the *Feist* standard is akin to the Canadian test of originality. On this point, however, *Tele-Direct* has been overruled by *CCH*.

arrangement of materials is protected, then second comers will be able to extract data from a compilation provided they rearrange the data and do not copy a substantial part of the first compiler's selection.[155]

In attempting to satisfy the criterion of an 'author's own intellectual creation' (whether that standard is akin to the *Feist* standard, or a civil law standard, or a new European standard) databases pose particular difficulties for showing an original selection or arrangement of materials.[156] The 'selection' in a database is represented by which fields of data are chosen to be included and the range of individual records that are included.[157] For those databases whose commercial value lies in their exhaustive nature, there is arguably little selection involved since the creator has simply covered the field.[158] Database creators may be faced with trading off commercial appeal and value against copyright protection.[159] Nevertheless, the problem may not be as acute for multimedia works that are to be protected as 'databases'. Since multimedia works combine different genres of material, this widens the scope for the selection to be creative in a way that text-only databases are not.[160] If there is a database of telephone listings, the product is valuable only if it is comprehensive but it does not take much creativity to decide that listings for all persons having a telephone line should be included.[161] This may be contrasted with a multimedia CD-Rom that aims, for example, to be a history of the Australian rock and roll music industry.[162] If the product is to be valuable, it too must be reasonably comprehensive in its scope. However, because the range of material available to illustrate musical eras and biographies of Australian rock artists would be larger and more varied (ie, images, graphics, video clips, music clips, sounds and text), it is more likely that creative 'selection' will be employed.

The notion of 'arrangement' has two possible interpretations. Both entail problems for multimedia works.[163] The term 'arrangement' could relate to the physical ordering of the database contents or to the presentation of the contents to the user (the conceptual or logical arrangement). The physical arrangement can differ from the conceptual arrangement.

---

[155] J Ginsburg, 'No "Sweat"? Copyright and other Protection of Works of Information After *Feist v Rural Telephone*' (1992) 92 *Columbia L Rev* 338, 348–49. This is assuming there is no other complementary protection for databases, such as unfair competition or database right (as in the EU).

[156] Laddie, *et al*, (2000) para 30.27 observe that skill and labour in gathering (as opposed to selection) or verifying of contents is no longer relevant.

[157] Austin (1988) paras 29, 30.

[158] Ginsburg (1992) p 345. See also Cornish and Llewelyn (2003) para 19–37.

[159] But see Ginsburg (1992) p 347 that 'value-adding' to exhaustive compilations could result in them being classed as 'original'.

[160] Beutler (1996) p 325.

[161] See *Feist Publications Inc v Rural Telephone Service Co* (1991) 499 US 340, 363–63; *Unauthorised Reproduction of Telephone Directories on CD-Rom* [2002] ECDR 3, p 30.

[162] See Australia, Department of Communications and the Arts, *Real Wild Child: Australian Rock Music and Culture 1950s–90s*, 1998, Multimedia CD Rom ('Real Wild Child CD-Rom').

[163] Beutler (1996) p 325.

In terms of conceptual arrangement, the user of a multimedia work can considerably influence how it is presented.[164] The degree to which users interact with a multimedia work is dictated by the underlying software and is manifested via user interface options. Consequently, the originality requirement for a database is hard to satisfy because these factors involve questions of originality concerning the computer program or user interface. However, the author of a database does determine some of the conceptual arrangement since 'the selection of data provided in the data records . . . facilitate[s] a computer program in portraying and/or accomplishing the logical arrangement'.[165] However, this is really a question of 'selection' and not 'arrangement'. It seems that for multimedia works, which are to be protected as 'databases', originality will be judged mainly according to the creativity applied to 'selection' and not 'arrangement' of materials.

In summary: multimedia works are hindered from qualifying as (non-database) compilations because they may comprise only restricted materials, which is not the case for databases. The difficulties for multimedia works qualifying for protection as databases relate to the requirements of 'independent works' and the necessity for these works, data, or other materials to be 'individually accessible'. These two requirements will exclude multimedia video games and also those multimedia works that rely on dynamic user interfaces from qualifying as a 'database'. There is also the uncertainty of whether the originality standards of 'labour, skill or judgement' and an 'author's own intellectual creation', which apply respectively to (non-database) compilations and databases, are qualitatively different. Even if there is a difference, most multimedia works will be able to demonstrate sufficient creative selection, but probably not arrangement. If multimedia works cannot satisfy the originality threshold, then there is the possibility of demonstrating 'substantial investment', which is the threshold test for the *sui generis* database right. Whether multimedia works can be protected under the *sui generis* database regime is discussed in the next section.

3. *Sui generis* Databases

The Database Directive, in addition to introducing the copyright reforms discussed in the previous section, established a new *sui generis* right for databases. This right has been implemented in the UK by the 1997 Database Regulations.[166]

---

[164] Beutler (1996) p 326.

[165] Austin (1998) para 46.

[166] Those databases completed before 1 January 1983 are subject to the old copyright law only. Databases completed between 1 January 1983 and 27 March 1996 inclusive, are subject to the database right and 'old copyright law'. Databases created since 27 March 1996 are subject to the database right and 'new copyright law'. No act done before commencement of the Database Regulations or after commencement, in pursuance of an agreement made before commencement shall be regarded as an infringement of a database right in a database: see Part IV of Database Regulations.

This new regime does not fall strictly under the umbrella of copyright.[167] However, it may provide an effective form of protection for multimedia works.

According to Regulation 12(1) of the Database Regulations, 'database' has the same meaning as that given by section 3A(1) of the CDPA. This means that materials comprising a database must be independent, systematically or methodically arranged, and individually accessible. The problems of satisfying these requirements (explained in the previous section) will also arise in the *sui generis* context. Briefly to reiterate, multimedia video games and reference multimedia works that utilise a moving user interface will face difficulties in satisfying the requirements that works, data, or other materials be 'independent' and 'individually accessible'.

Assuming that a multimedia work satisfies the threshold definition of database, it must also result from *substantial investment* in *obtaining, verifying or presenting the contents* of the database.[168] In contrast to the originality requirement of 'author's own intellectual creation' for copyright protection contained in Article 3(1),[169] the type and degree of effort that must be applied in order for the database right to subsist appears to be significantly different.[170] The language of investment is explicitly used,[171] thereby revealing the economic basis of the database right. The types of investment that are contemplated include human, financial and technical resources.[172] Further, according to Article 7(1), 'substantial investment' includes assessments of quantity and/or quality.

Three main issues have emerged in relation to this threshold requirement. First, the question of what may be classed as *substantial* investment. Second, what is meant by *obtaining, verification and presentation* of the database contents, in particular what is meant by 'obtaining'? Third, can the database be a *'spin-off'* from investment not directed at producing a database?

(a) Substantial Investment

What constitutes *substantial* investment is difficult to predict.[173] According to Article 7(1) of the Database Directive it includes assessments of *quantity* and/or *quality*. Further, recital 19 of the Directive indicates that a compilation of several

---

[167] Although see Davison (2003) pp 84–85, 90–91, who argues that the *sui generis* database regime overlaps considerably with copyright protection of databases.

[168] Art 7(1), Database Directive; reg 13(1), Database Regulations.

[169] The ECJ has reiterated that 'nothing in the directive points to the conclusion that a database must be its maker's own intellectual creation to be classified as [a database]': *OPAP* (ECJ) para 26.

[170] Cf Davison (2003) p 84.

[171] See also recitals 7–8, 39–40, 42, Database Directive.

[172] Recital 40, Database Directive.

[173] See Davison (2003) p 153; Powell (1997) p 1238; N Thakur, 'Database Protection in the European Union and the United States: The European Database Directive as an Optimum Global Model?' [2001] *IPQ* 100, 128 and G Westkamp, 'Protecting Databases Under US and European Law— Methodical Approaches to the Protection of Investments Between Unfair Competition and Intellectual Property Concepts' (2003) 34 *IIC* 772, 781.

recordings of musical performances on a CD will not represent a substantial enough investment to be eligible for protection under the database right.[174]

What amounts to 'substantial investment' was raised in the reference to the ECJ in *Fixtures Marketing v Svenska* ('*Svenska*').[175] Fixtures Marketing brought an action against Svenska, claiming infringement of database right in two football fixture lists (one for all the divisions in England and one for all the divisions in Scotland) under Paragraph 49 of the Swedish Copyright Law. Fixtures Marketing claimed that Svenska, which operates football betting pools, had used fixtures data as part of its services and thereby extracted and/or re-utilised the data from its fixture lists in an infringing manner. Fixtures Marketing were unsuccessful in the lower courts. On appeal to the Högsta Domstolen (Supreme Court of Sweden), the Court decided to stay proceedings and referred several questions to the ECJ for a preliminary ruling. The Högsta Domstolen observed that the Database Directive was unclear about whether the purpose of the database was relevant to determining whether it is protected under the *sui generis* right. Further, it was unclear what sort of human or financial investment can be taken into account in assessing 'substantial investment'. The Högsta Domstolen referred, *inter alia,* the following questions:

(1) In assessing whether a database is the result of a 'substantial investment' within the meaning of Article 7(1) of the directive can the maker of a database be credited with an investment primarily intended to create something which is independent of the database and which thus does not merely concern the 'obtaining, verification or presentation' of the contents of the database? If so, does it make any difference if the investment or part of it nevertheless constitutes a prerequisite for the database?

(2) Does a database enjoy protection under the database directive only in respect of activities covered by the objective of the database maker in creating the database?[176]

In her Opinion,[177] Advocate General Stix-Hackl expressed the view that 'substantial investment' is to be construed in relative terms, 'first in relation to costs and their redemption and secondly in relation to the scale, nature and contents of the database and the sector to which it belongs.'[178] Thus, high value investment in absolute terms is not the guiding factor. On the other hand, Advocate General Stix-Hackl explained that, 'the criterion "substantial" cannot be construed only in relative terms. The Directive requires an absolute lower threshold for investments

[174] J Gaster, 'The New EU Directive Concerning the Legal Protection of Databases' (1997) 20 *Fordham International Law Journal* 1129, 1135 explains that this recital reflects a pragmatic compromise.

[175] C–338/02 *Fixtures Marketing Ltd v Svenska Spel AB*, (Grand Chamber, 9 November 2004), ('*Svenska* (ECJ)')

[176] Above, at para 18.

[177] *Fixtures Marketing Ltd v Svenska Spel AB* C–338/02 Opinion of the Advocate General delivered on 8 June 2004 ('*Svenska* (Opinion)').

[178] Above, at para 38.

worthy of protection as a sort of *de minimis* rule. That is implied by the 19th recital, according to which the investment must be "substantial enough".[179]

Recital 19 appears to support a *de minimis* rule with regard to substantial investment. According to Advocate General Stix-Hackl this should be set at a low level, particularly since a high threshold level 'would undermine the intended purpose of the Directive, which was to create incentives for investment.'[180] However, the purpose of the Database Directive could equally support a high threshold, since sizeable investments are much less likely to be pursued if they are vulnerable to free-riders. In other words, it could be argued that the Directive is concerned to provide incentives for riskier types of investment. Further, applying a high threshold of protection would ensure that a database right attaches to only those databases worthy of strong legal protection. Practically speaking, however, a low threshold of substantial investment may be easier to apply than a high threshold level and thus create less uncertainty about whether databases qualify for protection. If a low threshold is adopted, then it argued that the *level* of investment would have to form a key part of the infringement analysis, in order to minimise the risk of databases being easily protected and easily infringed. As will be discussed in chapter 4, the ECJ has ruled that the investment in the part of the database contents that is extracted or re-utilised is the key consideration in assessing whether it is a 'substantial part'.

In answering the *Svenska* reference, the ECJ observed that:

> Investment in the creation of a database may consist in the deployment of human, financial or technical resources but it must be substantial in quantitative or qualitative terms. The *quantitative assessment refers to quantifiable resources and the qualitative assessment to efforts which cannot be quantified, such as intellectual effort or energy,* according to the 7th, 39th and 40th recitals of the preamble to the Directive.[181] (Emphasis supplied)

The ECJ (unlike the Advocate General) emphasised the *non-financial* aspects of investment, in the form of intellectual effort or energy. The Court did not, however, express any views on whether *substantial* investment is to be measured in absolute and/or relative terms or whether the threshold of investment is low. It may be argued that the ECJ's finding in *Svenska* that the football fixture lists did not reflect substantial investment supports the existence of a low threshold or, at least, does not support the existence of a high threshold. In *Svenska* the investment by Fixtures Marketing was primarily directed at creation of the data that went into the fixture list. The ECJ ruled that investment in *creation of data*, as opposed to collection of data, is not investment in *obtaining* contents (discussed below).[182]

---

[179] Above, at para 39.
[180] Above. *Cf* Westkamp (2003) pp 781–83.
[181] *Svenska* (ECJ) para 29. See also C–46/02, *Fixtures Marketing Ltd v OY Veikkaus Ab*, (Grand Chamber, 9 November 2004) ('*Veikkaus* (ECJ)') para 38; *OPAP* (ECJ) para 44.
[182] *Svenska* (ECJ) paras 24–25.

Therefore, this investment was not relevant.[183] In terms of investment in *verification* of data, the ECJ held that 'verification of the accuracy of the contents of fixture lists during the season simply involves, according to the observations made by Fixtures, adapting certain data in those lists to take account of any post-ponement of a match or fixture date decided on by or in collaboration with the leagues.'[184] This verification could not be regarded as requiring substantial invest-ment.[185] As for investment in *presentation* of data, the ECJ observed that presen-tation of a football fixture list is closely linked to the creation of data which comprise the list. Investment in creation of data was irrelevant and there was no investment independent of that applied in the creation of the data that went towards presentation of contents. Thus, the ECJ concluded that there was no substantial investment in either the obtaining, verification or presentation of the contents of a football fixture list.[186] This finding is consistent with the view taken by the Advocate General that the *de minimis* threshold of substantial investment is low. Apart from investment in creating the football fixture data (which was irrele-vant), there was minimal investment applied to verification or presentation of the fixture lists. Nonetheless, it would have been helpful if the ECJ had indicated whether the threshold of substantial investment is low and also whether invest-ment is to be judged in relative and/or absolute terms.

(b) Obtaining, Verification and Presentation of the Database Contents

(i) Obtaining

In *Svenska* the ECJ was asked to rule on when a database is to be considered the result of a substantial investment. The defendant in *Svenska* argued that 'invest-ment in . . . the obtaining . . . of the contents' of a database should be interpreted to mean the resources used to seek out existing independent materials and collect them in a database. According to the defendant, Fixtures Marketing had expended substantial investment, but *only in creation,* and *not collection,* of the fixtures data. Fixtures Marketing submitted that it was not possible to distinguish between the investment in creating the fixtures (ie, investment for the purpose of planning the game) from that in compiling the fixtures (ie, investment in drawing up the fixture lists).

In *Fixtures Marketing v Veikkaus* ('*Veikkaus*')[187] the claimant (who was the same claimant in *Svenska* and *OPAP*) brought an action against Veikkaus who organised gambling activities in Finland. Fixtures Marketing argued that use of around 200 matches per week by Veikkaus in order to organise its betting activities in relation

---

[183] Above, at para 33.
[184] Above, at para 34.
[185] Above.
[186] Above, at para 36.
[187] *Veikkaus* (ECJ).

to football involved an infringement of its database as protected by Article 49 of the Copyright Law. In the light of the uncertainty as to whether the fixture list was a protected database, the Finnish Court (Vantaan Käräjäoikeus) stayed proceedings and referred three questions to the ECJ. The first of these questions was:

> May the requirement in Article 7(1) of the directive for a link between the investment and the making of the database be interpreted in the sense that the 'obtaining' referred to in Article 7(1) and the investment directed at it refers, in the present case, to investment which is directed at the determination of the dates of the matches and the match pairings themselves and, when the criteria for granting protection are appraised, does the drawing up of the fixture list include investment which is not relevant?

In the third of the cases involving Fixtures Marketing, *OPAP* (discussed above in relation to the definition of 'database'), the Greek Court referred a question to the ECJ on whether football fixtures would be protected as databases.[188]

The interpretation of 'obtaining' in Article 7(1) was also considered by the ECJ in *British Horseracing v William Hill* ('*British Horseracing*').[189] This case concerned a dispute between the governing authority for the British racing industry, the British Horseracing Board (BHB) and one of the leading providers of off-course betting services in the UK and elsewhere, William Hill. BHB was formed in June 1993 and its functions include the compiling of data related to horseracing, establishing the dates and programme contents for race fixtures and creating the fixture list for each year's racing. William Hill mainly provides fixed odds bets on sporting and other events (of which horseracing is the most popular) from its Licensed Betting Offices. Additionally, it provides on-line betting services, which were the source of the dispute in this case.

Racing information in the BHB Database was distributed in two ways. First, via a company called Racing Pages Ltd, which operated a Declarations Feed (DF). The DF contained a list of races, declared runners and jockeys, distance and name of races, race time and number of runners in each race together with other information. This data was forwarded to subscribers usually on the day before the race. The second form of distribution was via Satellite Information Services (SIS), one of Racing Pages' subscribers, who was allowed to supply this data to its own subscribers in the form of a raw data feed (RDF). William Hill subscribed to both the DF and the RDF and used it for the purpose of its betting operations. The dispute in this case arose from William Hill's use of data from the DF and RDF in relation to its on-line betting services. BHB claimed that William Hill's activities amounted to unauthorised extraction or re-utilization of a substantial part of the contents of

---

[188] *OPAP* (ECJ), question 2: 'In the light of the definition of the scope of the directive, do lists of football fixtures enjoy protection as databases over which there is a *sui generis* right in favour of the maker and under what conditions?'

[189] C–203/02, *British Horseracing Board Ltd v William Hill Organization Ltd*, (Grand Chamber, 9 November 2004) ('BHB (ECJ)').

its database contrary to Article 7(1) of the Directive or else repeated and systematic extraction or re-utilization of insubstantial parts of the contents of the database contrary to Article 7(5). BHB succeeded in the High Court before Laddie J.[190] On appeal, the Court of Appeal referred a series of questions to the ECJ for interpretation.[191] One of these questions was: 'What is meant by "obtaining" in Article 7(1) of the directive? In particular, are the [facts as stated in the reference] capable of amount to such obtaining?'

To determine what is meant by 'obtaining' in Article 7(1), Advocate General Stix-Hackl examined the different language versions of Article 7(1). She observed that in the German version, the term 'Beschaffung' can only concern existing data. Further, the wording of the Portugese, French, Spanish and English versions of Article 7(1) are 'all based on the Latin "obtenere", to receive', which also suggests that 'obtaining' can only apply to existing data. A narrow interpretation of 'obtaining' was also suggested by the Finnish and Danish versions of Article 7(1).[192]

Advocate General Stix-Hackl considered the 39th recital of the preamble of the Database Directive, which is the introductory recital for the subject of the *sui generis* right. She noted that it refers to, 'the financial and professional investment made in *obtaining and collection* (sic) the contents.'[193] (Emphasis supplied) However, the Advocate General noted that the various language versions of recital 39 also differ. The majority of the versions use the same term for 'obtaining' as that used in Article 7(1), but there are some language versions in which two different terms from those used in Article 7(1) are used. In order to reconcile these differences, Advocate General Stix-Hackl recommended that in the latter situation Article 7(1) is to be interpreted 'so that the two activities listed are viewed as subspecies of obtaining within the meaning of Article 7(1) of the Directive'.[194] Whereas, in the former situation,

> the same term in the 39th recital as in Article 7(1) of the Directive will have to be construed so that the term obtaining in the 39th recital is understood in a narrow sense, whereas the term used in Article 7(1) of the Directive is to be understood in a wide sense, in other words as also encompassing the other activity listed in the 39th recital.[195]

---

[190] *BHB* (ChD).

[191] *British Horseracing Board Ltd v William Hill Organization Ltd* [2002] ECDR 4 ('BHB (CA)').

[192] *British Horseracing Board v William Hill* C–203/02, Opinion of the Advocate General delivered on 8 June 2004 ('*BHB* (Opinion)') para 42. See also *Svenska* (Opinion) para 52; *OPAP* (Opinion) para 68; C–46/02, *Fixtures Marketing Ltd v OY Veikkaus Ab*, Opinion of the Advocate General delivered on 8 June 2004 ('*Veikkaus* (Opinion') para 62.

[193] *BHB* (Opinion) para 43; *Svenska* (Opinion) para 53; *OPAP* (Opinion) para 69; *Veikkaus* (Opinion) para 63.

[194] *BHB* (Opinion) para 44; *Svenska* (Opinion) para 54; *OPAP* (Opinion) para 70; *Veikkaus* (Opinion) para 64.

[195] *BHB* (Opinion) para 45; *Svenska* (Opinion) para 55; *OPAP* (Opinion) para 71; *Veikkaus* (Opinion) para 65.

Thus, Advocate General Stix-Hackl concluded that *all* language versions of Article 7(1) allow for the interpretation that 'obtaining' does *not* cover the mere generation of data, and thus excludes the preparatory phase of making the database. However, the Advocate General went on to create a narrow exception to this rule, where the creation of the data coincides with its collection and screening.[196] In *British Horseracing* she explained this exception as follows: 'The expression 'obtaining' in Article 7(1) of the Directive must be interpreted as meaning that it also covers data created by the maker if the creation of the data took place at the same time as its processing and was inseparable from it.'[197] (emphasis supplied)

In each of the four references, the ECJ followed the Advocate General's opinion and ruled that investment in 'obtaining' refers to the resources used in seeking out and collecting *existing* independent materials and not those resources used in the creation of such materials.[198] However, the Court did not follow the Advocate General's narrow exception that 'obtaining' includes creation of data where it is contemporaneous and inseparable with the collection and processing of data. According to the ECJ, the interpretation of 'obtaining' as meaning the gathering of *existing* data was consistent with the purpose of the database right 'to promote the establishment of storage and processing systems for existing information and not the creation of materials capable of being collected subsequently in a database.'[199] The ECJ further stated that this interpretation was confirmed by the different language versions of recital 39, as the Advocate General had explained.[200] Finally, the Court drew support for this view from recital 19, according to which the compilation of several recordings of musical performances on a CD does not represent a substantial enough investment to qualify for the database right. Recital 19 was said to illustrate that the resources used for the creation of such recordings included in the database (ie, the CD) is not investment in 'obtaining' the contents of the database.[201]

In *Svenska*, *Veikkaus* and *OPAP* the ECJ ruled that resources used to establish dates, times and the team pairings for the various football matches in the league concerned the *creation* of materials and thus had to be excluded from the assessment of 'substantial investment'.[202] In *British Horseracing* the ECJ ruled that the resources used to draw up a list of horses in a race did not constitute investment

---

[196] *BHB* (Opinion) paras 46, 49; *Svenska* (Opinion) para 56; *OPAP* (Opinion) para 72; *Veikkaus* (Opinion) para 66.

[197] *BHB* (Opinion) para 157.

[198] *BHB* (ECJ) para 31; *Svenska* (ECJ) para 24; *Veikkaus* (ECJ) para 34; *OPAP* (ECJ) para 40.

[199] *BHB* (ECJ) para 31; *Svenska* (ECJ) para 24; *Veikkaus* (ECJ) para 34; *OPAP* (ECJ) para 40. See also recitals 10 and 12, Database Directive.

[200] *BHB* (ECJ) para 32; *Svenska* (ECJ) para 25; *Veikkaus* (ECJ) para 35; *OPAP* (ECJ) para 41.

[201] *BHB* (ECJ) para 33; *Svenska* (ECJ) para 26; *Veikkaus* (ECJ) para 36; *OPAP* (ECJ) para 42.

[202] *Svenska* (ECJ) para 37; *Veikkaus* (ECJ) para 49; *OPAP* (ECJ) para 53.

in 'obtaining' contents of the database because that investment related to the *creation* of data.[203]

While the ECJ's ruling on the interpretation of 'obtaining' is clear, and avoids reliance on the 'spin-off' doctrine (discussed below), it gives rise to two obvious difficulties.

The first problem is how to distinguish between *creating* data and *collecting existing* data. The potential difficulty of this exercise is highlighted by the divergence of views in *Svenska, OPAP* and *Veikkaus*. In her Opinions, Advocate General Stix-Hackl observed in relation to the football fixture list:

> It is primarily a matter of classifying the data and its handling from its receipt to its inclusion in the database at issue in the proceedings. That entails the assessment of the drawing up of the fixture lists, in other words, essentially tying up the pairings with the place and time of the individual games. *The fact that the fixture list is the outcome of negotiation between several parties, in particular, the police, associations and fan clubs, suggests that the present case is concerned with existing data.* The fact that, as many of the parties have pointed out, *the data were obtained for a purpose other than the creation of a database similarly suggests that these are existing data.*[204]

In contrast, the ECJ concluded that establishing the date, time and team pairings that comprised the fixture list involved generating data, as opposed to gathering data.[205]

A similar divergence of opinion could arise in the case of telephone directories. On the one hand, the names, addresses and telephone numbers of subscribers may be seen as existing data which telephone companies merely collect. On the other hand, it could be argued that subscribers' details (of name, address and telephone number) do not come into existence until requested by telephone companies and thus are generated data. Another example is radio or television listings. Radio or television listings reflect choices made about which programmes should be shown from the catalogue of content available to a broadcaster. On the one hand, those listings reflect a selection from *existing* data (ie, available programmes). On the other hand, the listings reflect *generated* data (ie, what programmes will be shown on a particular day).

The second difficulty arises where A commissions B to create material for A's database or A pays B for material to be used in A's database. In both instances, it appears that the money paid by A would constitute investment in *gathering*

---

[203] *BHB* (ECJ) paras 38, 42: '[I]nvestment in the selection, for the purpose of organising horse racing, of the horses admitted to run in the race concerned relates to the creation of the data which make up the lists for those races which appear in the BHB database.'

[204] *Svenska* (Opinion) paras 58–59; *OPAP* (Opinion) paras 74–75; *Veikkaus* (Opinion) paras 68–69.

[205] *Svenska* (ECJ) para 31: 'the resources deployed for the purpose of determining, in the course of arranging the football league fixtures, the dates and times of and home and away teams playing in the various matches represent . . . an investment in the creation of the fixture list.' See also *OPAP* (ECJ) para 47 and *Veikkaus* (ECJ) paras 42–44.

existing material, as opposed to *creating* material. Payment is made in exchange for materials that have been created (and thus exist) and the payment made by A may not necessarily reflect the costs incurred by B in generating the material. But where A creates material (rather than paying B for the material) the resources applied to this task would not constitute relevant investment according to the ECJ's ruling. Yet is it realistic or possible to distinguish between each investment by A? If no, then the distinction between investment in collecting, as opposed to creating, works, data or other material seems somewhat arbitrary. If yes, then it seems possible for A to circumvent the ECJ's interpretation of 'obtaining' by 'outsourcing' the task of creating works, data or other materials. Certainly, the consequence of the ECJ's ruling on 'obtaining' for creators of multimedia works wishing to obtain database right protection is that they should either purchase existing materials or commission third parties to create the materials for the multimedia work, rather than seek to create those works themselves.

In addressing the issue of 'obtaining', the ECJ could have adopted an interpretation which included both *generating* and/or *collecting* materials.[206] However, if the Court had adopted this interpretation it is argued the following requirement would have been necessary: that the main purpose of the investment in 'obtaining' contents was creating a database. Arguably, this is an implicit requirement of the Database Directive. The objective of the Directive is to prevent the misappropriation of investment in making databases so that *incentives to produce databases* are not diminished by free-riding. This is made clear by recitals 7, 9, 39 and 40, which state respectively:

> (7) Whereas the making of databases requires the investment of considerable human, technical and financial resources while such databases can be copied or accessed at a fraction of the cost needed to design them independently.
>
> (9) Whereas databases are a vital tool in the development of an information market within the Community; whereas this tool will also be of use in many other fields.
>
> (39) ... this Directive seeks to safeguard the position of makers of databases against misappropriation of the results of the financial and professional investment made in obtaining and collection the contents by protecting the whole or substantial parts of a database against certain acts by a user or competitor.
>
> (40) Whereas the object of this *sui generis* right is to ensure protection of any investment in obtaining, verifying or presenting the contents of a database for the limited duration of the right ...

If that is the objective of the Directive, then it is a short leap of logic to argue that the investment must be directed at *producing* a database. In other words, there must be a causal link between the investment and the making of the database.

---

[206] *Cf* E Derclaye, 'Databases "Sui Generis" Right: Should We Adopt the Spin-Off Theory?' [2004] *EIPR* 402, 409.

(ii) Verification

The Court of Appeal in *British Horseracing* referred a question to the ECJ on the meaning of 'verification' in Article 7(1) of the Database Directive.[207] The ECJ ruled that 'investment in . . . the . . . verification . . . of the contents' of a database refers to the resources applied to 'ensuring the reliability of the information contained in that database, to monitor the accuracy of the materials collected when the database was created and during its operation.'[208] Excluded from consideration are resources used for verification during the stage of creating data. This is because the resources are used in *creating* a database and cannot therefore be taken into account.[209]

BHB had undertaken prior checks on data relevant to entering a horse on a list for a race (ie, checks to the identity of the person making the entry, the details of the horse and the classification of the horse, its owner and jockey). The ECJ held that these checks were made at the stage of *creating the list* for the race in question and thus were resources applied to creation of the contents and not their verification.[210]

The consequence of the ECJ's interpretation of 'verification' is that investment in 'verification' can only ever relate to a database that *already exists* and which is either dynamic or updated from time to time. Investment in verification of data *before* it is entered in a newly created database will be irrelevant. However, this type of investment might be useful, or necessary, to producing a valuable database. For example, imagine a situation in which A wants to create an electronic directory of solicitors practising in London. A hard copy 2003 directory of solicitors practising in London already exists and is published by B. A obtains a license from B to use B's hard copy directory for the purpose of producing an electronic directory for 2005. When A is compiling its electronic directory it takes the data from B's directory and verifies whether or not the solicitors listed are still practising in London. If they are not, their names are not included in A's directory. According to the ECJ's ruling, the investment applied to checking whether solicitors are still practising in London would be considered irrelevant because it is not carried out in relation to information contained in an existing (electronic) database, but rather to deciding whether information should go into a (newly created) electronic database or not. Yet investment of this nature is important to producing a current database. It could be argued that the investment in verification of data prior to its inclusion in the database is investment in 'obtaining' (along with the investment

---

[207] See question 3 as cited in *BHB* (ECJ) para 22.

[208] *BHB* (ECJ) para 34. This ruling is consistent with the opinion of the Advocate General: *BHB* (Opinion) paras 51–52. See also *OPAP* (ECJ) para 43; *Svenska* (ECJ) para 27; *Veikkaus* (ECJ) para 37.

[209] *BHB* (ECJ) para 34. See also *OPAP* (ECJ) para 43; *Svenska* (ECJ) para 27; *Veikkaus* (ECJ) para 37.

[210] *BHB* (ECJ) paras 39–41.

reflected in payment of the licence fee) insofar as it relates to selecting or choosing which contents should be included in the database.

(iii) Presentation

On what constitutes 'investment in . . . the . . . presentation of the contents', the ECJ in *Svenska, OPAP* and *Veikkaus* observed that this referred to 'the resources used for the purpose of giving the database its function of processing information, that is to say those used for the *systematic or methodical arrangement of the materials* contained in that database and the organisation of their *individual accessibility*.'[211] (Emphasis supplied)

From the above observations it is clear that the ECJ links the notion of 'presentation' to the definition of 'database'.[212] In *Svenska, OPAP* and *Veikkaus* the ECJ indicated that there was no relevant investment in 'presentation' of the football fixtures. The Court commented that the presentation of the football fixture list was too closely linked to the creation of data to involve investment independent of the creation of data.[213]

What is unclear is how this interpretation of 'presentation' will affect the relationship between investment in *presentation* of contents in a database and the prohibition on software being considered a database. Article 1(3) of the Database Directive states that protection under the Directive 'shall not apply to computer programs used in the making or operation of databases accessible by electronic means'. However, the recitals to the Database Directive indicate that thesauruses and indexation systems may nevertheless form part of a database.[214] In the case of electronic databases, 'individual accessibility', ie, searchability and interactivity, and the conceptual arrangement of materials will be achieved via the underlying software. The prohibition in Article 1(3) of the Directive may simply mean that the underlying software cannot constitute a database. Or else it may go further and exclude investment which is applied to designing and creating the software from consideration of 'substantial investment'. If so, then it is difficult to envisage what kind of investment could be applied to presentation of the contents in an electronic database that does not relate to the design of the underlying software. A better view is to consider investment applied in designing the functional features of software, which enables the contents in an electronic database to be presented effectively, as relevant investment. However, investment in *coding* the instructions

---

[211] *Svenska* (ECJ) para 27; *OPAP* (ECJ) para 43 and *Veikkaus* (ECJ) para 37.

[212] This is consistent with the interpretation of 'presentation' adopted by the Advocate-General: *OPAP* (Opinion) para 78; *Svenska* (Opinion) para 62; *Veikkaus* (Opinion) para 72.

[213] *Svenska* (ECJ) para 35; *OPAP* (ECJ) para 51; *Veikkaus* (ECJ) para 46.

[214] Recital 20, Database Directive states that protection under this Directive 'may also apply to the material necessary for the operation or consultation of certain databases such as thesaurus and indexation systems.' See also Bainbridge (1999) p 187, who regards these elements as non-literal elements of a database.

which implement the functional features should not be considered relevant invest-ment because it relates to the software *per se*.

(c) 'Spin-off' Doctrine

The 'spin-off' doctrine or 'spin-off' theory, as it has been variously called, first emerged in Dutch case law.[215] According to the 'spin-off' doctrine, a database that is a consequence (or 'spin-off') of commercial activity not aimed at producing a database cannot be considered to have met the standard of 'substantial invest-ment'.[216] The argument being that 'investment' must be a conscious act directed towards a particular end, namely, the creation of a database.[217]

In her Opinions in *Svenska* and *Veikkaus* Advocate General Stix-Hackl sought to clarify the relevance of the 'spin-off' doctrine to the interpretation of the *sui generis* right in the Directive. Citing Hugenholtz, she explained that the doctrine:

> can be traced back, first, to the purpose implied by the 10th to 12th recitals of the Directive, which is to provide incentives for investment by improving the protection of investment. However, it is also based on the idea that investments should be repaid by profits from the principal activity. The 'spin-off theory' is also bound up with the idea that the Directive only protects those investments which were necessary to obtain the contents of a database.[218]

While noting that the above arguments had merit,[219] the Advocate General emphasised that the provisions of the Database Directive were decisive in its inter-pretation.[220] According to the Advocate General the issue turned on whether or not protection of a database is contingent on its purpose. She concluded that 'the purpose of the investment is not material. Investment for the purpose of drawing up the fixture lists in a database must also be taken into account.'[221] The Advocate General appears to have two main reasons for this view. First, the purpose of the investment is not a requirement contained within the express requirements of

---

[215] Early cases in which the spin-off doctrine was applied include: *Algemeen Dagblad v Eureka Internetdiensten* [2002] ECDR 1 (District Court, Rotterdam); *NV Holdingmaatschappig De Telegraaf v Nederlandse Omroep Stichting (NOS)* [2002] ECDR 8 (Ct of Appeal of The Hague, Netherlands). In *Societe Tigest* the spin-off doctrine was unsuccessfully argued. For a discussion of the background to the 'spin-off' theory see Derclaye (2004).

[216] Derclaye (2004) p 402 explains that: 'Spin-off databases are collections of data which are by-products ("spin-offs") of a main or other activity of the producer (such as event schedules, television or radio programmes, train and plane timetables, telephone subscriber data, stock prices, football or horseracing fixtures, scientific data resulting from research or experimentation, sports results)' (footnotes omitted).

[217] See also Derclaye (2004) pp 407–8.

[218] *Svenska* (Opinion) para 41; and *Veikkaus* (Opinion) para 51.

[219] For a pithy description of the arguments in favour and against the 'spin-off' doctrine see Derclaye (2004) pp 406–7.

[220] *Svenska* (Opinion) para 41; *Veikkaus* (Opinion) para 51.

[221] *Svenska* (Opinion) para 135.

Article 1 or Article 7, nor is it mentioned in the recitals.[222] Second, makers of databases may pursue several purposes in making a database such that investments made cannot be attributed to a certain single purpose or are inseparable. If the criterion of purpose were used either it would be impractical to apply or would run counter to the object of the Directive to provide incentives for investment if it excluded databases that serve several purposes.[223]

The ECJ in each of the four references rejected the 'spin-off' doctrine. The Court held that the key question was whether the maker of the database had applied substantial investment to obtaining, verification or presentation of the contents of the database, in the senses described above. If this occurred it was immaterial that 'the creation of a database is linked to the exercise of a principal activity in which the person creating the database is also the creator of the materials contained in the database'.[224] This is because investment in *creation* of data is not a relevant consideration under the Database Directive. In other words, the ECJ preferred to focus on the language of Article 7(1) of the Directive. Having interpreted 'obtaining' to exclude creation of data, resort to the 'spin-off' doctrine was unnecessary.

The view of the ECJ finds support in *Societe Tigest Sarl v Societe Reed Expositions France.*[225] In this case, the Paris Court of Appeal rejected the argument that directories of trade exhibitors were simply a 'spin-off' of the claimant's main commercial business of hosting trade exhibitions. This was because investments had been made in verifying and updating the directories, and in determining their layout and publication.[226]

As has been discussed above, the ECJ could have interpreted 'obtaining' to include creation and collection of materials. This would alleviate the difficulties associated with differentiating created materials from collected materials. However, this interpretation would have required the retention of the 'spin-off' doctrine or, more accurately, a causal requirement that substantial investment was aimed primarily at obtaining, verifying or presenting the contents of the database.

Conclusion

The rulings of the ECJ have clarified the meaning of the threshold requirement for protection under the *sui generis* right. The 'spin-off' doctrine has been firmly rejected and the ECJ has emphasised that the key issue is whether there is substantial investment in the obtaining, verification or presentation of the contents of a database. 'Obtaining' does *not* include the generation of data. However, investment in creation of data does not preclude protection under the database right *provided* there is *independent* investment in the collection, verification or presentation

---

[222] *Svenska* (Opinion) para 42; *Veikkaus* (Opinion) para 52.
[223] *Svenska* (Opinion) para 44; *Veikkaus* (Opinion) para 54.
[224] *Svenska* (ECJ) para 29; *BHB* (ECJ) para 35; *OPAP* (ECJ) para 45; *Veikkaus* (ECJ) para 39.
[225] *Societe Tigest Sarl v Societe Reed Expositions France* [2002] ECC 29 ('Societe Tigest').
[226] *Societe Tigest* paras 23–25.

of the database contents. Where the investment in collection, verification or presentation is inextricably tied to *creation* of the data, then it must be ignored.

The relevance of the ECJ's rulings to the protection of multimedia works as databases is that multimedia producers should use existing materials, rather than create their own materials. This is to ensure that their investment is applied to 'obtaining' contents. Further, a multimedia producer's investment in the presentation of the contents to the user will be highly relevant. Thus, investment in developing a user friendly visual user interface will be of great significance and should be considered as relevant investment in 'presentation' of the contents.

4. Film

A 'film' is defined in section 5B(1) of the CDPA as:

> ... a recording on any medium from which a moving image may by any means be produced.

This definition differs from the previous definition of film (ie, 'cinematograph film') contained in the Copyright Act 1956,[227] because it is more straightforward. However, it is also more limited because the subject matter resides in the *visual recording* or embodiment, as opposed to the sequence of visual images or underlying visual work.[228] For this reason, there is no originality requirement for film works,[229] although it is stipulated that copyright will not 'subsist in a film which is, or to the extent that it is, a copy taken from a previous film.'[230] This provision ensures that copyright in a film is not indefinitely extended by the simple act of duplicating it.[231]

To assess whether multimedia works can be protected as films, it is necessary to consider several issues concerning the scope of the above definition: (i) whether

[227] Section 13(10), Copyright Act 1956 (UK) defined a cinematograph film as: 'any sequence of visual images recorded on material of any description (whether translucent or not) so as to be capable, by the use of that material, (a) of being shown as a moving picture, or; (b) of being recorded on other material (whether translucent or not), by the use of which it can be so shown.' This definition bears some similarity to the definition of 'cinematograph film' in s 10(1), Australian Copyright Act 1968 (Cth): 'the aggregate of the visual images embodied in an article or thing so as to be capable by the use of that article or thing: (a) of being shown as a moving picture; or; (b) of being embodied in another article or thing by the use of which it can be so shown.'

[228] Thus, under s 5B cinematographic and audiovisual works are only protected via their recordings: P Kamina, *Film Copyright in the European Union* (CUP, Cambridge, 2002) 66 and 89; Laddie, *et al*, (2000) para 7.60; Cornish and Llewelyn (2003) para 10–23. See also Rattee J, obiter, in *Norowzian v Arks Ltd (No 2)* [1999] FSR 79, 86: '[T]he reference in section 1(1) [of CDPA] is to the actual material recording—the celluloid or videotape—and not the subject-matter of the recording, that is to say what is recorded on the celluloid or videotape.'

[229] Laddie, *et al*, (2000) para 7.60. Kamina (2000) p 97 argues that the absence of an originality criterion 'does not unreasonably extend the range of works protected'—only security camera recordings and fortuitous films would be probably excluded by an originality criterion.

[230] S5B(4), CDPA.

[231] On how to apply this criterion, see Kamina (2000) pp 97–99.

the recording is medium specific; (ii) whether the recording is restricted to certain types of material; (iii) what constitutes a moving image; and (iv) and whether a particular quantity of moving images must be produced?

The requirements of section 5B appear to be technology-neutral,[232] since the recording may be 'on *any* medium' provided a moving image 'may by *any means* be produced'. The relevant medium could be CD-Rom, DVD-Rom, or digital binary code provided a moving image may be produced.[233] This means that the format of multimedia works will not affect their ability to qualify as 'films'.

Is the 'recording on any medium' restricted to certain sorts of material? Nothing in the definition of film appears to restrict the recording to specific subject matter, in particular visual images.[234] This view is supported by the fact that the sound track accompanying a film is treated as part of the film for certain purposes.[235] The fact that films are not restricted to visual images is helpful in terms of protecting multimedia works which, by their very nature, involve a diversity of inputs:

> Thus [the definition of film] would seem to cover many 'multi-media' digital recordings. These may make much greater use of text, alongside visual images and a sound-track, than a traditional film, and they may include opportunities for interactivity; nevertheless, so long as moving images are part of their make-up, they fall to be treated as films.[236]

It can be queried whether images generated by computer software, as opposed to those retrieved from digital storage, can qualify as a recording, given that they are *generated*, as opposed to *recorded*.[237] A computer video game is the sort of multimedia work that squarely raises this issue. However, there has been no UK ruling on protection of video games as films.[238] Nonetheless, section 5B emphasises that the

---

[232] See Laddie, *et al*, (2000) para 7.16.

[233] Cornish and Llewelyn (2003) para 10–23; Stamatoudi (2002) pp 109, 142.

[234] Cornish and Llewelyn (2003) para 10–25. This is unlike the previous definition in s 13(10) of Copyright Act 1956, which referred to any sequence of *visual images*.

[235] See ss 5B(2) and (3)(a) CDPA. On the history of protection of film soundtracks under UK copyright law, see Kamina (2000) pp 94–96.

[236] Cornish and Llewelyn (2003) para 10–25.

[237] An example of computer generated images is the Australian decision *Galaxy Electronics Pty Ltd v Sega Enterprises Ltd* (1997) 37 IPR 462 ('*Galaxy Electronics*'), which held that a video game could be protected as a cinematograph film. In this case, the images on the screen were the result of computer calculations done according to a particular model, as opposed to the retrieval of pre-existing images. This aspect of the decision has been criticised by MJ O'Connor, 'Squeezing into Traditional Frames: Intellectual Property Law in the Shadow of the Information Society' (1998) 12 *IPJ* 285, 314–16.

[238] Note that in *Sega Enterprises Ltd v Richards* [1983] FSR 73, Goulding J granted interlocutory relief in respect of a video game, 'Frogger', which he held was protected as a computer program (ie a literary work) under the Copyright Act 1956 (UK) and was being infringed by the defendant's computer program. The plaintiff also argued that its video game constituted a cinematograph film under s 13(10), however, for the purposes of the interim application, Goulding J did not consider it necessary to determine this matter. Video games have been protected as films or audiovisual works in other jurisdictions. In Australia see *Galaxy Electronics*, and *Kabushiki Kaisha Sony Computer Entertainment v Stevens* (2003) 57 IPR 161, 209 (per Lindgren J) but cf *Aristocrat Leisure Industries Pty Ltd v Pacific Gaming Pty Ltd* [2000] 105 FCR 153, 168 where Tamberlin J held that electronic gaming machines did not constitute a 'cinematograph film' since they were 'simply moving pictures of static symbols which simulate the

production of a moving image may occur 'by any means'. This language suggests that this includes the generation of images via the interaction of stored digital data with software, the operating system, the relevant hardware, or with the user.[239]

In order for the 'recording' to qualify as a 'film', there must be 'a moving image' capable of being produced from it. Obviously, still images would not constitute a 'moving image'.[240] It has been suggested that movement of a single frame or the scrolling of text on screen would also fail to qualify as a moving image.[241] There remains the important question of *what quantity of moving images* needs to be produced in order for the *entirety* of the work (in this case, multimedia work) to qualify for protection as a 'film'? Provided a single moving image is displayed, would the entirety of the work be protected? Cornish and Llewelyn indicate that a multimedia work would need to produce a significant portion of moving images in order to qualify as a 'film':

> Where, for instance, does one place an electronic encyclopedia which can illustrate its basic text by films, recordings of music and of animal sounds, and which offers the user the capacity to re-draw and re-colour artistic works? Like songs and films before it, such a compendium can be conceived as a coalescence of different copyrights. In so far as it is a film, as well as constituting an accumulation of contributory copyrights, the digitised encyclopedia will also be a work in itself. *But large parts of it may not produce moving images; the whole* (or perhaps those parts*) may therefore not fit* within the definition of *film.*[242] (Emphasis supplied)

It seems reasonable to require the production of a significant quantity of moving images in order to protect the total recording as a 'film'. Otherwise, any 'recording' that merely produced *a* single moving image could be protected and this would make the 'film' category too wide. Unfortunately, this requirement creates a potential barrier for reference-type multimedia works[243] that include large

spinning of reels' and 'there is no element of progression or movement in the symbols themselves as there is in a traditional movie film, which is comprised of a series of marginally different pictures, which when repeated quickly, give the impression of motion'. In South Africa, see *Nintendo v Golden China TV-Game* (1993) 28 IPR 313. In the United States, see decisions such as *Stern Electronics v Kaufman* 669 F 2d 852(2nd Cir, 1982); *Midway Manufacturing Co v Artic International Inc* 704 F 2d 1009(7th Cir, 1983). Protection of multimedia video games as audiovisual works is discussed in more detail in ch 6.

[239] This view is also supported by Kamina (2000) pp 89–90; and Stamatoudi (2002) p 135.
[240] Stamatoudi (2002) p 133.
[241] Kamina (2000) p 92.
[242] Cornish and Llewelyn (2003) para 19–47.
[243] And *not* multimedia generally, which is what Stamatoudi (2002) p 141 argues:

> Multimedia presents a different picture. A variety of images are projected onto a television or computer screen. Still images, such as photographs and text, are combined with moving images. The images as such, and especially the moving images, are not the essence of a multimedia product. Not only are non-moving images involved, but the sound element is also of equal importance to the final product.

See also p 145—'moving images are rarely the prevailing element in a multimedia work. Multimedia works combine different types of works, and it is usually either text or still images which are their major element'.

quantities of static inputs, such as text, photographs, drawings or artistic images, or sound inputs.[244] To the extent that multimedia works utilise such static or sound inputs, they will not be protected as a film.[245] In addition, if the multimedia work has a stationary visual user interface, then it would also seem to be excluded by the definition of film.

Some commentators have argued that the film category is inappropriate for protecting multimedia works because it cannot accommodate *interactivity*, which is a key feature of these works.[246] How might interactivity prevent a multimedia work from qualifying as a film? The main concern is that interactivity will seriously hinder moving images from being displayed in a linear sequence.[247] A high degree of user interactivity will inhibit a flow of consecutive moving images because the user will largely determine the order in which they view the material within the multimedia work. The moving images might be displayed in a random or non-linear sequence. Certain types of multimedia works, such as reference-type works, are particularly problematic, since they are in no way a continuous blend of video, audio, and data with only a few still images interpolated. Rather, they are collections of diverse inputs (including still and moving images) which are disjunctively presented to the user as they determine. Indeed, the goal of this type of work is to make available a body of information with maximum flexibility to the user: ie, data that can be approached and expanded in a variety of ways and from a range of angles.[248]

The above concern assumes that a (linear) *sequence* of moving images is required by the definition of 'film'. Is this assumption justified? The express language of section 5B does *not* support such a requirement. Stamatoudi has argued that it is implicit in section 5B: 'Even if that requirement [of sequence of moving images] is not mentioned expressly in the law, it must purposively be derived from it, especially if it is referred to in relation to the notion of a film, which represents a certain form in our minds.'[249]

Stamatoudi argues that Parliament must have intended to include the traditional notion of films, namely works of moving images with a linear, narrative

---

[244] A similar barrier exists in relation to the Australian definition of 'cinematograph film': see T Aplin, 'Not in our Galaxy: Why "Film" Won't Rescue Multimedia' (1999) 12 *EIPR* 633. See also, G Wei, 'Multimedia and Intellectual and Industrial Property Rights in Singapore' (1995) 3 *Intl J of L & Information Technology* 214, 248 and Aust Copyright Law Review Committee, *Simplification of the Copyright Act 1968, Part 2: Categorisation of Subject Matter and Exclusive Rights, and Other Issues* (AGD, Canberra, 1999) ('SR:2') para 7.13.

[245] See also M Turner, 'Do the Old Legal Categories fit the New Multimedia Products?: a Multimedia Cd-Rom as a Film' [1995] *EIPR* 107, 108; Kamina (2000) p 92.

[246] See O'Connor (1998) p 316; J Lahore and F Phillips, 'The Notion of an Audiovisual Work: International and Comparative Law' [1996] 7 *AIPJ* 208, 219; J Douglas, 'Too Hot to Handle? Copyright Protection of Multimedia' [1997] 8 *AIPJ* 96, 100–1; Stamatoudi (2002) pp 136–40, 145.

[247] See also Stamatoudi (2002) pp 136–41; Turner (1995) p 108.

[248] N Negroponte, *Being Digital* (Hodder Stoughton, London, 1995) 70–71.

[249] Stamatoudi (2002) p 139.

quality, along with analogous works. Although interactivity is not entirely alien to the traditional notion of film,[250] multimedia works are not analogous works because they are highly interactive and non-linear in nature. Support for Stamatoudi's argument is found in Article 2(1) of the Berne Convention, which states that protection for 'literary and artistic works' includes 'cinematographic works to which are assimilated works expressed by a process analogous to cinematography'. Works expressed by a process analogous to cinematography have so far been extended only to televisual and videographic works.[251] However, there are two reasons why there is no implicit requirement of the kind suggested by Stamatoudi. First, Article 2(1) of the Berne Convention does not preclude Berne Union members from extending the subject matter protected as 'film'. This has obviously occurred in those jurisdictions that have protected computer video games as films or audiovisual works.[252] It was therefore open to the UK to create a category of film work of wider ambit than that envisaged by Article 2(1) of the Berne Convention. Second, given that the previous definition of film in section 13(10) of the Copyright Act 1956 referred to a 'sequence of visual images' and the express language of the new definition in section 5B of the CDPA omits such a reference, it seems unlikely that this is now an implicit requirement.[253]

In conclusion, the definition of 'film' in section 5B of the CDPA will prove problematic for reference-type multimedia works that include a large quantity of static inputs. However, similar obstacles do not exist for multimedia video games, particularly since the definition of 'film' can accommodate user interactivity.[254]

5. Dramatic Work

Copyright may subsist in an original dramatic work that is recorded in writing or otherwise.[255] A dramatic work is defined to include 'a work of dance or mime'[256] and cannot be static,[257] but 'must have movement, story or action'.[258] It seems unlikely that a multimedia work would qualify for protection as a dramatic work. However, after the Court of Appeal decision in *Norowzian v Arks (No 2)* ('*Arks (No*

---

[250] As noted by Stamatoudi (2002) p 137. See also the Software Report, para 14.86: 'it does not seem that interacting with a multi-media production is different in essence from editing a celluloid film, in much as making it infinitely more possible to modify the multi-media production in an infinite variety of ways.' However, the CLRC later revised their view on this issue: see SR:2, para 7.13.

[251] Ricketson (1987) pp 559–62.

[252] See eg, Australia and the United States, n 238 above.

[253] See also Kamina (2000) pp 89–90 and Cornish and Llewelyn (2003) para 10–25.

[254] Turner (1995) p 108. Although, Stamatoudi (2002) pp 183–85 argues that video games have low interactivity, as opposed to sophisticated interactivity of sampling, blurring and morphing.

[255] Ss 1(1)(a) and 3(2), CDPA.

[256] s 3(1), CDPA.

[257] *Creation Records v News Group Newspapers* [1997] EMLR 444.

[258] Cornish and Llewelyn (2003) para 10–11.

*2)')*²⁵⁹ the ambit of 'dramatic work' has been extended to include film works.²⁶⁰ This may open up the protection that is available for multimedia works.

The case concerned a short film called 'Joy' and an advertisement for Guinness produced by Arks called 'Anticipation'. The short film had no dialogue and involved a man dancing in a quirky manner in a bland setting. The visual impact was particularly striking because of the filming and editing techniques employed by the film director, Mr Norowzian, which resulted in sudden changes of position by the man that never could have been performed in reality. 'Anticipation' showed a man dancing in a similarly frenzied style waiting for his pint of Guinness to settle. The advertisement had been inspired by 'Joy' and, in fact, Arks had been given a copy of 'Joy' to preview and had asked Mr Norowzian to direct 'Anticipation', but he refused.

Mr Norowzian brought proceedings against Arks claiming that 'Anticipation' infringed copyright in 'Joy' as a dramatic work and a film. The claim in respect of film copyright was struck out at an interlocutory stage.²⁶¹ However, his claim in respect of dramatic copyright went to trial before Rattee J, who dismissed the action on two grounds: first, that 'Joy' did not constitute either a dramatic work or a recording of a dramatic work; and second, that even if 'Joy' was or comprised a dramatic work, 'Anticipation' did not reproduce a substantial part of it.²⁶²

Significantly, the Court of Appeal reversed the decision of Rattee J on the issue of whether a film could constitute a dramatic work,²⁶³ although the appeal was ultimately dismissed on the basis that 'Anticipation' was not a substantial reproduction of 'Joy', since only the filming and editing techniques had been reproduced.²⁶⁴ Nourse LJ delivered the leading judgment²⁶⁵ and held that 'dramatic work' must be given its ordinary and natural meaning, which amounted to 'a work of action, with or without words or music, which is capable of being performed before an audience.'²⁶⁶ Nourse LJ held that a film will often, but not always, be a work of action that it is capable of being performed before an audience.²⁶⁷ At first instance, Rattee J took a contrary view for a number of reasons: (i) section 1(1) of the CDPA treats films and dramatic works separately; (ii) section 48 of the Copyright Act 1956 (UK) excluded a cinematograph film from the definition of

---

²⁵⁹ *Norowzian v Arks (No 2)* [1999] FSR 79 (Rattee J); [2000] FSR 363 (CA) (*'Arks (No 2)'*).

²⁶⁰ See Kamina (2000) pp 36–37; 66–74.

²⁶¹ See *Norowzian v Arks (No 1)* [1998] FSR 394.

²⁶² *Norowzian v Arks (No 2)* [1999] FSR 79, 88 and 90.

²⁶³ *Arks (No 2)*, 366–67 (Nourse LJ). Nourse LJ at 367 agreed with Rattee J that 'Joy' was not a recording of a dramatic work, since it was not a recording of anything that was, or could be, performed by anyone.

²⁶⁴ *Arks (No 2)*, 368 (Nourse LJ).

²⁶⁵ Brooke LJ dismissed the appeal for the reasons given by Nourse LJ: see *Arks (No 2)*, 368.

²⁶⁶ *Arks (No 2)*, 367 (Nourse LJ).

²⁶⁷ Above.

'dramatic work';[268] and (iii) unlike the previous 1956 Act, the CDPA permits a dramatic work to be recorded by film.[269] Nourse LJ dismissed these reasons, stating that section 1(1) does not express any mutual exclusivity between films and dramatic works and that it was unsafe to rely upon the 1956 Act to interpret the material provisions of the CDPA.[270] Buxton LJ also agreed that a film *per se* might amount to a dramatic work, in the ordinary sense of that phrase indicated by Nourse LJ.[271] However, Buxton LJ went further by stating in *obiter dicta* that, if the CDPA is to be interpreted consistently with the UK's international obligations under Article 14*bis* of the Berne Convention (protection of cinematographic works), the category of 'dramatic work' must embrace 'not only drama in any traditional or normal sense but also cinematography' and that this is so 'even in cases where the natural meaning of "dramatic work" does not or might not embrace the particular film in question'.[272]

After the *Arks (No 2)* decision, a film can be protected as a dramatic work, provided it also satisfies the requirement of originality.[273] Kamina argues that fictional cinematic works and certain non-fictional cinematic works, such as documentaries, would qualify as 'dramatic works' because they convey some kind of story. A sporting event[274] would not be protected as a dramatic work since it 'does not tell a *story* and lacks the unity characteristic of a dramatic work.'[275] A televisual production of a live dramatic work (on stage) would also not be protected, since it is a copy of the play and not a new dramatic work.[276]

Can a multimedia work qualify for protection as a dramatic work? A preliminary question is whether multimedia works must fall within the definition of 'film' before they can qualify as dramatic works. In *Arks (No 2)*, the claimant sought to protect his film 'Joy' as a dramatic work because of the limited scope of protection available for film works. However, it was never in doubt that 'Joy' fell within the definition of film in section 5B. Given the facts of *Arks (No 2)*, it is arguable that for a film to qualify as a 'dramatic work' it must also satisfy the definition of 'film' in section 5B of the CDPA. This view is supported by Buxton LJ's comments

---

[268] In Australia, the definition of 'dramatic work' expressly excludes a cinematograph film, as distinct from the scenario or script for a film: see s 10(1), Copyright Act 1968 (Cth).

[269] *Norowzian v Arks (No 2)* [1999] FSR 79, 87.

[270] *Arks (No 2)*, 367 (Nourse LJ).

[271] *Arks (No 2)*, 369 (Buxton LJ).

[272] *Arks (No 2)*, 369 (Buxton LJ). Brooke LJ also agreed with these observations of Buxton LJ.

[273] For discussion of the Court of Appeal decision in *Arks (No 2)* see: R Arnold, '*Joy*: A Reply' [2001] *IPQ* 10; J Hughes and M Parry, 'An Unsettling Feeling: a Second View of the *Norowzian* Decision' [2000] *Entertainment L Rev* 56; Kamina (2002) pp 69–71; M James, 'Some *Joy* at Last for Cinematographers' [2000] *EIPR* 131; H Porter, 'A "Dramatic Work" Includes . . . a Film' [2000] *Entertainment L Rev* 50; T Rivers, '*Norowzian* Revisited' [2000] *EIPR* 389; I Stamatoudi, '"*Joy*" for the Claimant: Can a Film Also Be Protected as a Dramatic Work?' [2000] *IPQ* 117.

[274] As opposed to television productions of sporting events, which arguably would be protected as a dramatic work: Kamina (2000) pp 73–74.

[275] Kamina (2000) p 73 (emphasis original).

[276] Kamina (2000) pp 71–74.

stressing the importance of properly protecting *cinematographic works*, as set out in Article 14*bis* of the Berne Convention. The decision in *Arks (No 2)* may be viewed as a means of improving protection of films beyond that acquired under a 'film' copyright. If this view is correct, multimedia works would have to surmount the dual hurdle of establishing that they are film *and* dramatic works. However, those multimedia works that fail to satisfy the definition of 'film' because they involve a large quantity of static inputs are also unlikely to constitute *works of action*, so that this dual hurdle (if it indeed exists) will not operate harshly.

The type of multimedia work that is most likely to fall within the notion of 'dramatic work' (and also 'film') is a multimedia video game, or other multimedia work that employs a narrative of some description.[277] This type of work would constitute a work of action and would be capable of being performed before an audience. Certainly, if a film such as 'Joy' is capable of being performed before an audience (presumably by the film being shown in public), then a multimedia work will also satisfy this requirement if it can be shown (ie, displayed) in public.

The real difficulty with categorising multimedia works as dramatic works arises when trying to ascertain the scope of that protection. If protection does not extend to techniques of production (as in *Arks (No 2)*) then the value for multimedia works will be limited. This issue is explored further in chapter 4 when discussing the scope of protection of multimedia works.

6. Broadcasts

The Copyright and Related Rights Regulations[278] ('Copyright Regulations') implemented the Directive 2001/29/EC on the harmonisation of certain aspects of copyright and related rights in the information society[279] ('Information Society Directive') and came into effect on 31 October 2003. Prior to this, the CDPA recognised *both* broadcasts and cable programmes as categories of copyright works.[280]

---

[277] See also Kamina (2000) p 79 for a multimedia work to convey a dramatic audiovisual work it would have to carry 'a scenario or story (even if this scenario can be modified to a certain extent by the input of the user). The audiovisual dramatic work would be distinct from the underlying script (itself a dramatic work), since new elements have been added (sound effects, images, animations, etc) and original choices have been made by the persons in charge of the project.' Scripts and stories for videogames could also attract protection as dramatic works. *Cf, Aristocrat Leisure Industries Pty Ltd v Pacific Gaming Pty Ltd* [2000] 105 FCR 153, 167 where Tamberlin J held that the specifications for electronic gaming machines did not give rise to any 'dramatic work' under the Australian Copyright Act 1968 (Cth) since they lacked, 'the element of *performance* by characters, and are insufficiently predetermined . . . There is no apparent plot, nor is there any choreography, script, characterisation or interaction between characters and there is a strong element of unpredictability and randomness.'

[278] SI 2003/2498.

[279] OJ L167 22/6/2001, pp 10–19.

[280] See CDPA prior to commencement of the Copyright Regulations ('CDPA 1988 provisions'), s 1(1)(b) and ss 6 (broadcasts) and 7 (cable programmes). For a discussion of how new technologies, such as digital broadcasting, video-on-demand and on-line delivery, fitted within the old scheme of 'broadcasts' and 'cable programmes' see Kamina (2000) pp 114–16.

The former was concerned with transmissions by wireless telegraphy,[281] whereas the latter concerned transmissions by means of a telecommunications system, other than by wireless telegraphy. As a result of the Copyright Regulations, the category of 'cable programme' has been deleted from the CDPA,[282] whilst the category of 'broadcast' has been retained, albeit in a substantially amended and expanded form. This change was a consequence of introducing a new general 'communication to the public' right (discussed in the next chapter).[283]

Under the law as it stood prior to the Copyright Regulations, there was some support for the view that websites could qualify for protection as 'cable programmes'.[284] It was arguable that on-line multimedia works, in the form of websites, could obtain protection in their entirety via the route of 'cable programmes'. According to the transitional provisions, the Copyright Regulations apply, *inter alia*, to copyright works made before or after commencement (ie, 31 October 2003).[285] From a plain reading of the transitional provisions, it seems that a work which would have qualified for protection as a cable programme under section 7 will *no longer* be protected, unless it can fit within one of the (now) eight categories of protected works.[286] This is where the scope of amended section 6 of the CDPA becomes relevant, since it might be possible to fit on-line multimedia works within this category.

Section 6 of the CDPA, as amended by the Copyright Regulations, defines 'broadcast' as follows:

(1) In this Part a 'broadcast' means an electronic transmission of visual images, sounds or other information which—

(a) is transmitted for simultaneous reception by members of the public and is capable of being lawfully received by them, or

---

[281] According to Laddie, *et al* (2000) para 7.14 wireless telegraphy excluded signals transmitted by a dedicated material pathway.

[282] See Copyright Regulations, Part 2, reg 5 deleting s 7 and amending s 1(1)(b) of the CDPA 1988 provisions. T Cook, and L Brazell, *The Copyright Directive: UK Implementation* (Jordans, Bristol, 2004) comment, para 3.18: 'The change brings UK copyright law closer to the international mainstream, which does not recognise separate protection for cable programmes, and draws a line under an interesting, but flawed experiment in the creation of a new type of right.'

[283] See para 3.6, *Consultation on UK Implementation of Directive 2001/29/EC on Copyright and Related Rights in the Information Society: Analysis of Reponses and Government Conclusions* ('Consultation Paper') available at: http://www.patent.gov.uk/about/consultations/responses/copydirect/index.htm.

[284] See *Shetland Times v Wills* [1997] EMLR 277 (Scottish Court of Session), 281–82 (Lord Hamilton on an application for an interim interdict) and *Sony Music Entertainment (UK) and others v Easyinternetcafe Ltd* [2003] EWHC 62, para 48 in which Peter Smith J in granting summary judgment approved in obiter the *Shetland Times* decision. However, it is submitted this view was erroneous because many websites would fall foul of the exemption in 'old section 7(2)(a)' relating to interactive facilities that are an essential feature of a cable programme service. See also HL MacQueen, 'Copyright and the Internet' in L Edwards and C Waelde (eds), *Law and the Internet: A Framework for Electronic Commerce* (Hart Publishing, Oxford, 2000) 181, 191–93 on this issue.

[285] Part III, regs 30–32, Copyright Regulations.

[286] The Government believes that many 'cable programmes' are likely to be protected under other categories: see para 3.6, Consultation Paper.

(b) is transmitted at a time determined solely by the person making the transmission for presentation to members of the public, and which is not excepted by subsection (1A); and references to broadcasting shall be construed accordingly.

It is significant that the new definition of broadcast refers to *electronic transmission*, rather than transmission by wireless telegraphy, of 'visual images, sounds, or other information'. Broadcast is now redefined in a technologically neutral way to encompass *both* wireless and wire transmissions.[287] However, the appropriateness of describing transmissions in terms of whether they are *electronic* has been questioned, largely because it is not clear whether the expression is wide enough to embrace optical fibre transmissions,[288] along with future modes of transmission.[289] Nonetheless, Ross argues that it is clear that in terms of identifying broadcasts as subject matter, the emphasis has shifted from 'the medium by which the transmission is made . . . [to] whether the transmission is interactive (ie, the consumer can choose the start time) or not.'[290]

It is also notable that 'internet transmissions' are exempt from the definition of 'broadcast',[291] except in three narrow situations (discussed below). In assessing whether on-line multimedia works are capable of falling within the definition of 'broadcast', a key preliminary question is whether they are in fact 'internet transmissions' and thus *prima facie* exempt. In turn, this raises the question: what constitutes an internet transmission? The Copyright Regulations do not define 'internet transmission', suggesting that the draftsman must have been confident that this was a well-understood phenomenon. To some extent, this confidence does not seem misplaced. The Internet forms an important feature of people's daily activities, and it could be said that we intuitively recognise Internet transmissions when we see them.[292] Nevertheless, it is worth exploring the meaning of this term further.

The 'Internet'[293] is widely understood to be a 'network of networks' that operates according to TCP/IP Internet Protocol Suite (usually referred to as TCP/IP after its two main standards Transmission Control Protocol and Internet

---

[287] See para 3.6, Consultation Paper. A similar approach was adopted in Australia, following the DAA—see the new definition of 'broadcast' in s 10(1), Copyright Act 1968 (Cth).

[288] A Ross, 'Implementation of the Copyright Harmonisation Directive in the United Kingdom' (2004) 15 *Entertainment L Rev* 47.

[289] See Australian Copyright Council, 'Comments on draft Copyright Amendment (Digital Agenda) Bill 1999', 19 March 1998 (sic) ('ACC Comments') at http://www.copyright.org.au.

[290] Ross (2004) p 47.

[291] In Australia, certain activities are exempt from the definition 'broadcast' and 'broadcasting', namely, teletext services and services that make programs available on-demand, on a point-to-point basis—see s 10(1), Copyright Act 1968 (Cth).

[292] A Terrett and I Monaghan, 'The Internet—An Introduction for Lawyers' in L Edwards and C Waelde, (eds), *Law and the Internet: a Framework for Electronic Commerce* (Hart Publishing, Oxford, 2000) 1.

[293] For a good account of the history of the Internet, see J Naughton, *A Brief History of the Future: The Origins of the Internet* (Phoenix, London, 2000).

Protocol).[294] Describing the Internet as a 'network of networks' is meant to convey the fact that the 'Internet is not a single physical or tangible entity, but rather a complex series of interconnected computer networks forming a widespread information infrastructure . . .'[295]

The Internet is a combination of numerous backbone networks (high capacity networks),[296] their interconnections, and a huge number of internal networks within organisations that are connected to one of the backbone networks.[297] This 'network of networks' is not controlled by a central computer or server, but is made possible by TCP/IP.[298] TCP/IP may be described as a standard, or suite of protocols, that enables information to be communicated or exchanged across interconnected networks. TCP/IP operates at different network layers. Network layers are typically broken down into seven levels.[299] However, it is typical to describe TCP/IP in terms of only four: the data link, network, transport, and application layers.[300] TCP/IP is non-proprietary in nature, which is crucial to the openness of the Internet.[301]

One of the most important features of TCP/IP is that it creates a packet-switched, as opposed to circuit-switched, network. The latter type of network functions by creating a dedicated connection (circuit) between two points—a typical example is a telephone system. Whereas, with a packet switched network data is transferred across a network by disassembling it into smaller pieces, called packets, and these packets may travel different routes in order to arrive at their destination. This means the packets must be identified, delivered, and then reassembled. It is these tasks which are facilitated by TCP/IP.[302]

Internet transmissions may therefore be understood as transmissions that occur across external networks (as opposed to across internal networks), via a packet-switched system, according to TCP/IP.

---

[294] S Biegel, *Beyond Our Control? Confronting the Limits of Our Legal System in the Age of Cyberspace* (MIT Press, Cambridge, MA, 2003) 189–90; DE Comer, *Internetworking with TCP/IP— Volume 1: Principles, Protocols and Architecture*, 3rd edn (Prentice Hall, NJ, 1995) 2–3; L Lessig, *Code and Other Laws of Cyberspace* (Basic Books, New York, 1999) 101–2; Naughton (2000) pp 19–21; C Reed, *Internet Law: Text and Materials* (Butterworths, London, 2000) 10–14; AL Shapiro, *The Control Revolution: How the Internet is Putting Individuals in Charge and Changing the World that We Know* (Century Foundation, New York, 1999) 16–17.

[295] Biegel (2003) pp 189–90.

[296] One of the key Internet Backbone networks is NSFNet—for further details see Comer (1995) pp 40–43.

[297] J Nielsen, *Multimedia and Hypertext, the Internet and Beyond* (AP Professional, Boston, 1995) 165.

[298] Naughton (2000) p 21. Although note that TCP/IP can be used to communicate information across intranets or internal networks, ie, those networks that have no connection to outside networks: Comer (1995) p 2.

[299] According to the International Organisation for Standardization Reference Model of Open System Interconnection (ISO–7 layer)—(7) Application; (6) Presentation; (5) Session; (4) Transport; (3) Network; (2) Data Link; (1) Physical Hardware Connection: see Comer (1995) p 163.

[300] Biegel (2003) p 191; Comer (1995) pp 165–66; Lessig (1999) p 101.

[301] Shapiro (1999) pp 16–17; Lessig (1999) p 101.

[302] Comer (1995) p 18; and Naughton (2000) pp 20–21.

Multimedia websites, along with multimedia works made available via the Internet, *prima facie* will not qualify as 'broadcasts' because they will invariably involve Internet transmissions. Only if the multimedia works fall within the exempt Internet transmissions specified in section 6(1A) will they qualify as 'broadcasts'.[303] Sections 6(1A)(a) and (b) refer respectively to a 'transmission taking place simultaneously on the internet and by other means' and 'a concurrent transmission of a live event'. These provisions appear to encompass the situations where there is a recorded programme that is simultaneously being webcast[304] and broadcast or cable-cast (in the old technologically specific sense) and where there is a live event that is simultaneously being webcast and broadcast or cablecast (again, in the old technologically specific sense). Section 6(1A)(c) refers to another kind of Internet transmission that may qualify as a broadcast, namely:

> a transmission of recorded moving images or sounds forming part of a programme service offered by the person responsible for making the transmission, being a service in which programmes are transmitted at scheduled times determined by that person.

This provision appears to encompass non-interactive services, such as video-on-demand (eg, BSkyB Movies), which are transmitted via the Internet.

As discussed above, the great majority of on-line multimedia works will be Internet transmissions. However, few of them will be of the exempt kind. This is because most multimedia websites do not offer *simultaneous* delivery of recorded or live (traditional) forms of broadcast.[305] As websites such as http://news.bbc.co.uk/ and also http://edition.cnn.com/ show, the tendency is to include stored audio and video files of news reports and programmes which users can access when they choose.

In conclusion, there appears to be little chance of fitting on-line multimedia works within the newly amended category of 'broadcast'.

Authorship and Ownership

Another matter to be considered when assessing the suitability of existing copyright categories is whether the provisions on authorship and ownership relating to

---

[303] Cook and Brazell (2004) p 37 comment that only those Internet transmissions 'which are of a conventional broadcast character will qualify as broadcasts.'

[304] 'Webcast' is defined in *Hutchinson Dictionary of Computing, Multimedia and the Internet*, 3rd edn (Helicon, Oxford, 1999) 291 as: 'the World Wide Web equivalent of a radio or television broadcast. Any service that is regularly or continuously updated—such as sports results and share price information—can be described as a Webcast, but the term is increasingly used for *live* events where sounds and images are transmitted in a format such as RealAudio or RealVideo.'

[305] An example of a website that does offer such simultaneous transmission is http://www.bbc.co.uk/worldservice/index.shtml where it is possible to listen to a live news broadcast.

computer programs, films, dramatic works, compilations and copyright data-bases,[306] along with authorship and ownership of *sui generis* databases, actually relate to the reality of multimedia production. This section outlines the participants in multimedia creation, and then examines the authorship and ownership principles for each relevant category of work.[307]

1. Participants in Multimedia Creation

Multimedia production usually involves the following persons: the designer, the producer, the project manager, creators of the content, programmers, and technical specialists.[308] The *designer* is the person who develops the idea for, and designs, the work. The *producer* is the person who supplies the necessary investment to bring the idea to fruition. The *project manager* is the person who organises and oversees the entire production process, and is responsible for the following activities: preparing budgets and schedules, co-ordinating any permissions that may be required, and employing a production team responsible for programming, and the contents. The content *creators* are those persons who have created the individual inputs that comprise the work—ie, audio, video, graphics and animation—remembering that the content may be pre-existing or may be specially produced for the work. *Programmers* are the persons who write and test the software that underlies the multimedia work. The *technical specialists* are the persons who are in charge of formatting and assembling the contents of the multimedia work.

2. Authorship of Multimedia Works Protected under Copyright

For all copyright works, the author is the *person who creates* the work.[309] For some works, that person is stipulated in the legislation.[310] A work may be jointly authored.[311] This requires collaboration between two or more authors, and that

---

[306] But not broadcasts as it is highly unlikely that any element of on-line multimedia works will fall within this category.

[307] For an analysis under French law see Laitreille (2001) and Stamatoudi (2002) pp 196–203.

[308] See W Cotton and R Oliver, *Understanding Hypermedia: from Multimedia to Virtual Reality* (Phaidon, London, 1992) 78–81; JR Pardo, *Copyright and Multimedia* (Kluwer, The Hague, 2003) 98–99; and, to a lesser extent, Stamatoudi (2002) pp 33–35 for support. Stamatoudi's notion of 'editor' probably equates to 'designer' and her notion of 'maker or developer', probably equates to the project manager and possibly also encompasses the programmer and technical specialists.

[309] S 9(1), CDPA.

[310] For a sound recording, it is the producer; for a film, it is the producer and principal director, for a broadcast, it is the person making that broadcast and for a typographical arrangement of a published edition, it is the publisher: s 9(2), CDPA.

[311] Note that films are deemed to be works of joint authorship unless the principal director and producer are the same person: s 10(2), CDPA.

their respective contributions are significant (ie, original) and not distinct.[312] Generally speaking, the author is the first owner of copyright. This is the case *unless* the work is created by an employee in the course of employment and there is no agreement to the contrary.[313]

(a) Computer Programs

In the case of computer programs, the author usually will be the person who programmes the code. However, contributions to the design of the program or to the program's workability will not suffice to make a person a joint author. This is illustrated by *Fylde Microsystems Ltd v Key Radio Systems Ltd* ('*Fylde Microsystems*').[314] In this case, the plaintiff's business was the development and manufacture of telecommunications equipment and related computer software. The defendant's business involved the importation and manufacture of mobile and portable radios. The plaintiffs and defendants had cooperated in the design of software to be used in a new generation of radios to be sold by the defendant. In an action for infringement of copyright in the software, the defendant argued, *inter alia*, that the software was a work of joint authorship and thus jointly owned by them. It was not disputed that the plaintiff had written the relevant software. However, the defendant argued that it had made significant contributions to the development of the software. These contributions included testing the software and reporting faults, making suggestions as to what was causing some of the faults, error fixing, providing technical information about the hardware into which the software would be fitted, setting the specification for what the software was supposed to achieve, and setting the parameters and timings within the software.[315] Laddie J held that the defendant's contributions were 'extensive and technically sophisticated' and 'took a lot of time and were very valuable',[316] but that they were not contributions to the *writing* of the software. The defendant had made significant contributions, but of the wrong type of skill and labour,[317] and so was not a joint author (or owner) of the computer program.

For multimedia works that are protected as computer programs, the author will be the programmer who writes the software underlying the multimedia work. The

---

[312] See s 10(1) CDPA and *Robin Ray v Classic FM* [1988] FSR 622; *Stuart v Barrett* [1994] EMLR 448; *Godfrey v Lees* [1995] EMLR 307; *Hadley v Kemp* [1999] EMLR 589; and *Beckingham v Hodgens* [2003] ECDR 6 (ChD); [2003] EMLR 18 (CA); *Bamgboye v Reed* [2004] EMLR 5.

[313] S 11, CDPA. On what constitutes an 'employee' see *Beloff v Pressdram Ltd* [1973] RPC 765, 769–72, 775 (Ungoed-Thomas J). On what is 'made in the course of employment' see *Noah v Shuba* [1991] FSR 14, 25–27 (Mummery J). Note also that a long-standing practice allowing employees to retain copyright can amount to an implied agreement to the contrary within section 11(2): see *Noah v Shuba* [1991] FSR 14, 26–27 (Mummery J).

[314] *Fylde Microsystems Ltd v Key Radio Systems Ltd* [1998] FSR 449 ('*Fylde Microsystems*').

[315] Above, at 459–60.

[316] Above.

[317] Above, at 456.

effect of *Fylde Microsystems* is that a person who contributes to setting the program specifications or testing the program will not be recognised as a joint author. Nor will persons such as the designer, creators and technical specialists be recognised as joint authors.

(b) Compilations

In the case of compilations, the author will be the person who expended the skill and labour in obtaining, selecting, or arranging the contents of the compilation. For multimedia works that are protected as compilations, this is most likely to be the designer, ie, the person who plans the overall work. The project manager might also be classified as a joint author, as the person who expends skill and labour in obtaining the contents of the multimedia work. However, the programmer, technical specialists, creators, and producer will not be recognised as authors of the work.

(c) Copyright Databases

In the case of copyright databases, the author will be the person responsible for the selection or arrangement of the contents. As discussed above, for multimedia works that are protected as databases, the originality assessment will focus on the selection, rather than the arrangement, of contents. The author will be the person responsible for selecting what will comprise the multimedia database. This is most likely to be the designer. This means that the contributions of the programmers, the creators, the technical specialists, the project manager and the producer will not be recognised.

(d) Films

For films, the principal director and producer are deemed co-authors of the work.[318] A 'producer' is the person who undertakes the arrangements necessary for the making of the film.[319] This was elaborated upon in *Beggars Banquet Records Ltd v Carlton Television Ltd*.[320] The plaintiff was a record company that had commissioned the second defendant, a video production company, to make a film about a rave. A teenager at the rave died as a result of ecstasy use. Following a dispute between the parties, the video was not completed. The production company gave its footage to the first defendant, a broadcasting company, who broadcast a current affairs programme about the rave warning of the dangers of ecstasy, in

---

[318] S 9(2), CDPA.

[319] S 178, CDPA.

[320] *Beggars Banquet Records Ltd v Carlton Television Ltd* [1993] EMLR 349 ('*Beggars Banquet*'). This case concerned the law as it stood prior to implementation of the Directive 93/83/EEC of 29 October 1993 harmonising the term of protection of copyright and related rights OJ L 290, 24 November 1993, pp 9–13 ('Term Directive'). In other words, it related to producers as sole authors of a film, whereas, after 1 July 1994, s 9, CDPA was amended to refer to producer and principal director.

which excerpts of the footage were used. Following broadcast of the programme, the plaintiff brought an action for copyright infringement. In an application for interlocutory relief, the plaintiff claimed that it was the owner of the film, by virtue of being the producer (ie, author). To sustain its claim, the plaintiff relied on three factors: that it had financed the making of the footage; that it had arranged for the video production company to have access to the rave site; and that it had chosen the production company to do the filming.[321] Justice Warner held that these factors did not necessarily amount to the plaintiff being the person who undertook the arrangements necessary for the making of the film. It was argued that the person directly responsible for paying the production costs, rather than the person from whom the responsible person obtains the money, is the person who undertakes the arrangements necessary for making of a film.[322] Further, that arranging access to the rave differed from arranging locations for the making of the film, and so did not conclusively point to the plaintiff being the producer.[323] Finally, that choosing the production company to undertake the filming was akin to commissioning the film, and did not necessarily mean that the plaintiff thereby undertook the necessary arrangements.[324]

For multimedia works that are protected as films, the producer (within the meaning of section 9, CDPA) may not correspond to the multimedia producer if that person simply provides the finance.[325] The project manager is more likely to be the person who undertakes the arrangements necessary for the making of the film, insofar as the project manager determines the scheduling, costs, workload, task distribution, and permissions associated with the production of the multimedia work. The principal director of a multimedia work probably would be the designer. However, it seems that the contributions of creators, programmers and technical specialists will not be recognised.

(e) Dramatic Works

For audiovisual works that are protected as dramatic works, there are a number of creative contributors that could be recognised as co-authors. Kamina has explored in detail authorship of dramatic audiovisual works.[326] He argues there is little doubt that the director would qualify as an author[327] and further that, where a script is commissioned for a film, the screenwriter would be a co-author.[328] The

---

[321] *Beggars Banquet*, 361–62.
[322] Above, at 361.
[323] Above, at 362.
[324] Above.
[325] Above, at 361.
[326] Kamina (2002) pp 144–52.
[327] Above, at 146.
[328] Above, at 147. That the script is commissioned for the making of a film is necessary because joint authorship requires collaboration, 'and there cannot be collaboration in handing an unsolicited script to a producer.'

editor could be a co-author, assuming his contribution is substantial enough,[329] along with the director of photography (ie, the cinematographer), who is responsible for the film's aesthetic appeal.[330] Finally, an individual producer might qualify as a co-author, if he or she 'undertakes substantial rewriting of the script and directs the editing'. This level of contribution appears specific to the television industry, in particular television series.[331] Other contributors to the dramatic audiovisual work could include persons such as the art director, who is in charge of the construction or design of the décor, music composers, performers, and technicians such as camera operators and chief electricians. All of these persons are unlikely to be considered co-authors because their contributions are either distinct or are not significant enough.[332]

For multimedia works that are protected as dramatic (audiovisual) works, who would be recognised as the author or co-authors? This category of work has the potential to accommodate several categories of persons who contribute to the multimedia production process. The designer, who can be equated to the film director, should be protected as an author. In addition, the programmer should be recognised as co-author, if this role is seen as equivalent to that of a screenwriter. Finally, creators of content should be co-authors if their contributions are not distinct and are made for the purpose of the multimedia work. However, if we follow Kamina's analysis discussed above, technical specialists and producers (if they are production companies) would not be recognised as co-authors.

3. Authorship of Multimedia Works Protected by the Database Right

In the case of *sui generis* databases, the owner of the database right is the 'maker' of the database. The 'maker' is the person who 'takes the initiative in obtaining, verifying or presenting the contents of the database *and* assumes the risk of investing' in that process.[333] Where a database is made by an employee in the course of employment, then the employer shall be regarded as the maker of the database.[334] The notion of 'maker' ensures that the person who commercially drives a database project reaps the benefit of the database right. This is consistent with a regime that seeks to protect investment in the production of databases.

---

[329] Above, at 149.

[330] Above, at 150.

[331] Above, at 145.

[332] For musical composers and art directors it tends to be that the contributions are distinct, whereas for performers and technicians the problem is with whether the contribution is substantial enough: see above, at 148, 150–52.

[333] Database Regulations, reg 14(1). 'Maker' is not defined in the Database Directive, but guidance as to its meaning is provided in recital 41.

[334] Database Regulations, reg 14(2).

A database may be jointly made by co-makers:

> ... if two or more persons acting together in collaboration take the initiative in obtain-ing, verifying or presenting the contents of the database and assume the risk of investing in that obtaining, verification or presentation.[335]

Unlike joint authors (and thus joint owners[336]) under copyright law,[337] the con-tribution of each co-maker of the database does not to have to be indistinct in nature from that of the other co-makers. Thus, one person could be responsible for collecting the contents of the database; another responsible for checking the accuracy of those contents; someone else charged with the design of how those contents will be available to the user; and finally another person whose contribu-tion is financing the project.[338] The provisions concerning jointly made databases have the potential to embrace a wide range of contributors to a multimedia work. Arguably, the designer, the project manager, the producer, the technical specialists and (where the contents are purpose-made for the project) the creators, could be classed as joint makers of a database. This would only leave out the programmer as a possible co-maker.

Article 11 of the Database Directive imposes territorial qualifications on makers (or rightholders) of *sui generis* databases. A maker or rightholder must be a national of a Member State or else have their habitual residence in the Community.[339] Where the maker or rightholder is a company formed in accord-ance with the law of Member State, their registered office, central administration or principal place of business must be within the community.[340] Article 11 of the Directive is implemented by regulation 18 of the Database Regulations.[341]

Article 11(3) of the Database Directive provides that the database right can be extended to databases made in third countries (ie, non-EEA countries of ori-gin).[342] However, such an extension shall be made only on the basis of material

---

[335] Database Regulations, reg 14(5).

[336] S 10(3) and s 11, CDPA.

[337] S 10(1), CDPA.

[338] See Rees and Chalton (1998) p 62; Bainbridge (1999) p 203; Davison (2003) p 147.

[339] Article 11(1), Database Directive.

[340] Article 11(2), Database Directive. Gaster (1997) p 1148 explains that '[t]he underlying reason for this is that the European Community has no power to grant *sui generis* rights outside its territorial juris-diction. The required link is thus territorial or personal sovereignty.'

[341] Reg 18, Database Regulations requires that the maker, or one of the makers (if there is joint authorship), is an EEA (European Economic Area) national or habitually resident in the EEA, or, if a business, has its significant business connection with the EEA. If a corporation, it has to be incorpo-rated under the law of an EEA state and have a principal business or central administration within EEA; or have its registered office within the EEA and its operations linked on an ongoing basis with the econ-omy of an EEA state. If an unincorporated body, it must have its central administration or principal place of business within the EEA.

[342] This is concluded by the European Council of Ministers acting on a proposal from the European Commission: Article 11(3), Database Directive.

reciprocity.[343] Thus, the principle of national treatment[344] is not followed in the Directive.[345] Of particular concern is how this affects one of the largest producers of databases, the United States, and whether it leaves US databases vulnerable to 'free-riding' within Europe.[346] US copyright law protection of databases is not comparable to the database right,[347] since copyright extends only to databases which reflect a minimal level of creativity in the selection or arrangement of their contents and the scope of protection is correspondingly 'thin'.[348] In addition, repeated attempts to legislate for *sui generis* protection for databases have not met with success.[349] To the extent that some of these legislative proposals reflect a mis-appropriation or unfair competition approach, there is also the concern that this level of protection is not comparable.[350]

Conclusion

The authorship and ownership rules for *sui generis* databases and dramatic (audiovisual) works have the potential to accommodate a significant number of multimedia contributors. The film category is the next most favourable, followed by compilations. The least favourable categories, from the point of view of

---

[343] See recital 56, Database Directive. Ricketson (1987) para 1.27 explains that 'material reciprocity' is where country A accords protection to works from country B, if the latter gives substantially equiv-alent protection to works from country A. According to J Wald, 'Legislating the Golden Rule: Achieving Comparable Protection Under the European Database Directive' (2000) 25 *Fordham Intl L J* 987, 1025, the requirement of material reciprocity serves the functions of giving the EU an advan-tage in bilateral negotiations with trading partners and encourages database production within the EU.

[344] The principle of national treatment is reflected in Article 5(1) of the Berne Convention: 'Authors shall enjoy, in respect of works for which they are protected under this Convention, in countries of the Union other than the country of origin, the rights which their respective laws do now or may hereafter grant to their nationals . . .' On the development and scope of the principle of national treatment in the Berne Convention see Ricketson (1987) paras 5.54–5.68. The principle of national treatment is also contained in the TRIPs Agreement, Article 3: 'Each Member shall accord to the nationals of other Members treatment no less favourable than that it accords to its own national with regard to the pro-tection of intellectual property, subject to the exceptions already provided in . . . the Berne Convention (1971) . . .'

[345] Although see the argument by Davison (2003) pp 223–24, that the database right is *in effect* a form of copyright protection and therefore is subject to the principle of national treatment under the Berne Convention and the TRIPs Agreement.

[346] Davison (2003) ch 5; FW Grosheide, 'Database Protection—the European Way' (2002) 8 *Washington U J L & Pol'y* 39, 71–72; G M Hunsucker, 'The European Database Directive: Regional Stepping Stone to an International Model?' (1997) 7 *Fordham Intellectual Property Media & Entertainment L J* 697; J Lipton, 'Balancing Private Rights and Public Policies: Reconceptualizing Property in Databases' (2003b) 77 *Berkeley Technology L J* 1246–47; JH Reichman and P Samuelson, 'Intellectual Property Rights in Data?' (1997) 50 *Vanderbilt Law Review* 51, 96; Thakur (2001) p 125.

[347] See Powell (1997) p 1246; Grosheide (2002) p 70.

[348] This is after *Feist*. See J Ginsburg, 'No "Sweat"? Copyright and other Protection of Works of Information after *Feist v Rural Telephone*' (1992) 92 *Columbia L Rev* 338. See also Reichmann and Samuelson (1997) pp 62–63.

[349] For a detailed account see Davison (2003) pp 190–216.

[350] Grosheide (2002) pp 71–72. For a discussion of whether the various US legislative proposals would provide comparable protection see: Wald (2002) pp 1025–38.

accommodating contributors as co-authors, are those of copyright databases and computer programs.

Duration

1. Copyright Works

Apart from the operation of authorship and ownership rules, the category of work into which multimedia works are fitted affects the length of protection that is available to them. For computer programs, compilations, copyright databases, and dramatic works, the general rule is that copyright protection lasts for 70 years from the end of the year in which the author dies.[351] Where these works are jointly authored, the term of protection will be 70 years after the death of the last joint author to die. If a multimedia work is protected as a dramatic work, in which several creative contributors are recognised as joint authors, then the multimedia work potentially would be protected for a long period of time.

In the case of films, the term of protection is 70 years from the end of the calendar year of the death of the last of the following persons to die: the principal director; the author of the screenplay, the author of the dialogue, or the composer of music specially created for, and used in, films.[352] This is the case even though the latter three persons are not recognised as co-authors of the film. If the contributors to a multimedia work could map onto these persons, then the film category would provide a long period of protection for multimedia works. Realistically, the designer could equate to the principal director, but there would be difficulties in equating the other contributors to screenplay author, dialogue author, and music composer. Possibly the programmer could be equated to the author of the screenplay, and if music were especially created for the multimedia work, then that creator could be equated to the composer of music.

2. *Sui Generis* Databases

Article 10 of the Directive establishes that the database right lasts for fifteen years.[353] This term is calculated from the first of January of the year following the

---

[351] S 12(2), CDPA.

[352] S 13B, CDPA This section implements Article 2 of the Term Directive. For a discussion of the impact of the Term Directive see B Sherman and L Bently, 'Balance and Harmony in the Duration of Copyright: the European Directive and its Consequences' in P Parrinder and W L Chernaik, (eds), *Textual Monopolies: Literary Copyright and the Public Domain* (OHC, Centre for English Studies, London, 1997) pp15–37.

[353] Implemented in the UK by reg 17(1), Database Regulations.

date of completion of the database. Alternatively, where the database is not yet completed, from the first of January of the year following the date when the database was first made available to the public.[354] A point of contention has been Article 10(3), which provides for a *further* term of fifteen years if a substantial new investment is made to the database.[355] Commentators have expressed concern that this provision leaves open the way for rolling terms of protection, such that databases may be protected perpetually.[356]

Article 10(3) of the Directive provides:

> *Any substantial change,* evaluated qualitatively or quantitatively, to the contents of a database, *including* any substantial change resulting from the *accumulation of successive additions, deletions or alterations,* which would result in the database being considered to be a *substantial new investment,* evaluated qualitatively or quantitatively, shall qualify the *database resulting from that investment* for its own term of protection (emphasis supplied)

This provision deals with the problem raised by dynamic databases, which require a steady stream of maintenance to ensure their currency, which maintenance in turn demands continuing investment.[357] In addition, it may also benefit owners of static, but long term, databases where what is required is ongoing verification of material.[358] However, there is some ambiguity over how Article 10(3) will operate; namely, is the database 'resulting from that investment' referring to the *entirety* of the new (modified) database or only the *new part* of the database that is created with the later investment?

The scope of Article 10(3) was considered in *British Horseracing.* The defendants argued that in updating and verifying the BHB Database, new databases came into existence, each of which was protected for its own new term. Consequently, the defendant argued that it had not infringed the database right because it had made an insubstantial extraction or re-utilization from a series of related databases, as opposed to repeated insubstantial extractions or re-utilizations from the same database. The Court of Appeal in *British Horseracing* referred the following question on Article 10(3) to the ECJ:

> Does Article 10(3) of the Directive mean that, whenever there is a 'substantial change' to the contents of a database, qualifying the resulting database for its own term of protection, the resulting database must be considered to be a new, separate database, including for the purposes of Article 7(5)?

[354] See Article 10(1) and (2), Database Directive. See reg 17(1) and (2), Database Regulations.
[355] See reg 17(3), Database Regulations.
[356] WR Cornish, 'Protection of and Vis-à-Vis Databases' in M Dellebeke (ed), *Copyright in Cyberspace: Copyright and the Global Information Infrastructure* (Otto Cramwinckel, Amsterdam, 1997) 435–42, 440; Davison (2003) p 93; Reichmann and Samuelson (1997) pp 85–86; Thakur (2001) p 115.
[357] *BHB* (ChD), 241–42.
[358] See recital 55, Database Directive.

Advocate General Stix-Hackl opined that the above question should be answered in the positive. In other words, the resulting database is a new, separate database, including for the purposes of Article 7(5). In the case of dynamic databases, the Advocate General took the view that there is only ever one database, namely, the most recent version, since the database is being 'constantly transformed into a new one.'[359] This raises the important question of what is the object of protection of the new term. The Advocate General opined that it is the most recent version of the database, namely, the *whole* database. This is because the object of the substantial changes is to update the database, which in turn means that 'the whole database is the object of the new investment.'[360] This approach is also justified as a practical solution and because it is consistent with the objective of the Database Directive to provide an incentive for investment in making databases, including dynamic databases.[361]

Advocate General Stix-Hackl's approach to Article 10(3) potentially will result in a 'rolling' *sui generis* right in the case of dynamic databases and thus sacrifice public domain interests to practical concerns.[362] Moreover, her approach creates an anomaly where a database is published both as a hard copy and as a dynamic database. An example is a telephone directory, which is published annually in hard copy format (and updated each time), but which is also made available on-line and regularly updated.[363] Following the Advocate General's approach, one could envisage a situation in which a competitor copied and published listings (for say, law firms) from a yellow pages hard copy directory published in 2000 in the year 2016. That would not amount to a substantial extraction or re-utilisation because database protection would have expired in 2015. Yet, because the on-line database in 2016 would be treated as the most recent version of the database, the entirety of which is protected, the competitor's actions could well amount to a substantial (indirect) extraction or re-utilisation of the on-line database and infringe the *sui generis* right in that database. Such a result seems odd, to say the least. Possibly a way of avoiding such a result and also curbing the potentially infinite term of protection is to adopt the approach of Laddie J at first instance in *British Horseracing*, which is reflected in the following passage from his judgment:

> In my view the BHB Database is a single database which is in a constant state of refinement . . . An attempt to split it into a series of discrete databases, besides being impossible to do, would not reflect reality. Its contents change with time and without any

---

[359] *BHB* (Opinion) para 152.

[360] *BHB* (Opinion) para 149.

[361] *BHB* (Opinion) paras 153–54.

[362] Lipton (2003b) p 839 has queried whether constantly renewing terms of protection is in fact necessary to sustain incentives for investment in dynamic databases. She argues that the initial term of protection is sufficient to give a database producer its lead-time and that a 'database producer should not be able to claim ongoing proprietary rights in a database simply for keeping the database up-to-date'. Davison (2003) pp 280–81, has suggested a term less than 15 years is more appropriate.

[363] In the UK, see the Yellow Pages Directory and www.yell.co.uk.

obvious break. So too, the term of protection changes. As new data are added so the data-base's term of protection is constantly being renewed. *However, an unlicensed third party who takes only older data from it only faces a database right which runs from the date when all of that older data was present in the database at the same time.*[364] (Emphasis supplied)

While this approach may be difficult to apply in practice, at least it allows judges to apply the Directive yet at the same time retain enough flexibility to avoid a never-ending monopoly on data or the odd result that might arise in the case of co-existing hard copy and dynamic databases. Unfortunately, the ECJ did not con-sider it necessary to reply to the question referred on Article 10(3), because of the answer that it had given to the question on the scope of Article 7(5)[365] (discussed in chapter 4). This important issue therefore remains unresolved.

Conclusion

This chapter examined the categories of work under UK copyright law that may embrace *entire* multimedia works, and demonstrated that no satisfactory solution is offered by any single category.

A computer program underlying a multimedia work is eligible for copyright protection as a literary work. However, the notion of computer program does not extend to visual user interface features and digital data. Accordingly, this sub-category of literary work does not incorporate the following features of a multi-media work: the multiple digital media that are combined together, the way those digital inputs are integrated, and how a user may interact with those digital media. Moreover, the author and owner of a multimedia work to be protected as a computer program would be limited to the programmer and would ignore the other creative contributors to the multimedia work.

The problem with protecting multimedia works as (non-database) compila-tions is that this does not protect the digital media themselves, but rather the way in which they are combined. Further, the obtaining, selection, or arrangement of materials is restricted to certain types of material. Most multimedia works should be able to surmount the originality hurdle, but authorship and ownership would be limited to the designer and possibly also the project manager.

In the case of multimedia works protected as copyright databases, this looks encouraging insofar as the selection or arrangement may relate to a wide variety of materials. However, certain types of multimedia works, such as multimedia video games or those that utilise a dynamic user interface, will find it difficult to satisfy the threshold definition requirements of 'independent works' and the necessity for

---

[364] *BHB* (ChD), 242.
[365] *BHB* (ECJ) paras 95, 96.

the works, data or other materials that are combined to be 'individually accessible'. Whilst there is confusion over the requisite standard of originality for copyright databases, it seems that most multimedia works will be able to satisfy the criterion of 'author's own intellectual creation'. However, authorship and ownership of the multimedia work would be restricted to the designer, and the creative or financial contributions of other persons would not be recognised.

The s*ui generis* database right is a promising form of protection for multimedia works. Protection will occur if there has been a substantial investment in obtaining, verifying or presenting the contents contained in the multimedia work. Substantial investment is judged according to the quality and quantity of human, financial, or technical resources that are applied. Whether the hurdle of 'substantial' investment is high or low remains unclear. However, the ECJ has clarified that investment in 'obtaining' data does *not* include investment in creation of data. Further, that where investment in collection, verification or presentation of data is inextricably tied to investment in creation of the data then it must be ignored. In other words, to gain protection there must be investment, independent of investment in creation, in the collection, verification or presentation of the database contents. A consequence of the ECJ's ruling for creators of multimedia works wishing to rely upon *sui generis* database protection is that they should either purchase existing materials or commission independent contractors to create the materials for the multimedia work, rather than create the materials themselves.

The major problem for multimedia works qualifying for this form of protection is in satisfying the definition of database, which definition corresponds to the one adopted for copyright databases. Only reference type multimedia works that have a static user interface appear capable of satisfying the requirements that works, data, or other materials be 'independent' and 'individually accessible'. An advantage of this form of protection is that it has the potential to accommodate several multimedia contributors as co-makers and co-owners of the database. Further, dynamic multimedia works that are continually updated or verified have the potential to attract ongoing protection.

The multiple digital media comprising a multimedia work may be protected if they are combined to produce a moving image, thus falling within the category of film. This category has been expanded in other jurisdictions to embrace multimedia video games. Although a similar precedent has not been set in the UK, it appears that the UK definition of film would extend to such works. For other multimedia works, namely reference type works or works that adopt a static user interface, there is a problem in showing that a moving picture or moving image is capable of being produced. Moreover, the interactive nature of multimedia works will often undermine a linear moving sequence being shown, but this may not be problematic in terms of the UK definition. In terms of authorship and ownership, the creative contribution of the designer would be recognised, along with the efforts of the project manager, but not the contributions of the other participants in multimedia production.

In the UK, there is the added possibility of certain multimedia works qualifying for protection as a dramatic work. The likelihood of successfully gaining protection under this category is affected by two factors. First, the recent extension of the scope of dramatic works occurred in respect of films, and so a further extension that also embraces multimedia works may be unacceptable. However, if a multimedia work first qualifies as a 'film', then there seems to be no reason why it could not also qualify as a 'dramatic work', provided that it is a work of action. Second, the requirement that a multimedia work be a work of *action* is one which multimedia databases or works with static interfaces are unlikely to satisfy. An advantage of protection under this category is that, after *Arks (No 2)*, there is the potential to recognise several multimedia contributors as authors and owners of the dramatic (audiovisual) work.

Finally, the protection of multimedia works under the new category of 'broadcast' was considered. Whereas under the previous law it was possible to argue that on-line multimedia works were cable programmes, it is now highly unlikely that multimedia works fit within the definition of 'broadcast'.

Thus, it seems that reference type multimedia works or those that utilise a static user interface are most likely to be protected as compilations or databases (copyright or *sui generis*). Multimedia video games and multimedia works that feature a moving user interface are most likely to be protected as films or dramatic works. Any type of multimedia work should be able to gain protection for the underlying software.

The next chapter will investigate the scope of protection for multimedia works that qualify as a computer program, compilation, copyright database, *sui generis* database, dramatic work, or film. This will provide a better appreciation of how multimedia works are protected under different categories of work in copyright law. The exploration in chapter 5 of how certain royalty free exceptions apply to multimedia works will serve a similar purpose. Drawing on the conclusions of chapters 3 to 5, chapter 6 will investigate whether or not to introduce minor reforms to existing copyright categories, or alternatively, whether a new category of multimedia work is desirable.

4

Scope of Protection for
Multimedia Works

Introduction

Owners of copyright works and *sui generis* databases acquire exclusive rights which they are entitled to exercise in respect of their works. The precise bundle of rights attaching to a multimedia work will depend on whether it qualifies for copyright protection as a computer program, compilation, database, dramatic work, or film, or qualifies for *sui generis* database protection. Chapter 4 will examine the scope of exclusive rights relevant to multimedia works. This is significant for two reasons. First, it permits the relative strengths of protecting multimedia works under different categories (literary or dramatic work[1] versus film[2]) and different schemes of protection (copyright versus *sui generis* database right) to be evaluated. Second, it reveals at a more general level whether copyright law has adapted successfully to changes wrought by digital and networking technologies, which technologies profoundly affect multimedia works.

This chapter will consider, in turn, the following exclusive rights under UK copyright law: reproduction, adaptation, issuing copies to the public, rental or lending, performance, playing or showing in public and communication to the public. It will then consider at length the rights of extraction and re-utilisation under the EU and UK database right regime. The final part of this chapter will address whether hyperlinking and framing amounts to copyright (or database right) infringement under UK law, since these are activities that are central to the use of on-line multimedia works, along with digital material generally.

---

[1] These works attract the following exclusive rights: the right to copy, the right to issues copies of the work to the public; the right to rent or lend the work to the public; the right to perform the work in public; the right to communicate the work to the public; the right to make an adaptation of the work: see ss 16(1), 17(1), 18(1), 18A(1)(a), 19(1), 20(a), as well as 21(1) and (2), Copyright Designs and Patents Act 1988 (UK) ('CDPA').

[2] Films attract the above rights sans the right of adaptation: see ss 16(1), 17(1), 18(1), 18A(1)(c), 19(3), 20(b), CDPA.

Right to Copy

As UK law is heavily influenced by EU law, it is useful first to consider the reproduction right under EU law before turning to discuss the right to copy under UK law.[3]

1. EU Law

Relevant here are the Software Directive,[4] Database Directive[5] and Information Society Directive.[6] The Software and Database Directives harmonise provisions concerning computer programs and databases,[7] respectively. Whereas the Information Society Directive goes further, in that it harmonises aspects of copyright law in a 'horizontal' manner, and seeks also to implement the central obligations of the WCT and WPPT.[8] In addition, the Information Society Directive strives to cater for the challenges presented by digital technology. This is evidenced by recital 5, which states:

> Technological development has multiplied and diversified the vectors for creation, production and exploitation. While no new concepts for the protection of intellectual property are needed, the current law on copyright and related rights should be adapted and supplemented to respond adequately to economic realities such as new forms of exploitation.

Article 4 of the Software Directive stipulates that the rightholder of copyright in a computer program (as a literary work) has the right to do or to authorise:

> the permanent or temporary reproduction of a computer program by any means and in any form, in part or in whole. Insofar as loading, displaying, running, transmission or storage of the computer program necessitate such reproduction, such acts shall be subject to authorisation by the rightholder.[9]

---

[3] See s 17, CDPA.
[4] Directive 91/250/EEC on the legal protection of computer programs OJ L122 17 May 1991, pp 42–46 ('Software Directive').
[5] Directive 96/9/EC on the legal protection of databases OJ L77 27 March 1996, pp 20–28 ('Database Directive').
[6] Directive 2001/29/EC on the harmonisation of certain aspects of copyright and related rights in the information society OJ L167 22 June 2001, pp 10–19 ('Information Society Directive'). Adopted on 22 May 2001, entered into force on 22 June 2001 and the deadline for implementation was 22 December 2002.
[7] See recitals 3 and 4, Database Directive.
[8] See recital 15, Information Society Directive.
[9] Article 4(a), Software Directive.

In respect of copyright databases, Article 5(a) of the Database Directive states that the author shall have the exclusive right to carry out or to authorise, 'temporary or permanent reproduction by any means and in any form, in whole or in part.' The reference to 'in part', in the absence of an explicit substantiality requirement, has led to the suggestion, 'that an act of reproduction in relation to any part of an original database—however small or inconsequential—potentially infringes copyright, perhaps subject only to the principle of *de minimis non curat lex*.'[10] However, given that the originality threshold for databases is stringent in requiring 'intellectual creation', courts are more likely to require 'some part of the personal creative input to have been appropriated.'[11]

Article 2 of the Information Society Directive applies to works, fixations of performances, phonograms, first fixation of films and fixations of wire or wireless broadcasts, and obligates Member States to provide:

> the exclusive right to authorise or prohibit direct or indirect, temporary or permanent reproduction by any means and in any form, in whole or in part.[12]

Read in the light of recital 21,[13] Article 2 clearly shows that the reproduction right is to be broadly construed in EU Member States. This may be contrasted with the WCT, which saw considerable debate over the scope of Article 9(1) of the Berne Convention[14] in the digital environment, but failed appropriately to resolve the issue.[15] The most that was achieved was an agreed statement that:

> The reproduction right, as set out in Article 9 of the Berne Convention, and the exceptions permitted thereunder, fully apply in the digital environment, in particular to the use of works in digital form. It is understood that the storage of a protected work in digital form in an electronic medium constitutes a reproduction within the meaning of Article 9 of the Berne Convention.[16]

---

[10] G Tritton, *Intellectual Property in Europe*, 2nd edn, (Sweet & Maxwell, London, 2002) para 4–104.

[11] Tritton (2002) para 4–104.

[12] Tritton (2002) p 361, n 87, points out that Information Society Directive, Art 2, like the Database Directive, contains no express substantiality requirement and suggests that, unlike the Database Directive, there is no specific originality requirement for copyright protection and thus small or inconsequential reproductions may constitute infringement.

[13] Recital 21, Information Society Directive states: 'This Directive should define the scope of the acts covered by the reproduction right with regard to the different beneficiaries. This should be done in conformity with the acquis communautaire. A broad definition of these acts is needed to ensure legal certainty within the internal market.'

[14] Berne Convention for the Protection of Literary and Artistic Works 1886 ('Berne Convention').

[15] For details see M Ficsor, *The Law of Copyright and the Internet: the 1996 WIPO Treaties, their Interpretation and Implementation* (OUP, Oxford, 2002) 135–43; TC Vinje, 'The New WIPO Copyright Treaty: a Happy Result in Geneva' [1997] 5 *EIPR* 230, 233; and P Samuelson, 'The US Digital Agenda at WIPO' (1997) 37 *Virginia J Intl L* 369, 382–92.

[16] H Rosenblatt, 'Protocol to the Berne Convention: the WIPO Diplomatic Conference—the Birth of Two New Treaties' (1997) 13 *CL&SR* 307, 310: 'Having been approved only on a roll-call vote, the Statements may carry less interpretative weight than those adopted by consensus. The vexed question of whether transient or temporary storage constituted a reproduction thus remains unanswered.' A Dixon and MF Hansen, 'The Berne Convention Enters the Digital Age' (1996) 11 *EIPR* 604, 608–9.

More success was achieved under the WPPT. Thus, Article 7 of the WPPT stipulates that 'Performers shall enjoy the exclusive right of authorising the direct or indirect reproduction of their performances fixed in phonograms, in any manner or form' and Article 11 provides for the same right in respect of producers of phonograms. An agreed statement to the WPPT states that:

> The reproduction right, as set out in Articles 7 and 11, and the exceptions permitted thereunder under Article 16, fully apply in the digital environment, in particular to the use of performances and phonograms in digital form. It is understood that the storage of a protected performance or phonogram in digital form in an electronic medium constitutes a reproduction within the meaning of these Articles.

An important issue is the interrelationship between the Information Society and Software and Database Directives. In other words, do the provisions of the Information Society Directive apply also to computer programs or databases? In relation to the reproduction right, whether or not Article 2 of the Information Society Directive applies to computer programs and databases is not especially important, given that Article 2 is very similar in terms to Article 4(a) of the Software Directive and Article 5(a) of the Database Directive. However, where provisions in the Software or Database Directive are absent from, or conflict with, provisions in the Information Society Directive, the relationship between the Directives takes on particular significance. For example, the exception for temporary reproduction in Article 5(1) of the Information Society Directive is one such point of conflict where it is necessary to know the scope of application of this provision to computer programs or databases.

The Information Society Directive provides guidance as to its relationship with earlier Directives, such as the Software and Database Directives. Article 1(2) states that 'this Directive *shall leave intact and shall in no way affect* existing Community provisions relating to (emphasis supplied)' computer programs, rental and lending, satellite broadcasting and cable retransmission, term of protection and databases. In relation to the Rental Right Directive[17] and the Satellite Directive,[18] Article 11 of the Information Society Directive makes specific amendments.[19] Further, recital 20 of the Information Society Directive indicates that the Directive 'is based on principles and rules already laid down in the Directives currently in

---

[17] Directive 92/100/EEC of 19 November 1992 on rental and lending right and on certain rights related to copyright in the field of intellectual property OJ L 346, 27/11/1992, pp 61–66 ('Rental Right Directive').

[18] Directive 93/83/EEC of 27 September 1993 on the coordination of certain rules concerning copyright and rights related to copyright applicable to satellite broadcasting and cable retransmission OJ L248, 6/10/1993, pp 15–21 ('Satellite Directive').

[19] Article 11, Information Society Directive deletes Article 7 from the Rental Right Directive and replaces Article 10(3) of the Rental Right Directive with the following provision: 'the limitations shall only be applied in certain special cases which do not conflict with a normal exploitation of the subject-matter and do not unreasonably prejudice the legitimate interests of the rightholder.' Article 11 of the Information Society Directive also replaces Article 3(2) of the Satellite Directive dealing with duration.

force in this area' in particular the Software, Rental Right, Satellite, Term and Database Directives and 'develops those principles and rules and places them in the context of the information society. The provisions of this Directive should be *without prejudice* to the provisions of those Directives, unless otherwise provided in this Directive.' (emphasis supplied) In summary, the Information Society Directive 'shall leave in tact and in no way affect' provisions of the earlier Directives and is 'without prejudice' to those earlier provisions. Thus, it seems that one needs to look at whether or not there is a provision in an earlier Directive dealing with a particular issue and if there is, then the Information Society Directive does not apply to it. If there is no such provision in an earlier Directive, then the Information Society Directive may apply.[20]

Applying this approach, the position on the definition of reproduction is straightforward. Article 2 of the Information Society Directive cannot affect Article 4(a) of the Software Directive or Article 5(a) of the Database Directive because these provisions deal with the same issue. We turn next to consider the position of exceptions to temporary reproduction.

Article 5(1) of the Information Society Directive obligates Member States to introduce an exemption in respect of *temporary* acts of reproduction.[21] The provision states:

> Temporary acts of reproduction referred to in Article 2, *which are transient or incidental,* which are an *integral* and *essential part* of a technological process *whose sole purpose* is to enable:
>
> a *transmission in a network* between third parties by an intermediary *or* a lawful use
>
> of a work or other subject matter to be made, and which have no independent economic significance, shall be exempted from the right provided for in Article 2. (Emphasis supplied)

Given the breadth of the definition of 'reproduction' in Article 2, the mandatory nature of the above exemption is entirely sensible, otherwise copyright owners would have a stranglehold over dissemination of copyright works.

Article 5(1) permits temporary, technical acts of reproduction that occur as part of a network transmission between third parties, as performed by an Internet Service Provider (ISP) (or, more accurately, a series of ISPs). The transmission of material across the Internet from an originating server, operated by a 'value-added'

---

[20] See L Bently, 'European Developments in Copyright' Unpublished paper delivered for the *Irish Centre for European Law* (copy held on file with the author), 43.

[21] An 'exception-based' approach to controlling the scope of the reproduction right has also been followed in Australia: see ss 43A and 111A, Copyright Act 1968 (Cth), discussed by T Aplin, 'Contemplating Australia's Digital Future: the Copyright Amendment (Digital Agenda) Act 2000' [2001] *EIPR* 565, 571–72 and looks likely to be followed in New Zealand, as discussed by J Smillie, 'Digital Copyright Reform in New Zealand' [2004] *EIPR* 302, 303–4.

ISP,[22] to a user, is made possible by packets of information being routed via a series of ISPs; the final link being made by a 'simple access' ISP,[23] with whom the user has its subscription. During transmission across the network the intermediate ISPs (or intermediaries) will store the packets of information routed via them for a fleeting moment.[24] It is this kind of reproduction that is exempted by Article 5(1).

Additionally, the exemption appears to permit temporary acts of reproduction that occur when a user is 'browsing' on-line material.[25] 'Browsing' material via the world wide web[26] involves a particular communication and interface process between computers connected to the Internet. The user 'browsing' must be connected to the Internet through an ISP and to access a document or 'page' on the web, the user enters a Uniform Resource Locator (URL), which is a specific numeric address for the file or webpage that the user wants to access. This request is sent to the remote web server that stores the document or webpage, whereupon that web server transmits a copy of the relevant file back to the user's computer. When a file is transmitted from a remote web server, it is actually downloaded temporarily to random access memory (RAM) in the user's computer.[27] This process enables the file or webpage to be viewed or 'browsed'.[28]

---

[22] The term 'value added' ISP is used to describe an entity that offers access to the Internet plus additional on-line services to their subscribers, in the form of hosting websites or operating proxy servers.

[23] A 'simple access' ISP is used to describe any entity who provides subscribers with basic access to the Internet, which means access to the facilities of email, world wide web, ftp, telnet, newsgroups and chat rooms. The terms simple access and value added ISPs are merely functional descriptions: thus, a telecommunications carrier who performed either of these functions would be classed as either a simple access or value added ISP in relation to this activity.

[24] M Makeen, *Copyright in a Global Information Society: The Scope of Copyright Protection Under International, US, UK and French Law* (Kluwer, London, 2000) at 309 remarks that the 'reproduction which is allegedly performed by servers along the chain of communication resembles in actual fact the task performed by relay stations in (sic) broadcasting context. Since the reproduction right has no application whatsoever to tasks performed by relay stations, similarly it should not be applied to network servers, as this might lead to an artificial distinction between the broadcasting medium and that of computer networks.'

[25] See recital 33, Information Society Directive. J Litman, *Digital Copyright* (Prometheus, New York, 2001) 178 comments: 'Today, making digital reproductions is an unavoidable incident of reading, viewing, listening to, learning from, sharing, improving, and reusing works embodied in digital media. The centrality of copying to use of digital technology is precisely why reproduction is no longer an appropriate way to measure infringement.'

[26] The world wide web is an information tool of the Internet: see AM Major, 'Copyright Law Tackles yet another Challenge: the Electronic Frontier of the World Wide Web' (1998) 24 *Rutgers Computer & Technology L J* 75, 78. The popularity of the web has come through its user-friendly interface, which allows non-technical people to secure access to information available on the Internet (a network of networked computers), without requiring a working knowledge of the various protocols that make this information accessible, see Major (1998) p 78, n 10. Users secure access to the web through a graphical interface, called a web browser, which enables navigating from site to site by a simple process of pointing and clicking with one's mouse: see Major (1998) p 79.

[27] Major (1998) pp 78–93.

[28] Makeen (2000) pp 309–10 comments that 'an equivalent process takes place on television screens. For information to be displayed on the television luminescent screen at the viewer's end, the cathode ray tube converts information from electrical form to light, which entails copying. However, such copying was never held to constitute reproduction in copyright terms.'

Relating 'browsing' to the terms of Article 5(1), any incidental reproduction is part of a technological process whose sole purpose is to enable a network transmission, since 'browsing' is the final link in the transmission process. Without 'browsing', the network transmission would not be complete.

Alternatively, 'browsing' may be a 'lawful use', that is, a use which 'is authorised by the rightholder or not restricted by law',[29] because of either an express or implied licence granted by the rightholder. The case law establishes a number of bases upon which a licence to do an exclusive act may be implied. In a contractual context, a term will be implied if it is necessary to give business efficacy to the contract and it satisfies the 'officious bystander' test.[30] Where there is a particular, non-contractual arrangement between the parties, a licence may be implied to give business efficacy to that arrangement.[31] A licence may also be implied from conduct, in the absence of any contractual relations.[32]

Access to a particular website may be possible only by entering into a 'click on' agreement with the website producer, however, this does not appear to represent the norm of Internet access at present. If a 'click on' agreement exists, it is likely that the express terms and conditions of such agreement would include viewing or 'browsing' the website contents (usually in return for a subscription or one-off fee). If there were no express terms to this effect, it would seem absolutely necessary to give effect to that agreement that the user be able to 'browse' or view the contents of the website, and such a licence would almost certainly be implied on the grounds of business efficacy.[33] If there was no 'click on' agreement between the parties, but a 'click on' subscription instead, where the user is able to access the website upon registering their personal details, thereby creating a bare licence, one

---

[29] Recital 33, Information Society Directive.

[30] K Garnett, J James and G Davies, (eds), *Copinger and Skone James on Copyright*, vol 1, 14th edn, (Sweet & Maxwell, London, 1999)('Copinger') para 5–208; *Robin Ray v Classic FM* [1998] FSR 622, 641; *Interstate Parcel Express Co Pty Ltd v Time-Life International (Nederlands) BV* (1977) 138 CLR 534, 548 (Stephen J); *Creative Technology Ltd v Aztech Systems Pte Ltd* [1997] FSR 491, 507 (Singapore CA). Lightman J in *Robin Ray v Classic FM* [1998] FSR 622 at 642 emphasises that the term that is implied must not exceed what is necessary in the circumstances.

[31] See *Fylde Microsystems Ltd v Key Radio Systems Ltd* [1998] FSR 449, where the defendants did not have a contractual relationship with the plaintiffs, but an ongoing business relationship, the defendants argued that for reasons of commercial efficacy there was an implied licence for them to use the software in question. Laddie J rejected this contention on the grounds that it was not necessary or reasonable to imply such a term. See also *Trumpet Software Pty Ltd v OzEmail Pty Ltd* (1996) 34 IPR 481, where Heerey J in the Federal Court of Australia determined that the doctrine of implied contractual terms could be applied analogously to determine any implied terms included in a software shareware licence. In this instance, an implied term must be necessary to give business efficacy or so obvious that it goes without saying.

[32] The payment and acceptance of royalties in respect of the exploitation of copyright can evidence the recipient's consent to the acts of the payer. This is to be adjudged viewing the words and conduct of the alleged licensor objectively: *Redwood Music Ltd v Chappell & Co* [1982] RPC 109. See also *Computermate Products (Aust) Pty Ltd v Ozi-Soft Pty Ltd* (1988) 20 FCR 46.

[33] Major (1998) p 91 observes that 'Web sites that limit access to users will defeat an implied license outside of the specific circle of allowed users'.

could probably identify an express permission to browse the website. In the absence of express permission, such a term would probably be implied into this bare licence on the basis of commercial efficacy.

In many cases of users 'browsing' the Internet, however, there is neither a 'click on' agreement nor subscription involved and the whole contents of a website are made available to a user upon entering the relevant URL. Here there is neither a contractual or other arrangement between the parties and one would have to rely on the conduct of the copyright owner in placing, or agreeing to place, those materials on-line to imply a licence to browse. This seems plausible, on the basis that it would be singularly nonsensical to place, or agree to place, materials on-line that were not intended to be viewed by those who used the Internet, since the whole purpose of this network is to operate as a global communications vehicle.[34]

The above arguments in favour of an implied licence to browse Internet material rest on the assumption that the copyright material has been placed on-line with the permission of the copyright owner. If the copyright owner has not consented to inclusion of their works in a website, then the basis for any implied licence to browse would be negated.

Finally, acts of local and proxy caching may be excused by Article 5(1). Caching broadly refers to copying a web page on the world wide web as an incidental process to first accessing a web page. More specifically, there are two types of caching, known as local or client caching and proxy caching.[35] Local caching refers to the situation where the web browser software of an Internet user stores recently accessed web pages. This allows a user to call up these web pages faster than if the computer had to fetch them from their source server over the Internet.[36] 'Proxy caching' occurs at the network level on proxy servers. Proxy servers act as intermediaries between local client servers and remote content servers.[37] They store copies of the most frequently requested pages, so that these copies can be delivered to users, rather than having to search out the data from the original source. This process has all sorts of benefits; it makes user access faster, reduces the bandwidth used by both users and server and generally reduces the amount of congestion on the Internet.[38] Unfortunately, caching impedes the ability of websites to calculate hits and page impressions, which information is crucial to selling advertising.

---

[34] See Major (1998) p 91: 'the strongest argument for an implied license is that the owner of the copyright posted the material for a large audience to read in a public forum.'

[35] PB Hugenholtz, 'Caching and Copyright: the Right of Temporary Copying' [2000] *EIPR* 482, 482–83.

[36] Hugenholtz (2000) p 483.

[37] *Hutchinson Dictionary of Computing, Multimedia and the Internet*, 3rd edn, (Helicon, Oxford, 1999) 228.

[38] Hugenholtz (2000) p 482; and A Morrison, 'Hijack on the Road to Xanadu: the Infringement of Copyright in HTML Documents via Networked Computers & the Legitimacy of Browsing Hypermedia Documents' [1999] 1 *J of Information, L & Technology* at http://www.law.warwick.ac.uk/jilt/99–1/morrison.html.

There is also a risk that stale documents will be accessed by Internet users.[39] While proxy servers may be configured so that their caches are regularly updated, there is no fixed schedule whereby this is guaranteed.

Caching should be exempt according to Article 5(1). This is emphasised by recital 33, which states:

> To the extent that they meet these conditions, this exception should include acts which enable browsing as well as *acts of caching* to take place, *including those which enable transmission systems to function efficiently,* provided that the intermediary does not modify the information and does not interfere with the lawful use of technology, widely recognised and used by industry, to obtain data on the use of information. (Emphasis supplied)

Local caching should be exempt as a temporary, technical act of reproduction whose sole purpose is to enable a lawful use, namely that of 'browsing'. In the case of proxy caching, the temporary acts of reproduction may be considered as an integral and essential part of a technological process whose sole purpose is to enable network transmissions. However, there may be an issue about whether proxy caching lacks independent economic significance. If proxy caching is viewed as 'ancillary to non-exploitative acts of network transmission',[40] this condition should be satisfied.

An important question is whether Article 5(1) applies also to computer programs and databases? It seems not.[41] First, Article 5 of the Information Society Directive concerns exceptions and limitations to the rights of reproduction, communication to the public and distribution conferred by Articles 2, 3 and 4 respectively. The rights conferred by Articles 2, 3 and 4 of the Information Society Directive do not apply to either computer programs or databases, since reproduction, adaptation and distribution of *computer programs* are governed by Articles 4 and 5 of the Software Directive and reproduction, communication and distribution of *databases* are governed by Article 5 of the Database Directive. Second, exceptions and limitations to computer programs are governed by Articles 5 and 6 of the Software Directive and, for databases, Article 6 of the Database Directive.[42]

An overlap exists between Article 5(1) of the Information Society Directive and Articles 12 and 13 of the E-Commerce Directive.[43] The E-Commerce Directive[44]

---

[39] Hugenholtz (2000) p 482.

[40] Hugenholtz (2000) p 488.

[41] This has led the Commission to suggest amending the Software Directive and Database Directive so that they are consistent with the scope of the reproduction right and the Article 5(1) exception in the Information Society Directive: see *Commission Staff Working Paper on the review of the EC legal framework in the field of copyright and related rights* Brussels, 19 July 2004 SEC (2004) 995 ('Working Paper') paras 2.1.1 and 2.1.3.2.

[42] See ch 5 below for discussion.

[43] Directive 2000/31/EC of 8 June 2000 on certain legal aspects of information society services, in particular electronic commerce OJ L178, 17/7/2000, pp 1–16 ('E-Commerce Directive').

[44] Implemented in the UK by the Electronic Commerce (EC Directive) Regulations 2002 SI 2002/2013, ('E-Commerce Regulations') in force on 21 August 2002.

seeks to provide a clear legal framework to ensure the free movement of information society services and thus ranges across several areas, including commercial communications, electronic contracts, the liability of intermediaries, and codes of conduct.[45] Articles 12–14 deal specifically with liability of intermediary service providers,[46] where they act as a mere conduit, cache or host material, and provide exemptions from liability subject to certain conditions being fulfilled. Whereas Article 5(1) of the Information Society Directive creates an exemption from infringement of the reproduction right,[47] Articles 12–14 of the E-Commerce Directive create 'horizontal' exemptions from legal liability for service providers,[48] that is, exemptions that are not restricted to copyright[49] and, in the case of copyright, that are not limited to the reproduction right. Importantly, the E-Commerce exemptions for service providers do not extend to *injunctive relief*.[50] Article 5(1) of the Information Society Directive must be read in the light of Article 8(3), which obligates Member States to ensure that 'rightholders are in a position to apply for an injunction against intermediaries whose services are used by a third party to infringe a copyright or related right.' Article 8(3) of the Information Society Directive appears to create a standalone cause of action that

---

[45] See Art 1(2), E-Commerce Directive. The European Commission has published its *First Report on the application of Directive 2000/31/EC of the European Parliament and of the Council of 8 June 2000 on certain aspects of legal aspects of the information society, in particular electronic commerce in the Internal Market* Brussels 21 November 2003 COM (2003) 702 final ('First E-Commerce Report').

[46] These provisions are very similar to the safe harbour provisions introduced into the US Copyright Act 1976 by the Digital Millennium Copyright Act 1998, except that Articles 12–14 of the E-Commerce Directive are not limited to copyright liability and there is absent from the European regime an exemption for the use of information location tools, such as hyperlinks and search engines. See V McEvedy, 'The DMCA and the E-Commerce Directive' [2002] *EIPR* 65 for further details.

[47] Cf T Cook and L Brazell, *The Copyright Directive: UK Implementation* (Jordans, Bristol, 2004) para 5.11 who argue that Art 5(1) of the Information Society Directive, 'does not, unlike the provisions in the E-Commerce Directive, simply provide service providers with a defence. Instead, it wholly excludes certain types of reproduction from the scope of protection by copyright and related rights . . .'

[48] A 'service provider' is any natural or legal person providing an information society service and an 'information society service' refers to services within the meaning of Article 1(2) of the Directive 98/34/EC (Art 2, E-Commerce Directive), which 'covers any service normally provided for remuneration, at a distance, by means of electronic equipment for the processing (including digital compression) and storage of data, and at the individual request of a recipient of a service.' (recital 17, E-Commerce Directive). Recital 18, E-Commerce Directive indicates that

> Information society services span a wide range of economic activities which take place on-line . . . [and] extend to services which are not remunerated by those who receive them, such as those offering on-line information or commercial communications; or those providing tools allowing for search, access and retrieval of data; information society services also include services consisting of the transmission of information via a communication network, in providing access to a communication network or in hosting information provided by a recipient of the service.

[49] It would extend, for example, to defamation, misleading advertising or trade mark infringement: see recital 16, E-Commerce Directive. It would also extend to criminal liability: see First E-Commerce Report, para 4.6.

[50] See Arts 12(3), 13(2), 14(3) and recital 45, E-Commerce Directive. The exemptions apply to liability for damages, other monetary remedies and criminal sanctions.

is not contingent on the ISP engaging in any infringing act and 'is unspecific as to what activities the injunction that can thereby be secured is directed'.[51]

Article 12 of the E-Commerce Directive contains an exemption from liability for service providers for transmissions of information or the provision of access to a communication network. In other words, where the service provider acts as a 'mere conduit' in the transfer of information. This exemption is conditional upon the provider neither initiating the transmission, nor selecting the receiver of the transmission, nor selecting or modifying the information contained in the transmission.[52] The 'automatic, intermediate and transient storage' of the information insofar as it occurs for the sole purpose of effecting the transmission and is not stored for longer than is reasonably necessary to do so, is also covered by this exemption.[53]

Article 13 of the E-Commerce Directive is directed at storage of information by service providers for the purpose of caching. A service provider shall not be liable, 'for the automatic, intermediate and temporary storage of . . . information, performed for the sole purpose of making more efficient the information's onward transmission to other recipients of the service upon their request.' This is subject to a number of conditions being satisfied. These conditions seek to minimise the problems associated with caching by service providers (otherwise known as proxy caching), for example by requiring that the service provider complies with any rules regarding updating of information and does not interfere with technology used to gather data on the use of information.[54]

Articles 12 and 13 of the E-Commerce Directive clearly overlap with Article 5(1) of the Information Society Directive, but does this cause a problem? Recital 50 of the E-Commerce Directive stresses that the Information Society Directive and E-commerce Directive should 'come into force within a similar time scale with a view to establishing a clear framework of rules relevant to the issue of liability of intermediaries for copyright and related rights infringements at Community level.' Recital 16 of the Information Society Directive, states that the Directive is 'without prejudice to provisions relating to liability' in the E-Commerce Directive. This would seem to mean that where the E-Commerce Directive deals with particular issues, then provisions on the same issue in the Information Society Directive do not apply. Where the E-Commerce Directive does not have provisions on a particular issue, then the provisions of the Information Society Directive may

---

[51] Cook and Brazell (2004) para 5.14.

[52] See also recital 43, E-Commerce Directive. Note that recital 44, E-Commerce Directive states that 'A service provider who deliberately collaborates with one of the recipients of his services to undertake illegal acts goes beyond the activities of "mere conduit" or "caching" and as a result cannot benefit from the liability exemptions established for these activities.'

[53] See recital 42, E-Commerce Directive: 'this activity is of a mere technical, automatic and passive nature, which implies that the information society service provider has neither knowledge of nor control over the information which is transmitted or stored.'

[54] Hugenholtz (2000) p 491. See also recital 43, E-Commerce Directive.

apply. Given that Article 12 of the E-Commerce Directive clearly deals with service provider exemptions for transient storage of information and Article 13 with exemptions for caching of information, Article 5(1) should *not* apply to intermediaries, but arguably would still apply in the case of browsing and caching by users.

It is unclear whether or not Articles 12 and 13 of the E-Commerce apply to computer programs and databases. There is little in the E-Commerce Directive to assist in answering this question. Although Article 1(5) of the E-Commerce Directive stipulates that it shall not apply to certain fields and earlier Directives, and recital 11 stipulates that the E-Commerce Directive is without prejudice to earlier Directives, these earlier Directives do not concern copyright or related rights. Thus, it may be argued that Articles 12 and 13 of the E-Commerce Directive *do* apply in the case of computer programs and databases. This would create an exemption from liability only for the service provider and *not* for the user who is browsing or caching the program or database.

There is no overlap, however, between Article 14 of the E-Commerce Directive and Article 5(1) of the Information Society Directive. Article 14 provides that a service provider will not be held liable for information *stored* at the request of a recipient of an information society service.[55] This is conditional on the service provider not having actual knowledge or, in the case of civil liability, constructive knowledge, of illegal information or activity, or where such knowledge is obtained, acting expeditiously to remove or disable access to the information. Thus, Article 14 of the E-Commerce Directive potentially exempts ISPs from infringing the reproduction right and also the right of communication to the public where they permanently store material for third parties. Article 5(1) of the Information Society Directive, by way of contrast, is concerned only with exempting certain acts of temporary storage from being an infringing reproduction.

From the point of view of ISP liability, Article 5(1) of the Information Society Directive was unnecessary and, as argued above, does not apply to intermediaries. Rather, it applies to users who browse or cache works, other than computer programs or databases. Article 8(3) of the Information Society Directive was also unnecessary in the light of Articles 12 to 15 of the E-Commerce Directive, which do not create exemptions from injunctive relief and, in the case of Article 15(2), permit Member States to establish obligations on the part of ISPs to inform the relevant authorities of illegal activities undertaken or information provided by recipients of their service or to provide information identifying users of their service. Thus, Articles 5(1) and 8(3) of the Information Society Directive add an unnecessary layer of complexity to the framework of ISP liability.

Having reviewed EC law relating to the reproduction right, it is time to review the position under UK law, which we turn now to discuss.

---

[55] This is provided the recipient of the service is not acting under the authority or the control of the service provider: see Article 14(2), E-Commerce Directive.

2. UK Law

Section 17 of the CDPA offers some guidance as to what constitutes 'copying' under UK law. In relation to literary, dramatic, musical and artistic works, 'copying' means 'reproducing the work in any material form' and 'material form' includes storing the work in any medium by electronic means.[56] Clearly, *digital storage* of a multimedia work, protected as a literary or dramatic work, would count as reproduction in material form and thus copying of the work.[57] Moreover, 'reproducing the work in any material form' contemplates non-literal, as well as literal, copying. The scope of non-literal copying in relation to computer programs is discussed in further detail below.

For the remainder of copyright works, copying includes making substantial copies in the *same form*, but not making the work afresh.[58] This principle is aptly illustrated in relation to films by *Norowzian v Arks (No 1)('Arks (No 1)')*,[59] the facts of which were recounted in ch 3.[60] *Arks (No 1)* involved an interlocutory application to strike out that part of Mr Norowzian's claim for infringement of copyright based on copyright in his film, 'Joy'.

Acting Judge, AG Steinfeld QC articulated the issue as being, 'whether copyright in a film is infringed not by making an exact copy of the film itself but by making another film in a way which is designed to and which does closely resemble and imitate the film in which copyright subsists.'[61]

No English authority existed on this issue. After looking at the plain terms of the CDPA, secondary English material and Australian authorities, the judge concluded that what is prohibited is 'copying of the whole or a part of the film itself in the sense of a copying of the whole or a part of the *particular recording* of that film.'[62] Hence, re-shooting a film sequence that is very similar to an existing film does not infringe copyright in that film unless frames from it are taken,[63] which was not the case in *Arks (No 1)*.

In terms of a multimedia work protected as a film, either the medium from which the moving image may be produced (ie, the program or data code) or else the actual images produced from the medium would have to be copied. But if a

---

[56] S 17(2), CDPA.

[57] WR Cornish and D Llewelyn, *Intellectual Property: Patents, Copyright Trade Marks and Allied Rights*, 5th edn, (Sweet & Maxwell, London, 2003) para 11–23. The same position exists under Australian law: see ss 21(1A) and 21(6) of Copyright Act 1968 (Cth).

[58] Cornish and Llewelyn (2003) para 11–26. But note that films or broadcasts may be copied by making a photograph of the whole or any substantial part of any image forming part of that work: s 17(4), CDPA.

[59] *Norowzian v Arks (No 1)* [1998] FSR 394 ('*Arks (No 1)*').

[60] See above ch 3, p 78.

[61] *Arks (No 1)*, 395–96.

[62] *Arks (No 1)*, 400 (original emphasis).

[63] Kamina (2002) pp 219–20.

person imitated the navigational structure or user interface functions of a multi-media work, this would not involve *copying* a film and thus would not amount to an infringement.[64] However, *Norowzian v Arks (No 2)('Arks (No 2)')*[65] mitigates the effect of *Arks (No 1)*. This is because, for a multimedia work protected as an original dramatic work, the broader right of *non-literal* coping (reproducing the work in any material form) will apply. The question is *how* this broader right of copying would apply to multimedia works.

In *Arks (No 2)*, although the film, 'Joy', was held to be an original dramatic work, the Court of Appeal upheld Rattee J's decision that a substantial part of the dramatic work had not been reproduced by the advertisement, 'Anticipation'.[66] According to Rattee J, the subject matter of one film was very different from the other: the plots were wholly different, the settings were different, and there were different numbers of characters in each film.[67] At most, the filming and editing styles and techniques of the claimant had been reproduced. Rattee J described the striking similarities between the two films as follows: 'Both use a fixed or 'locked-off' camera position. Both use varying camera speeds and, in editing, both use jump cutting techniques which, together with the varying speeds and the sepia-tinted, colourless settings produce an effect of somewhat disturbing unreality or quirkiness.'[68]

The Court of Appeal reiterated the view of Rattee J that copyright could not subsist in filming or editing styles and techniques.[69] This aspect of the decision has been criticised by some commentators, who argue that camera work and editing comprise a large part of a director's creativity in making a film.[70] For example, Porter argues:

> [T]he film director's art resides in projecting to the audience his interpretation of what is usually a pre-existing work, whether in the form of a book, a screenplay, or other written work, in respect of which a major contribution is made by the camera work and editing. Indeed, film making is all about techniques—techniques in relation to lighting, set design, pace and mood, sound effects, colourisation of film, camera angles, etc . . . In the circumstances, it is difficult to see, from this case, where the boundaries of dramatic copyright protection should be drawn for a film director, particularly if the film is itself based on a pre-existing work.[71]

---

[64] The same position exists under Australian law: see s 14(1)(a) of Copyright Act 1968 (Cth) and *Telmak Teleproducts Australia Pty Ltd v Bond International Pty Ltd* (1985) 5 IPR 203; (1986) 6 IPR 97.

[65] *Norowzian v Arks (No 2)* [2000] FSR 363 ('*Arks (No 2)*').

[66] *Arks (No 2)*, 367–68 (Nourse LJ), and 370, (Buxton LJ).

[67] *Norowzian v Arks (No 2)* [2000] FSR 363 (CA); [1999] FSR 79, 89 (Rattee J).

[68] Above.

[69] *Arks (No 2)*, 368 (Nourse LJ), and 370 (Buxton LJ).

[70] See H Porter, 'A "Dramatic Work" Includes . . . a Film' [2000] *Entertainment L Rev* 50, 53; J Hughes and M Parry, 'An Unsettling Feeling: a Second View of the *Norowzian* Decision' [2000] *Entertainment L Rev* 56, 58.

[71] Porter (2000) p 53.

However, as was highlighted by Nourse LJ in the Court of Appeal,[72] protection of such (commonplace) techniques would preclude the production of many other creative works. By way of counter-argument, it could be argued that there is a difference between denying protection to any technique and to commonplace techniques, so that if a film technique was particularly creative it should be deserving of protection. On the other hand, even protection of non-commonplace techniques might be seen as providing too much of a monopoly and therefore moving into the realm of protecting ideas rather than expression. In any event, the ratio of the Court of Appeal in *Arks (No 2)* succeeds in increasing the protection of films, by opening up the possibility of non-literal infringement of films (protected as dramatic works), even if infringement was not found on the facts of the case.[73]

How does this increased protection under *Arks (No 2)* affect multimedia works that qualify for protection as dramatic works? Multimedia video games are the type of multimedia work most likely to qualify as a 'dramatic work'. Reasoning by analogy with *Arks (No 2)*, the scope of protection is likely to extend to features such as similar sequences of images, similar characters and similar scenery or backgrounds to the central action. Thus, to a certain extent, visual user interface features may be protected. However, protection would not extend to programming techniques that produced certain striking visual effects, such as increased speed of play or a three-dimensional visual appearance. Nor would protection extend to non-visual user interface features, such as commands or functional operations.

(a) Temporary Copying

Section 17(6) of the CDPA provides that copying, for any type of work, includes *transient* and *incidental* copies. It appears to be well accepted that the scope of this provision extends to loading software into the RAM of a computer[74] and is thus consistent with Article 4(a) of the Software Directive, discussed above. Similarly, loading a database into the RAM of a computer would also be covered by section 17(6). This, in turn, means that Internet activities which are based on temporary copying in computer RAM, such as browsing or non-persistent local caching, are captured by the right to copy.[75] Persistent local caching and proxy caching are also activities which involve temporary, if not permanent, copying. Further, saving to disk or printing out substantial parts of a multimedia work undoubtedly will amount to unlawful copying of these works, unless a licence exists or an exception is applicable.

[72] *Arks (No 2)*, 368.

[73] Kamina (2002) p 220 arguing that *Arks (No 2)* also strengthens protection against adaptations.

[74] See H Laddie, *et al*, *The Modern Law of Copyright and Designs*, 3rd edn, (Butterworths, London, 2000) para 14.8; and HL MacQueen, 'Copyright and the Internet' in L Edwards and C Waelde, (eds), *Law and the Internet: a Framework for Electronic Commerce* (Hart Publishing, Oxford, 2000) 181, 195.

[75] MacQueen (2000) pp 195–96; S Lai, 'Substantive Issues of Copyright Protection in a Networked Environment' (1999b) 8 *Information and Communications Technology Law* 127, 139.

As for whether section 17(6) also encompasses transient acts of reproduction that occur during transmissions across a network[76] Laddie argues that section 17(6) is intended to cover such things as storage in a dynamic computer memory.[77] Laddie gives the example of dynamic RAM, which operates on the basis that each cell in the memory, because it is only capable of holding information for a very brief fraction of second, is constantly 'refreshed' by the circuit.[78] If this sort of transience is contemplated by section 17(6), then it is certainly arguable that fleeting copies incidental to network transmissions amount to 'copying' within section 17(6).

However, it is also arguable that some limit needs to be placed on the right to copy,[79] otherwise the scope of this right would be distorted to cover acts of transmitting copyright material, and this in turn would lead to considerable overlap between the reproduction and communication rights.[80] The notion of preserving subject matter for an 'appreciable time' to enable it to be perceived[81] may provide the appropriate limitation on temporary copying.[82] In the case of RAM storage, although exceptionally transient in nature, the storage time is appreciable enough for the copyright work (program or data) to be perceived by the user.[83] Whereas, transmission copies, at the point of passing through ISPs network connections, are not capable of being perceived. The inability to perceive the ephemeral copy is heightened because the data being copied is in the form of a 'packet'. That is, information sent across the Internet is broken down into bundles called 'packets' and is routed through different computers.[84] This fact makes it even less likely for the copyright work (or, indeed, a substantial part of the work) to be perceived at a particular point along the transmission chain.[85] Based on this chain of reasoning, one could argue that network transmission copies are not temporary copies for the purposes of section 17(6) of the CDPA.

[76] Lai (1999b) p 132, 'we are left with no clarification whatsoever on the liability which potentially arises with temporary reproduction in the provision of networked services'.

[77] Laddie, *et al*, (2000) para 14.8. See also MacQueen (2000) p 195.

[78] Laddie, *et al*, (2000) para 14.8.

[79] For example, see Smillie (2004) p 304.

[80] Of course, this says nothing about the need for criminal law specifically directed to these sorts of computer activities.

[81] This formulation is drawn from *R v Gold and Schifreen* [1988] 2 WLR 984, 991 (Lord Brandon of Oakbrook).

[82] Makeen (2000) pp 308–14 goes further and argues that, in relation to network transmissions, reliance on the reproduction right is neither necessary nor desirable. Rather, only the right of communication to the public should be applicable.

[83] See D Loundy, 'Revising the Copyright Law for Electronic Publishing' (1995) 14 *John Marshall J of Computer & Information L* 1, 12: 'What is important is not the length of time that the work is available in a computer's RAM, but rather what can be done with the work once it is in the computer's RAM (fn omitted) In other words, "transitory duration" is a term that must be defined in context, and in the computer context, a very short duration may constitute a fixation.' Note that this is in relation to the fixation requirement in the US Copyright Act 1976.

[84] C Gringas, *The Laws of the Internet* (Butterworths, London, 1997) 188.

[85] Cf Gringas (1997) p 189.

However, the plain words of section 17(6) can sustain an interpretation that transient copies made during network transmissions amounts to 'copying' and, on balance, the better view is that it does. The UK Patent Office, during consultations regarding implementation of the Information Society Directive, expressed the view that section 17 of the CDPA was consistent with Article 2 of the Information Society Directive.[86] As such, it was thought unnecessary to amend section 17 and this section was left unchanged by the Copyright and Related Rights Regulations 2003[87] ('Copyright Regulations').[88]

With regards to the exemption in Article 5(1) of the Information Society Directive, the Copyright Regulations inserted new section 28A into the CDPA.[89] This section states:

28A Making of temporary copies

Copyright in a literary work, *other than a computer program or a database*, or in a dramatic, musical or artistic work, the typographical arrangement of a published edition, a sound recording or a film, is not infringed by the making of a temporary copy which is transient or incidental, which is an integral and essential part of a technological process and the sole purpose of which is to enable—

(a) a transmission of the work in a network between third parties by an intermediary; or

(b) a lawful use of the work;

and which has no independent economic significance. (emphasis supplied)

The plain terms of section 28A clearly state that it does not apply to computer programs or databases, which appears to be a correct implementation of Article 5(1) of the Information Society Directive, as was discussed above. The exceptions relevant to computer programs and databases are contained in sections 50A–50D of the CDPA and are explored in chapter 5. Thus, section 28A will be relevant only to those multimedia works that are protected as a compilation, dramatic work or film. This means that browsing, local caching, proxy caching and network transmissions of such works should be exempt from being an infringing reproduction, provided that the conditions stipulated are satisfied. These conditions are quite onerous such that the impact of section 28A on rightholders is likely to be limited.[90]

---

[86] See para 2.3 of *Consultation on UK Implementation of Directive 2001/29/EC on Copyright and Related Rights in the Information Society: Analysis of Responses and Government Conclusions* ('Consultation Paper').

[87] SI 2003/ 2498.

[88] But note the Copyright and Related Rights Regulations 2003 SI 2498 ('Copyright Regulations'), reg 8(3) inserted s 182A(1A), CDPA: 'In subsection (1), making a copy of a recording includes making a copy which is transient or is incidental to some other use of the original recording.'

[89] See reg 8(1), Copyright Regulations. Regulation 8(2) inserted a similar provision in respect of performances in Schedule 2.

[90] Cook and Brazell (2004) para 5.11.

The Copyright Regulations have implemented Article 8(3) of the Information Society Directive in the form of sections 97A and 191JA of the CDPA. These sections respectively provide that the Court shall have the power to grant an injunction against a service provider, where it has *actual knowledge* of another person using its service to infringe copyright or a performer's property right. When determining whether the service provider has actual knowledge the court shall take into account, *inter alia*, whether the service provider has received a notice through contact details provided under Regulation 6(1)(c) of the Electronic Commerce (EC Directive) Regulations 2002 No 2013 ('E-Commerce Regulations')[91] and the extent to which any notice includes the full name and address of the sender of the notice and details of the infringement in question.

The E-Commerce Regulations have implemented Articles 12 to 15 of the E-Commerce Directive in language very similar to those provisions.[92] With respect to the exemption for caching and hosting, regulation 22 states that for the purpose of determining actual knowledge of the service provider, a court shall have regard to whether the service provider has received a notice through contact details provided under regulation 6(1)(c) and the extent to which any notice includes the full name and address of the sender of the notice; details of the location of the information in question; and details of the unlawful nature of the activity or information in question. The relationship between Articles 12 to 15 of the E-Commerce Directive and earlier Directives is such that implementation of the service provider exemptions should also extend to computer programs and database (and thus multimedia works protected as such). Thus, it appears that service providers will be not be liable, other than for injunctive relief,[93] for their role in transmitting works, such as databases or computer programs, or storing them on a proxy cache, provided the conditions stipulated are satisfied.

(b) Copying of Computer Programs

For multimedia works that are protected as computer programs, it is important to determine the scope of protection under this sub-category of literary work.

In *John Richardson Computers Ltd v Flanders* ('*Flanders*')[94] Ferris J held that at the stage at which substantiality of any copying falls to be assessed, similarities beyond the text of the code may be considered.[95] To determine whether such non-literal similarities represented copying of a substantial part, Ferris J recommended

---

[91] That is, 'the details of the service provider, including his electronic mail address, which make it possible to contact him rapidly and communicate with him in a direct and effective manner.'

[92] See regs 17–20 and 22 of the E-Commerce Regulations. The Commission has observed that Member States have, in general transposed Articles 12–14 correctly and many have opted to transpose the provisions quasi-literally: see First E-Commerce Report, p 13.

[93] See reg 20, E-Commerce Regulations.

[94] *John Richardson Computers Ltd v Flanders* [1993] FSR 497 ('*Flanders*').

[95] *Flanders*, 527.

that the abstraction-filtration-comparison test relied upon in the US case *Computer Associates International Inc v Altai Inc*[96] be adopted.[97] This test requires that first the non-literal elements of a program, at varying degrees of abstraction, are ascertained. The next step is to filter out those elements that are not protected by copyright, such as unprotectable ideas, features that are dictated by considerations of efficiency or by external factors or which are taken from the public domain. After this process, one should be left with the core of protectable expression, which can be compared with the defendant's program. Ferris J believed that this test addressed the same issue addressed by substantiality, ie, the originality of the part of the program copied. However, Ferris J did admit to facing difficulties in applying the *Altai* test in this particular case.[98]

In the end, Ferris J held that the defendant's program infringed the plaintiff's program in a few minor ways; namely, by copying the line editor, amendment routines and dose codes.[99] Even though the defendant's main menu featured the same functions as the plaintiff's menu, this was held to be merely similar in concept or idea and not the proper subject of copyright.[100] Other irrelevant similarities included the selection of various options by pressing a key identified by a letter against each option and the unconventional use of the 'Escape' key (to switch between the labelling screens and another screen), because the keys were either a standard method of choice or standard keys.[101]

Flanders therefore highlights how (non-visual) user interface features[102] may potentially fall within the scope of copyright protection of computer programs, although not many did in this particular case.

In *IBCOS Computers Ltd v Barclays Mercantile Highland Finance Ltd* ('*IBCOS*'),[103] Jacob J (as he then was), in considering infringement of the suite of programs as a compilation, held that it was relevant to consider the 'program structure as a whole and the design features as a whole as part of the work, in addition to the literal bits of code and the program structure within an individual program.'[104]

Jacob J found that the close correspondence in both software packages of the distribution of functions amounted to copying of a substantial part of the compilation of programs.[105] Also present were similarities in design features of the

---

[96] *Computer Associates International Inc v Altai Inc* 23 USPQ 2d 1241 (1992).

[97] See S Lai, *The Copyright Protection of Computer Software in the United Kingdom* (Hart Publishing, Oxford, 2000) 32–34 for further discussion.

[98] *Flanders*, 527.

[99] Above, at 558–59.

[100] Above, at 541–42.

[101] Above, at 542.

[102] See Lai (2000) 78–80 discussing this as a user interface case.

[103] *IBCOS Computers Ltd v Barclays Mercantile Highland Finance Ltd* [1994] FSR 265 ('*IBCOS*').

[104] Above, at 292–93.

[105] Above, at 304.

software package; however, his Lordship did not regard those features as forming part of the copyright compilation: they were at a level of generality such that they involved minimal originality, the copying of which would be copying of general idea and not expression.[106] Further, Jacob J found that a large number of individual programs were infringed by the defendant's package (approximately 30). He reached this conclusion by comparing the quantity of identical variables (active and redundant), labels, remarks, code lines and code in each pair of programs. Although Jacob J recognised that this approach was somewhat mechanical and had its drawbacks, he believed that the quantity of the literal elements copied was sufficiently large to reflect copying of a substantial part. He added that, in many places, the individual programs also demonstrated structural similarities.[107]

In respect of the file transfer programs, these were held to infringe because they reproduced the file record layouts in the plaintiff's software package and these layouts formed a substantial part of the package.[108] This was so, despite the fact that data compatibility was necessary for the defendant's package to compete successfully with the plaintiff's.[109]

Finally, Jacob J expressed his agreement with Ferris J's view in *Flanders* that consideration of copyright in computer programs extends beyond the text of the code; however, he disagreed that the *Altai* test (or indeed any US approach) should be invoked to determine whether there has been copying of a substantial part.[110] Rather, he suggested the question of substantial part, 'is a question of degree where a good guide is the notion of over-borrowing of skill, labour and judgment which went into the copyright work.'[111] As *IBCOS* was concerned primarily with copying of literal elements[112] (ie, the structure of a compilation and the code of individual programs), Jacob J's remarks may be considered obiter.[113] Thus, this case is mainly concerned with copying *literal* elements of computer programs. To the extent that it deals with non-user interface features (ie, data compatibility) these features may be protected as a compilation, rather than as part of the program.

In *Cantor Fitzgerald International v Tradition (UK) Ltd* (*'Cantor'*),[114] Pumfrey J held that a substantial part of a computer program should be judged by the originality of the part copied, and not according to the essential or critical nature of

---

[106] Above, at 305.

[107] Above, at 305–13.

[108] Above, at 313.

[109] Above. This case was decided before s 50C was inserted into the CDPA by the Copyright (Computer Programs) Regulations 1992, SI 1992/3233 ('Software Regulations'). Even if s 50C had been applicable, it seems this would not have affected the outcome on this issue, since copying the file record layouts was an infringement of the compilation and not of the individual programs.

[110] *IBCOS*, 302.

[111] Above.

[112] Lai (2000) pp 25–26.

[113] See also D Bainbridge, *Software Copyright Law*, 4th edn (Butterworths, London, 1999) 133.

[114] *Cantor Fitzgerald International v Tradition (UK) Ltd* [2000] RPC 95 (*'Cantor'*).

the part[115] or the amount of use the system makes of the copied code.[116] Further, the substantiality of what is taken is to be judged in relation to all of the modules as a whole.[117] Pumfrey J also commented obiter that the 'architecture' of a computer program may be protected if it resulted from sufficient skill, labour and judgement; meaning, the structure of the program or, in other words, the way in which the functions in the program are allocated.[118]

Thus, *non-literal features* of programs may be protected in the form of the structure of the program code and limited non-visual user interface features. *Non-user interface* features may be separately protected as a compilation. The implications for multimedia works are twofold. First, the user interface of a multimedia work can be imitated, provided the underlying code, including the way it is structured, is not copied. Second, creators of multimedia works may prevent others from marketing competing, compatible multimedia works that require certain data tables or file layouts in order to be compatible.

(c) Compilations and Databases

It is the scope of copyright protection for compilations and databases that is the major drawback of relying on this form of protection in respect of multimedia works. A person will infringe copyright in a compilation or database by copying the selection or arrangement of the contents, as opposed to the contents themselves.[119] Nevertheless, there is authority under the previous Copyright Act 1956 (UK) which suggests that protection beyond the selection or arrangement of the *compilation* may occur.

Waterlow Publishers Ltd v Rose[120] involved copyright in a work published by Waterlow, known as the 'Solicitors' Directory and Diary', which included lists of solicitors and barristers and a diary portion. The Court of Appeal upheld the finding of the lower court that a rival work produced by a competitor was a copyright infringement of the Solicitor's Diary. The case was solely concerned with issues of authorship and infringement. Infringement was found to have occurred

---

[115] Which was the approach adopted by the High Court of Australia in *Autodesk v Dyason [No 1]* (1993) 173 CLR 330, 336 (Mason CJ, Brennan and Deane JJ), and 346 (Dawson J); *Autodesk [No 2]* (1993) 176 CLR 300, 312 (Brennan J), and 330 (Gaudron J). However, the High Court of Australia later disapproved this approach in *Data Access Corporation v Powerflex Services Pty Ltd* (1999) 202 CLR 1 (*'Data Access'*). It held that it was an impracticable test for determining substantial reproduction because *any* part of a computer program could be classified as 'essential' or 'critical' to a program, since without any part a program would not work, or at least not work properly. Rather, the High Court preferred to assess whether there is a reproduction of a substantial part by considering the originality of the part allegedly taken: *Data Access*, 33 (Gleeson CJ, McHugh, Gummow and Hayne JJ).

[116] *Cantor*, 131 and 135.

[117] *Cantor*, 135.

[118] *Cantor*, 134–35.

[119] See Article 5, WIPO Copyright Treaty 1996 ('WCT').

[120] *Waterlow Publishers Ltd v Rose* (1989) 17 IPR 493.

on the basis that the defendant extracted the information on solicitors and used this information to make his own compilation.[121]

Similarly, in *Waterlow Directories Ltd v Reed Information Services Ltd*,[122] which was decided under the CDPA, the plaintiff, who published the Solicitors and Barristers Directory succeeded in obtaining an interlocutory injunction against the defendant who had consulted and used the plaintiff's directory to publish a more comprehensive Butterworths Law Directory. Only infringement of copyright was in issue on this motion and Aldous J (as he then was) held that by copying names and addresses of solicitors and organisations onto a word processor, so that they might approach these people to invite them to appear in the defendant's directory, there was a reproduction of the plaintiff's work.[123] Whether it was reproduction of a substantial part remained a serious issue to be tried.

There is mixed opinion on whether the above cases indicate that strong protection of compilations existed in the UK,[124] which, in any case, has been undercut by the Copyright and Rights in Databases Regulations 1997 ('Database Regulations').[125] The better view seems to be that the scope of protection for compilations was equivocal, based on the few cases on this topic. Regardless of what might have been the position for compilations, it is now the case that protection of compilations and databases extends only to the selection or arrangement of their contents.[126] As discussed in chapter 3, the scope of this protection is particularly limited where there is only a minimal degree of creativity expended on the selection or arrangement of materials—a result that is likely to occur in the case of comprehensive databases. However, the scope of protection should be stronger in the case of multimedia works, given that they are more likely to involve significant creativity in determining the materials to be included within the work and the way they are arranged (although arguably arrangement is not assessed as part of the originality requirement). Even so, creators of multimedia works wishing to protect the entirety of their products will find frustrating the absence of protection for the contents of a multimedia work. The new *sui generis* database right may provide an adequate alternative. Indeed, the justification for *sui generis* protection of databases was that they were not sufficiently protected in Member States of the European Union by existing legislation.[127] Further, that while copyright was 'an

---

[121] Above, at 505–7.

[122] *Waterlow Directories Ltd v Reed Information Services Ltd* [1992] FSR 409.

[123] Above, at 414, 417. See also *Elanco Products Ltd v Mandops Ltd* [1979] FSR 46.

[124] Cf Bainbridge (1999) p 181; and C Rees and S Chalton (eds), *Database Law* (Jordans, Bristol, 1998) 86.

[125] SI 1997/3032 ('Database Regulations'). These came into force on 1 January 1998.

[126] See Article 5, WCT; Article 10(2), Agreement on Trade Related Aspects of Intellectual Property Rights 1994 ('TRIPs Agreement'); Database Directive and Database Regulations.

[127] Recital 1, Database Directive. See also D Fewer, 'A Sui Generis Right to Data? A Canadian Position' (1998) 30 *Canadian Business L J* 165, 168–69.

appropriate form of exclusive right for authors who have created databases', 'other measures are required in addition to prevent the unauthorised extraction and/or re-utilisation of the contents of a database.'[128] The scope of protection under the *sui generis* right is discussed later in this chapter.

Right to Make an Adaptation

Under UK law, the adaptation right applies only to literary, dramatic and musical works.[129] Where such a work is adapted, there is also the right to do all of the exclusive acts of copyright in relation to the adapted work.[130]

The adaptation right will be most relevant to multimedia works that are protected as literary works, specifically computer programs and databases. In respect of computer programs, an 'adaptation' according to section 21(ab) of the CDPA means 'an arrangement or altered version of the program or a translation of it'. This provision was inserted by the Software Regulations[131] in order to implement Article 4(b) of the Software Directive, which provides that the rightholder shall have the right to do or authorise, 'the translation, adaptation, arrangement and any other alteration of a computer program and the reproduction of the results thereof, without prejudice to the rights of the person who alters the program.'[132] According to section 21(4) of the CDPA, 'translation' includes a 'version of the program in which it is converted into or out of a computer language or code or into a different computer language or code'.[133] As such, 'translation' includes conversion from source code into object code or vice versa,[134] along with conversion into different higher programming languages. What then would be covered by an *arrangement* or *altered version* of the program? Would it cover a situation where one set of instructions (ie, program code) is devised to perform the same functions as another set of instructions (program code), but which are not objectively similar? If the original program code has been used only to identify the underlying ideas or functions performed by the program, then it is submitted this would not amount to infringing adaptation, since otherwise protection would extend too far

---

[128] Recitals 5 and 6, Database Directive.

[129] S 21(1), CDPA.

[130] S 21(2), CDPA.

[131] Software Regulations, reg 5(2).

[132] Reg 5 of the Software Regulations repealed from s 21(4) those words that exempted translation incidental to running a program since this was inconsistent with Article 4(a), Software Directive.

[133] S 21(4), CDPA.

[134] Cf situation in Australia where conversion between object and source code is classed as 'reproduction': see s 21(1A), Copyright Act 1968 (Cth). Thus, adaptation relates only to *versions* of a computer program, other than a compilation or decompilation.

into the non-literal realm.[135] However, if the original code is used *beyond* merely identifying the underlying ideas or functions of a program and 'as an aid to devising the descriptions of the activities (and any accompanying data) which together comprise the allegedly infringing program'[136] then this might amount to an arrangement or altered version of the program.

In summary, the owner of copyright in the program underlying a multimedia work would be able to prevent others from translating the program code into different programming languages. They would not, however, be able to prevent a competitor from imitating the program's user interface or the functions of a program, where the coded instructions have been used only as an aid to understanding the program's idea or function.

An adaptation of a database[137] may be an arrangement, altered version or translation of it.[138] As these words are not defined, their ordinary dictionary meaning would apply. An 'arrangement' is defined to mean 'the action of arranging', namely, 'to put (the parts) into order; to adjust'.[139] 'Alter' is defined as 'to make otherwise or different in some respect, without changing the thing itself; to modify'[140] and 'version' is defined as 'a translation' or 'a particular form or variant of something'.[141] Finally, 'translation' is defined as 'the action or process of turning from one language into another' or 'transformation, alteration, change; changing or adapting to another use'.[142]

An adaptation of a database could occur in several ways. First, updating a database could result in a modified version of the original database being produced. If so, a third party would be prohibited from updating a database or, in relation to an updated database, prohibited from carrying out any exclusive acts in relation to the modified selection or arrangement of the database contents. Second, making a database available in another language could amount to an adaptation of the database, depending on whether the language translation related to the selection

---

[135] The High Court of Australia has held that the right of adaptation in relation to computer programs does not cover situations where, although the functionality of a computer program is copied, original code has been written to perform the same function. Although the defendant's macros performed the same function as the plaintiff's macros, they were written in original source code and were held not to be infringing adaptations: *Data Access*, 39.

[136] *Coogi Australia Pty Ltd v Hysport International Pty Ltd* (1998) 157 ALR 247, at 279 (Drummond J).

[137] Note, this definition is limited to 'databases' and does not extend to non-database compilations (see s 3(1)(a) and s 3(1)(d) of CDPA, which distinguishes between these two sorts of works). For non-database compilations, it is merely stated that there is the right to make an adaptation or do any of the exclusive acts in relation to an adaptation: s 16(1)(e), CDPA.

[138] S 21(3)(ac), CDPA inserted by Art 7 of Database Regulations to implement Art 5(b) of Database Directive granting the author of a database the exclusive right to carry out or to authorise: 'translation, adaptation, arrangement and any other alteration.'

[139] *Shorter Oxford English Dictionary on Historical Principles*, 3rd edn, (Clarendon Press, Oxford, 1991) ('SOED') 106.

[140] SOED, p 53.

[141] SOED, p 2467.

[142] SOED, p 2347.

or arrangement of the contents, as opposed to the contents themselves. If the *contents* themselves were translated—for example, a database of reported Dutch cases on copyright was translated into English—this would not amount to an adaptation of the database. However, if the *user interface* is translated from one language to another, then this would amount to a translation of the *arrangement* of the contents. This is because arrangement may be understood as including the presentation of the contents to the user.[143] Finally, there is the situation where a person copies the contents of a database, but rearranges or reorders the contents, perhaps even adding to the copied contents. Under the right to copy discussed in the previous section, this is unlikely to be an infringement because the selection or arrangement of those contents has not been copied. However, if the adaptation right gives the copyright owner the right to produce a modified version of the database, this arguably extends to producing a modified 'selection or arrangement' of independent works, data or other materials. The difficulty will be in determining the extent to which the selection or arrangement of the database's contents may be modified pursuant to the adaptation right.

In summary, where a multimedia work is protected as a database, the copyright owner should be able to prevent third parties producing updated versions of the work, translating the user interface into different languages and, to a certain extent, copying the contents and then reordering and rearranging them.

Right to Issue Copies to the Public

Section 16(2)(b) of the CPDA grants owners of copyright works the right to issue copies of the work to the public. This right did not appear in the earlier Copyright Act 1956 (UK); rather, copyright owners had a right to publish, which was limited to making public a work which had been previously unpublished.[144] Whereas, under the CDPA, the right to issue copies of the work to the public confers on the copyright owner 'a right to control a series of acts, that is the issue of each and every copy, rather than the single act of bringing the work from its unpublished state into the public domain'.[145]

Section 18 of the CDPA defines the scope of this right and this section has undergone several amendments in order to give effect to the Software Directive and the Rental Rights Directive. It now reads:

---

[143] See ch 3, p 49 above in relation to definition of 'database'.

[144] See *Infabrics Ltd v Jaytex Ltd* [1982] AC 1, 17 (Lord Wilberforce), and 25 (Lord Scarman). See also J Phillips and L Bently, 'Copyright Issues: The Mysteries of Section 18' [1999] 3 *EIPR* 133.

[145] Phillips and Bently (1999) p 133.

(1) The issue to the public of copies of the work is an act restricted by the copyright in every description of copyright work.

(2) References in this Part to the issue to the public of copies of a work are to—

    (a) the act of putting into circulation in the EEA copies not previously put into circulation in the EEA by or with the consent of the copyright owner, or

    (b) the act of putting into circulation outside the EEA copies not previously put into circulation in the EEA or elsewhere.

(3) References in this Part to the issue to the public of copies of a work do not include—

    (a) any subsequent distribution, sale, hiring or loan of those copies previously put into circulation (but see section 18A: infringement by rental or lending), or

    (b) any subsequent importation of such copies into the United Kingdom or another EEA state,

except so far as paragraph (a) of subsection (2) applies to putting into circulation in the EEA copies previously put into circulation outside the EEA.

(4) References in this Part to the issue of copies of a work include the issue of the original.

The distribution right is obviously relevant to *off-line* multimedia works disseminated in CD-Rom or DVD-Rom format. The relevance of this right to *on-line* multimedia works depends largely on whether it is aimed solely at distribution of *tangible* copies or not. If so, it is hard to see how ISPs or persons uploading material to a web server could be engaged in an activity of distribution, because the materials transmitted or made available would be *intangible* copies. However, it is not apparent from the terms of the section that it is restricted to tangible copies.[146] Other sections of the CDPA, namely section 17, appear to support the view that *intangible* copies may be issued to the public.[147] Section 17(2) makes clear that copying includes 'storing the work in any medium by electronic means'. Thus, 'copies' could include storage of a work in an electronic (intangible) format in multiple quantities.[148]

A basis upon which to exclude digital copies from the scope of this right is that it involves the act of issuing 'copies' to the public. If 'copies' refers only to the plural then placing a (single) copy on a web server and making it available to the

---

[146] See GJH Smith (ed), *Internet Law and Regulation*, 2nd edn (FT Law & Tax, London, 1997) 22. *Cf* Lai (1999b) p 138, who approaches it from a different angle: 'it is debatable whether by merely placing infringing files on a network the service provider can be said to have issued them to the public. Since "issuing" is an active verb, it is arguable that it requires a positive act to transfer the infringing file.'

[147] *Cf* MacQueen (2000) p 197 who argues that 'section 18, unlike section 17 which deals with copying, makes no reference to the notion of a "transient copy"; the copies required for the purposes of section 18 may therefore be limited to those which are non-transient, which would go beyond mere "on-demand" transmission.'

[148] S 17(1), CDPA states that references to copying and copies shall be construed as set out in that section. Thus, the plural of the noun 'copy' could be interpreted in this way, based on the definition of the verb 'copying' in s 17(2).

public would not satisfy the requirement of 'copies'. *Microsoft Corporation v Electro-wide Ltd*[149] is the only case to have touched on this issue. Microsoft had sued the defendants, who were original equipment manufacturers (OEMs), for infringement of copyright in various operating systems software. The facts showed that the defendants had sold to their customers personal computers with pre-installed Microsoft operating systems software, but without transferring the relevant floppy disks or CD-Roms containing the software, the authentic manual, end-user licence agreement or Certificate of Authenticity. There existed a special licence agreement between Microsoft and OEMs that would allow OEMs to pre-install Microsoft software onto personal computers, provided the materials accompanying the software were also supplied with the personal computer. In an application for summary judgment before Laddie J, Microsoft argued that the unlicensed loading of its software onto various personal computers was an act of substantial copying. Further, that the subsequent supply of the computer loaded with the software was an unlawful act of issuing copies of the work to the public.[150] In relation to this latter issue, the defendant's counsel argued that section 18 required an issue of 'copies', with the use of the plural in that section being deliberate and thereby preventing the issue of a single copy. Laddie J did not decide this point of law, notwithstanding the strong arguments made to the contrary by the plaintiff, and assumed that the defendant's position was correct.[151] It was unnecessary for Laddie J to decide the application on this basis since unlawful copying had clearly occurred. Thus, the weight that can be attached to this case in respect of section 18 of the CDPA is slight.

Phillips and Bently posit the contrary view that section 18 does not require a plurality of copies.[152] Their view is based on section 18(4), which states that issuing copies of a work includes the issue of the *original*, which by nature is a single item. If this view is correct, then placing a copyright work on-line, which has not previously been issued to the public, may well involve this right.

The issue should now be settled by implementation of the Information Society Directive, which clearly reflects the intention to restrict the distribution right to *tangible* copies,[153] as do the recent WIPO Treaties.[154] Article 4(1) of the

---

[149] *Microsoft Corporation v Electro-wide Ltd* [1997] FSR 580 ('*Electro-wide*').

[150] Above, at 590.

[151] Above, at 591.

[152] Phillips and Bently (1999) p 140. See also Laddie, *et al*, (2000) para 15.18. Another confusion with section 18, identified by Phillips and Bently (1999) pp 134–35, is at what point does the relevant 'issuing' occur?

[153] See recital 19 and Article 4(2) of Information Society Directive.

[154] See Article 6 of WCT and Agreed Statement: 'As used in these Articles, the expressions "copies" and "original and copies," being subject to the right of distribution and the right of rental under the said Articles, refer exclusively to fixed copies that can be put into circulation as tangible objects.' See also Articles 8 and 12 of WIPO Performances and Phonograms Treaty 1996 ('WPPT') and the accompanying Agreed Statement.

Information Society Directive provides authors, in respect of the original of their works or of copies thereof, with the 'exclusive right to authorise or prohibit any form of distribution to the public by sale or otherwise'. Recital 28 indicates that this right governs the distribution of the work incorporated in a *tangible* article (such as a CD-Rom), as opposed to distribution of on-line services.[155]

Thus, the distribution right contained in Article 4 of the Information Society Directive does not appear to encompass on-line or electronic distribution and section 18 of the CDPA should be interpreted consistently with the Directive. Confining the right of distribution in this way does not deprive the copyright owner of exclusive rights relevant to an on-line environment, since the new right of communication to the public and the right of reproduction will successfully cover this ground. The new right of communication to the public is discussed later in this chapter.

Rental or Lending of the Work to the Public

For multimedia works that attract copyright protection as a literary work (ie, as a program, compilation or database), dramatic work or film, the right to rent or lend copies of the work to the public is relevant. Rental means 'making a copy of the work available for use, on terms that it will or may be returned, for direct or indirect economic or commercial advantage.'[156] Lending refers to a similar activity, except that it must be done other than for direct or indirect economic or commercial advantage, and through an establishment which is accessible to the public.[157]

Clearly, this right is relevant to copies of multimedia works that are distributed in *off-line* format. Less clear is whether it extends to *on-line* distribution of multimedia works. The recent WIPO Treaties, but not the Information Society Directive, indicate that the expression 'copies' in respect of the rental right refers to tangible copies.[158] Interpreting the provisions of section 18A, it is arguable that making works available on-line constitutes 'making a copy of the work available for use.' This is because when data is transmitted to a user of the world wide web from the host server, a copy of that data is made and sent to the requesting party.

---

[155] Recital 29, Information Society Directive is consistent with this view. See also K Murray, 'The Draft Directive on the Harmonisation of Certain Aspects of Copyright' [1998] *Entertainment L Rev* 190, commenting on an earlier version of the Directive.

[156] S 18A(2)(a), CDPA.

[157] S 18A(2)(b), CDPA.

[158] See Article 7 of WCT and accompanying Agreed Statement, 'the expressions "copies" and "original and copies" . . . refer exclusively to fixed copies that can be put into circulation as tangible objects'. See also Articles 9 and 13 of WPPT and accompanying Agreed Statement.

However, it is not usually the case that such a transmission is made on the basis that the copy sent will be returned.[159] Moreover, in only a limited number of instances are websites made accessible for a fee (ie, commercial advantage).[160]

Certain activities are expressly excluded from being rental or lending. These include making available for on the spot reference use and making available for the purpose of communication to the public.[161] Arguably, browsing material on-line strongly resembles 'on-the-spot reference use' and so is excluded on this basis. Alternatively, and perhaps more clearly, since transmissions over the Internet will usually involve the right of communication to the public (discussed below), this would exclude the operation of the rental or lending right for on-line activities.

Performance, Showing or Playing of the Work in Public

Sections 16(1)(c) and 19 establish the right to perform, show or play a work in public. For multimedia works that are protected as literary works, it is the right to *perform* the work in public that is applicable,[162] whereas for multimedia works protected as films, it is the right to *play or show* the work in public.[163] Accessing a multimedia work on-line and in the process of so doing displaying it on a computer screen could qualify as showing or performing[164] the work. However, it may be problematic to demonstrate that such showing or performing has occurred 'in public'.[165] The notion of 'in public' is reasonably broad and the courts have not laid down any strict rules about what amounts to a performance 'in public'. Particular emphasis is placed, however, on the character of the audience, as one that is brought together by an aspect of their public life, as opposed to a domestic or private tie,[166] and the relationship of the audience to the copyright owner.[167] However, if any meaningful distinction between acts done 'in public', as distinct from 'to the public', is to exist, the former would have to connote reception of the performance in the same geographical location. According to this interpretation the point-to-point and on-demand nature of Internet transmissions is unlikely to

---

[159] MacQueen (2000) p 197.

[160] MacQueen (2000) pp 197–98.

[161] See s 18A(3), CDPA. The latter exclusion was inserted by Copyright Regulations, sch 1(1) para 6(2)(a) as an amendment consequential upon implementing Article 3 of the Information Society Directive.

[162] S 19(1), CDPA.

[163] S 19(3), CDPA.

[164] Since s 19(2)(b), CDPA defines 'performance' to include 'any mode of visual or acoustic presentation, including by means of a sound recording, film or broadcast of the work.'

[165] MacQueen (2000) p 198.

[166] See *Jennings v Stephens* [1936] Ch 469, 479 (Lord Wright MR), and 481–82 (Romer LJ); and *APRA v Commonwealth* (1992) 40 FCR 59, 74.

[167] *Jennings v Stephens* [1936] Ch 469, 485 (Greene LJ).

be considered as 'in public'.[168] Internet transmissions are more likely to fall within the new right of communication to the public, which is discussed in the following section.

Right of Communication to the Public

A key feature of the Copyright Regulations is the substitution of a new section 20 in the CDPA.[169] Whereas, previously, section 20 referred to the right of broadcasting the work and the right to include a work in a cable programme service,[170] the new section 20 replaces these rights with a right of communication to the public of the work.[171] Before considering the new UK communication right, it is important to discuss the background to its introduction, including the WIPO Treaties and Article 3 of the Information Society Directive.

1. International Context[172]

By the early 1990s, concerns were being voiced about the implications of digital transmissions for copyright owners, in particular, whether or not the exclusive rights contained in the Berne Convention enabled an author to control exploitation of her work via the Internet or similar sort of digital network.[173] By the mid 1990s, concerns about the ability of regional and national copyright laws to embrace new forms of digital dissemination of works were also being raised.[174] A solution to the

---

[168] Cf MacQueen (2000) pp 198–99.

[169] See reg 6, Information Society Directive.

[170] For a pithy discussion of the scope of the previous rights of broadcasting and cable transmission see Makeen (2000) pp 143–47 and 232–33, respectively.

[171] A similar reform was introduced into the Australian Copyright Act 1968 (Cth) by the Copyright Amendment (Digital Agenda) Act 2000, which replaced the rights to broadcast and transmit to subscribers to a diffusion service with a broader right of communication to the public, which includes making available online. For details, see T Aplin, 'Contemplating Australia's Digital Future: The Copyright Amendment (Digital Agenda) Act 2000' [2001] *EIPR* 565, 565–66.

[172] For a detailed historical background to the right of communication to the public and the making available right see Ficsor (2002) ch 4.

[173] See WIPO, *WIPO Worldwide Symposium On The Impact Of Digital Technology On Copyright And Neighboring Rights*, Harvard University, Cambridge, MA, 31 March 1993 to 2 April 1993. See also F Macmillan and M Blakeney, 'Internet and Communication Carriers' Copyright Liability' [1998] 2 *EIPR* 52, 53–54.

[174] EC, *Green Paper on Copyright and Related Rights in the Information Society*, Brussels, 19 July 1995 COM (95) 382 final. Information Infrastructure Task Force (IITF), *Intellectual Property and the National Information Infrastructure: Preliminary Draft of the Working Group on Intellectual Property Rights* (Washington DC, 1994) and Information Infrastructure Task Force (IITF), *Intellectual Property and the National Information Infrastructure: The Report of the Working Group on Intellectual Property Rights* (Washington DC, 1997).

perceived problem of digital dissemination of copyright works and related subject matter was first provided at the International level, in the form of the WIPO Treaties, concluded at the WIPO Diplomatic Conference in December 1996.

Article 8 of the WCT provides for a broad right of communication to the public:[175]

> Without prejudice to the provisions of Articles 11(1)(ii), 11*bis*(1)(i) and (ii), 11*ter*(1)(ii), 14(1)(ii) and 14*bis*(1) of the Berne Convention, authors of literary and artistic works shall enjoy the exclusive right of authorising any *communication to the public of their works, by wire or wireless means,* including the *making available to the public* of their works in such a way that members of the public may access these works from a place and at a time individually chosen by them. (Emphasis supplied)

This right supplements the existing rights of communication in the Berne Convention and introduces, as part of an author's broader right of communication to the public, the right of making available to the public.

The WIPO Performances and Phonograms Treaty 1996 ('WPPT') bifurcates the concepts expressed above in Article 8 into two free standing rights. Articles 10 and 14 of the WPPT grant performers and phonogram producers, respectively, *the right of making available to the public,* via wire or wireless means, their performances fixed in phonograms and phonograms, from a place and at a time individually chosen by members of the public. Article 15(1) gives performers and phonogram producers a right to equitable remuneration for broadcasting or communication to the public of phonograms.[176]

The solution provided by Article 8 WCT came after much debate about the appropriate means to protect authors from unauthorised transmission of their works over digital networks. In the lead-up to adoption of the Final text of the WCT, various solutions had been proposed, such as treating digital dissemination as an act of distribution, an act of public display or rental, an act of communication to the public, or establishing a new specific digital transmission right.[177] In the end, an 'umbrella' solution was adopted, namely, to create an obligation to grant an exclusive right to authorise on-demand transmission, but described in a neutral way so that the legal characterization of the right granted would be left to national law.[178] This was confirmed by a statement made by a US delegate that was silently accepted by the other delegations.[179]

---

[175] This right was introduced because Article 11*bis*(1) and Articles 11(1), 11*ter*(1), 14(1) and 14*bis*(1) of the Berne Convention do not comprehensively cover all types of communications to the public of all the different types of copyright works.

[176] Arguably, the bifurcation of these two concepts in the WPPT is disappointing since Article 8 of the WCT might otherwise have suggested an international consensus that making available to the public at a time chosen by individual members of the public is an aspect of communication to the public: Macmillan and Blakeney (1998) p 55.

[177] For further details see Ficsor (2002) pp 233–47; and Makeen (2000) pp 285–92.

[178] Ficsor (2002) pp 208–9, 500–1.

[179] See Ficsor (2002) pp 249, 496–98; and J Reinbothe and S von Lewinski, *The WIPO Treaties 1996* (Butterworths, London, 2002) 108. But note Makeen (2000) p 291 who argues that Article 8 of the

The first part of Article 8 WCT seeks to supplement the provisions of the Berne Convention in respect of the (traditional) right of communication to the public. This is made clear by the words, 'Without prejudice to the provisions of Articles 11(1)(ii), 11*bis*(1)(i) and (ii), 11*ter*(1)(ii), 14(1)(ii) and 14*bis*(1) of the Berne Convention'. These provisions refer to several exclusive rights for different types of works. Authors of dramatic, dramatico-musical and musical works enjoy the right of authorising any communication to the public *of the performance* of their works (Art 11(1)(ii)). Authors of literary and artistic works have the exclusive right of *broadcasting* their works or otherwise communicating their work to the public by means of wireless diffusion. Further, they have the right of *communication to the public by wire of the broadcast* of the work, or by *rebroadcasting the broadcast* of the work (when this communication is made by an organisation *other* than the original one) (Art 11*bis*(1)(i) and (ii)). Authors of literary and artistic works also have the exclusive right of authorising the *public performance and communication to the public by wire* of their works which have been cinematographically adapted and reproduced (Art 14(1)(ii)). Authors of literary works have the exclusive right of *communication to the public of the recitation* of their works. (Art 11*ter*(1)(ii)) and owners of copyright in a cinematographic work shall enjoy the exclusive right of *public performance and communication to the public by wire* (Art 14*bis*(1)).

The casuistic gaps left by the above provisions have been eliminated by the first part of Article 8.[180] Thus, the communication right in Article 8 of the WCT, aside from the making available right, will supplement Article 11*bis*(1) of the Berne Convention in the following ways. Importantly, for literary and artistic works, Article 8 WCT grants the exclusive right of communication to the public via wire (including cable transmission);[181] also the right to retransmit by cable originated cable transmissions; and the exclusive right to rebroadcast, or retransmit, a broadcast made by the same organisation which emitted the original programme.[182] Article 8 WCT further embraces 'transmission of originated cable programs incorporating any kinds of works *not* covered by Article 11(1)(ii), 11*ter*(1)(ii), 14(1)(ii) and 14*bis*(1) Berne Convention(those include musical, dramatic and dramatico-musical works other than in the form of a performance or recitation.'[183] Finally, Article 8 WCT extends protection under Article 11*ter*(1) and Article 14(1), in giving the exclusive right to the communication to the public of text and images.[184]

WCT 'is no longer an umbrella solution but rather a specific right . . . Had it been a mere umbrella solution, there would have been no point in defining the term "public" unequivocally in the body of the Treaty to include people chronologically dispersed.'

[180] Ficsor (2002) p 495.
[181] Macmillan and Blakeney (1998) p 55.
[182] Reinbothe and von Lewinski (2002) pp 106–7.
[183] Reinbothe and von Lewinski (2002) p 106.
[184] Macmillan and Blakeney (1998) p 55.

In terms of what will amount to a communication *to the public,* no guidance is provided by either the Berne Convention or the WCT.[185] Commentators have suggested, however, that it will not include acts 'within the close circle of a family and closest social acquaintances'.[186] Thus, it will be left to national law to determine what is 'public'.[187]

Guidance as to what amounts to a *communication* is sought to be provided by the Agreed Statement to Article 8 WCT which states:

> It is understood that the mere provision of physical facilities for enabling or making a communication does not in itself amount to communication within the meaning of this Treaty or the Berne Convention.

It is unclear what would amount to 'mere provision of physical facilities'. Probably it would cover the activities of a common carrier, but it remains debatable whether it would also cover the activities of a simple access or valued added ISP.[188] Moreover, the possibility of common carriers or ISPs being held liable for authorising infringement still remains.[189]

The second part of Article 8 WCT (and also Articles 10 and 14 of the WPPT) refers to the act of *making available to the public.* According to Reinbothe and von Lewinski this would cover *offering* of works or subject matter for access, along with the entire *transmission* to the user, if such transmission takes place.[190] The 'making available' has to be such 'that members of the public may access these works from a place and at a time individually chosen by them.' This embraces *on-demand* situations,[191] such as websites that offer MP3 files or news stories for download by Internet users.[192] It excludes, however, broadcasting via traditional means or via digital networks (ie, webcasting or simulcasting) where pre-determined programmes are offered to the public at specified times; pay-per-view services; or services which repeatedly broadcast a series of works at regular intervals.[193] The making available right also includes works distributed via electronic mailing lists (eg, articles via news subscriptions) or works distributed via peer-to-peer

---

[185] Cf Makeen (2000) p 291 who argues that 'public' was defined to include persons who were geographically *and* chronologically dispersed.

[186] Reinbothe and von Lewinski (2002) p 107. See also S Ricketson, *The Berne Convention for the Protection of Literary and Artistic Works: 1886–1986* (Kluwer, London, 1987) para 8.71.

[187] K Weatherall, 'An End to Private Communications in Copyright? The Expansion of Rights to Communicate Works to the Public' [1999] *EIPR* 342; [1999] *EIPR* 398, 349; T Dreier, 'Copyright in Audiovisual Works vis à vis Digital Technology and Databases' in H Cohen Jehoram, P Keuchenius and J Seignette (eds), *Audiovisual Media and Copyright in Europe* (Kluwer, Deventer, 1994) 5, 53–74, 67. See also Working Paper, para 3.3.

[188] Reinbothe and von Lewinski (2002) p 112.

[189] Macmillan and Blakeney (1998) pp 55, 58–59. See also Ficsor (2002) p 509.

[190] Reinbothe and von Lewinski (2002) pp 108, 338, 369.

[191] JAL Sterling, *World Copyright Law*, 2nd edn (Sweet & Maxwell, London, 2003) para 9.30.

[192] Eg see http://www.napster.co.uk, http://www.mycokemusic.com/.

[193] Reinbothe and von Lewinski (2002) p 109; Sterling (2003) para 9.30.

networks (such as audio or video files via KaZaa).[194] In terms of members of the public being able to choose the place from which they want to access the works, this would include using personal computers from home, work, an internet café or library.[195]

In terms of what constitutes making available *to the public*, there is no guidance provided in the WCT or WPPT and it is left to be determined by national law.[196] Commentators have suggested that the concept of 'public' excludes the close family circle and closest social acquaintances, such that material stored on domestic intranets would not constitute making available to the public.[197] If this is correct then situations where material is placed on the Internet, but without being accessible to anyone but family or friends, should also be excluded. The notion of 'public' would not necessarily exclude material made available via school or company intranets.[198] Further, 'making available to the public' would clearly embrace placing a protected work, performance or recording on an Internet server, without restriction, along with an individual accessing that work, performance or recording.

A final and problematic issue is identifying *where* the act of making available occurs. The WCT and WPPT are silent on this matter. However, a virtually identical issue has arisen with direct broadcasting by satellite ('DBS')[199] because (as with Internet transmissions) reception of direct satellite broadcasts can occur in multiple jurisdictions. Thus, the literature and debates concerning the place where DBS occurs may be usefully referred to here.[200] Makeen emphasises that, in the case of DBS, it becomes necessary to identify the place where the relevant act of broadcasting occurs where the applicable law is determined by the *lex loci delicti* (as opposed to the *lex fori*).[201] Makeen also explains that two main theories emerged to resolve where the satellite broadcast takes place: the 'emission theory' and the 'communication theory'.[202] The 'emission theory' describes the relevant act of broadcasting as occurring from the country of emission.[203] According to this theory, the sole applicable law is that of the country of emission of the

---

[194] Which Reinbothe and von Lewinski (2002) p 110 respectively characterise as examples of 'push' and 'pull' technology.

[195] Reinbothe and von Lewinski (2002) p 111.

[196] Above.

[197] Above.

[198] Above.

[199] On the history and definition of direct broadcasting by satellite see Makeen (2000) pp 175–85.

[200] Cook and Brazell (2004) paras 4.48–4.52 briefly refer to the earlier debates concerning satellite broadcasting.

[201] Makeen (2000) pp 185–92, esp 192.

[202] Makeen (2000) pp 194–203. See also Ficsor (2002) paras 4.42–4.48 and Ricketson (1987) paras 8.81–8.83.

[203] Makeen (2000) p 199, n 112 makes the point that advocates of the emission theory do not agree on whether it is the country of actual emission (ie, place where the program is emitted towards the satellite) or the country of the headquarters of the broadcasting organisation.

broadcast signal.[204] By contrast, the 'communication theory'[205] considers that 'broadcasting' covers the whole process of transmission and potential reception to the public. In other words, it includes both the emission stage (upleg towards the satellite) and the reception stage (downleg towards the footprint of the satellite). According to the 'communication theory', the applicable law is both the law of the country of emission *and* the law of the country/countries of reception.[206] In fact, the 'communication theory' was refined to mean that generally the law of the country of emission would be the sole applicable law, on condition that it granted the exclusive right of broadcasting. However, where the country of emission did not provide such an exclusive right or provided for a compulsory licence in relation to broadcasting then the laws of the countries of reception would become relevant.[207] In relation to Article 11*bis*(1) of the Berne Convention, WIPO has expressed a preference for the 'communication theory' over the 'emission theory', however, Berne Union members are free to follow either approach.[208]

Commentators have attempted to use the 'emission theory' and 'communication theory' to determine the applicable law in relation to the new right of making available to the public. As Makeen has emphasised in relation to DBS, this only arises in relation to network communications where the applicable law is determined by the *lex loci delicti*.

Following an emission theory, the sole applicable law in the context of the making available right would be the law of the country from which the interactive transmission originates. However, it is not immediately clear which is the country from which the interactive transmission originates. It could be the place from which material is transmitted or uploaded to an Internet server or is provided for on-line transmission to an end user ('place of upload') or it could be the place where the Internet server hosting the material is located ('place of server').[209] The problem with nominating the place of server as the point of emission is that not every act of making available to the public involves an Internet server. For example, distributing material via a mailing list or peer-to-peer model does not involve storing material on a server.[210] Another difficulty with attempting to apply the emission theory to the act of making available to the public is that, unlike satellite

---

[204] Makeen (2000) p 199.

[205] As Makeen (2000) pp 194–96 explains, the communication theory evolved from the 'Bogsch Theory'.

[206] Makeen (2000) p 195. Makeen (2000) p 195 also highlights the key difference between the 'Bogsch Theory' and 'Communication Theory' which is that under the former the law of the country of emission was ignored whereas under the latter 'the law of the country of emission as well as that of each country covered by the footprint should be applicable.'

[207] Makeen (2000) pp 195–96.

[208] Ricketson (1987) para 8.83. On the merits of each theory see Makeen (2000) pp 199–203.

[209] Sterling (2003) p 396; L Bently and B Sherman, *Intellectual Property Law*, 2nd edn, (OUP, Oxford, 2004) 145 describe these two possibilities.

[210] For details of peer-to-peer technology see A Oram, (ed), *Peer-to-Peer: Harnessing the Benefits of a Disruptive Technology* (O'Reilly, Sebastopol, 2001).

broadcasting, it is not always straightforward to identify the point of initial transmission since the material may be uploaded from several places or stored on different servers.[211] Given that one of the main benefits of the emission theory (in the context of broadcasting) is said to be its practicality, that benefit seems to be lacking in the context of the right of making available to the public. Further, there is the concern that Internet servers may be relocated to places where copyright laws are weak, or the initial upload may be made in a place where copyright laws are weak. Finally, Ficsor argues that the emission theory approach 'would contradict the concept of "communication to the public" '.[212]

There is support for a 'communication theory' approach adapted to the situation of on-demand transmissions.[213] There appear to be two possibilities. First, the sole applicable law could be the laws of the countries where the work may be accessed or is accessed (ie, countries of reception).[214] Second, the applicable law could be the law of the country of emission (whether place of upload or place of server) *and* the laws of the countries of reception. In this second situation, it would only be necessary to determine the applicable law according to the laws of the countries of reception where the country of emission does not provide for the right of making available to the public.

The question of how to determine the applicable law (according to the *lex loci delicti*) in the context of the right of making available to the public has not yet been resolved. It is argued that the better view is to follow a communication theory approach, specifically the second situation described above (which is almost an exact analogy to the communication theory in the broadcasting context). This is for two reasons. First, the communication theory approach has fewer flaws than the emission theory approach. Second, the communication theory approach is more consistent with the notion of *making available to the public.*

2. European Context

Apart from seeking to harmonise certain substantive aspects of copyright law to prevent distortion of the internal market,[215] the Information Society Directive seeks to implement a number of the new international obligations under WCT and WPPT.[216] Article 8 WCT and Articles 10 and 14 WPPT are implemented by Article 3 of the Information Society Directive which provides:

---

[211] Sterling (2003) p 395 argues 'that it is not practical or logically sound to apply the "emission theory" in this context, since the transmission system of the Internet, involving as it does multiple transmission points, is entirely different from the satellite broadcast transmission system, which basically involves an identifiable transmission point.'

[212] Ficsor (2002) pp 508–9.

[213] See Ficsor (2002) pp 508–9; Sterling (2003) para 9.33.

[214] For this formulation see Sterling (2003) p 396.

[215] Recital 2, Information Society Directive.

[216] Recital 15, Information Society Directive.

(1) Member States shall provide authors with the exclusive right to authorise or prohibit any communication to the public of their works, by wire or wireless means, including the making available to the public of their works in such a way that members of the public may access them from a place and at a time individually chosen by them.

(2) Member States shall provide for the exclusive right to authorise or prohibit the making available to the public, by wire or wireless means, in such a way that members of the public may access them from a place and at a time individually chosen by them;

   (a) For performers, of fixations of their performances;
   (b) For phonogram producers, of their phonograms;
   (c) For the producers of the first fixations of films, of the original and copies of their films;
   (d) For broadcasting organisations, of fixations of their broadcasts, whether these broadcasts are transmitted by wire or over the air, including by cable or satellite.

(3) The rights referred to in paragraphs 1 and 2 shall not be exhausted by any act of communication to the public or making available to the public as set out in this Article.

Article 3 of the Information Society Directive ensures that all rightholders will have an exclusive *right to make available to the public* copyright works or subject matter by way of interactive on-demand transmissions, which are 'characterised by the fact that members of the public may access them from a place and at a time individually chosen by them'.[217] Authors of traditional works,[218] however, will acquire this right as part of the right of communication to the public, which right is to be:

> ... understood in a broad sense covering all communication to the public not present at the place where the communication originates . . . [and] should cover any such transmission or retransmission of a work to the public by wire or wireless means, including broadcasting.[219]

Article 3 of the Information Society Directive, like the WIPO Treaties whose obligations it seeks to implement, does not address *where* the act of making available takes place, thus leaving Member States to determine this issue via national law. The above discussion of this issue (under 'International context') is equally applicable here. In terms of where *broadcasting* takes place, guidance is provided

---

[217] Recital 25, Information Society Directive.

[218] This does not include computer programs or databases: see Art 1(2) Information Society Directive. However, for databases, this would be covered by Article 5(d), Database Directive and, by a wide interpretation of Article 4(c), Software Directive, which refers to 'any form' of distribution to the public for computer programs. However, the Commission in its Working Paper has suggested that the applicability of a right of communication to the public to computer programs be clarified (para 2.2.1.2).

[219] Recital 23, Information Society Directive.

by the Satellite Directive[220] which mandates the emission theory in relation to satellite broadcasts.[221] This is made clear by Article 1(2)(b) of the Satellite Directive:

> The act of communication to the public by satellite occurs solely in the Member State where, under the control and responsibility of the broadcasting organisation, the pro-gramme-carrying signals are introduced into an uninterrupted chain of communication leading to the satellite and down towards the earth.[222]

Thus, Members States are obliged to treat satellite broadcasts originating *within* the European Union as occurring in the country of uplink. To avoid forum shop-ping, 'the Directive required member states to provide neighbouring right holders with a strong set of rights.'[223] For other broadcasts, Member States are free to apply either the emission theory or the communication theory.

Recital 27 to the Information Society Directive seeks to clarify the ambit of the right of communication to the public in relation to service providers in terms sim-ilar to those contained in the Agreed Statement concerning Article 8 of the WCT. Recital 27 states:

> The mere provision of physical facilities for enabling or making a communication does not in itself amount to an act of communication to the public within the meaning of this Directive.

The comments made above in relation to the Agreed Statement are equally applic-able to the above recital.

Article 14 of the E-Commerce Directive (discussed above under 'Reproduction') is more likely to provide an exemption for service providers in relation to the right of communication to the public. Article 14 of the E-Commerce Directive provides that a service provider will not be held liable (other than for an injunction) for information *stored* at the request of a recipient of an information society service.[224] This is conditional on the service provider not having actual knowledge or, in the case of civil liability, constructive knowledge, of illegal information or activity, or

---

[220] Makeen (2000) p 216 comments: 'One of the main reasons behind enacting the Cable and Satellite Directive was to settle the legal uncertainty that surrounded the applicable law issue, which hindered the promotion of European cross-border satellite broadcasting.'

[221] Art 1(2)(a) states: 'For the purpose of this Directive, "communication to the public by satellite" means the act of introducing, under the control and responsibility of the broadcasting organisation, the programme-carrying signals intended for reception by the public into an uninterrupted chain of com-munication leading to the satellite and down towards the earth.' Makeen (2000) p 217 explains that '[t]he adopting of the Emission Theory stemmed not from a common belief among member states that it was legally sounder than the Bogsch or the Communication Theory, but because it was more suitable for a common market; it avoids the cumulative application of several national laws to one single act of broadcasting' (footnotes omitted).

[222] See also recital 14, Satellite and Cable Directive.

[223] Makeen (2000) p 217.

[224] This is provided the recipient of the service is not acting under the authority or the control of the service provider: see Article 14(2), E-Commerce Directive.

where such knowledge is obtained, acting expeditiously to remove or disable access to the information. This potentially exempts ISPs from infringing the right of communication to the public where they permanently store (or 'host') material for third parties.

3. UK Context

The UK appears to have successfully implemented Article 3 of the Information Society Directive.[225] According to section 20(1) the new right of communication to the public applies to all categories of works, with the exception of typographical arrangements.[226] The scope of this right is indicated in section 20(2), which provides:

> (2) References in this Part to communication to the public are to *communication to the public by electronic transmission*, and in relation to a work include—
>
> (a) the *broadcasting* of the work;
> (b) the *making available to the public* of the work by electronic transmission in such a way that members of the public may access it from a place and at a time individually chosen by them. (Emphasis supplied)

Thus, the right of communication to the public *includes* but is not restricted to *broadcasting* and *making available to the public*. As discussed in ch 3, 'broadcasting' refers to wire or wireless transmission of visual images, sounds or other information, *excluding internet transmissions*, except of a limited kind akin to traditional broadcasting. The right of *making available to the public* will therefore be relevant to on-demand and Internet transmissions. As discussed above, this will embrace websites that offer copyright works for download by Internet users, along with the distribution of works via electronic mailing lists or via peer-to-peer networks, such as Grokster or KaZaa.

In terms of *where* the right of communication to the public takes place, section 6(4) provides guidance only in respect of satellite broadcasting (and thus implements Article 1(2)(b) of the Satellite Directive discussed above). Section 6(4) designates that a wireless broadcast is made from the place 'where, under the control and responsibility of the person making the broadcast, the programme-carrying signals are introduced into an uninterrupted chain of communication (including, in the case of a satellite transmission, the chain leading to the satellite and down towards the earth)'. Section 6(4) is subject to the safeguard provision section 6A which applies where the place from which a satellite broadcast is made is located in a country outside the EEA and the law of that country fails to provide a

---

[225] This was by no means an easy exercise for the legislative draftsmen: contrast the proposed ss 6 and 20, CDPA in the Consultation Paper with the Copyright Regulations as finally adopted.
[226] See s 20(1), CDPA.

minimal level of protection. No guidance is provided in respect of communication to the public *other* than satellite broadcasting and, in particular, in relation to making available to the public. It has been argued that the fact that the emission theory applies to satellite broadcasts does not preclude the communication theory being applied to making available to the public in section 20, CDPA.[227] As was argued above, it is preferable to adopt a 'communication theory' approach to Internet transmissions. This means that the law of the country of emission *and* the law of the country/countries of reception are applicable.

In respect of liability of service providers for infringing communications to the public, regulation 19 of the E-Commerce Regulations will be relevant, since it implements quasi-literally Article 14 of the E-Commerce Directive (discussed above). However, this will not preclude a court from granting an injunction against a service provider. This is emphasised also by sections 97A and 191JA of the CDPA. These sections respectively provide that the Court shall have the power to grant an injunction against a service provider, where it has *actual knowledge* of another person using its service to infringe copyright or a performer's property right.

Sui Generis Database Right

Chapter 3 examined whether multimedia works would qualify for protection as *sui generis* databases. It was argued that multimedia works that feature dynamic user interfaces or which display their contents in a highly interrelated and integrated way will have difficulty satisfying the definition of 'database'. Whereas, reference type multimedia works are far more likely to fall within the definition of 'database'. This section explores the scope of the rights available under the *sui generis* regime, in order to assess the effectiveness of protecting multimedia works as databases.

1. Extraction and Re-utilisation

Article 7(1) of the Database Directive provides the maker of a database with the right to prevent extraction or re-utilisation of the whole or of a substantial part of the contents of the database[228] and, according to Article 7(5), the right to prevent repeated and systematic extraction and/or re-utilisation of insubstantial parts of the database contents.[229]

---

[227] Cook and Brazell (2004) para 4.52.
[228] Implemented in the UK by reg 16(1), Database Regulations.
[229] Implemented in the UK by reg 16(2), Database Regulations.

Article 7(2)(a) of the Database Directive defines 'extraction' to mean:

> the permanent or temporary transfer of all or a substantial part of the contents of a database to another medium *by any means or in any form* (emphasis supplied).[230]

Article 7(2)(b) of the Database Directive defines 're-utilisation' to mean:

> *Any form of making available to the public* all or a substantial part of the contents of a database by the distribution of copies, by renting, by on-line or other forms of transmission. The first sale of a copy of a database within the Community be the rightholder or with his consent shall exhaust the right to control resale of that copy within the Community (emphasis supplied).[231]

The meaning of 'extraction' and 're-utilisation' were the subject of references in *British Horseracing v William Hill* ('*British Horseracing*').[232] In delivering its judgment, the ECJ in *British Horseracing* emphasised that the terms 'extraction' and 're-utilisation' must be interpreted in the light of the objective of the Database Directive, which is to 'afford protection to the maker of the database and guarantee a return on his investment in the creation and maintenance of the database.'[233] The Court also noted that the language used to define extraction ('by any means or in any form') and re-utilisation ('any form of making available to the public') indicates that these concepts are to be given a wide definition.[234] The ECJ concluded:

> In the light of the objective pursued by the directive, those terms must therefore be interpreted as referring to any act of appropriating and making available to the public, without the consent of the maker of the database, the results of his investment, thus depriving him of revenue which should have enabled him to redeem the cost of the investment.[235]

Advocate General Stix-Hackl observed that the reference to a 'substantial part' in the definition of the concepts of extraction and re-utilisation highlighted an error in the structure of the Database Directive. This is because Article 7(2) unnecessarily repeats the requirement of 'whole or substantial part' which is contained in

---

[230] See reg 12(1), Database Regulations.

[231] Above.

[232] C–203/02, *British Horseracing Board Ltd v William Hill Organization Ltd* (Grand Chamber, 9 November 2004) ('*BHB* (ECJ)'), questions 7–9.

[233] *BHB* (ECJ) para 46. See also para 45: '[The Directive] is intended to protect the maker of the database against "acts by the user which go beyond [the] legitimate rights and thereby harm the investment" of the maker, as indicated in the 42nd recital of the preamble to the directive.'

[234] *BHB* (ECJ) para 51. Commentators have also expressed the view that the re-utilisation right is broadly defined and covers various activities, including on-line transmission and distribution or renting of copies of databases. See MJ Davison, *The Legal Protection of Databases* (CUP, Cambridge, 2003) 88; CD Freedman, 'Should Canada Enact a New *Sui Generis* Database Right?' (2002) 13 *Fordham Intellectual Property Media & Entertainment L J* 35, 94; FW Grosheide, 'Database Protection—The European Way' (2002) 8 *Washington U J of L & Pol'y* 39, 56; L Kaye, 'The Proposed EU Directive for the Legal Protection of Databases: A Cornerstone of the Information Society' [1995] *EIPR* 583, 586.

[235] *BHB* (ECJ) para 51. It is irrelevant that the act of extraction or re-utilisation is to create a competing database or is for a commercial or non-commercial purpose: see *BHB* (ECJ) paras 47 and 48.

Article 7(1). Further, Article 7(2) contradicts Article 7(5), since the latter provision deals with the prohibited activities in relation to *insubstantial* parts.[236] The ECJ agreed with the Advocate General's observation that the reference to the substantial nature of the extracted or re-utilised part in Article 7(2) 'does not concern the definition of those concepts as such but must be understood to refer to one of the conditions for the application of the *sui generis* right laid down by Article 7(1) of the directive.'[237]

The Court of Appeal in *British Horseracing* referred questions to the ECJ on whether extraction includes *indirect* transfer of the database contents and whether re-utilisation includes making available to the public the contents of the database *indirectly* from the database.[238] These questions arose because the defendant, William Hill, had obtained the racing fixtures data *indirectly* via newspapers published the day before the race and from one of BHB's licensed distributors.

Advocate General Stix-Hackl expressed the view that extraction is limited to the transfer of contents *directly* from the database to another medium.[239] This was because the prohibition of extraction 'presupposes knowledge of the database'[240] and must not be 'so widely construed as also to cover indirect transfer.'[241] The Advocate General's primary reason for adopting this interpretation was to avoid the risk of protecting data *per se*.[242] The same risk arises in relation to re-utilization.[243] Yet the Advocate General concluded that *re-utilisation* may occur via *indirect* means, particularly since the words 'any form' in Article 7(2)(b) indicate that re-utilisation is to be construed widely.[244]

According to the ECJ, limiting the database right to *direct* extraction and re-utilisation would expose the maker of the database to the risk of unauthorised copying from a copy of the database.[245] Further, unauthorised acts of extraction

---

[236] C–203/02, *British Horseracing Board v William Hill*, Opinion of the Advocate General delivered on 8 June 2004 ('*BHB* (Opinion)') para 90.

[237] *BHB* (ECJ) para 50.

[238] See *BHB* question 7: 'Is "extraction" in Article 7 of the directive limited to the transfer of the contents of the database directly from the database to another medium, or does it also include the transfer of works, data or other materials, which are derived indirectly from the database, without having direct access to the database?' See also *BHB* question 8: 'Is "re-utilisation" in Article 7 of the directive limited to the making available to the public of the contents of the database directly from the database, or does it also include the making available to the public of works, data or other materials which are derived indirectly from the database, without having direct access to the database?' A similar question was referred in C–338/02, *Fixtures Marketing Ltd v Svenska Spel AB* (question 4), however, the ECJ did not feel the need to reply to this question, given its finding that the football fixture list did not reflect substantial investment in obtaining, presentation or verification of the contents in the database: see C–338/02, *Fixtures Marketing Ltd v Svenska Spel AB*, (Grand Chamber, 9 November 2004) ('*Svenska* (ECJ)').

[239] *BHB* (Opinion) para 157.

[240] Above, at para 96.

[241] Above, at para 100.

[242] Above, at para 94.

[243] Rees and Chalton (1998), 22.

[244] *BHB* (Opinion) para 110.

[245] *BHB* (ECJ) para 52.

or re-utilisation carried out indirectly by third parties are equally likely to harm the investment of the database maker as such acts carried out directly from the database. Against the background that the concepts of 'extraction' and 're-utilisation' should be construed widely, the ECJ ruled that those terms *do not imply direct access* to the database concerned.[246] This interpretation of extraction and re-utilisation should be welcomed since it is consistent with the language and objective of the Database Directive. Further, it avoids the easy circumvention of the prohibition in Article 7(1).[247] However, to minimise the risk of protecting data *per se,* a careful approach to what constitutes a 'substantial part' of the database contents must be taken. The ECJ has adopted such an approach, which is discussed in the following section.

The ECJ stressed that the protection granted by extraction and re-utilisation does not cover *consultation of a database* where the maker of a database has made the contents of the database available to the public or authorised a third party to re-utilise the contents of the database, ie, to distribute it to the public.[248] This aspect of the ECJ's judgment minimises the risk that the right of extraction will operate as an electronic access right.[249] However, the fact that the contents of a database were made accessible to the public by its maker or with his consent does not exhaust the *sui generis* right. The maker will still retain the right to prevent acts of extraction and/or re-utilisation of the whole or a substantial part of the contents of a database. According to the ECJ, this view is confirmed in relation to the extraction right by recital 44 which states: 'when on-screen display of the contents of a database necessitates the permanent or temporary transfer of all or a substantial part of such contents to another medium, that act should be subject to authorisation by the rightholder.' In relation to the re-utilisation right this view is confirmed by recital 43 which provides that 'in the case of on-line transmission, the right to prohibit re-utilisation is not exhausted either as regards the database or as regards a material copy of the database or of part thereof made by the addressee of the transmission with the consent of the rightholder.' Thus, to the question referred: 'is "re-utilisation" in Article 7 of the directive limited to the first making available to the public of the contents of the database?', the ECJ firmly answered 'no'.[250] This amounts to a sensible interpretation of Article 7(2) since it

[246] Above, at paras 53 and 67.

[247] As with copyright law, the innocence of an infringing party may be accommodated by disentitling the claimant to damages—see eg, reg 23, Database Regulations and s 97, CDPA.

[248] *BHB* (ECJ) paras 54–56.

[249] Several commentators had expressed the fear that running an electronic database would involve extraction and thus have the potential to operate as an electronic access right: see Davison (2003) p 97; Grosheide (2002) p 56; Kaye (1995) p 585; M Powell, 'The European Union's Database Directive: An International Antidote to the Side Effects of *Feist*?' (1997) 20 *Fordham Intl L J* 1215, 1239.

[250] Advocate General Stix-Hackl also took the view that re-utilisation is not limited to first making available to the public of the contents of the database because the rules on exhaustion only apply to physical objects and not through other, non-tangible means of on-line transmission: *BHB* (Opinion) paras 109, 157.

avoids restricting the scope of the prohibitions to a level that would provide little protection for database makers.

2. Substantial Part of the Contents of a Database

Article 7(1) of the Database Directive stipulates that for an unauthorised extraction or re-utilisation to be infringing, it must relate to *all*[251] or a *substantial* part of the contents of a database. Substantiality is to be evaluated quantitatively or qualitatively or via a combination of the two.[252] The Court of Appeal in *British Horseracing* referred questions to the ECJ about the meaning of 'a substantial part, evaluated qualitatively and/or quantitatively, of the contents of that database'.[253]

The ECJ ruled that the expression 'substantial part, evaluated quantitatively' means 'the volume of data extracted from the database and/or re-utilised and must be assessed in relation to the total volume of the contents of the database'.[254] In relation to the expression 'substantial part, evaluated qualitatively', the ECJ ruled that this 'refers to the scale of the investment in the obtaining, verification or presentation of the contents of the subject of the act of extraction and/or re-utilisation, regardless of whether that subject represents quantitatively substantial part of the general contents of the protected database.'[255] Thus, a quantitatively negligible part of the contents of the database could still amount to a substantial part if that part reflected, 'in terms of obtaining, verification or presentation, significant human, technical or financial investment.'[256] An 'insubstantial part', as referred to in Article 7(5), is a part which does not fulfil the definition of a substantial part, evaluated both quantitatively and qualitatively.[257]

Advocate General Stix-Hackl opined that a substantial part evaluated qualitatively should be interpreted as meaning that the technical or economic value of the affected part is relevant.[258] Assessing the economic value of an affected part would usually be measured by the drop in demand 'caused by the fact that the affected part is not extracted or re-utilised under market conditions, but in some other

---

[251] *Unauthorised Reproduction of Telephone Directories on CD-Rom* [2002] ECDR 3 (BGH) is an example of where the database right was infringed by extracting the entire contents of the database, ie, copying the complete subscriber details from the claimant's telephone directories.

[252] See Article 7(1), Database Directive. Freedman (2002) p 97 criticises the Database Directive for providing little guidance on what constitutes a substantial part.

[253] See questions 4 and 6, as set out in *BHB* (ECJ) para 22. See also *Svenska* (ECJ) para 18, question 3; and C–46/02, *Fixtures Marketing Ltd v OY Veikkaus Ab*, (Grand Chamber, 9 November 2004) ('*Veikkaus* (ECJ)') para 19, question 3. However, the ECJ in *Svenska* and *Veikkaus* did not feel it necessary to reply to these questions.

[254] *BHB* (ECJ) paras 70 and 82.

[255] Above, at paras 71, 82.

[256] Above, at para 71.

[257] Above, at para 73.

[258] *BHB* (Opinion) paras 77, 157.

way.'[259] It could also be measured according to what the wrongdoer has saved.[260] In the light of the objective of the Database Directive to protect investment, the investment of the maker would have to be taken into account (such as the cost of obtaining data).[261] However, the question of whether there is a 'substantial' part should not be determined by whether there is significant detriment to the database maker.[262]

The ECJ rejected as a relevant criterion the intrinsic value of the materials affected by the act of extraction or re-utilisation.[263] The reason for doing so was that the database right does not give rise to a new right in the works, data or materials themselves.[264] Instead, the Court focussed on the scale of the investment in obtaining, verification or presentation of the database contents as the sole criterion. The approach adopted by the ECJ is preferable to that suggested by the Advocate General since it relates more directly with the objective of the Database Directive. Thus, even if there is a low threshold of substantial investment to qualify for the database right, the level of investment will be critical to determining whether or not infringement occurs. This goes a considerable way to ensuring that the *sui generis* scheme is not an 'easy to protect/easy to infringe' model.

The ECJ applied its reasoning to the facts and indicated that William Hill had *not* extracted and re-utilised a substantial part of the BHB database. The information displayed by William Hill on its Internet betting website concerned details of the race: the names of the horses running in the race concerned, the date, time and name of the race and the name of the racecourse.[265] As the data represented only a very small proportion of the whole of the BHB database, the ECJ held that it did not constitute a substantial part, evaluated quantitatively, of the contents of the BHB database.[266] In terms of assessing whether the data constituted a substantial part, evaluated *qualitatively*, the intrinsic value of the data had to be ignored. Thus, it was irrelevant that the data extracted and re-utilised by William Hill was essential to the organisation of the horse races organised by BHB and others.[267] The

---

[259] Above, at para 78.

[260] Above, at para 78. In *British Horseracing Board v William Hill* [2001] CMLR 12 ('*BHB* (ChD)'), Laddie J at 235 commented that 'the significance of the information to the alleged infringer may throw light on whether it is an important or significant part of the database'. In *Sa Prline v SA Communication & Sales and Sarl News Invest* [2002] ECDR 2 (Tribunal de Commerce De Nanterre), although the extractions were quantitatively small, they were qualitatively substantial because the extractions were used by a competitor and enabled the competitor to expand its database.

[261] *BHB* (Opinion) paras 79–80.

[262] Above, at para 82.

[263] This interpretation deals with the concern of Davison (2003) at 89–90 that 'qualitative could mean one work, piece of data or other material that is regarded as extremely useful or valuable' and thereby create an overlap in the copyright in the single item contained in the database and the *sui generis* right in the contents of the database.

[264] *BHB* (ECJ) para 72.

[265] Above, at paras 19 and 75.

[266] Above, at para 74.

[267] Above, at para 78.

issue was whether the human, technical and financial efforts put in by the maker of the database in obtaining, verifying and presenting the extracted and/or re-utilised data constituted a substantial investment.[268] Resources used in the creation of the data could not be taken into account, since 'obtaining' was interpreted by the ECJ to refer to collection, and not creation, of materials.[269] The ECJ concluded:

> The resources deployed by BHB to establish, for the purposes of organising horse races, the date, the time, the place and/or name of the race, and the horses running in it, represent an *investment in the creation of materials* contained in the BHB database. Consequently, and if, as the order for reference appears to indicate, *the materials extracted and re-utilised by William Hill did not require BHB and Others to put in investment independent of the resources required for their creation*, it must be held that those materials do not represent a substantial part, in qualitative terms, of the BHB database.[270] (Emphasis supplied)

The Advocate General did not address whether the 'contents' of the database which are extracted or re-utilised must reflect the maker's investment. In contrast, the ECJ clearly ruled that the *type of investment reflected in the contents that are extracted or re-utilised* will be highly relevant to determining whether they constitute a substantial part, qualitatively speaking.[271] According to the ECJ, William Hill had not extracted or re-utilised contents from the BHB database which reflected substantial investment in obtaining, verifying or presenting and therefore had not infringed BHB's database right.

In *British Horseracing* the defendant also argued that its acts did not infringe the database right because they had not made use of the arrangement of the contents of the database or the way in which the maker had rendered the contents individually accessible. That is, the defendant had not extracted or re-utilised the *form* or *structure* (or, to put it another way, the presentation of the contents) of the database. Laddie J, at first instance, dismissed this argument as erroneous. To restrict the concept of infringement in this way would confuse subsistence requirements with the scope of protection.[272] Further, this interpretation would confuse copyright and database right and run counter to the clear purpose of the database right

---

[268] Above, at para 76.

[269] Above, at para 79.

[270] Above, at para 80.

[271] See above, at para 82: 'The expression "substantial part, evaluated qualitatively . . . of the contents of [a] database" refers to the scale of the investment in the obtaining, verification or presentation of the contents of the subject of the act of extraction and/or re-utilisation, regardless of whether that subject represents a quantitatively substantial part of the general contents of the protected database.' See also *BHB* (ChD), where Laddie J at 236 seemed to adopt a similar approach: 'William Hill is relying on and taking advantage of the completeness and accuracy of the information taken from the RDF, in other words the product of BHB's investment in obtaining and verifying that data. This is a substantial part of the contents.'

[272] *BHB* (ChD), 233.

to protect investment in databases.[273] The Court of Appeal referred a question to the ECJ on this issue:

(1) May either of the expressions:

—'substantial part of the contents of the database'; or
—'insubstantial parts of the contents of the database'

in Article 7 of the directive include works, data or other materials derived from the database but which do not have the same systematic or methodical arrangement of and individual accessibility as those to be found in the database?[274]

Advocate General Stix-Hackl concluded that: 'the view that the Directive does not protect data which are compiled in an altered or differently structured way is fundamentally mistaken.'[275] She reasoned that Article 7, by omitting reference to systematic or methodical arrangement or individually accessibility, makes it clear that such a requirement was not intended. Further, such a requirement would be contrary to the purpose of the Database Directive since it would mean that Article 7 could be easily circumvented by rearrangement of the contents of the database.[276] The ECJ, however, did not consider it necessary to reply to this question, in the light of its conclusion that a substantial part of the contents of the BHB database had not been extracted or re-utilised by William Hill.[277] However, the ruling of the ECJ on the meaning of 'substantial part, evaluated qualitatively . . . of the contents of [a] database' indicates how this question should be answered. The systematic and methodical arrangement and individual accessibility of the contents of the database relates to the *presentation* of the contents.[278] Thus, infringement would arise where substantial investment in presentation of the contents has occurred and the contents reflecting the investment in presentation have been extracted or re-utilised. However, infringement would not arise if the presentation of the contents was not copied and there was no relevant substantial investment in the obtaining or verification of the database contents.

---

[273] *BHB* (ChD), 234.

[274] See also C–444/02, *Fixtures Marketing Ltd v Organismos Prognostikon Agnon Podosfairou (OPAP)*. (Grand Chamber, 9 November 2004) ('*OPAP* (ECJ)') para 10, question 3: 'How exactly is the database right infringed and is it protected in the event of rearrangement of the contents of the database?' However, in the light of the ECJ's ruling on the first two questions referred (on the definition of database and whether a football fixture list enjoys protection as a database), the Court found it unnecessary to reply to the third question.

[275] *BHB* (Opinion) para 70.

[276] Above, at paras 62–70.

[277] *BHB* (ECJ) para 81: 'The change made by the person making the extraction and re-utilisation to the arrangement or the conditions of individual accessibility of the data affected by that act cannot, in any event, have the effect of transforming a part of the contents of the database at issue which is not substantial into a substantial part.'

[278] See *Svenska* (ECJ) para 27; *OPAP* (ECJ) para 43; and *Veikkaus* (ECJ) para 37.

3. Scope of Article 7(5)

The Court of Appeal in *British Horseracing* referred questions to the ECJ on the scope of Article 7(5) of the Database Directive, which prohibits:

> The repeated and systematic extraction and/or re-utilisation of insubstantial parts of the contents of the database implying acts which conflict with a normal exploitation of that database or which unreasonably prejudice the legitimate interests of the maker of the database.

The Court of Appeal asked what was meant by 'insubstantial parts of the database'.[279] It also asked what was meant by 'acts which conflict with a normal exploitation of that database or unreasonably prejudice the legitimate interests of the maker of the database' and whether the facts stated in the reference were capable of amounting to such acts.[280] On the question of what constitutes an *insubstantial part*, the ECJ ruled (following the Advocate General) that this is any part which does not fulfil the definition of a substantial part, evaluated both quantitatively and qualitatively.[281]

The ECJ also stated that Article 7(5) is an exception to the general rule set out in Article 8(1) that a lawful user of a database, which has been made available to the public by the database maker, has the right to extract and/or re-utilise insubstantial parts of the database contents. The Court referred to the Common Position (EC) No 20/95 of the Council[282] in which the Council explained in its reasons that Article 7(5) introduced a 'safeguard clause'.[283] The ECJ went on to interpret Article 7(5) narrowly, as a provision designed to prevent circumvention of the prohibition in Article 7(1) of the Directive. The objective of Article 7(5) is 'to prevent repeated and systematic extractions and/or re-utilisations of insubstantial parts of the contents of a database, *the cumulative effect* of which would be to seriously prejudice the investment made by the maker of the database *just as the extractions and/or re-utilisations referred to in Article 7(1) of the directive would.'*[284] Thus, the ECJ elaborates:

> 'acts which conflict with a normal exploitation of [a] database or which unreasonably prejudice the legitimate interests of the maker of the database' refer to unauthorised actions *for the purpose of reconstituting, through the cumulative effect of acts of extraction,*

---

[279] *BHB* (ECJ) para 22, questions 5 and 6.

[280] See *BHB* (ECJ) para 22 question 10. See also *Svenska* (ECJ) para 18, question 5: 'How should the terms "normal exploitation" and "unreasonably prejudice" in Article 7(5) be interpreted?' However, the ECJ in *Svenska* did not consider it necessary to reply to this question: *Svenska* (ECJ) para 38.

[281] *BHB* (ECJ) para 82.

[282] Adopted on 10 July 1995 (OJ 1995 C288, p14).

[283] Common Position (EC) no 20/95 of the Council adopted on 10 July 1995 (OJ 1995 C288, p 14) at p 26.

[284] *BHB* (ECJ) para 86 (emphasis supplied).

the whole or a substantial part of the contents of a database protected by the *sui generis* right and/or of *making available to the public, through the cumulative effect of acts of re-utilisation, the whole or a substantial part of the contents of such a database,* which thus seriously prejudice the investment made by the maker of the database.[285] (Emphasis supplied)

The ECJ applied its ruling to the facts and held that William Hill's acts of extraction and re-utilisation were repeated and systematic because they were carried out each time a race was held.[286] However, the Court held that the acts were not intended to circumvent Article 7(1) of the Directive. The cumulative effect of William Hill's acts 'would not reconstitute and make available to the public the whole or a substantial part of the contents of the BHB database and thereby seriously prejudice the investment made by BHB in the creation of that database.'[287]

The ECJ appears to require that each insubstantial taking of the contents is retained, as opposed to deleted or discarded. This is suggested by their ruling that the cumulative effect of insubstantial extractions or re-utilisations is to *reconstitute* the whole or a substantial part of the contents of the database. The use of the word 'reconstitute' suggests that through cumulative insubstantial takings, the alleged infringer will have extracted or re-utilised a substantial part of the contents of the database. This interpretation of 'reconstitute' would result in Article 7(5) having an extremely limited application. It would not, for example, cover the scenario in *Svenska* or *Veikkaus* where the data about football fixtures was used on a weekly basis and then (presumably) deleted because it was no longer relevant. Thus, it is argued that the ECJ must have intended 'reconstitute' to mean that if the series of insubstantial extractions or re-utilisations are taken together, they would reflect a substantial part of the database contents, regardless of whether all of those insubstantial takings are still retained or being used.

Conclusion

In summary, the rights of 'extraction' and 're-utilisation' are broad in scope. Those acts must be carried out in relation to a 'substantial part' of the database contents. What is 'substantial' will not be judged by the value of the parts taken, but rather the level of investment reflected in the contents taken and/or re-used. This interpretation of what can constitute a *substantial part* is in keeping with the purpose of the Database Directive to protect the investment of the maker and ensures that the database right provides strong, but not overreaching protection. It seems fair to conclude that for those multimedia works that qualify as a *sui generis* database they will be well protected.

---

[285] Above, at para 89.
[286] Above, at para 90.
[287] Above, at para 91.

Hyperlinking and Framing

For on-line multimedia works, and digital works in general, the question of liability for hyperlinking ('linking') and framing is an important one.[288] This section discusses the potential liability under UK law[289] faced by a person who inserts a hyperlink to, or who frames, a copyright work, without the permission of the copyright owner. Before analysing the copyright (and database right) infringement issues raised by linking and framing, the next section briefly outlines these two activities.

1. Hyperlinking and Framing

A hyperlink ('link') is a staple tool of the on-line environment and has been defined as:

> A programmed link between items of information in different sections of a programme, or in physically different locations within a network. Hyperlinks make it easy for the user to follow cross-references or access glossary definitions, for instance by clicking on the prompt word, which is usually differentiated from normal text by colour or by typographical treatment.[290]

A large number of websites are created by the use of Hypertext Mark Up Language (HTML). A HTML hyperlink is created by using a Hypertext Reference (HREF) command. For example, a hyperlink to the website of the World Intellectual Property Organisation would be created as follows: <A HREF = 'http://www.wipo.int' World Intellectual Property Organisation</A>. The words 'World Intellectual Property Organisation' would appear as text, highlighted and underlined, on the screen. By clicking on the highlighted text, the user's web browser is instructed to send a request for transfer of the files located at the given Universal

---

[288] For a comprehensive analysis of the issues see SE Strasser, *Digital Technologies and Law: Linking and Framing on the World Wide Web* (unpublished D Phil thesis, Bodlean Law Library, Oxford, 2002).

[289] For discussion of liability under UK law see GJH Smith (ed), *Internet Law and Regulation*, 3rd edn (Sweet & Maxwell, London, 2002) 32–40; and Sterling (2003) pp 534–37. For a discussion of liability under US copyright law see WA Effross, 'Withdrawal of the Reference: Rights, Rules, and Remedies for Unwelcomed Web-Linking' (1998) 49 *South Carolina L Rev* 651; M Jackson, 'Linking Copyright To Homepages' (1997) 49 *Federal Communications L J* 731; B Wassom, 'Copyright Implications of "Unconventional Linking" on the World Wide Web: Framing, Deep Linking and Inlining' (1998) 49 *Case Western Reserve L Rev* 181. For a comparison of liability under US copyright law and European copyright law see IJ Garrote, 'Linking and Framing: A Comparative Law Approach' [2002] *EIPR* 184 and under UK and US copyright law see Strasser (2002) ch 3.

[290] W Cotton and R Oliver, *The Cyberspace Lexicon: An Illustrated Dictionary of Terms from Multimedia to Virtual Reality* (Phaidon, London, 1994) 98.

Resource Locator (URL) address,[291] in this example 'http://www.wipo.int'. As with any Internet transmission, the files at the specified URL are transmitted to the requesting party and temporarily stored in the RAM of the user's computer. The same result may be achieved by simply typing the relevant URL directly into a web browser in the 'Location' box.[292] A hyperlink may be used to connect to another part of the same web page, to material hosted on the same server or to material located on any other server.[293] Further, the link may be inserted to the *homepage* of a website (known as 'surface linking') or to the *sub-pages* of a website (known as 'deep linking').[294] Thus, a link to http://www.wipo.int would be to the homepage of WIPO, whereas a link to http://www.wipo.int/treaties/en/ip/berne/index.html would constitute a 'deep link' to a sub-page of the WIPO website at which a copy of the Berne Convention is made available.

It is not only text documents to which a hyperlink may be applied: hyperlinks may also connect to image files. This is done using the HTML IMG command, namely <IMG SRC . . .>, and is known as 'inlining' or 'in-line linking'.[295] The command tells the web browser the URL of the image and instructs the browser to load that image. Thus, when a user browses a web page with an inline link, the graphic is loaded automatically into the page and it may in fact originate from another location on the Internet.[296]

'Framing'[297] has similarities with deep linking, in that it can give the impression that the material that is brought up on the screen is, or is connected to, the

---

[291] Note that URL addresses are expressed in domain names, which domain names substitute for having to remember the IP address of the web page. To find the IP address of the URL, the local name server contacts the root domain name server for the particular Top Level Domain, in above example 'org'. The root domain name server for 'org' then returns the primary name server for 'wipo.org'. The local name server then contacts the primary name server for the IP address of 'www.wipo.org' and the requesting party uses this IP address to request the files stored at that address: see C-H Wu and JD Irwin, *Emerging Multimedia Computer Communication Technologies* (Prentice Hall, New Jersey, 1998) 245–46.

[292] See also Effross (1998) pp 653–54; Jackson (1997) pp 736–37 for a description of hyperlinking.

[293] See Jackson (1997) p 737; and also Smith (1997) p 25.

[294] Wassom (1998) pp 192–93; J Lambrick, 'Protecting Content in an On-Line Environment' (1999) 1(2) *Digital Technology L J* at http://wwwlaw.murdoch.edu.au/dtlj/, para 40.

[295] Wassom (1998) p 193.

[296] Smith (1997) pp 25–26; Wassom (1998) p 193; Jackson (1997) p 737. In *Kelly v Arriba Soft Corp*, 336 F 3d 811(9th Cir, 2003) the US Court of Appeals for the Ninth Circuit at p 816 described in-line linking:

> In-line linking allows one to import a graphic from a source website and incorporate it in one's own website, creating the appearance that the in-lined graphic is a seamless part of the second web page. The in-line link instructs the user's browser to retrieve the linked-to image from the source website and display it on the user's screen, but does so without leaving the linking document. Thus, the linking party can incorporate the linked image into its own content.

One of the issues to be determined at trial is whether in-line linking to full size images constitutes an infringing reproduction and display of the artistic works, which can be excused as a fair use. The defendant, however, obtained summary judgment from the District Court that its use of thumbnail images constituted fair use of the copyright works which was upheld by the Court of Appeals.

[297] See Wassom (1998) pp 191–92 for a description of 'framing'.

original web page in some way. However, framing and deep linking are different processes. Web browsers enable websites to be split into a number of different areas (or frames) and each frame can be displayed on a separate portion of the screen and be made to act independently of the others. The advantage of using frames is that it breaks up large documents into smaller information packets to facilitate transferring, storing and displaying of these documents.[298] It is possible for frames (usually border frames) to be retained even where a user has clicked on a hyperlink and the content located at the URL symbolised by the link is downloaded from another website. This process risks obscuring advertisements and trade marks present on other websites and may create confusion as to the association between the framing website and the framed website.

2. Hyperlinking as Infringement

(a) Surface and Deep Linking

Linking may result in copyright infringement in several ways. If the hyperlink tag itself qualifies as a copyright work, inserting a hyperlink may amount to an infringing reproduction of that work. Infringement may also occur as a result of what follows from clicking on a hyperlink, namely, transmission of copyright works or making temporary copies of such works to enable browsing. Finally, the person who inserts a hyperlink may be liable for authorising the doing of exclusive acts.[299]

The only case in the UK to have dealt with liability for hyperlinking is *Shetland Times v Wills*.[300] In this case, Shetland News engaged in deep linking by linking directly to Shetland Times stories, without first routing users through the home page of the Shetland Times. The hyperlinks which the Shetland News inserted comprised the headlines of the stories. Lord Hamilton, in granting the interim edict in favour of Shetland Times, held that it was at least arguable that the headlines, which formed the hyperlinks, were literary works and were reproduced

---

[298] Morrison (1999); Smith (1997) p 28.

[299] S 16(2), CDPA.

[300] *Shetland Times v Wills* [1997] EMLR 277 ('*Shetland Times*'). Linking has generated more litigation in other jurisdictions, such as the US. See, for example, Case 97–3055 DDP, *Ticketmaster Corp v Microsoft Corp* Complaint, (CD Cal, Filed April 18, 1997); *Intellectual Reserve Inc v Utah Lighthouse Ministry Inc*, 75 F Supp 2d 1290 (D Utah, 1999); *Universal Studios v Corley* 273 F 3d 429 (2nd Cir, 2001); *Kelly v Arriba Soft Corp*, 336 F 3d 811 (9th Cir, 2003); *Ticketmaster Corp v Tickets.com, Inc*, 2003 WL 21406289 (CD Cal, 2003). It has also been considered in various European civil law countries. See, for example, *Koda, NCB, Dansk Artist Forbund and IFPI Danmark v Anders Lauritzen and Jimmy Egebjerg* [2002] ECDR 25 (Court of Appeal, Denmark); *Algemeen Dagblad v Eureka Internetdiensten* [2002] ECDR 1 (District Court, Rotterdam); *Olsson* [2002] 23 *EIPR* 55 (Supreme Court, Sweden); *IFPI Vzw and Polygram Records Nv v Belgacom Skynet Nv* [2002] ECDR 5 (Court of Appeal, Brussels); *Danske Dagblades Forening (DDF) v Newsbooster* [2003] ECDR 5 (City Court, Denmark).

without permission.[301] However, in most situations, and contrary to *Shetland Times,* it is unlikely that hyperlinks will be protected as literary works since they are usually, although not necessarily, short forms of text. As such, they are not capable of affording information or instruction in the form of literary enjoyment,[302] or do not satisfy a *de minimis* test,[303] or lack originality.[304] However, the possibility remains that if a hyperlink is in some stylised form or graphic, it may be an artistic work[305] and reproduction of that artistic work as a hyperlink tag probably would infringe copyright.[306]

As mentioned above, when a user clicks on a hyperlink this triggers the transmission of content located at that URL to the RAM of the user's computer. An important question is whether insertion of the hyperlink constitutes *making available to the public* the copyright works located at the particular URL.[307] Take the following example: assume MP3 files of popular songs that are protected as musical and literary works are stored and available for download from a music website, freely available to all Internet users, called 'Zakstar'. Unless the person in charge of 'Zakstar' obtained permission to upload these songs onto their website, this would constitute an infringing communication to the public, contrary to section 20 of the CDPA. Assume also that a cluster of music aficionados operate their own personal websites and on these websites they include links to interesting

---

[301] *Shetland Times,* 282. Lord Hamilton held that it was arguable that the website was a cable programme within the meaning of section 7 of the CDPA and that hyperlinking infringed copyright in the cable programme service. This aspect of the decision is no longer relevant after the Copyright Regulations deleted section 7, CDPA and amended sections 6 and 20, CDPA. See above ch 3 at pp 80–84.

[302] See for example *Exxon Corporation v Exxon Insurance Consultants International Ltd* [1982] Ch 119, where the word 'Exxon' was held not to be the subject of copyright. See also JP Connolly and S Cameron, 'Fair Dealing in Webbed Links of Shetland Yarns' [1998] 2 *J of Information, L and Technology* at http://elj.warwick.ac.uk/jilt/copright/98_2conn/, paras 4.4.1–4.4.3; and Strasser (2002) pp 57–58.

[303] *Francis Day and Hunter, Ltd v 20th Century Fox Corp, Ltd* [1940] AC 112, 123 where Lord Wright, delivering the opinion of the Privy Council stated: 'in general a title is not by itself a proper subject-matter of copyright. As a rule a title does not involve literary composition and is not sufficiently substantial to justify a claim to protection. That statement does not mean that in particular cases a title may not be on so extensive a scale, and of so important a character, as to be a proper subject of protection against being copied.' In that case, however, the title of a song, 'The Man Who Broke The Bank At Monte Carlo' was held not to be protected as a literary work. See also Strasser (2002) p 58.

[304] Under US copyright law, Jackson (1997) p 742 argues that a hyperlink merely reproduces an URL, which in turn is a fact and not protected by copyright and that, to the extent that a hyperlink includes short forms of expression, titles and names are generally not copyrightable. Note that in *Ticketmaster Corp v Tickets.com, Inc,* 2003 WL 21406289 (CD Cal, 2003), in granting summary judgment to the defendant on, *inter alia,* the copyright claim, the court held at p 5 that: 'A URL is simply an address, open to the public, like the street address of a building, which, if known, can enable the user to reach the building. There is nothing sufficiently original to make the URL a copyrightable item, especially the way it is used . . . There appear to be no cases holding the URLs to be subject to copyright. On principle, they should not be.'

[305] See definition of 'artistic work' in s 4, CDPA.

[306] A Christie, 'Copyright Protection for Web Sites' in A Fitzgerald, *et al* (eds), *Going Digital: Legal Issues for Electronic Commerce, Multimedia and the Internet* (Prospect Media, NSW, 1998) 1, 8.

[307] See Bently and Sherman (2004) p 146.

music sites, including a link to 'Zakstar'. It seems misconceived to say that the links to Zakstar also constitute making available to the public the musical and literary works since it is not the aficionados who have uploaded the MP3 files—all they have done is *referred* other users to where the files may be readily found.[308] In other words, they have provided a form of citation to the copyright works. The ability to cite/hyperlink is a key feature of the way the Internet operates[309] and could also be seen as a fundamental aspect of a user's freedom of expression.[310] Thus, it is submitted that inserting a hyperlink in this manner would *not* and should not constitute making available to the public.

Assume a different scenario, namely, literary works in the form of lecture notes are posted on a college intranet, so that only students of that college are able to access the notes and not the general Internet public. Assume also that someone bypasses the firewalls of the intranet and sets up a link to the lecture notes such that students from other colleges can access the material. Bently and Sherman suggest that inserting this type of hyperlink might constitute making a work available to a *new* public.[311]

Clicking on a hyperlink will result in the information stored at that location being transferred to the RAM of a user's computer. As argued above, such storage will amount to a transient reproduction and thus, *prima facie,* amount to an infringement. However, the person *inserting* the hyperlink cannot be said to carry out the act of reproduction. Rather, it is the *user* who temporarily reproduces the copyright work as a result of clicking on the hyperlink.[312] As such, this is unlikely to amount to an infringing reproduction because of the exemption created by section 28A of the CDPA.[313] In other words, either the reproduction constitutes a transient reproduction which is an integral and essential part of a technological process whose sole purpose is to enable a transmission in a network between third parties by an intermediary *or* it is a lawful use. One means of establishing a lawful use is to imply a licence to browse.[314] In the case of deep linking, the scope of the implied licence to browse would have to include browsing webpages in random

---

[308] *Cf Koda, NCB, Dansk Artist Forbund and IFPI Danmark v Anders Lauritzen and Jimmy Egebjerg* [2002] ECDR 25 (Court of Appeal, Denmark); and *Olsson* (2002) 23 *EIPR* 55 (Supreme Court, Sweden).

[309] Lambrick (1999) para 37, 'linking is the very essence of the World Wide Web'.

[310] DL Burk, 'Proprietary Rights in Hypertext Linkages' [1998] 2 *J of Information, L and Technology* at http://elj.warwick.ac.uk/jilt/intprop/98_2burk/. See also Litman (2001) p 183 who argues: 'the public has always had, and should have, a right to cite. Referring to a copyrighted work without authorization has been and should be legal. Referring to an infringing work is similarly legitimate . . . Posting a hypertext link should be no different.'

[311] Bently and Sherman (2004) p 146.

[312] See also Garrote (2002) p 187.

[313] Discussed above ch 3 at p 114.

[314] Discussed above ch 3 at pp 104–5. See also Gringas (1997) p 190 in respect of a website protected as a computer program. This kind of browsing could also be classified as fair dealing for the purpose of research or private study: see below ch 5 at pp 194–5.

order, as opposed to homepage first followed by subpages. It seems unduly restrictive to suggest that users can only browse if they browse in a particular order, especially since this contradicts the interactive and non-linear nature of websites. Thus, it seems reasonable to accept that if an implied licence to browse exists, this would include browsing web pages non-sequentially.

The possibility of authorising an infringement should also be considered. According to section 16(2) of the CDPA, a person may infringe copyright if they authorise another to do any of the acts restricted by copyright. This is a form of primary, as opposed to contributory liability, however, it is contingent upon another person having carried out an infringing act *within* the UK.[315]

'Authorise' has been given its dictionary meaning of 'sanction, countenance or approve' by Bankes LJ in *Falcon v Famous Players Film Co.*[316] In the same case, Atkin LJ proffered an alternative formulation of 'authorise' as: 'to grant or purport to grant a third person the right to do the act complained of, whether the intention is that the grantee shall do the act on his own account or only on account of the grantor.'[317]

The House of Lords in *CBS Songs Ltd v Amstrad* ('*CBS v Amstrad*')[318] expressly applied Atkin's LJ dicta on the meaning of authorise.[319] The background to this case is that Amstrad manufactured particular audio systems, which featured a double cassette deck that permitted high speed recording between the two decks. The marketing of these machines had especially drawn this design feature to the attention of potential consumers. *CBS v Amstrad* case was the climax of an ongoing dispute between Amstrad and members of the music industry regarding the lawfulness of manufacturing, advertising and offering for sale these audio systems, which had been earlier litigated in *Amstrad Consumer Electronics Plc v British Phonographic Industry Ltd* ('*Amstrad v BPI*').[320]

In *Amstrad v BPI*, the British Phonographic Industry had complained to Amstrad about the advertising and sale of these machines, to which Amstrad responded by initiating proceedings for declaratory relief that their behaviour was not unlawful. One of the grounds of alleged unlawfulness was that Amstrad had authorised the copyright infringements made by persons using their machines.

[315] Authorisation occurring abroad has been held to be within the jurisdiction of English courts provided the infringing act occurs within the UK: *ABKCO Music and Records Inc v Music Collection International Ltd* [1995] RPC 657.
[316] *Falcon v Famous Players Film Co* [1926] 2 KB 474, 491. This case involved s 1(2) of Copyright Act 1956 (UK), a materially similar provision to s 16(2) of CDPA.
[317] *Falcon v Famous Players Film Co* [1926] 2 KB 474, 499.
[318] *CBS Songs Ltd v Amstrad Plc* [1988] 1 AC 1013 ('*CBS v Amstrad*').
[319] See *CBS v Amstrad*, 1054 (per Lord Templeman delivering the leading speech). See also *Amstrad Consumer Electronics Plc v British Phonographic Industry Ltd* [1986] FSR 159, 207 (Lawton LJ), and 211 (Slade LJ), where both judges approved Atkin LJ's dicta, believing that this formulation came closer to the ordinary meaning of 'authorise' than the synonyms of 'sanction, approve and countenance'.
[320] *Amstrad Consumer Electronics Plc v British Phonographic Industry Ltd* [1986] FSR 159 ('*Amstrad v BPI*').

The first instance decision before Whitford J was unsuccessful, along with Amstrad's appeal. The appeal was unsuccessful on a point of law not raised at first instance. However, the Court of Appeal overturned other points of law, including the issue of 'authorisation'. The Court held that Amstrad could not be said to authorise acts of copyright infringement by purchasers of their audio systems since Amstrad was no longer in control of the machines post-sale.[321]

CBS v Amstrad was heard after the decision in *Amstrad v BPI*. In *CBS v Amstrad*, the plaintiffs sued on behalf of themselves and other copyright owners in the music trade, claiming that the manufacturing, advertising, offering for sale, selling or supplying these audio systems was unlawful behaviour on the part of Amstrad. The defendants applied to strike out the writ and statement of claim, which application was refused. On cross-appeal by the defendants, a majority of the Court of Appeal ordered that the writ and statement of claim should be struck out. The plaintiffs then appealed to the House of Lords. Lord Templeman, delivering the leading speech of the House, held that Amstrad had not authorised copyright infringements carried out by purchasers of its machines. In arriving at this conclusion, his Lordship chose not to rely on the statement of principle articulated in *University of NSW v Moorhouse*[322] and distinguished the case on the basis that the machines were no longer in control of Amstrad once they were sold. Further, his Lordship approved the dicta of Atkin LJ in *Falcon v Famous Players Film Co*, along with the statements of principle on authorisation made by the Court of Appeal in *Amstrad v BPI*.[323] Thus, his Lordship emphasised that one needs *actually* to authorise an infringement, rather than merely provide a person with the means to carry out one.

It seems unlikely that a person who inserts a hyperlink will be liable for authorising infringement. If inserting a hyperlink *does* amount to making a work available to the public, then there is no need to rely on authorisation. If inserting a hyperlink does *not* constitute making available to the public, then one must go on to consider authorisation of an infringement by the user. However, as argued above, it is unlikely that clicking on a link and thereby calling up web material onto one's screen amounts to an infringing reproduction. Even if it did, because section 28A of the CDPA did not apply or a licence to browse could not be implied, it is unlikely that the person who inserted the link has authorised this reproduction. This is because they do not have control over the means of infringement or much

---

[321] *Amstrad v BPI*, 207 (Lawton LJ), 211 (Slade LJ), and 217 (Glidewell LJ).

[322] (1975) 133 CLRI, 13 per Gibbs J: "a person who has under his control the means by which an infringement of copyright may be committed—such as a photocopying machine—and who makes it available to other persons, knowing, or having reason to suspect, that it is likely to be used for the purpose of committing an infringement, and omitting to take responsable steps to limit its use to legitimate purposes, would authorise any infringement that resulted from its use."

[323] *CBS v Amstrad*, 1055.

ability to prevent the infringement.[324] The person inserting a link has no control over the user or her personal computer, and the user can *independently* trigger the copying of the website through entering the particular URL into her Internet browser. In the same way that a person who recommends a book does not purport to authorise its subsequent photocopying, nor should the presence of a hyperlink be construed as seeking to grant the right to temporarily reproduce a website in the RAM of a user's computer.

If links are inserted to a multimedia work that is protected as a *sui generis* database, then the question arises whether this constitutes unlawful extraction or re-utilisation.[325] This issue was raised in *Danske v Newsbooster*.[326] In this case the defendant's search engine, in response to search criteria, generated a list of news headlines that represented deep links to the relevant articles on the newspapers' websites. In granting interim relief to the claimant (who was the representative body for all Danish newspapers) the Denmark City Court held that Newsbooster's deep-linking amounted to repeated and systematic extraction or re-utilisation of insubstantial parts of the contents of the database (in breach of Article 7(5), Database Directive).[327]

It seems dubious that inserting a hyperlink can amount to *extraction* of the contents of the database. Article 7(2) of the Database Directive defines extraction as: 'the permanent or temporary *transfer* of all or a substantial part of the contents of a database to another medium by any means or in any form' (emphasis supplied). The person who inserts a hyperlink to the contents of a database does not *transfer* any of the contents to another medium. Rather, it is the person who clicks on a hyperlink who triggers the transfer of the contents to the RAM of her computer and thus would be carrying out the act of extraction.[328]

It also seems unlikely that inserting a hyperlink to a database amounts to re-utilization of the database contents. Article 7(2)(b) of the Database Directive

---

[324] *Cf* Strasser (2002) p 85:

> In the unlikely situation that a user selecting a link violates the reproduction right in the target page, the linking website will almost certainly be liable for authorising the infringement. It is difficult to argue that posting a link does not encourage a user to view (and thus reproduce) a web page. Although the website author posting the link cannot be said to exert perfect control over the user, it is not only foreseeable that a user might reproduce the URL and target page, but expected and desired. Depending on the context, links may be perceived as an invitation to view a target file, regardless of whether the website author endorses its content.

[325] Freedman (2002) p 94; and see generally R Lubens, 'Survey of Developments in European Database Protection' (2003) 18 *Berkeley Technology L J* 447; and Strasser (2002) pp 186–89.

[326] *Danske Dagblades Forening (DDF) v Newsbooster* [2003] ECDR 5.

[327] *Cf Algemeen Dagblad v Eureka Internetdiensten* [2002] ECDR 1 where the District Court, Rotterdam held that linking to the claimants' news website, assuming it was protected as *sui generis* database did not amount to substantial extraction or re-utilisation of the database.

[328] Lubens (2003) p 471. Freedman (2002) p 94 warns that an overly broad application of extraction will prohibit deep-linking.

defines re-utilization as: 'Any form of making available to the public all or a substantial part of the contents of a database by the distribution of copies, by renting, by on-line or other forms of transmissions.' Inserting a hyperlink should not be classed as making available to the public the contents of a database where those contents are freely available to users. This is because, in this type of situation, all the person inserting the hyperlink is doing is providing a reference or citation, as opposed to posting or uploading content.[329] The position is slightly more complicated where the contents of the database are not freely available to users, such as where they are only accessed via password. In this type of situation, inserting a hyperlink to a copy of the contents could well amount to making available the contents to a *new* (albeit unintended) public.

(b) In-line Linking

Liability for in-line linking has not arisen before UK courts,[330] however, it is arguable that it does amount to infringing activity under UK copyright law.

An in-line link differs from a surface or deep link, insofar as it is not directly triggered by a user. With surface or deep links, the user activates a transmission of the content located at the relevant URL by clicking on the link. Whereas, with an in-line link, the user's browser software is instructed to retrieve the image from the relevant URL and typically the user will be unaware that this is happening. Thus, the user only *indirectly* triggers the calling up of images by deciding to access a web page that contains in-line links. As such, it seems strange that the user would be treated as having carried out an act of temporary reproduction. Even if the user is considered to have carried out such an act, it should be exempt under section 28A. It is also not possible to say that the person inserting the in-line link has reproduced the copyright work, since that person does not copy the work, but merely instigates a transmission of a work that is stored somewhere on a server. Thus, it seems that the person inserting an in-line link, along with the user who is browsing a webpage that contains in-line links, will not be liable for infringing reproduction.[331]

However, inserting an in-line link arguably constitutes making available to the public the linked to image. Unlike surface or deep linking, this type of linking goes beyond including a reference to where the linked to image is located on the Internet, in that it actually delivers that image to the user without his or her positive request. Thus, the image is being made available to a *new* public. This does not seem to be an unfair conclusion from a policy perspective insofar as in-line

---

[329] Lubens (2003) p 471.

[330] *Cf* US—*Kelly v Arriba Soft Corp*, 336 F 3d 811(9th Cir, 2003).

[331] In addition, inserting an in-line link will not constitute an adaptation since this exclusive right does not extend to artistic works: see s 21, CDPA. *Cf* US copyright law where it has been suggested that in-line linking of an image can infringe the derivation right: see Wassom (1998) pp 220–22.

linking to an image is the functional equivalent of actually copying an image into a webpage (but without technically copying it) and if the image had been copied without permission this would constitute a *prima facie* infringement. In other words, the work is being exploited in manner that a copyright owner would expect to control, so it does not offend against common sense to find that an in-line link amounts to an infringing communication to the public of a work.

(c) ISP Liability for Linking

An interesting issue is whether an ISP will be held liable for hosting a website of one its subscribers on which hyperlinks to illegal material are contained. In the European cases pre-implementation of the E-Commerce Directive, courts have leaned towards exempting an ISP from liability in this type of situation, provided it did not have notice that its subscriber was infringing copyright.[332] Following implementation of the E-Commerce Directive, a similar approach will be adopted. It must first be asked, however, on what basis would an ISP be held liable under UK copyright law for hosting the infringing hyperlinks of a third party? Where the ISP has knowledge that a third party's material is infringing copyright, the most likely basis for liability would be *authorisation* of infringement. Given an ISP has control over whether or not to store the information of the third party, failure to remove the information that it knows to be infringing could be seen as approving of the third party's act. To avoid monetary liability for authorisation of infringement, an ISP would have to show that it does not have actual or constructive knowledge of its subscribers' infringement, or, where it does have knowledge, acts expeditiously to remove or disable access to such infringing material.[333]

Even where it is not possible to establish that an ISP is liable for authorising an infringement, it may still be possible to obtain an injunction against the ISP, relying on section 97A of the CDPA. According to this section, a court can grant an injunction against a service provider where an ISP has *actual knowledge* of another person using its service to infringe copyright. This is so, even if the ISP is not itself engaging in infringing acts. When determining whether the service provider has actual knowledge the court shall take into account, *inter alia*, whether the service provider has received a notice through contact details provided under Regulation

---

[332] Eg, *Church of Spiritual Technology v Dataweb BV (and XS4ALL)* [2004] ECDR 25 (Ct Appeal of The Hague), *IFPI Vzw and Polygram Records Nv v Belgacom Skynet Nv* [2002] ECDR 5 (Ct Appeal, Brussels).

[333] See Art 14, E-Commerce Directive. *Cf* the position in the US where service providers have, in addition to an exemption from monetary liability for infringement of copyright by hosting third party material, an exemption from liability 'for infringement of copyright by reason of the provider referring or linking users to an online location containing infringing material or an infringing activity, by using information location tools, including a directory, index, reference, pointer, or hypertext link' see s 512(d), USC. In the First E-Commerce Report, the European Commission has commented at p 12 that it will monitor the need to adapt Articles 12–15 of the E-Commerce Directive to include an additional limitation on liability for activities such as the provision of hyperlinks and search engines.

6(1)(c) of the Electronic Commerce (EC Directive) Regulations 2002 No 2013 (E-Commerce Regulations)[334] and the extent to which any notice includes the full name and address of the sender of the notice and details of the infringement in question.

3. Framing

The question of framing has not been dealt with by UK courts but has arisen before the US courts.[335] The first case was *Washington Post Company v Total News Inc*,[336] which concerned an extreme form of framing. It will be discussed briefly here in order to illustrate what framing entails. The Total News website used framing technology to link a number of news services together in one site. This website brought together over 1,000 news organisations using their trade marked logos as hyperlinks. When the user clicked on one of these hyperlinks, information from the particular news organisation was delivered to the user, but while retaining the Total News border around the screen and obscuring the border of the website being linked to. The Total News border featured its own advertising, whilst the advertising on the framed sites was either juxtaposed with theirs or obscured. Various news providers objected to what they felt was parasitic activity and brought an action for injunctive relief against Total News. The case was settled on terms that forced Total News to cease framing and from doing anything that might cause confusion to Internet users. Simple surface linking, however, was permitted by the terms of the settlement.[337]

Framing most obviously raises issues relating to passing off, because the juxta-position of different websites within the one frame may cause confusion over which site is actually being accessed or the relationship between the two websites. It is less obvious that framing risks infringing copyright.[338] The framing website does not, for example, reproduce the content of the website that is being framed. Rather, when a user browsing the Internet clicks a hyperlink which calls up that content within the frame, there is a temporary storage of the content in the RAM

---

[334] That is, 'the details of the service provider, including his electronic mail address, which make it possible to contact him rapidly and communicate with him in a direct and effective manner.'

[335] For a comprehensive analysis of liability for framing under UK and US law, see generally Strasser (2002).

[336] *Washington Post Company v Total News Inc* No 97 Civ 1190 (PKL) (SDNY 20 February 1997) (Complaint).

[337] See http://www.jmls.edu/cyber/cases/shetld2.html for details of the settlement. See also *Futuredontics Inc v Applied Anagramics Inc* 1998 WL417413 (9th Cir (Cal)) where the plaintiff claimed that the defendant had infringed copyright by creating a hyperlink which caused content from the plaintiff's website to appear in one of the several frames on the defendant's website. An application for a preliminary injunction against the defendant was denied by the District Court and this was affirmed by the US Court of Appeals for the Ninth Circuit on the ground that the plaintiff had failed to prove harm from the framed link.

[338] See also Strasser (2002) pp 27–31, 101–5.

of the user's computer.[339] In other words, the user makes a temporary reproduction and, as discussed above, this is arguably exempt under either section 28A of the CDPA or an implied licence to browse. Although, in terms of an implied licence the issue is whether it is conditional upon the information not being reproduced or transmitted in the form of frames. However, this would be an impossible condition to implement since users have no control over whether the information browsed is framed or not. Thus, it is argued that the implied licence to browse would include browsing within frames.[340]

In the context of US copyright law, commentators have argued that framing might result in the creation of a derivative work and thus infringe the adaptation right.[341] A similar argument has been made in relation to civil law countries.[342] This sort of argument is unlikely to succeed under UK copyright law. As discussed above, the adaptation right is a narrowly drawn right (more so than under US copyright law) and applies to only certain types of works, namely literary, dramatic and musical works. The adaptation right is most likely to be relevant to multimedia works protected as literary works, namely, computer programs or databases. To make an infringing adaptation of a computer program or database, requires an unauthorised arrangement or altered version or translation of the program or database.[343] If one characterises the framed web page (B), which is written in a certain programming code, such as HTML, as a computer program, then would an altered version of B be produced when it is called up and framed within another web page (A), which may also be characterised as a computer program? Arguably not, since all that occurs is that B is obscured from view. B remains intact and is not altered in any way by its inclusion within a frame of A.[344] If one characterises the framed web page (B) as a database, it is possible that its inclusion within the framing web page (A) amounts to an altered version of a database? Once again, it may be said that B remains in tact, but is simply partly obscured by A and thus an altered version of a database does not arise.[345] In addition, it may be argued that the temporary nature of framing is such that an altered version of either a computer program or database is never produced. In other words, there is a lack of fixation of the adaptation, such that a new work cannot be said to arise. The basis for this argument is that a literary work does not arise 'unless and until it is recorded, in writing or otherwise'.[346] In arguing that a literary work is adapted, one is essentially arguing that a new literary work has arisen, thus it seems plausi-

---

[339] See also Wassom (1998) p 201.
[340] Cf Christie (1998) p 11.
[341] Wassom (1998) pp 202–7.
[342] Garrote (2002) pp 196–97.
[343] See s 21(ab), CDPA for computer programs; and s 21(ac), CDPA for databases.
[344] See also Jackson (1997) p 752. *Cf* Garrote (2002) pp 196–97.
[345] Cf Garrote (1997) p 197.
[346] S 3(2), CDPA.

ble that this adapted work should also satisfy the fixation requirement. Although material form can include electronic form, storage within the RAM of a user's computer is unlikely to be permanent enough to satisfy the requirement of being 'recorded'.

Summary

There is limited guidance from case law about whether hyperlinking or framing will infringe copyright or the database right. The better view seems to be that neither activity is likely to infringe the reproduction right and, in the case of framing, this is unlikely to infringe the adaptation right. However, when it comes to (surface or deep) linking to copyright works that have limited availability to the public, arguably this will be an infringing communication to the public. In the case of in-line linking it seems even clearer that this activity will infringe the right of communication to the public.

Assuming a multimedia work is protected as a *sui generis* database, linking to the database should not infringe the extraction right, although it may infringe the re-utilisation right if the database contents are not readily available to the public. Finally, ISPs who store infringing links inserted by third parties should be able to rely on the exemption created by Article 14 of the E-Commerce Directive.

From a policy perspective, whether linking should constitute copyright infringement is a different matter since linking may be characterised as a technologically sophisticated form of citation. Moreover, to allow copyright owners to control linking would reduce drastically the freedoms associated with Internet usage and its virtue of enabling a vast network of resources. Finally, if copyright owners object to their works being linked to they could choose not to upload them or else upload them with some sort of copy-protection or technological measure attached which, if circumvented, could be actionable under the anti-circumvention provisions recently introduced into UK law in order to implement Article 6 of the Information Society Directive.[347]

In respect of the concerns raised by framing, these seem to be more appropriately dealt with under the umbrellas of passing off and trade mark infringement, than copyright law.

Conclusion

The digital environment, in particular the transmission of material over computer networks such as the Internet, has created pressure to expand the existing rights

---

[347] Strasser (2002) pp 209–15.

available under copyright law. In the EU and UK, the main focus of expansion has been the reproduction[348] and communication[349] rights.

Article 2 of the Information Society Directive dictates an extremely wide reproduction right that embraces any form of technical copying. Section 17 of the CDPA reflects a broad approach to reproduction under UK copyright law, so this provision did not require amendment. However, a wide reproduction right catches activities, such as browsing and caching, which are essential features of Internet use and do not really threaten the economic interests of a copyright owner. The solution, therefore, has been to cut down the scope of the reproduction right by including an exemption for copies made in the process of transmitting or receiving a network transmission.[350] This exemption should be welcomed, however, its relationship with the E-Commerce Directive, Articles 12 and 13 may be criticised. From the point of view of ISPs, the exemption created by Article 5(1) of the Information Society Directive is unnecessary in the light of Articles 12 and 13 of the E-Commerce Directive. Further, as Article 5(1) of the Information Society Directive does not apply to computer programs or databases, Articles 12 and 13 of the E-Commerce Directive have a role to play for these types of works.

The communication right has been extended considerably by virtue of Article 3 of the Information Society Directive, which creates a right of communication to the public that includes on-line making available to the public. This has been translated into the UK context as new section 20 of the CDPA which defines communication to the public as including broadcasting the work and making a work available to the public. The expanded communication right allows the on-line distribution of works to be controlled by the copyright owner and also has the potential to restrict certain types of hyperlinking to copyright material. What remains unclear for the time being and needs to be resolved at an EU level is where the act of making available to the public takes place.

Thus, broadly speaking, it is possible to conclude that copyright law has responded adequately to the demands of on-line exploitation of works. Copyright law at one level seeks to maintain a distinction between tangible and intangible distribution of works, for example by restricting the distribution right to tangible copies of works and having the communication right apply to intangible transmission of works. However, the expansion of the reproduction right to include technical copies made during transmission risks considerable overlap with the communication right. This overlap is reduced significantly by the existence of

---

[348] JH Spoor, 'The Copyright Approach to Copying on the Internet: (Over)Stretching the Reproduction Right?' in PB Hugenholtz, (ed), *The Future of Copyright in a Digital Environment* (Kluwer, The Hague, 1996) 67, 75–79.

[349] For the position in France see J Passa, 'The Protection of Copyright on the Internet under French Law' in F Pollaud-Dulian, (ed), *The Internet and Authors' Rights* (Sweet & Maxwell, London, 1999) 25–72.

[350] See Hugenholtz (1996) p 89; and Dreier (1994) p 69 who support this approach.

Article 5(1) of the Information Society Directive and its equivalent in UK copyright law, section 28A. Nonetheless, there remains some murkiness to the boundaries between the two rights.

In considering the scope of exclusive rights under UK and EU copyright and database law, it is possible to draw some conclusions about which category of work provides the strongest form of protection for multimedia works.

For multimedia works that are protected as a computer program, the scope of protection will extend to the program structure and limited non-visual user interface features. This means that the user interface features and functions of a multimedia work will remain substantially unprotected and open to imitation.

Protecting multimedia works via the film category means that the visual sequence of images will be protected, but only if those images are copied, as opposed to imitated. In other words, the thin protection available for films means that the navigational structure and user interface functions of a multimedia work would not be protected. Reliance on the category of dramatic works is better, insofar as the scope of the reproduction right is wider, such that visual user interfaces features are more extensively protected. However, protection would not extend to programming techniques that produced certain striking visual effects. Nor would protection extend to non-visual user interface features, such as commands or functional operations.

Possibly the weakest protection under copyright law comes from classifying multimedia works as a either a database or compilation. This is because the scope of protection will not extend to the contents of the multimedia work, but will focus on prohibiting a substantially similar selection or arrangement of materials.

The strongest form of protection available to multimedia works sits adjacent to copyright law in the form of the database right. If a multimedia work is protected as a *sui generis* database then a substantial part of the contents, and in some circumstances an insubstantial part of the contents, may not be extracted or re-utilised without permission. The database right offers the most robust protection for the contents of a multimedia work, together with protection for the presentation of the contents, namely the visual user interface.

The scope of protection available for multimedia works must also be judged in the light of the exceptions that are available under copyright law and the database right regime. The following chapter considers in detail the exceptions relevant to multimedia works.

5

Exceptions and Multimedia Works

Introduction

In order to fully appreciate the scope of protection available for multimedia works under copyright law and the database right regime, this chapter examines the permissible uses of multimedia works that are protected as computer programs, copyright databases and *sui generis* databases. This chapter will then consider certain royalty free exceptions in relation to literary works (other than computer programs), dramatic works and films. At various points the relevance of exceptions to creation of multimedia works also will be considered.

Computer Programs

Exceptions to infringement of computer programs are contained in sections 50A–50C of the Copyright Designs and Patents Act 1988 ('CDPA'). These exceptions relate to back up copies, decompilation, reverse engineering other than decompilation and error correction, and seek to give effect to Articles 5 and 6 of the Software Directive.[1] As software forms an essential component of multimedia works, these exceptions have a clear relevance to what users of multimedia works may do. The following section discusses each of these exceptions.

1. Reverse Engineering other than Decompilation

The concept of 'reverse engineering' embraces a wide variety of activities, all of which are aimed at investigating the functionality and underlying ideas of a

---

[1] Directive 91/250/EEC on the legal protection of computer programs, [1991] OJ L122/42 ('Software Directive'). H Laddie, *et al*, *The Modern Law of Copyright and Designs*, 3rd edn, (Butterworths, London, 2000) para 34.57 are generally critical of the scheme of exceptions established by the Software Directive.

computer program. These activities include: reading program documentation (such as user manuals); running a computer program and observing what it does and how it operates (sometimes referred to as 'black box' testing);[2] and decompilation, which is disassembling object code (which is in binary notation) in an attempt to recreate the source code.[3]

(a) EU Law

The Software Directive draws a distinction between reverse engineering that involves studying the operation of a computer program ('black box' testing) and reverse engineering that involves decompilation. Article 5(3) deals with the former situation whereas Article 6 deals with the latter.

Studying a computer program involves running a computer program which in turn involves reproduction of the program in the RAM of the computer. Unless the person running a computer program (or copy thereof) has the copyright owner's permission to do so, this temporary reproduction will constitute a *prima facie* infringement of copyright.[4] It may also amount to an infringing adaptation. Relevant to this type of situation is Article 5(3) of the Software Directive which provides:

> The person having a right to use a copy of a computer program shall be entitled, without the authorisation of the rightholder, to observe, study or test the functioning[5] of the program in order to determine the ideas and principles which underlie any element of the program if he does so while performing any of the acts of loading, displaying, running, transmitting or storing the program which he is entitled to do.

Article 5(3) should be read in tandem with Article 1(2) of the Software Directive which provides that, 'Ideas and principles which underlie any element of a computer program, including those which underlie its interfaces, are not protected by

---

[2] See S Lai, *The Copyright Protection of Computer Software in the United Kingdom* (Hart Publishing, Oxford, 2000) 222:

> The entire plaintiff's computer program/chip is viewed as a black-box, and the engineer in this instance merely observes what it does and how it performs, with a view to inferring what must be going on inside the program. Through the empirical observation of program inputs and outputs, the programmer is only making a reasonable guess as to how the program's coding is structured. This inspection fails to ascertain information as fact, and moreover is unable to reveal the precise cause for apparent errors.

[3] For a more detailed explanation of reverse engineering see Lai (2000) pp 218–32.

[4] As discussed in ch 4 above at pp 99, 113–4. Note that B Czarnota and R Hart, *Legal Protection of Computer Programs in Europe: a Guide to the EC Directive* (Butterworths, London, 1991) 69–70 argue that this exception was based on a misconception, namely, that such transient reproduction would constitute infringing reproduction. They argue that a musical work on compact disc requires an act of reproduction for the object code in its machine readable form to be converted into analog but that it was never suggested that a purchaser should be unable to carry out the act of reproduction necessary in order to use the work. Laddie, *et al*, (2000) para 34.50 express similar scepticism about the validity of this type of reproduction amounting to an infringement.

[5] Czarnota and Hart (1991) p 70 stress that it is observing, studying or testing the *functioning* of the program and not the program itself.

copyright under this Directive.' These provisions thus recognise that ideas and principles underlying software are not protected by copyright law.[6]

Only 'the person having a right to use a copy of a computer program', can rely on the exception created by Article 5(3) of the Software Directive. Slightly different terminology is used in paragraphs (1) and (2) of Article 5: these provisions respectively refer to a 'lawful acquirer' of a computer program and 'a person having a right to use the computer program'. However, all three expressions are understood to refer to the same concept of 'lawful user': that is, a person who lawfully acquires the program (for example, via sale, gift, public lending and rental contracts).[7] Thus, to rely on this exception, an illicit copy of the program cannot be used.[8]

Article 9(1) of the Software Directive emphasises that any contractual provisions contrary to Article 5(3)[9] are null and void. Thus, it appears that the owner of copyright in the program cannot override the user's right to reverse engineer. However, the terms of Article 5(3) which state that the reverse engineering has to occur 'while performing any of the acts of loading, displaying, running or transmitting or storing the program *which he is entitled to do*' (emphasis supplied), read in combination with recital 19 which provides that the acts of reverse engineering 'do not infringe copyright in the program' suggest that the copyright owner could license the use of the program in such a way that restricted the user's ability to carry out acts of reverse engineering.[10]

(b) UK Law

The Software Directive was implemented into UK law via the Copyright (Computer Programs) Regulations 1992 ('Software Regulations').[11] The Software Regulations

---

[6] See also Art 9, Agreement on Trade Related Aspects of Intellectual Property Rights 1994 ('TRIPs Agreement').

[7] V Vanovermeire, 'The Concept of the Lawful User in the Database Directive' (2000) 31 *IIC* 63, 72. See also *Report from the Commission to the Council, The European Parliament and the Economic and Social Committee on the implementation and effects of Directive 91/250/EEC on the legal protection of computer programs*, Brussels 10/4/2000 COM (2000) 199 Final ('Commission Report') p 12 where the Commission states that 'lawful acquirer' in Article 5 of the Software Directive means a purchaser, licensee, renter or a person authorised to use the program on behalf of one of these persons. See also Czarnota and Hart (1991) p 64.

[8] Czarnota and Hart (1991) p 64; Lai (2000) p 99.

[9] Along with Article 5(2) and Article 6, Software Directive.

[10] Laddie, *et al*, (2000) para 34.53 state:

It would therefore appear that art 5(3) is a tame provision indeed since the copyright owner surely must be at liberty to license the use of his program for a limited purpose. It would seem to follow in those circumstances that, although the user is entitled to observe the operation of the program while using it in the ordinary course, and although this right cannot be excluded by contract since art 9(1) says so, he is not allowed to use the software in an abnormal manner as would be required by a proper, comprehensive research programme.

[11] Copyright (Computer Programs) Regulations 1992 SI 1992/3233 ('Software Regulations'), which came into force on 1 January 1993. For discussion see S Chalton, 'Implementation of the Software Directive in the United Kingdom: The Effects of the Copyright (Computer Programs) Regulations 1992' [1993] *EIPR* 138.

did not, however, insert an express provision into the CDPA implementing Article 5(3) of the Software Directive. Presumably this was because such acts were not considered to infringe copyright in a computer program[12] or else were thought excusable under the exception of fair dealing for research and private study in section 29, CDPA.[13] Rather, Article 5(3) was indirectly implemented via section 296A(1)(c), which stated that where a person was using a computer program pursuant to an agreement, the use of a term or condition which prohibited or restricted, 'the use of any device or means to observe, study or test the functioning of the program in order to understand the ideas and principles which underlie any element of the program' was void. The Commission criticised this provision on the basis that the language used did not restrict the acts to those which the user is entitled to do.[14] This criticism has been addressed by the Copyright Regulations,[15] specifically Regulation 15 which inserts a new section 50BA[16] into the CDPA, which states:

(1) It is not an infringement of copyright for a lawful user of a copy of a computer program to observe, study or test the functioning of the program in order to determine the ideas and principles which underlie any element of the program if he does so while performing any of the acts of loading, displaying, running, transmitting or storing the program which he is entitled to do.

(2) Where an act is permitted under this section, it is irrelevant whether or not there exists any term or condition in an agreement which purports to prohibit or restrict the act (such terms being, by virtue of section 296A, void).

A lawful user of a copy of a computer program is defined as a person who has a right to use the program, whether under a licence to do any acts restricted by the copyright or otherwise.[17] This would apparently include the purchaser of a program and any person claiming through the purchaser and it could also include a person having a right to use the program pursuant to one of the permitted exceptions.[18]

Section 29(4A), CDPA[19] inserted by Regulation 9 of the Copyright Regulations, makes it clear that exceptions to infringement by observing, studying or testing a

---

[12] This could be on the basis that ideas and principles are not protected by copyright law: WR Cornish and D Llewelyn, *Intellectual Property: Patents, Copyright, Trade Marks and Allied Rights*, 5th edn, (Sweet & Maxwell, London, 2003) para 19–11.

[13] Lai (2000) p 106.

[14] Commission Report, p 13.

[15] Copyright and Related Rights Regulations 2003 SI 2498 ('Copyright Regulations').

[16] A similar provision is included in Australian law—see s 47B(3), Copyright Act 1968 (Cth).

[17] S 50A(2), CDPA.

[18] K Garnett, JR James and G Davies, (eds), *Copinger and Skone James on Copyright*, 14th edn, (Sweet & Maxwell, London, 1999) ('Copinger') para 9–60. If this is right, then the concept of lawful user under UK law is arguably wider than under the Software Directive.

[19] Section 29(4A), CDPA provides: 'It is not fair dealing to observe, study or test the functioning of a computer program in order to determine the ideas and principles which underlie any element of the program (these acts being permitted if done in accordance with section 50BA (observing, studying and testing)).'

program are to be regulated by section 50BA and not the fair dealing exception. The new section 50BA appears to have been needed because (as is discussed below) section 29 of the CDPA is now limited to fair dealing for non-commercial research and study purposes and Article 5(3) of the Software Directive is not limited in this manner.[20]

If a lawful user of software wishes to undertake reverse engineering that exceeds observing, studying or testing the functioning of the program, then she will have to rely upon the exception for decompilation,[21] which is discussed next.

2. Decompilation

Decompilation allows a software engineer or programmer to access the original source code, or a version as near as possible to the source code, so that he can appreciate the ideas and principles underlying a computer program, how the program functions and the interfaces of the program. This may allow a competitor to imitate the program, design a competing program which improves upon the existing program, or create a program or hardware device that complements the existing program, in the sense that it is compatible (or interoperable) with that program. However, decompilation necessarily involves either a reproduction or adaptation[22] of the computer program and, in the absence of an applicable exception or express licence, this will constitute a *prima facie* infringement of copyright.[23]

(a) EU Law

Article 6 of the Software Directive creates an exception for decompilation.[24] The provision is fairly detailed and sets out the permissible purpose of decompilation, together with the permissible circumstances in which decompilation may occur and the permissible uses of information obtained from the decompilation process. These will be analysed in turn.

Article 6(1) states that the rightholder's permission is not required for reproduction or translation of a computer program where these acts are '*indispensable* to obtain the information necessary to achieve the *interoperability* of an *independently created computer program* with other programs' (emphasis supplied). The

---

[20] L Bently and B Sherman, *Intellectual Property Law*, 2nd edn, (OUP, Oxford, 2004) 221, n 210.

[21] Czarnota and Hart (1991) p 70.

[22] See above ch 4 at pp 120–1.

[23] See further Laddie, *et al*, (2000) para 34.45.

[24] This was keenly debated during the passage of the Software Directive: see J Berkvens and G Alkemade, 'Software Protection: Life after the Directive' [1991] *EIPR* 476; M Colombe and C Meyer, 'Interoperability still Threatened by EC Software Directive: A Status Report' [1990] *EIPR* 325; T Dreier, 'The Council Directive of 14 May 1991 on the Legal Protection of Computer Programs' [1991] *EIPR* 319; Laddie, *et al*, (2000) para 34.48.

decompilation must be 'indispensable'[25] to obtaining the relevant information, which means, for example, that the information needed to achieve interoperability cannot already be obtained by 'black-box' testing in reliance upon Article 5(3).[26] The purpose of decompilation must be interoperability and Article 6(1) makes clear that the independently created program may be one which competes with the program that is decompiled.[27] It has been argued that Article 6 confines interoperability to software-to-software interoperability and not interoperability between hardware and software.[28] However, recitals 10 to 12 of the Software Directive suggest that software-to-hardware interoperability is permissible:

(10) Whereas the function of a computer program is to communicate and work together with other components of a computer system and with users, and for this purpose, a logical and, where appropriate, physical interconnection and interaction is required to permit all elements of software and hardware to work with other software and hardware and with users in all the ways in which they are intended to function;

(11) Whereas the parts of the program which provide for such interconnection and interaction between elements of software and hardware are generally known as 'interfaces'

(12) Whereas this functional interconnection and interaction is generally known as 'interoperability'; whereas such interoperability can be defined as the ability to exchange information and mutually to use the information which has been exchanged

In other words, the recitals define 'interoperability' as functional interconnection and interaction and envisage that these activities can occur between elements of software and hardware.

Certain circumstances have to exist before a person can rely on Article 6 of the Software Directive. First, according to Article 6(1)(a), the person performing the acts of reproduction or translation must be the licensee, or another person having a right to use a copy of a program, or a person authorised by the licensee or a person having a right to use the program.[29] Second, Article 6(1)(b) stipulates that the

---

[25] Lai (2000) p 101 queries whether this requirement was even necessary given that decompilation tends to be a measure of last resort, given its complexity. Czarnota and Hart (1991) p 77 argue that 'indispensable', 'imposes a high burden of proof on the decompiler to demonstrate that other means to achieve the same objective were not available or were not sufficient for his purposes.'

[26] Dreier (1991) p 324.

[27] Above.

[28] R Hart, 'Interfaces, Interoperability and Maintenance' [1991] *EIPR* 111. However, Hart (1991) pp 114–15 argues that there is no need for the exception to extend to hardware devices since there will always be a physical link between a hardware device and the hardware device storing and executing the program to be interfaced with, such that the functions of the interface can be discerned by monitoring the signals communicated across the physical interface. See further Czarnota and Hart (1991) p 85. *Cf* Lai (2000) pp 100–1, who argues that it is unrealistic to draw a distinction between software-to-software compatibility and software-to-hardware compatibility and that the latter is within the intention of Article 6 of the Software Directive.

[29] Thus, hackers or those who possess pirated copies are excluded: Czarnota and Hart (1991) p 79.

information necessary to achieve interoperability has not previously been readily available to the persons just mentioned. It is not clear when information will be considered 'readily available'. For example, it is unclear whether there is an obligation on the developer to request interface information from the rightholder, or to offer to pay a licence fee for that information.[30] It is also unclear whether information is readily available where a developer (in good faith) did not know that the information was published or could not after a good faith attempt obtain the information.[31] If rightholders want to minimise the effect of Article 6, then they can do so by publishing the specifications of one particular interface freely.[32] Finally, Article 6(1)(c) states that the acts of reproduction and translation must be 'confined to the parts of the original program which are necessary to achieve interoperability.'[33] Lai queries the utility of this condition since, '[t]he inherent difficulty and expense of decompilation is such that this particular technique of reverse engineering will not be used to analyse more of a program than necessary.'[34] There is also the criticism that it is not always possible to ascertain at the beginning of the decompilation process which parts of the work are essential to achieving interoperability.[35]

Once information necessary to achieve interoperability has been obtained, Article 6(2) imposes further obligations on what may be done with this information. First, the information obtained cannot be used for purposes 'other than to achieve interoperability of the independently created computer program'.[36] Second, the information cannot be passed onto others, except when necessary for the interoperability of an independently created computer program.[37] Finally, the information cannot be used to create a substantially similar computer program, 'or for any other act which infringes copyright.'[38]

Article 9(1) of the Software Directive emphasises that any contractual provisions contrary to Article 6 are null and void.[39] Even so, it is arguable that Article

---

[30] Dreier (1991) p 324 is of the view that interface information is not 'readily' available if a developer either has to ask for it or can only obtain it upon payment. *Cf* Copinger (1999) para 9–62 who takes the view that information will be 'readily available' if information regarding a program's interfaces is available from the program's manufacturers. See also Czarnota and Hart (1991) p 80. Laddie, *et al* (2000) para 34.49 take the view that this requirement should be interpreted to mean that the developer can find out the information by making obvious and straightforward enquiries.

[31] Colombe and Meyer (1990) p 329.

[32] E R Kroker, 'The Computer Directive and the Balance of Rights' [1997] *EIPR* 247, 249. See also Czarnota and Hart (1991) p 80.

[33] Laddie, *et al* (2000) para 34.49 emphasise that the provision should be read as acts which are necessary *to obtain the information* to achieve interoperability.

[34] Lai (2000) p 102.

[35] Kroker (1997) p 250.

[36] Article 6(2)(a), Software Directive.

[37] Article 6(2)(b), Software Directive.

[38] Article 6(2)(c), Software Directive.

[39] L Guibault, *Copyright Limitations and Contracts* (Kluwer, The Hague, 2002) 213–19, argues that Article 9 of the Software Directive was an attempt to guarantee certain imperative rights to the lawful users of computer programs, yet 'the margin of appreciation left to national legislatures in the

9(1) does not prohibit Article 6 being overridden by other forms of legal protection, such as confidential information.[40]

(b) UK Law

Section 50B[41] of the CDPA provides that it is not an infringement of copyright for a lawful user[42] of a copy of a computer program expressed in a low level language to convert it into a version expressed in a higher level language[43] or, incidentally in the course of so converting the program, to copy the program (in other words, to decompile the program). Two conditions must be satisfied. First, that it is necessary to decompile the program in order to obtain the information necessary to create an independent program which can be operated with the program decompiled or another program ('the permitted objective'). Second, that the information is not used for a purpose apart from the permitted objective. These conditions are not satisfied where the lawful user: 1) has readily available to him the information necessary to achieve the permitted objective; 2) does not limit the acts of decompiling to those necessary to achieve the permitted objective; 3) supplies the information obtained to persons to whom it is not necessary to supply it in order to achieve the permitted objective; or 4) uses the information to create a program which is 'substantially similar in its expression'[44] to the program decompiled or to do any act restricted by copyright. Any attempts to override acts permitted under section 50B by contract will be void.[45]

Section 50B departs from the language of Article 6 of the Software Directive in two key respects.[46] First, 'decompiling' is not described as 'reproduction of the code and translation, of its form' but rather in terms of converting a copy of a computer program expressed in a low level language into a version in a higher level language; or, incidentally while doing so, copying the program. Arguably the UK language has a more restricted meaning.[47] Second, section 50B refrains from using

---

implementation of their obligations under the Directives has resulted in varying degrees of "imperativeness".' (p 219).

[40] Laddie, *et al*, (2000) para 34.56.

[41] A similar provision is contained in Australian law—see s 47D, Copyright Act 1968 (Cth). However, unlike s 50B, CDPA, s 47D states that interoperability extends to making independently another program or an article that connects to or otherwise interoperable with the original program or with other programs.

[42] A lawful user of a computer program for the purposes of ss 50A-C, CDPA is a person who has a right to use the program, whether under a licence to do any acts restricted by the copyright in the program or otherwise.

[43] Copinger (1999) p 533, n 16, express the view that machine code, assembly code and object or source code represent ascending levels of language.

[44] Copinger (1999) para 9–62 argue that it seems likely that UK courts will interpret these words as being equivalent to 'which reproduces a substantial part'.

[45] S 296A, CDPA.

[46] Cornish and Llewelyn (2003) para 19–20. The differences in the UK implementation are also noted in the Commission Report, p 14.

[47] Chalton (1993) p 141. *Cf* Lai (2000) p 104.

the term 'interoperability', and instead refers to obtaining the information necessary *to create an independent program* which can be operated with the program
decompiled or another program. Lai argues that on a literal reading of section 50B,
where a reverse engineer's program already exists, he will not be permitted to
make use of such obtained information to adapt, correct or maintain the interoperability of his program.[48]

Section 29(4) of the CDPA makes clear that decompilation will not fall under
the fair dealing exception[49] for research and private study. This provision states
that acts permitted under section 50B do not fall within section 29 of the CDPA.
Thus, it is not a fair dealing to convert a computer program expressed in a low level
language into a version expressed in a higher level language, or incidentally in the
course of converting the program to copy it. Even so, there are some situations in
which section 29 may retain relevance for decompilation. These include decompilation occurring before the enactment of section 29(4) (on 1 January 1993) or
the enactment of the Software Directive (on 14 May 1991) or where the act
complained of involves a 'hex dump', which is a conversion of ordinary binary
notation into hexadecimal notation.[50]

To the extent that a person wishes to decompile a computer program in order
to create an independent multimedia work that is interoperable with that program
or another program, this will be permitted under section 50B, subject to the conditions discussed above being fulfilled. Stamatoudi, however, is critical of the way
in which this exception relates to multimedia works. She argues that this exception
does not allow anything other than the software in a multimedia work to be
decompiled: 'there is nothing that can be decompiled in relation to the visual
effect/compilation of sound, images, text, etc.'[51] However, it is difficult to appreciate why a competitor would need to decompile the *contents* of a multimedia
work, as opposed to the underlying *software*, in order to ensure compatibility with
different operating systems or other computer programs.[52] Further, if a competi-

---

[48] Lai (2000) p 105. Although he notes that a UK court would have to interpret section 50B against
its literal meaning or look to apply section 50C.

[49] Cf the situation in the US where the defence of fair use in s 107 US Copyright Act 1976 has been
applied to decompilation of video game programs for the purpose of developing compatible game cartridges that would run on the plaintiff's game consoles, even though this involved circumventing the
technical protection measures used in relation to the original game cartridges: see *Sega Enterprises v
Accolade Inc* 977 F 2d 1510(9th Cir, 1992). *Cf Atari Games Corp v Nintendo of America Inc* 975 F 2d 832
(Fed Cir, 1992) where reverse engineering of a program in order to understand its ideas, processes and
methods of operation was recognised as capable of constituting a fair use. However, there was no fair
use on the facts of the case because an unauthorised copy of the program had been used in the reverse
engineering process. Laddie, *et al*, (2000) para 34.47 and 34.50 take the view that it is not clear that the
Software Directive required the UK to abolish the fair dealing defence in relation to decompilation.

[50] Lai (2000) pp 128–29.

[51] I Stamatoudi, *Copyright and Multimedia Works: a Comparative Analysis* (CUP, Cambridge, 2002)
158.

[52] Which Stamatoudi (2002) p 158 appears to appreciate when she writes: 'The interoperability of
the multimedia product is solely regulated by its technical base.'

tor wanted to appreciate the contents within a multimedia work, they would be able to achieve this by running the multimedia work. One issue that does arise, however, is whether it is permissible to reproduce the contents of a multimedia work in order to appreciate how the work functions or whilst analysing or studying the underlying computer program. The decompilation exception in Article 6 of the Software Directive, implemented in section 50B of the CDPA, clearly states that the activities which are excused are reproduction or adaptation of the *computer program*. This means that, unless the digital content is classed as part of the computer program[53] temporary reproduction of the contents would not be exempt under this exception. If, however, the multimedia work is classed as a database, then the lawful user exception expressed in Article 6(1) of the Database Directive,[54] and implemented in section 50D CDPA,[55] may operate to allow a reverse engineer to temporarily reproduce those contents where the act involves studying the operation of the multimedia work (ie, software plus contents).

Stamatoudi also fears that the decompilation exception will permit reverse engineers of multimedia works to extract and re-use the digital code of the contents.[56] She argues that it is odd that this type of activity would be prohibited under the database right but permitted by the decompilation exception. However, this should not be a concern: while decompilation might technically facilitate access to, and use of, contents within the multimedia work, the terms of Article 6 do not sanction this activity. This is because Article 6(2) does not allow information obtained through decompilation to be used for goals other than achieving interoperability of the independently created computer program and reproducing the contents of a multimedia work would not be for the purpose of achieving interoperability. Further, the information may not be used to do any other act which infringes copyright and arguably re-use of the contents of a multimedia work would involve unlawful reproduction of individual copyright works.

A clear weakness with the decompilation exception under EC and UK law is that it does not permit the reproduction of data tables which do not form part of the computer program,[57] but which are necessary in order to achieve interoperability. This may be compared with the position under Australian law, where the

---

[53] See above at pp 41, 117.

[54] Directive 96/9/EC on the legal protection of databases OJ L 77 27/3/96, pp 20–28 ('Database Directive').

[55] See below at p 178 for a discussion.

[56] Stamatoudi (2002) p 158: 'decompilation would create havoc in relation to the collection of works that is contained in the multimedia product.' Further, 'the whole concept of interoperability, especially as a tool to mark the borders of what is allowed, makes no sense whatsoever in relation to multimedia works.'

[57] V Bouganim, *The Legal Protection of Databases: from Copyright to Dataright* (UL unpublished PhD thesis, 1999), 67 suggests that where data is intended to control the flow, processing, manipulation and presentation of objects held in computer storage, it would form part of the computer program. But when data is the object to be processed, manipulated or presented it does not constitute part of the computer program.

definition of computer program, for the purposes of the permitted exceptions (including decompilation) in Division 4A, Part III of the Copyright Act 1968 (Cth), is defined to include any literary work that is incorporated or associated with a computer program and essential to the effective operation of a function of that program. Consequently, a person is able to reproduce data tables in order to achieve interoperable software.[58]

3. Back-up Copies

Article 5(2) of the Software Directive stipulates that '[t]he making of a back-up copy by a person having a right to use the computer program may not be prevented by contract insofar as it is necessary for that use.'[59] This is implemented in section 50A(1) of the CDPA which creates an exception for a lawful user of a copy of a computer program, 'to make any back up copy of it which it is necessary for him to have for the purposes of his lawful use.' The right to make a back up copy cannot be excluded by contract.[60] What amounts to a 'back-up' copy is not defined in Article 5(2) of the Software Directive or section 50A of the CDPA, but it seems that it 'refers to a copy made by the user as a reserve in case of loss of or damage to the original.'[61] While it may be desirable to make a back-up copy, it is questionable whether it is generally necessary to do so.[62] The requirement of 'necessity' probably limits the lawful user to making only one back up copy.[63]

4. Error Correction

Article 5(1) of the Software Directive provides that a lawful acquirer of a computer program may carry out the acts of reproduction, translation, adaptation, and any other alteration of a computer program (ie, the acts referred to in Article 4(a) and (b), 'where they are necessary for use of the computer program by the lawful acquirer in accordance with its intended purpose, including for error correction.'[64] According to Article 5(1) this exception applies in the absence of specific contrac-

---

[58] See s 47D, Copyright Act 1968 (Cth). *Cf* the position prior to this amendment as reflected in *Data Access Corporation v Powerflex Services Pty Ltd* (1999) 202 CLR 1.

[59] The Commission Report, p 13 notes that the provision has been implemented in all Member States.

[60] S 50A(3), s 296A, CDPA.

[61] Copinger (1999) para 9–60.

[62] According to Czarnota and Hart (1991) p 68 it might be difficult to establish that making a back-up copy is a necessity where the program is embedded in the hardware in a manner such that it cannot duly be damaged or altered in normal use or if the manufacturer provides a security copy under the terms of the agreement with the user. A private copy for personal or home use would not be classified as a necessary back up copy.

[63] Czarnota and Hart (1991) p 68; Lai (2000) pp 136–37. See also Commission Report, p 18.

[64] According to Czarnota and Hart (1991) p 65, error correction is not defined but is to be understood as including the detection and location of the error as well as the measures taken to correct it.

tual provisions. Thus, it appears permissible to exclude via contract the right to correct errors. Yet recital 18 introduces some ambiguity into this field because it provides that 'the acts of loading and running necessary for the use of a copy of a program which has been lawfully acquired, and the act of correction of its errors may not be prohibited by contract'.[65] According to the Commission, what is intended by Article 5(1) is that lawful acquirer of a program is able to do any of the acts required for the use of the program in accordance with its intended purpose or for correcting errors. However, a contract may include specific provisions that 'control' the restricted acts which may be carried out by the user of the program[66] or, in other words, the conditions under which the program is to be used.[67]

Section 50C seeks to implement Article 5(1) of the Software Directive. This provision states:

(1) It is not an infringement of copyright for a lawful user of a copy of a computer program to copy or adapt it, provided that the copying or adapting—

(a) is necessary for his lawful use; and
(b) is not prohibited under any term or condition of an agreement regulating the circumstances in which his use is lawful.

(2) It may, in particular, be necessary for the lawful use of a computer program to copy it or adapt it for the purpose of correcting errors in it.

(3) This section does not apply to any copying or adapting permitted under section 50A or 50B.

There are a few differences between section 50C of the CDPA and Article 5(1) of the Software Directive. First, section 50C refers to acts of copying and adaptation, whereas Article 5(1) refers to those acts mentioned in Article 4(a) and (b) of the Software Directive.[68] However, given the way in which 'adaptation' is defined in section 21 of CDPA, there is less difference than first appears. Second, section 50C(2) refers to error correction as forming part of the lawful use of the program (and lawful use may be regulated by contract) whereas Article 5(1) refers to acts necessary for the use of the computer program in accordance with its intended purpose, including for error correction. However, the Commission comments that it 'is not aware that any practical difficulties have arisen as a result of this shortcoming.'[69] Third, section 50C does not refer to 'in the absence of specific contractual provisions', however, the Commission takes the view that this is not inconsistent with the Directive, on the basis that the UK applies a comprehensive concept freedom of contract.[70]

---

[65] See Copinger (1999) para 9–64.
[66] Commission Report, p 12.
[67] Czarnota and Hart (1991) pp 64–65.
[68] Lai (2000) p 137.
[69] Commission Report, p 12.
[70] Commission Report, p 12.

Lai argues that 'error correction', although undefined, will be construed strictly so as not to cover 'improvements' and 'modifications' to software packages. However, it probably will cover detection and location of the error as well as the measures taken to correct it.[71] Lai also makes the point that this particular exception will come in useful only where the lawful user has a copy of the source code of the program. If a copy of the source code is not available, then it is unlikely that the lawful user will be able to decompile the program in order to obtain such a copy. This is because 'error correction' falls outside the permitted objective in section 50B, CDPA. Further, section 50C(2) will not be applicable since it excludes either copying or adaptation and decompilation involves both activities.[72]

5. Right to Repair

A common law 'right to repair' or 'spare parts exception' was recognised by the House of Lords in *British Leyland v Armstrong,*[73] and subsequently interpreted narrowly by the Privy Council in *Canon Kabushiki Kaisha v Green Cartridge.*[74] The scope of the defence in relation to reverse engineering of software was considered in the case of *Mars v Teknowledge.*[75] The claimant, Mars, is a leading company in the design and manufacture of coin receiving and changing mechanisms for coin-operated machines. The machines included 'coin discriminators', whose function was to ascertain the authenticity and denomination of coins fed into the machine. The claimant had designed a new 'Cashflow' coin discriminator which could be reprogrammed to take account of new coin data. Data about different denominations of coins was recorded on an electronically erasable programmable read only memory (EEPROM). To inhibit reprogramming of the 'Cashflow' discriminator by persons other than Mars or their approved agents, the discriminator was encrypted. Nonetheless, the defendant, through a process of reverse engineering the EEPROM of the discriminator, discovered how to recalibrate or reprogram the discriminators, without further reference to the claimant. In other words, the defendant developed its own re-programming software for the 'Cashflow'.

The claimant issued proceedings on the basis that the defendant's actions amounted to infringement of copyright and database right, breach of confidence and infringement of section 296 of the CDPA. The defendant conceded that it had infringed the claimant's copyright and database right by reproducing the coin data, and the claimant's copyright by reproducing the discrimination algorithms within its software and making transient copies of the Mars' software in the course

---

[71] Lai (2000) p 138.
[72] Lai (2000) p 139.
[73] *British Leyland v Armstrong* [1986] AC 577.
[74] *Canon Kabushiki Kaisha v Green Cartridge* [1997] FSR 817.
[75] *Mars v Teknowledge* [2000] ECDR 99 ('*Mars*').

of developing and operating its reprogramming software. The parties agreed that the real issue was whether or not the defendant's infringements could be excused by reliance on the common law 'spare parts exception'.[76] Jacob J held that this defence could *not* be relied upon, given that EC law, as implemented into UK law, provided a completed statutory code. Mr Justice Jacob explained:

> That code in relation to computer programs is contained in sections 50 A–C of the Act. These provisions were inserted by the Copyright (Computer Programs) Regulations 1992. Those Regulations were made to implement Council Directive on the Legal Protection of Computer Programs 91/250/EEC. Nothing in the Directive, and consequently in sections 50A–C, provides for any 'repair' or update exception, although a whole variety of detailed acts are permitted . . . It is not for national judge-made laws (which may vary from country to country) to override or add to what are clearly intended to be Community wide rules. Were that not so, then there would be little point in having Directives requiring Member-States to align their laws in a specific area.[77]

Jacob J went on to say that even if he were wrong on this point, the recalibration activities of the defendant would not fall within the scope of this defence.[78]

Thus, the 'spare parts' exception appears to have limited or no relevance to computer programs under UK copyright law.[79]

Copyright Databases

As discussed in chapter 3, some types of multimedia works are likely to be classified as databases and, as such, attract copyright protection. Therefore, exceptions to infringement of copyright in a database become important to determining the use that may be made of multimedia works protected as databases. Article 6 of the Database Directive governs the exceptions to infringement of copyright databases.[80] Five categories of exception are included in Article 6.[81] Only one of

---

[76] Mars chose not to advance a case under s 296, CDPA. However, they did advance a case under breach of confidence.

[77] *Mars*, 106–7.

[78] *Mars*, 108–9.

[79] G Llewelyn, 'Does Copyright Law Recognise a Right to Repair' (1999) 21 *EIPR* 596, 599.

[80] J Gaster, 'The New EU Directive Concerning the Legal Protection of Databases' (1997) 20 *Fordham Intl L J* 1129, 1138 notes that the exceptions to copyright protection of databases 'was the subject of extensive horse trading in the Working Party'.

[81] Although note the suggestion from the European Commission that Article 6 of the Database Directive be amended to include an exception for the benefit of people with a disability, similar to that available under Article 5(3)(b) of Directive 2001/29/EC on the harmonisation of certain aspects of copyright and related rights in the information society OJ L167 22/6/2001, pp 10–19 ('Information Society Directive'). See *Commission Staff Working Paper on the review of the EC legal framework in the field of copyright and related rights* (Brussels, 19 July 2004) SEC (2004) 995, ('Working Paper') para 2.2.4.1.

these exceptions, however, relating to normal use of the database, is mandatory, with the remaining four exceptions being optional. Article 6(3) emphasises that the exceptions contained within Article 6, 'may not be interpreted in such a way as to allow its application to be used in a manner which unreasonably prejudices the rightholder's legitimate interests or conflicts with normal exploitation of the database.' The following sections will discuss these exceptions, and their implementation into UK law.

1. Mandatory Lawful User Exception

Article 6(1) of the Database Directive provides as follows:

> The performance by a lawful user of a database or of a copy thereof of any of the acts listed in Article 5 which is *necessary for the purposes of access to the contents of the database* and *normal use of the contents by the lawful user* shall not require the authorisation of the author of the database. Where the lawful user is authorised to use only part of the database, this provision shall apply only to that part. (Emphasis supplied)

The acts listed in Article 5 of the Database Directive are comprehensive, as they cover the following activities in relation to the database: reproduction, translation, adaptation, arrangement and any other alteration, distribution to the public (subject to exhaustion), any communication, display or performance to the public, and any reproduction, distribution, communication, display or performance to the public of an adapted database. The doing of these copyright acts, however, must be *necessary* in order to access the database contents and for normal use of the contents. What constitutes 'normal use' of the database contents is likely to be governed by the agreement with the rightholder.[82] Any contractual provision that seeks to override the exception in Article 6(1) will be null and void, according to Article 15. Importantly, the acts must be carried out by the *lawful user* and it is this concept which appears to give rise to the most difficulty in interpretation.

The concept of 'lawful user' is important to Article 6(1), along with Article 8 which grants lawful users of a *sui generis* database the right to extract or re-utilise insubstantial parts of the contents of database[83] and Article 9 which provides optional exceptions to the database right. The failure to define 'lawful user' has been criticised by Vanovermeire, who argues that 'by not defining the term, the Commission has overlooked one of the opportunities to enforce desired uniformity through harmonisation, thereby endangering one of the major goals of the Directive, certainty and stability in the legal regime of databases.'[84]

---

[82] See Gaster (1997) p 1140 and recital 34, Database Directive.

[83] Provided the database has been made available to the public and the acts do not conflict with the normal exploitation of the database or unreasonably prejudice the legitimate interests of the maker of the database.

[84] Vanovermeire (2000) p 81.

However, it may be argued that because the exceptions in Article 6(2), along with Article 9, are optional, harmonisation in the area of exceptions is not particularly important.

Three possible interpretations of 'lawful user' have been suggested.[85] The first (and broadest) interpretation of lawful user is any person who uses a database relying upon exceptions provided by the licence *or* those permitted by law (ie, the traditional exceptions to copyright and those mentioned in Articles 6, 8 and 9 of the Directive).[86] The second (and narrowest) interpretation is that the lawful user is a licensee, that is, 'the person having obtained a specific authorisation by contract, setting out the conditions of use'.[87] The third interpretation of lawful user is any person who lawfully acquires the database (for example, via sale, gift, public lending and rental contracts).[88]

The preferable interpretation of 'lawful user' is the third interpretation.[89] This is based on the history of Article 6 and is also supported by Articles 8 and 9 of the Directive, which include the condition of the database having been made available to the public.[90] This condition suggests 'lawful use can only be made of a licit copy of the database, ie, a copy manufactured and made available with the consent of the rightholder, obtained through the distribution channels authorised by the rightholder or by the law, ie, lawfully acquired.'[91] Another argument in favour of this interpretation is that is consistent with Article 5 of the Software Directive, governing exceptions to infringement of copyright in computer programs. Article 5 of the Software Directive talks of a 'lawful acquirer', a 'person having a right to use the computer program' and 'person having a right to use a copy of a computer program', which were discussed above as meaning a lawful acquirer.[92] In addition, the Commission has recently indicated that:

> 'lawful acquirer' [in Article 5 of the Software Directive] did in fact mean a purchaser, licensee, renter or a person authorised to use the program on behalf of one of the above. *This argument also draws from Articles 6 and 8 of the database Directive (Directive 96/9/EC) which use the term 'lawful user' and which were modelled along the lines of Article 5(1) of the computer programs Directive* (emphasis supplied).[93]

---

[85] Vanovermeire (2000); FW Grosheide, 'Database Protection—the European Way' (2002) 8 *Washington U J of L & Pol'y* 39; MJ Davison, *The Legal Protection of Databases* (CUP, Cambridge, 2003).
[86] Vanovermeire (2000) p 66; Davison (2003) p 78.
[87] Vanovermeire (2000) p 69; Davison (2003) p 77.
[88] Vanovermeire (2000) p 72; Davison (2003) p 78.
[89] Vanovermeire (2000) p 80; Grosheide (2002) p 69.
[90] Vanovermeire (2000) pp 72–74.
[91] Vanovermeire (2000) pp 74–75.
[92] Vanovermeire (2000) p 76; Grosheide (2002) p 69.
[93] See Commission Report, p 12.

Article 6(1) of the Database Directive has been implemented in UK law as section 50D of the CDPA.[94] That provision is similar in terms to Article 6(1), except that instead of referring to a 'lawful user' it refers to 'a person who has a right to use the database or any part of the database (whether under a licence to do any of the acts restricted by the copyright in the database or otherwise)'. Davison takes the view that the words 'or otherwise' introduce uncertainty, in that it includes some users who do not have a licence. These users may be limited to users of a tangible copy who obtain it from the original purchaser[95] or they may include those who are gaining access for the purposes of fair dealing.[96] Thus, the interpretation of 'lawful user' in section 50D appears open.[97]

Previously, section 29(5) of the CDPA stated that 'the doing of anything in relation to a database for the purposes of research for a commercial purpose is not fair dealing with a database.' However, this subsection was repealed by the Copyright Regulations, presumably because it was thought unnecessary after the amendment to section 29 which restricts the purpose of research to a non-commercial purpose.[98] Terms or conditions of any agreement that purport to prohibit or restrict the performance of an act permitted under section 50D are void by virtue of section 296B of the CDPA.[99]

2. Optional Exceptions

Article 6(2) allows Member States to introduce any of the following four exceptions to copyright protection of databases. First, reproduction for private purposes of a non-electronic database. Second, use for the sole purpose of illustration for teaching or scientific research, provided the source is indicated and to the extent justified by the non-commercial purpose. Third, use for the purposes of public security or for an administrative or judicial procedure. Finally, exceptions to copyright which are traditionally authorised under national law. The first three of these exceptions are mirrored in the *sui generis* regime.[100]

---

[94] According to Copinger (1999) para 9–65: 'This new permitted act was introduced to protect users of electronic databases who, in order to search a database, may find it necessary to download the whole or a substantial part of the database in the memory of a computer.'

[95] Bently and Sherman (2004) p 222. See also Laddie, *et al,* (2000) para 30.34.

[96] Davison (2003) p 145.

[97] C Rees and S Chalton, (eds), *Database Law* (Jordans, Bristol, 1998) 76 argue that the concept of 'lawful user' in s 50D could include a person who is relying on a statutory exception, such as section 56 of the CDPA, or an implied licence to use the database. Members States have adopted differing interpretations of 'lawful user' in implementing the Database Directive. For example, France has followed the second interpretation, namely that a lawful user is a licensee, whereas Germany follows the first interpretation, namely, that a lawful user is a person relying on either contract or acts permitted by law: Davison (2003) pp 114–115, 117, 125.

[98] Discussed below at pp 191–2.

[99] This implements Article 15, Database Directive. See also Copinger (1999) para 9–66.

[100] See Article 9(a), (b) and (c), Database Directive.

The first optional exception is limited, in that it exempts only the act of reproduction carried out in relation to non-electronic databases. It reflects a private use
type exception for hard-copy databases. This exception was not implemented into
the CDPA probably because a private use exception does not exist in UK copyright
law, as compared with certain civil law Member States.[101]

The scope of the second optional exception is difficult to ascertain. It is unclear,
for example, what will amount to '*illustration* for teaching or scientific research'.
Does 'illustration' confine the use to providing examples of what is being taught
or researched? If so, this would not allow a teacher or researcher to use the database simply in preparing their teaching or as an aid to their research. Further, does
'illustration for teaching' mean that use for the purpose of learning, in other
words, private study, is excluded?[102] Finally, illustration for teaching or scientific
research must be the sole purpose and must not exceed the non-commercial
purpose. Thus, it appears that the use must be non-commercial, which may be a
difficult requirement to satisfy in the light of realities of educational and research
institutions.[103] This exception was not specifically implemented in UK law.
However, the exception of fair dealing for the purpose of (non-commercial)
research and private study, along with the exceptions relating to copying by educational establishments in sections 32–36 of the CDPA will embrace the sorts of
activities contemplated by Article 6(2)(b) of the Database Directive.

The third optional exception, namely, Article 6(2)(c) concerning the purposes
of public security and administrative and judicial procedures, would appear to be
catered for by sections 45–50 of the CDPA. These provisions create exceptions
relating to public administration.

The fourth optional exception, namely, exceptions to copyright traditionally
authorised under national law, was the subject of consideration in *Mars v
Teknowledge* (discussed above in relation to computer programs). In *Mars*, Jacob
J considered that such exceptions had to be adopted by Member States and did not
encompass judge-made exceptions, such as the common law 'right to repair' or
'spare parts' exception that originated in *British Leyland v Armstrong*,[104] and was
subsequently narrowed by the Privy Council in *Canon Kabushiki Kaisha v Green
Cartridge*.[105] In relation to Article 6(2)(d) of the Database Directive, Jacob J commented—

[101] Eg, Germany, see German Law on Copyright and Neighbouring Rights 1965 ('German Law'),
Art 53 which includes exemptions for copies for private use and copies made for scholarly or scientific
use. For France see French Intellectual Property Code 1992 ('French Code'), Art L 122–5(2) dealing
with private reproduction and Art L 122–5(1) exempting free and private performances produced
exclusively within the family circle.
[102] Davison (2003) p 79.
[103] Davison (2003) p 80.
[104] *British Leyland v Armstrong* [1986] AC 577.
[105] *Canon Kabushiki Kaisha v Green Cartridge* [1997] FSR 817.

that provision is an option for Member States to adopt by way of limitation of database rights. It can hardly be for the judges of a particular Member State of their own to act as though they are exercising the option on behalf of that State. If Parliament had wanted to adopt an option in relation to the use of database rights for updating equipment, that is a matter for it, not the judges. I cannot regard section 173(2) (sic) as adopting such an option. Moreover it is far from certainly the case that the use of copyright in databases (which, before the Directive, were generally protected in the UK as literary works in form of compilations) was 'traditionally authorised' in this country.

Jacob J's comments about Article 6(2)(d), strictly speaking, are obiter dicta since the case concerned the applicability of the 'spare parts' defence to the *database right* and Article 6(2)(d) relates only to copyright databases.[106]

Database Right Exceptions

1. EU Law

Article 8(1) of the Database Directive emphasises that a lawful user of a database, which has been made available to the public by the database maker, has the right to extract and/or re-utilise insubstantial parts of the database contents. This right applies to that part of a database that a lawful user is authorised to extract or re-utilise. Article 8(2) emphasises that the acts of the lawful user must not conflict with normal exploitation of the database or unreasonably prejudice the legitimate interests of the maker of the database. Further, Article 8(3) stipulates that a lawful user 'may not cause prejudice to the holder of a copyright or related right in respect of the works or subject matter contained in the database.' Finally, Article 15 makes clear that any contractual provision seeking to override Article 8 is null and void.

The above 'right' of the lawful user must be considered in connection with Article 7 (discussed in ch 4), which prohibits extraction and/or re-utilisation of substantial parts of the contents of a database. The scope of the prohibition contained in Article 7(1) of the Database Directive is such that it should be obvious that a user of a database will be able to extract and/or re-utilise *insubstantial parts* of a the database contents.[107] In which case, what does Article 8 add in terms of the rights of the user? It seems that the effect of Article 8 is to ensure that any

---

[106] Llewelyn (1999) p 599 takes the view the 'spare parts defence' clearly does not apply to copyright databases.

[107] As discussed in ch 4 at pp 145–6, this is subject to Article 7(5), which prohibits repeated and systematic extraction and/or re-utilisation of insubstantial parts which would conflict with the normal exploitation of the database or unreasonably prejudice the legitimate interests of the maker of the database.

particular use of an insubstantial part of a database is not prohibited by contractual provisions in database licences.[108] This is limited, however, to lawful users, as opposed to any users, of a database. Thus, the concept of lawful user discussed above will also be relevant here.

In terms of the exceptions to the database right provided for in Article 9, these have been criticised for their failure to quite balance the wide protection that is provided for in Article 7.[109] The exceptions to the database right are listed in Article 9 of the Directive.[110] Since they are optional to implement, there is the risk that some Member States will implement a strong database right without corresponding balances in the form of exceptions.[111] However, for the Member States that have thus far implemented the Directive, this does not appear to have happened.[112] The exceptions provided for in Article 9 are also narrowly drawn. The three situations in which Member States may provide for exceptions to extraction or reutilisation are:

   i) extraction for private purposes of the contents of a non-electronic database;
  ii) extraction for the purposes of illustration for teaching or scientific research, provided the source is indicated and to the extent justified by the non-commercial purpose to be achieved; and
 iii) extraction or reutilisation for the purposes of public security or an administrative or judicial procedure.

The first type of exception, which is ostensibly a 'private use' exception, is limited to extraction from hard-copy databases. Thus, extraction from electronic databases, even for private purposes is excluded (unless it relates to an insubstantial part and falls within Article 8(1)). Re-utilisation from any type of database is also excluded (again, unless it falls within Article 8(1)).

In relation to the second exception, this creates a type of 'fair dealing' exception. However, it is limited to *extraction* and does not encompass re-utilisation. Thus, any on-line transmission, public performance or public display of a substantial part of the contents of a database for the purposes of non-commercial teaching or

---

[108] Davison (2003) p 91.

[109] Cornish and Llewelyn (2003) p 789; CD Freedman, 'Should Canada Enact a New Sui Generis Database Right?' (2002) 13 *Fordham Intellectual Property Media & Entertainment L J* 35, 97; J Lipton, 'Databases as Intellectual Property: New Legal Approaches' [2003] *EIPR* 139, 141–42; J Lipton, 'Balancing Private Rights and Public Policies: Reconceptualizing Property in Databases' (2003b) *Berkeley Technology L J* 773, 825–27; JH Reichman and P Samuelson, 'Intellectual Property Rights in Data?' (1997) 50 *Vanderbilt Law Review* 51, 93. *Cf* G M Hunsucker, 'The European Database Directive: Regional Stepping Stone to an International Model?' (1997) 7 *Fordham Intellectual Property Media & Entertainment L J* 697, 752–63, who argues that the exceptions, together with EC Competition Law, are enough to preserve the public's interest in competition.

[110] Although note the suggestion from the European Commission that Article 9, Database Directive be amended to include an exception for the benefit of people with a disability, similar to that available under Article 5(3)(b), Information Society Directive: see Working Paper, para 2.2.4.1.

[111] M J Bastian, 'Protection of "Noncreative" Databases: Harmonization of United States, Foreign and International Law' (1999) 22 *Boston College Intl & Comparative L Rev* 425, 455.

[112] See Davison (2003), ch 4.

research will not be exempt under this provision. Further, the purpose of 'illustration for teaching or research' is not the same as being able to extract or re-utilize the information for non-profit scientific[113] or educational *pursuits.*[114] In addition, purposes such as criticism or review or reporting current events are not catered for. Finally, for an extraction of this type to be exempt it must be non-commercial. This may be difficult for academics and others working within universities to satisfy. As Lipton comments, '[a] commercial purpose may be unclear in an era in which institutions such as universities have the potential to commercialize to an extent previously unpracticed research products and teaching materials in competition with other institutions.'[115]

The final type of exception is the widest in that it permits extraction or reutilisation of substantial parts of the database contents. This exception is directed at uses relating to public administration.

To the extent that technological protection measures are applied to *sui generis* databases, the Information Society Directive[116] prohibits circumvention of those measures[117] and the 'manufacture, import, distribution, sale, rental, advertisement for sale or rental, or possession for commercial purposes of devices . . . or the provision of services or trafficking in circumvention devices or services'.[118] Where national laws have implemented permissible exceptions to the database right, the question arises whether a lawful user of a database may circumvent such measures in order to rely on those exceptions. Article 6(4) of the Information Society Directive provides that where rightholders have not taken voluntary measures, such as via agreements, to ensure that beneficiaries of exceptions or limitations provided for in national law can take the benefit of such exceptions or limitations, then Member States shall take appropriate measures to ensure this is the case. The notion of 'voluntary measures' and 'appropriate measures' have been criticised for being vague.[119] Of particular concern, however, is the fact that Article 6(4) stipu-

---

[113] N Thakur, 'Database Protection in the European Union and the United States: the European Database Directive as an Optimum Global Model?' [2001] *IPQ* 100, 128 queries whether this exception would relate to researchers other than scientific researchers, such as historians.

[114] Reichman and Samuelson (1997) p 93. They argue that the exceptions in Article 9 of the Database Directive indicate that the 'sui generis provisions contain no real equivalents of the private use, fair use, and related exceptions that traditional copyright laws afford scientific and educational users of core literary and artistic works'. See also Lipton (2003b) p 829.

[115] Lipton (2003b) p 829.

[116] Directive 2001/29/EC on the harmonisation of certain aspects of copyright and related rights in the information society OJ L167 22/6/2001, pp 10–19 ('Information Society Directive').

[117] Technological protection measures are defined in Article 6(3), Information Society Directive.

[118] See Article 6(1) and (2), Information Society Directive. See also Article 6(3), Information Society Directive which specifically extends the protection against circumvention and trafficking in circumvention devices and services to *sui generis* databases.

[119] See, for example, M Hart, 'The Copyright in the Information Society Directive: an Overview' [2002] *EIPR* 58, 62–63; N Braun, 'The Interface Between The Protection of Technological Measures and the Exercise of Exceptions to Copyright and Related Rights: Comparing the Situation in the United States and the European Community' [2003] *EIPR* 496, 499–500, 502.

lates that this obligation on Member States shall not apply to databases 'made available to the public on agreed contractual terms in such a way that members of the public may access them from a place and a time individually chosen by them.'[120] Thus, the obligation on Member States to ensure that lawful users of databases can benefit from exceptions will apply to a limited range of databases, namely, *off-line* electronic databases. Further, it is not clear whether the right to extract or reutilise insubstantial parts of the database contents provided for in Article 8 would be classed as an 'exception or limitation', such that Article 6(4) of the Information Society Directive would apply. Consequently, there is the real likelihood that, in the case of on-line databases, the above exceptions can be overridden by the use of technological protection measures.

2. UK Law

No exception relating to reproduction of non-electronic databases for private purposes was introduced into UK law. Rather, the main exception to the database right is that of fair dealing. Regulation 20 provides that, where a database has been made available to the public in any manner, fair dealing with a substantial part of the database contents is not an infringement of the database right. This is provided the part is extracted by a *lawful user* of the database. The concept of lawful user is defined in Regulation 12(1) as, 'any person who (whether under a licence to do any of the acts restricted by any database right in the database or otherwise) has a right to use the database.'[121] In addition, the part must be *extracted* and it must be 'for the purpose of *illustration* for teaching or research and not for *any* commercial purpose' (emphasis supplied); and the source must be indicated. These provisos are consistent with Article 9(b) of the Database Directive and, as argued above, considerably limit the scope of this exception.

There are no indications of the factors that should be considered in determining whether the dealing with a substantial part of the database contents is *fair*. Probably the factors that are used in relation to fair dealing under copyright law[122] can be used in this context. Thus, the following factors may assist in determining whether the dealing is 'fair': the purpose of the extractions; the number and extent of the extractions; and the proportion of the extraction/s to the proportion of the work in which they are used. The purpose of the extractions will be constrained by the fact that they must be for illustration in teaching or research and not for any commercial purpose. This leaves the amount of the extractions and the substantiality of the

---

[120] Braun (2003), 501 comments that Article 6(4) para 4 of the Information Society Directive considerably narrows the scope of the intervention provided for in Article 6(4) paras 1 and 2.

[121] Laddie, *et al*, (2000) para 30.60 indicate that a lawful user could be a licensee, along with subsequent purchasers of copies of a database made available to the public.

[122] See discussion below at pp 192–4. See also Davison (2003) p 151.

extractions in relation to the context in which they are used as the relevant factors to be assessed.

An important consideration to bear in mind is that this fair dealing exception relates to the *contents* of the database in terms of the database right and not in terms of copyright. Thus, while an extraction of a substantial part of a database's contents for the purpose of (non-commercial) illustration for teaching or research may not infringe the database right, it may still infringe copyright in those individual works that are extracted or reproduced in the process.[123] This will depend on a number of things: whether fair dealing for the purpose of research or private study in respect of the individual copyright work can apply, or whether ownership of those individual works has been assigned to the database owner, or if the database owner has obtained from the various copyright owners licences that allow such dealings.

There are no fair dealing exceptions to the *sui generis* right that relate to reporting of current events or criticism or review.[124] However, lawful users of databases could use *insubstantial* amounts of the database contents for either of those purposes. Regulation 19(1) emphasises that a lawful user of a database, which has been made available to the public in any manner, is entitled to extract or re-utilise insubstantial parts of the contents of the database for any purpose.[125] Regulation 19(2) reiterates the importance of regulation 19(1): it states that where a term of an agreement, which gives a person the right to use a database or part thereof, seeks to prevent a person from extracting or re-utilising insubstantial parts of the contents of the database, this term will be void.

Other specific exceptions are contained in schedule 1 of the Database Regulations.[126] These relate to acts done for the purposes of public administration, including: anything done for the purposes of, or for reporting, parliamentary or judicial proceedings or the proceedings of a Royal Commission or statutory inquiry; extraction of information from public registers provided this is done with the authority of the appropriate person; use by the Crown of the contents of the databases which were communicated to it in the course of public business; and the doing of acts specifically authorised by Act of Parliament.

Finally, regulation 21 states that acts of extraction and re-utilisation of a substantial part of the contents of a database are permitted if it is not possible by reasonable inquiry to ascertain the identity of the database maker and it is reasonable to assume that the database right has expired.

---

[123] See also Article 8(3), Database Directive: 'A lawful user of a database which is made available to the public in any manner may not cause prejudice to the holder of a copyright or related right in respect of the works or subject matter contained in that database.'

[124] Laddie, *et al* (2000) para 30.63.

[125] Copyright and Rights in Databases Regulations 1997, SI 1997/3032 ('Database Regulations'), reg 19 implements Article 8, Database Directive.

[126] These exceptions reflect a complete code of permitted acts: see *Mars*, 107 (Jacob J) and also Laddie, *et al* (2000) para 30.62.

Fair Dealing and other Royalty-free Exceptions

There are numerous exceptions listed within chapter III of the CDPA, however, not all of these have an obvious relevance to multimedia works. Exceptions relating to software and databases (both copyright and *sui generis*) are highly relevant to multimedia works and these have already been discussed above. Other exceptions are also particularly applicable to multimedia works and these are the focus of the following section. Before turning to discuss these exceptions, however, it is necessary to consider how Article 5 of the Information Society Directive has sought to harmonise copyright exceptions.

1. EU Law[127]

The Information Society Directive, in addition to extending and seeking to harmonise the exclusive rights granted to authors,[128] also attempts to strike a fair balance between rightholders and users and to harmonise the copyright exceptions and limitations in Member States.[129] Article 5 of the Information Society Directive is the key provision here and a distinction must be drawn between Article 5(1) and Articles 5(2) and 5(3). Article 5(1) stipulates the only *mandatory* exception and relates to certain acts of temporary reproduction which form an integral and essential part of a technological process and whose sole purpose is to enable network transmissions or lawful use. The scope of this exception has already been discussed in detail in the chapter 4[130] and that discussion will not be repeated here. Articles 5(2) and 5(3), however, set out an *optional* yet *exhaustive* list of exceptions. In other words, Member States are not obliged to implement any of the exceptions contained in these provisions, however, they may not introduce, or retain, exceptions or limitations that are not contained within, or are inconsistent with, those listed in Articles 5(2) and 5(3).[131] The optional nature of these exceptions and the fact there are twenty exceptions in total undoubtedly thwarts the goal of harmonisation.[132] Further, an exhaustive list leaves little flexibility for

---

[127] See also T Cook and L Brazell, *The Copyright Directive: UK Implementation* (Jordans, Bristol, 2004) 18–25.

[128] Discussed above ch 4 at pp 100, 133–35.

[129] Recital 31, Information Society Directive.

[130] See above at pp 102–6.

[131] Hart (2002) p 59; E Derclaye, 'The Copyright Directive: How will the Statutory and Case Law of England and Wales be Affected?' [2001] *Copyright World* 19.

[132] G Davies, *Copyright and the Public Interest*, 2nd edn (Sweet & Maxwell, London, 2002) 316–17; G Kennedy, 'Copyright in the Information Society: A World of More Copies and Rights?' [1999] *Copyright World* 15, 18; PB Hugenholtz, 'Why the Copyright Directive is Unimportant and Possibly Invalid' [2000] *EIPR* 499, 500–1; Cook and Brazell (2004) p 21.

devising new exceptions and limitations that may be appropriate in future environments.[133] However, the advantage of having optional exceptions is that different legal traditions in Member States may comfortably co-exist and an exhaustive list of exceptions means that some headway is being made towards harmonisation.[134]

Article 5(2) of the Information Society Directive provides for exceptions and limitations that may be applied to the right of reproduction, whereas Article 5(3) concerns exceptions and limitations that may be applied to the right of reproduction, the right of communication to the public and the right of making available to the public. Where a Member State introduces an exception or limitation to the reproduction right, pursuant to Article 5(2) or 5(3), it may also provide a similar exception or limitation to the right of distribution, 'to the extent justified by the purpose of the unauthorised act of reproduction'.[135]

Some of the more noteworthy exceptions contained in Articles 5(2) and 5(3) of the Information Society Directive will be discussed here, as opposed to the entire list of twenty exceptions. Turning first to Article 5(2), this provision allows Member States to provide for five exceptions or limitations specifically relating to the reproduction right. Article 5(2)(a) permits exceptions or limitations in respect of reprographic copying (ie, reproductions on paper or any similar medium effected by photographic techniques) provided the rightholder receives *fair compensation*. The notion of fair compensation is also critical to Article 5(2)(b), which allows for private use exceptions. Article 5(2)(b) states that Member States may provide for exceptions or limitations in respect of:

> *reproductions on any medium* made by a natural person for *private use* and for ends that are *neither directly nor indirectly commercial*, on condition that the rightholders receive *fair compensation* which takes account of the application or non-application of technological measures referred to in Article 6 to the work or subject-matter concerned. (Emphasis supplied)

---

[133] T Heide, 'The Berne Three-Step Test and the Proposed Copyright Directive' [1999] 3 *EIPR* 105, 108; Hugenholtz (2000) p 501; Cook and Brazell (2004) p 21. PB Hugenholtz, 'Copyright and Freedom of Expression' in R Dreyfuss, DL Zimmerman and H First, (eds), *Expanding the Boundaries of Intellectual Property: Innovation Policy for the Knowledge Society* (OUP, Oxford, 2001) 343, 352 observes, 'that removing the "safety valve" of discretion to create new exceptions in the laws of the Member States . . . will put the copyright versus free speech conflict firmly on the map in Europe.' Davies (2002) p 317 comments that if a new exception is needed, the Information Society Directive will have to be revised and queries whether this is compatible with Article 10 WIPO Copyright Treaty 1996 ('WCT') and Article 16, WIPO Performances and Phonograms Treaty 1996 ('WPPT').

[134] See recital 32, Information Society Directive: the 'exhaustive enumeration of exceptions and limitations . . . takes due account of the different legal traditions in Member States, while, at the same time, aiming to ensure a functioning internal market.' See also G Tritton, *Intellectual Property in Europe*, 2nd edn, (Sweet & Maxwell, London, 2002) para 4–112.

[135] Art 5(4), Information Society Directive.

Articles 5(2)(a) and (b) represent exceptions which are new to UK copyright law, in that the CDPA does not contain parallel provisions.[136] In addition, the exceptions are conditional on the rightholder receiving 'fair compensation' and this concept, although not defined, is elaborated upon in recital 35, which states:

> In certain cases of exceptions or limitations, rightholders should receive fair compensation to compensate them adequately for the use made of their protected works or other subject matter. When determining the form, detailed arrangements and possible level of such fair compensation, *account should be taken of the particular circumstances of each case.* When evaluating these circumstances, a valuable criterion would be the *possible harm to the rightholders* resulting from the act in question. In cases where rightholders have already received payment in some other form, for instance as part of a licence fee, no specific or separate payment may be due. The level of fair compensation should take *full account of the degree of use of technological protection measures* referred to in this Directive. In certain situations where the prejudice to the rightholder would be minimal, no obligation for payment may arise. (Emphasis supplied)

From the above recital it seems that the concept of 'fair compensation' is reasonably flexible.[137] An issue that has arisen is whether or not existing levy systems in certain Member States, such as Germany, will satisfy the notion of fair compensation. Broadly speaking, these levy systems permit certain private copying provided a levy is paid. The levy is imposed on the manufacturer or importer of copying equipment (such as photocopiers, scanners and video recorders) and/or the media used to copy such works (such as blank tapes, blank CDs, and mini-discs) and the scheme is usually administered by a collecting society.[138] Whilst a levy system might be a practical method of ensuring that rightholders receive appropriate compensation, it can also be criticised as a crude tool, since all purchasers of recording equipment and media indirectly bear the levy, despite the fact that the equipment or media may not be used to make infringing copies.[139]

In terms of determining fair compensation, recital 35, read in conjunction with Article 5(2)(b), emphasises that the use of technological protection measures will be a relevant consideration. This is important, since otherwise levies would be paid for copying which cannot take place or which is strictly regulated.[140]

Article 5(2)(c) allows exceptions or limitations for publicly accessible libraries, educational establishments and museums, or archives, in respect of acts of reproduction which are not for direct or indirect economic or commercial advantage.

---

[136] See C Schaal, 'The Copyright Exceptions of Art 5(2)(a) and (b) of the EU Directive 2001/29' (2003) 14 *Entertainment L Rev* 117, 118; S Stokes, 'The UK Implementation of the Information Society Copyright Directive: Current Issues and Some Guidance for Business' (2004) 10 *Computer and Telecommunications Law Review* 5.

[137] Schaal (2003) p 118.

[138] Hart (2002) p 60; and Schaal (2003) pp 119–20 discussing the levy system in Germany.

[139] Hart (2002) p 60.

[140] Hart (1992) p 60; Cook and Brazell (2004) p 23.

This provision recognises the importance of allowing non-profit educational organisations to make reproductions; however, this exception does not extend to uses made in the context of on-line delivery of works or other subject matter.[141] While there are no direct parallels in the CDPA to this provision, several exceptions fall within the same terrain and were amended as a result of implementation of Article 5(2) of the Information Society Directive.[142]

Article 5(3) of the Information Society Directive contains a longer list of optional exceptions and limitations (fifteen in total) and these may apply to the reproduction right, along with the communication right and the right of making to the public. Some of the more significant exceptions will be discussed here. Article 5(3)(a) allows for exceptions or limitations where the use is for the *sole purpose* of illustration for teaching or scientific research. This is provided that, where possible, the source (including the author's name) is indicated and only to the extent justified by the non-commercial purpose to be achieved.[143] This provision recognises the importance of the use of copyright works to learning, dissemination of knowledge and developing new works. It is, however, strictly circumscribed by the fact that the sole purpose must be teaching or scientific research (including distance learning) and the use must not exceed its *non-commercial purpose*. Recital 42 of the Information Society Directive emphasises that the commercial/non-commercial nature of the activity will be determined by the activity as such, rather than according to whether the organisation is non-profit making or commercial. In respect of UK law, the prerequisite of non-commercial purpose represents a significant departure, since historically the fair dealing exception concerning research has not been limited to non-commercial research.[144]

Article 5(3)(c) permits exceptions or limitations relating to media activities. More specifically, it allows for the use of copyright material for reporting of current events. This is to the extent justified by the informatory purpose, and provided the source and author's name are indicated, unless this turns out to be impossible. This provision also permits the use of published articles or broadcasts on current economic, political or religious topics, again provided the source and author's name are indicated. The most direct parallel to this provision in UK law is section 30(2) of the CDPA, which creates an exception of fair dealing for the purpose of reporting current events.

Article 5(3)(d) is similar to Article 5(3)(c), in that it promotes freedom of expression, this time in relation to criticism and review, as opposed to reporting news. Thus, quotations for purposes such as criticism or review are permitted, *provided* the copyright work or subject matter has already been lawfully made

---

[141] See recital 40, Information Society Directive.
[142] See ss 38, 39, 43 61, CDPA.
[143] This language is virtually identical to that in Article 6(2)(b), Database Directive.
[144] See also Cook and Brazell (2004) p 24; Hart (2002) p 60.

available to the public and the use is in accordance with fair practice and to the extent required by the specific purpose. The source, including the author's name, must also be indicated, unless this turns out to be impossible. This exception is reflected in UK law in the form of section 30(1), which creates a fair dealing exception for the purpose of criticism or review.[145]

Finally, Article 5(3)(o) is a 'catch-all' provision, in that it permits 'uses in certain other cases of minor importance where exceptions or limitations already exist under national law.' Importantly, these exceptions or limitations can only concern analogue uses and must not affect the free circulation of goods and services within the Community. Further, they must be without prejudice to the other exceptions and limitations contained in Article 5.

Article 5(5) of the Information Society Directive stipulates that implementation of the exceptions or limitations provided for in Article 5 must be 'applied in certain special cases which do not conflict with a normal exploitation of the work or other subject-matter and do not unreasonably prejudice the legitimate interests of the rightholder'. Article 5(5) follows the wording of Article 9(2) of the Berne Convention[146] and Article 10(2) of the WCT[147] and effectively makes implementation of the exceptions or limitations subject to the 'three-step' test[148] in international copyright law.[149] Article 5(5) apparently operates as an additional safeguard so that if a member state implements one of the permissible exceptions under Article 5, it must ensure compliance with the 'three-step' test.[150]

---

[145] Other provisions in Article 5(3), Information Society Directive that promote freedom of expression include Article 5(3)(f) dealing with political speeches and 5(3)(k) dealing with use for the purpose of caricature, parody or pastiche.

[146] Art 9(2) of the Berne Convention for the Protection of Literary and Artistic Works ('Berne Convention') states: 'It shall be a matter for legislation in the countries of the Union to permit the reproduction of such works in certain special cases, provided that such reproduction does not conflict with a normal exploitation of the work and does not unreasonably prejudice the legitimate interests of the author.'

[147] Art 10(2) of the WCT states: 'Contracting Parties shall, when applying the Berne Convention, confine any limitations of or exceptions to rights provided for therein to certain special cases that do not conflict with a normal exploitation of the work and do not unreasonably prejudice the legitimate interests of the author.'

[148] For a discussion of the three-step test see M Senftleben, *Copyright, Limitations and the Three-Step Test* (Kluwer, The Hague, 2004), esp ch 4. See also S Ricketson, *The Berne Convention for the Protection of Literary and Artistic Works: 1886–1986* (Kluwer, London, 1987) 482–89; and S Ricketson, 'The Boundaries of Copyright: Its Proper Limitations and Exceptions: International Conventions and Treaties' [1999] *IPQ* 56.

[149] See recital 44, Information Society Directive. See also Senftleben (2004) pp 250, 255–56. Senftleben (2004) pp 245–46 argues that the three-step has now become part of the *acquis communtaire*, given that there is similar wording in Art 6(3), Database Directive and Art 6(3) Software Directive, and that Article 11(1), Information Society Directive incorporates a nearly identical version of Article 5(5), Information Society Directive into the Directive 92/100/EEC of 19 November 1992 on rental and lending right and on certain rights related to copyright in the field of intellectual property OJ L 346, 27/11/1992, pp 61–66 ('Rental Right Directive').

[150] Senftleben (2004) pp 255–56.

Senftleben makes three key observations about the application of Article 5(5) to the rest of Article 5. First, that to fulfil the condition that exceptions or limitations are applied in *certain special cases* Member States do not need to 'form special cases of the enumerated cases.'[151] In other words, Member States are not required to implement the limitations in Article 5 more narrowly than is set out in the Directive itself. Second, the obligation on Member States to provide for 'fair compensation' in three cases under Article 5(2) is independent from the obligation to provide payment of equitable remuneration pursuant to the three-step test.[152] As such, it is Senftleben's view that fair compensation may not be adequate in the case of copying by industrial undertakings of the type specified under Article 5(2)(a) and that a digital private use system administered by libraries (under Article 5(2)(b)) would also require fair compensation. Further, that the three-step test requires payment of monetary reward in respect of Article 5(3)(a) exemption for illustrating teaching or scientific research[153] and payment of equitable remuneration in the case of Article 5(3)(e) exception relating to uses for public security, performance or reporting of administrative, parliamentary or judicial proceedings.[154] Finally, Senftleben takes the view that although it is not necessary to implement the 'three-step' test in national legislation, it would be wise to do so, since it could help achieve the objective of harmonisation of copyright law.[155]

Having identified the main features of Article 5 of the Information Society Directive, we turn to consider the UK copyright exceptions that are relevant to multimedia works and which have been amended as a result of implementation of the Directive.[156]

---

[151] Senftleben (2004) p 291

[152] Senftleben (2004) pp 274–77.

[153] Note that in the draft version, Article 5(3)(a) of the Information Society Directive contained a requirement that rightholders receive fair compensation for this exempted use, however, the requirement was subsequently deleted since it was considered unnecessary in the light of the non-commercial purpose of the activities involved and the possibility open to member States of imposing a condition of fair compensation, should they so desire: see Amended Proposal for a European Parliament and Council Directive on the Harmonization of Certain Aspects of Copyright and Related Rights in the Information Society COM (1999) 250 Final OJ C180, 25 June 1999, p 6. See also para 30 of the European Council's reasons, included within its Common Position at OJ C 344, 1 December 2000, p 1.

[154] Senftleben (2004) pp 276–77.

[155] Senftleben (2004) pp 280–81.

[156] No new exceptions were introduced as a result of implementation of the Information Society Directive. Rather the Copyright Regulations amended the existing exceptions and limitations in the CDPA, mainly narrowing them in scope.

2. UK Exceptions

(a) Fair Dealing for the Purpose of Research or Private Study

Users of multimedia works may wish to rely on the exception of fair dealing for the purpose of research or private study in respect of certain activities.[157] This exception is contained in section 29 of the CDPA and is limited to literary, dramatic, musical or artistic works and the typographical arrangement of published editions.[158] As such, this exception will be relevant to multimedia works protected as literary works (ie, databases or compilations)[159] or as dramatic works, but *not* as films.

As a result of implementation of Article 5(3)(a) of the Information Society Directive, along with Article 6(2)(b) of the Database Directive, section 29 has undergone considerable narrowing in its scope.[160] In the case of fair dealing for the purpose of *research,* this is now limited to research for a *non-commercial purpose*[161] and Cook and Brazell suggest that 'it would be prudent to assume that any research with even an indirectly commercial purpose will require a licence for any copying involved.'[162] Moreover, use for a non-commercial purpose must be accompanied by a sufficient acknowledgment, although this is not required where

---

[157] Under the CDPA, fair dealing must relate to one of the purposes specified in ss 29 and 30 (ie, research or private study, criticism or review, or reporting of current events). This may be contrasted with the position in the US, where s 107 of the US Copyright Act 1976 sets out a 'fair use' defence which is not limited to specific purposes (its list of purposes is illustrative, rather than exhaustive).

[158] Ss 29(1), (1C), (2), CDPA.

[159] According to ss 29(4) and (4A), CDPA, acts of reverse engineering and decompilation in respect of computer programs are excluded from this fair dealing exception: see above at pp 165–66, 170.

[160] For discussion see Cook and Brazell (2004) pp 53–55; Bently and Sherman (2004) pp 197–200.

[161] S 29(1), CDPA, although not for typographical arrangements of published editions. For the position previously see Laddie, *et al,* (2000) para 20.12.

[162] Cook and Brazell (2004) p 53. This seems to be the only way of avoiding the difficulty of separating out research undertaken for commercial as opposed to non-commercial reasons. *Cf* the position in Canada, *CCH Canadian Ltd v Law Society of Upper Canada* [2004] 1 SCR 339 where a unanimous Supreme Court of Canada considered, *inter alia,* the scope of section 29 of the Canadian Copyright Act 1985, which creates an exception for fair dealing for the purpose of research or private study. The Supreme Court held that the fair dealing exceptions are 'users' rights' (para 48) and that in the context of section 29, 'research', 'must be given a large and liberal interpretation to ensure that users' rights are not unduly constrained' (para 51). Thus, research was *not* limited to non-commercial or private contexts and lawyers photocopying relevant cases could be considered as conducting 'research' within the meaning of section 29.

See also the position in the US, where the fair use defence in s 107, US Copyright Act 1976 refers to the purposes of, *inter alia,* teaching, scholarship or research. In Australia, the Copyright Law Review Committee ('CLRC') recommended that fair dealing for the purpose of commercial research should be permitted, since there is a public interest in allowing some commercial research to be covered and the distinction between private and commercial activities undertaken for research or study is often unclear. Moreover, the commercial nature of the research could be taken into account or weighed up as part of the fairness criteria: Aust Copyright Law Review Committee, *Simplification of the Copyright Act 1968, Part 1: Exceptions to the Exclusive Rights of Copyright Owners* (AGD, Canberra, 1998) ('SR:1') para 6.116.

'this would be impossible for reasons of practicality or otherwise'.[163] In relation to fair dealing for the purpose of *private study*, the Government sought to bring the exception into line with Article 5(2)(b) of the Information Society Directive by inserting a definition of 'private study' which states that it does not include 'any study which is directly or indirectly for a commercial purpose'.[164] The UK did not, however, feel the need to make this exception conditional on the payment of 'fair compensation'.[165]

Section 29 of the CDPA contemplates that persons, other than the researcher or student, may engage in copying on another person's behalf that amounts to fair dealing.[166] Where the person copying is a librarian, or a person acting on behalf of a librarian, that person must not do anything which would not be permitted under sections 38, 39 or 40 of the CDPA.[167] In short, these provisions allow librarians to make a copy of part of a published work, or of an article in a periodical, where it is for the *non-commercial* research or private study of a user; however, this copying must not amount to multiple copying. Where a person other than a librarian is doing the copying that person must not know, or have reason to believe, that the copying will result in multiple copies.[168]

The assessment of whether any dealing is 'fair' is a matter of degree[169] or fact and impression.[170] Unlike the situation in other common law jurisdictions, such as Australia[171] and the United States,[172] there are no guiding factors set out in the CDPA.[173] Nonetheless, case law offers guiding factors relevant to determining 'fairness'[174] which bear considerable similarity to the statutory factors in Australia and the United States.

---

[163] S 29(1B), CDPA.

[164] S 178, CDPA. See Consultation on UK Implementation of Directive 2001/29/EC on Copyright and Related Rights in the Information Society: Analysis of Reponses and Government Conclusions ('Consultation Paper') available at http://www.patent.gov.uk/about/consultations/responses/copydirect/index.htm, p 6.

[165] Which Senftleben (2004) pp 276–77 argues is contrary to the 'three-step' test.

[166] *Cf* the situation that existed previously under s 6(1) of the Copyright Act 1956 (UK); see also *Sillitoe v McGraw-Hill Book Company (UK) Ltd* [1983] FSR 545.

[167] S 29(3)(a), CDPA.

[168] S 29(3)(b), CDPA.

[169] *Hubbard v Vosper* [1972] 2 QB 84, 94 (Lord Denning MR).

[170] *Beloff v Pressdram Ltd* [1973] RPC 765, 786 (Ungoed-Thomas J); *Pro Sieben Media AG v Carlton Television Ltd* [2000] ECDR 110, 120 (Robert Walker LJ delivering judgment of CA).

[171] See ss 40(2) and 103C(2), Copyright Act 1968 (Cth), which set out a non-exhaustive list of factors to be taken into account when determining whether fair dealing for the purpose of research or study is 'fair'.

[172] Section 107, US Copyright Act 1976 sets out the 'fair use' exception and a non-exhaustive list of factors to be taken into account when determining whether a use, for purposes including teaching, scholarship or research, is 'fair'.

[173] This is also the case under the Canadian Copyright Act 1985, s 29 and the factors have been developed by the courts. For the most recent articulation see the Supreme Court of Canada in *CCH Canadian Ltd v Law Society of Upper Canada* [2004] 1 SCR 339, paras 53–60.

[174] For a discussion see Bently and Sherman (2004) pp 194–96; Laddie, *et al* (2000) para 20.16.

The purpose of the dealing is a relevant factor.[175] If the dealing is commercial in nature this will weigh against a finding of fairness.[176] The motives for the dealing may also be taken into account.[177] Thus, the court must 'judge the fairness by the objective standard of whether a fair minded and honest person would have dealt with the copyright work in the manner' in question.[178] Another relevant factor is whether or not the work is published. If the work is unpublished, this will weigh against a finding of fairness and, in the case of fair dealing for the purpose of criticism or review, the defence may not be invoked if the work has not been previously 'made available' to the public.[179] Linked to this factor is how the work is obtained. If the work is obtained surreptitiously, such as through being stolen or leaked, this may count against a dealing being fair.[180] The quantity and quality of the work that is dealt with is also highly relevant and the more substantial the dealing, the more likely it is that it will be considered unfair.[181] Further, the effect that the use has on the market for the work is particularly important.[182]

It has been suggested that, in the light of the Human Rights Act 1998 and its incorporation of the European Convention of Human Rights into UK law, particularly Article 10 concerning freedom of expression, courts should not adopt a rigid attitude towards the fair dealing factors.[183] Moreover, it is arguable that courts should take additional factors into account, such as the purpose of the use in a wider sense (eg, where the use deals with a matter of political importance)[184]

---

[175] *Hubbard v Vosper* [1972] 2 QB 84, 94 (Lord Denning MR), approved in *Beloff v Pressdram Ltd* [1973] RPC 765, 786 (Ungoed-Thomas J). See also *Hyde Park Residence Ltd v Yelland* [2001] Ch 143, 158 (Aldous LJ delivering majority judgment of CA); *Newspaper Licensing Agency Ltd v Marks & Spencer* [2001] Ch 257, 272 (Peter Gibson LJ), and 280 (Chadwick LJ).

[176] *Ashdown v Telegraph Group* [2002] Ch 149, 174 (Lord Phillips MR delivering judgment of CA).

[177] *Hyde Park Residence Ltd v Yelland* [2001] Ch 143, 158 (Aldous LJ); *Pro Sieben Media AG v Carlton Television Ltd* [2000] ECDR 110, 121 (Robert Walker LJ).

[178] *Hyde Park Residence Ltd v Yelland* [2001] Ch 143, 159 (Aldous LJ); *Newspaper Licensing Agency Ltd v Marks & Spencer* [2001] Ch 257, 272 (Peter Gibson LJ).

[179] S 30, CDPA. See *British Oxygen Co Ltd v Liquid Air Ltd* [1925] Ch 383, 393; *Hyde Park Residence Ltd v Yelland* [2001] Ch 143, 159 (Aldous LJ); *Ashdown v Telegraph Group* [2002] Ch 149, 173–74 (Lord Phillips MR). *Cf, Time Warner Entertainments Company LP v Channel Four Television Plc* [1994] EMLR 1, 10 per Neill LJ, who comments that the method of obtaining a work is relevant to unpublished works, but not those in the public domain.

[180] See *Beloff v Pressdram Ltd* [1973] RPC 765, 786 (Ungoed-Thomas J); and *Hyde Park Residence Ltd v Yelland* [2001] Ch 143, 159 (Aldous LJ).

[181] *Ashdown v Telegraph Group* [2002] Ch 149, 173 and 175 (Lord Phillips MR); and *Hubbard v Vosper* [1972] 2 QB 84, 94 (Lord Denning MR).

[182] *Ashdown v Telegraph Group* [2002] Ch 149, 174 (Lord Phillips MR); *Pro Sieben Media AG v Carlton Television Ltd* [2000] ECDR 110, 120 (Robert Walker LJ); *Newspaper Licensing Agency Ltd v Marks & Spencer* [2001] Ch 257, 272 (Peter Gibson LJ), and 280 (Chadwick LJ).

[183] *Ashdown v Telegraph Group* [2002] Ch 149, 173 (Lord Phillips MR). See also J Griffiths, 'Copyright Law After Ashdown—Time to Deal Fairly with the Public' [2002] *IPQ* 240, 250–55 criticising the Court of Appeal decision in *Ashdown*. MD Birnhack, 'Acknowledging the Conflict between Copyright Law and Freedom of Expression Under the Human Rights Act' (2003) 14 *Entertainment L Rev* 24, 33.

[184] Birnhack (2003) p 33.

and also the nature of the defendant's work—such as whether it is a work of 'low' as opposed to 'high' authorship.[185]

Users of instructional or educational multimedia works may be keen to rely on this particular fair dealing exception. Certainly there is an increasing amount of instruction occurring through CD-Rom based and on-line multimedia works, not least because it opens up 'exciting new possibilities for curricular design'.[186] Fair dealing with the multimedia work protected as a compilation, copyright database or dramatic work, as well as fair dealing with the individual works that comprise the multimedia work, will need to be considered by users.

In respect of multimedia works that qualify as (copyright) databases or compilations,[187] fair dealing for the purpose of research or private study must be directed towards the *structure* of the database or compilation and *not* its contents. Since multimedia works that qualify as databases or compilations are likely to involve more original selection than arrangement of contents, this leaves the *selection* of contents as the main aspect of the database or compilation that may be copied for the purposes of research or private study.

For multimedia works that qualify as dramatic works,[188] the dealing may relate to the content of the entire work, as opposed to simply the structure (or selection or arrangement of contents). The fact that many multimedia works that qualify as film works will also qualify as dramatic works compensates for the fact that fair dealing for the purpose of research or study does not extend to films. For users who wish legitimately to copy any of the individual works that comprise a multimedia work, they may also seek to rely upon this fair dealing exception.

Users of multimedia works will regularly engage in the activities of browsing, printing or saving the entire work, or parts thereof. This next section considers whether such acts can amount to *fair* dealing.

Browsing a multimedia work or parts thereof and thus temporarily copying its contents in the RAM of one's computer may be undertaken for the purpose of research or private study. However, a user browsing for research purposes must be able to show that this relates to non-commercial research. In terms of whether such dealing is 'fair', a relevant consideration will be the purpose of the temporary reproduction which, in this case, will be to make the work perceptible or accessible. This is hardly a commercial use. The nature of the works reproduced and the

---

[185] Griffiths (2002) pp 257–60.

[186] L Moran, 'Distance Education, Copyright and Communication in the Information Society' (1999) 33 *Copyright Bull* 3, 10–11 explains that computer based, multimedia content produced as CD-Rom or for on-line delivery is one of the two main educational strategies emerging in the digital environment. The other main strategy is computer-mediated communication, ie, electronic mail, file transfer, computer conferencing and remote computer access. See also A Monotti, 'University Copyright in the Digital Age: Balancing and Exploiting Rights in Computer Programs, Web-Based Materials, Databases and Multimedia in Australian Universities' [2002] *EIPR* 251.

[187] See ch 3 above at pp 41–59.

[188] See ch 3 above at pp 77–80.

amount and substantiality of the works reproduced will vary, depending on the sophistication and type of multimedia work and how much of it is browsed. In terms of the effect this type of reproduction has on the market for the work, arguably it will be minimal since 'browsing does not affect the market for the original work any more than the browsing allowed in public libraries'.[189] Thus, browsing a multimedia work, or its contents, could well fall within the scope of this exception.

In relation to copying a multimedia work, or parts thereof, through saving or printing, it is difficult to say with any certainty whether this will qualify as fair dealing since there are such varied amounts and types of saving and printing that may be carried out.[190] Nevertheless, some of the relevant considerations will be canvassed. As has already been mentioned, a key threshold criterion is whether the purpose is for *non-commercial* research or private study. Assuming this hurdle can be surmounted, the question becomes whether the dealing is fair. Relevant to this assessment is the purpose or character of the saving or printing. Thus, saving or printing may be carried out to permit a more convenient, later use of the work for the purposes of personal, non-commercial research, rather than having to read the work on-line or on-screen. However, where a person saves or prints material in order to accumulate an archive of material, this may be considered less of a personal, non-commercial purpose; particularly so where an institution is archiving material.[191] The nature of the work, whether it is factual or highly creative, will be relevant and this will require an assessment of what actually is the work being saved or printed. This raises the question as to whether, in addition to any individual works that may be downloaded, the multimedia work itself is capable of copyright protection and, if so, as a compilation, copyright database or dramatic work? In terms of the effect that saving or printing the multimedia work, or parts thereof, has on the market for the multimedia, this will depend on the work involved and how much of it is saved or printed. Broadly speaking, printing parts of a multimedia work is likely to have less of an effect on the market for the work than saving parts of the work. This is because saved copies of the multimedia work, or parts of it, are likely to operate as substitutes for purchasing the work. Whereas,

---

[189] JJ Marcellino and M Blakeslee, 'Fair Use in the Context of a Global Computer Network—Is a Copyright Grab Really Going On?' [1997] 6 *Information & Communications Technology Law* 137, 147. However, there is the counter-argument that continually calling up works on screen is a convenient substitute for purchasing the work and that it differs from browsing in libraries because it is more convenient to call up a work on-screen than to seek it out in the library. However, the argument that 'browsing' works is a substitute for purchasing them ignores the strain and difficulty of reading material on screen, which makes this activity unlikely to substitute for purchasing the actual work. Although, technological advances that make electronic viewing as portable and readable as books might alter this outcome.

[190] Marcellino and Blakeslee (1997) p 147.

[191] For example, in the context of photocopying articles, this has been a relevant factor in determining whether the US fair use defence applies: see *American Geophysical Union v Texaco Inc* (1994) 29 IPR 381.

printing out the multimedia work, or parts thereof, is not a complete substitute for the multimedia work.

For *creators or producers*, as opposed to users, of multimedia works, the fair dealing exception will be of limited use in permitting them to copy and make available copyright works as part of their multimedia work. This is because copying or making available a work as part of a multimedia work will probably fall outside the purpose of research or private study. A multimedia work is typically created for *commercial* distribution and, as such, is unlikely to be for research purposes. Even if it were for research purposes, this would be commercial, as opposed to non-commercial. The fact that users of a multimedia work intend to use it for the purpose of research or private study will not assist here. This is because the person doing the copying will know or have reason to believe that 'it will result in copies of substantially the same material being provided to more than one person at substantial the same time and for substantially the same purpose.'[192] In addition, a person other that the researcher or student may only *copy*, and not engage in the other exclusive rights such as making available, on behalf of the researcher or student.

This position reflects the restrictive nature of having specific fair dealing exceptions, and also the narrow scope of the purpose of research or private study. This may be contrasted with section 107 of the United States Copyright Act 1976 which sets out a 'fair use' defence which is not limited to specific purposes, but is open-ended in nature, and thus able to embrace new types of uses.[193] This is illustrated by the recent decision of *Kelly v Arriba Soft Corporation*[194] where the defendant operated an Internet search engine that displayed its results in the form of small pictures, namely thumbnail images. Some of these thumbnail images were of the plaintiff's photographs. The defendant had copied full sized photographs from the plaintiff's website and from these created thumbnail sized images. The District Court granted summary judgment in favour of the defendant holding that, although making thumbnail size copies of the plaintiff's photographs amounted to a *prima facie* infringement, it was permissible on the basis of fair

---

[192] S 29(3)(b), CDPA. There is a similar approach in the US context when assessing 'fair use'. See for example, *Princeton University Press v Michigan Document Services Inc* 855 F Supp 905 (ED Mich, 1994), where the defendant's practice of copying large amounts of copyright material for student coursepacks was 'pure copying for profit', not educational in any sense and thus not a 'fair use' of the material.

[193] Thus, 'time-shifting', ie, recording television broadcasts on video tapes, was recognised as a 'fair use' in *Sony v Universal City Studios, Inc* 464 US 417 (1984); and reverse engineering of computer programs was recognised as 'fair use' in *Sega Enterprises Ltd v Accolade Inc* 977 F 2d 1510 (9th Cir, 1992). Downloading MP3 files via peer-to-peer file sharing software was not, however, recognised as 'fair use'—*A&M Records, Inc v Napster, Inc* 239 F 3d 1004 (9th Cir, 2001). In the UK 'time-shifting' and 'reverse engineering' are dealt with under their own specific exceptions (s 70 and ss 50B, 50BA), as opposed to via the fair dealing exception.

[194] 336 F 3d 811 (9th Cir, 2003).

use.[195] On appeal to the US Court of Appeals for the Ninth Circuit, the court upheld the District Court's finding of fair use.[196] A similar factual scenario would not be excused under UK copyright law, either under the fair dealing or other exceptions in the CDPA.[197] The inflexibility of the fair dealing exceptions does not bode well for developers of on-line multimedia works, who may wish to utilise on-line materials in ways similar to the defendant's use in *Kelly v Arriba*.

(b) Performance of Dramatic Works; Playing of Films before Audiences of Educational Establishments

For multimedia works that qualify for protection as a *dramatic work* or *film*, the exception contained in section 34 of the CDPA may be relevant to where those works are used for educational purposes. Section 34(1) provides that the *performance* of a *dramatic work* before an audience comprising teachers and pupils at an educational establishment and other persons directly connected with the activities of the establishment is not an infringing public performance of the work. This is provided the performance is done by a teacher or pupil *in the course of the activities of the establishment* or *at* the establishment by any person *for the purposes of instruction*. In a similar vein, section 34(2) stipulates that *playing or showing a film* before such an audience at an educational establishment for the purposes of instruction, is not an infringing playing or showing of the work in public.

It is conceivable that instructional multimedia works may be used at educational establishments in the course of their activities or for the purposes of instruction. If this is the case, then where the multimedia work is classified as a dramatic work, certain performances may not amount to an infringement. Although a multimedia work can be classified as a dramatic work and its demonstration as 'performance', it does seem unusual to characterise the activity in such a manner when section 34 appears to contemplate activities such as a drama teacher or a drama class rehearsing parts of a play. This once again highlights the awkward consequences of *Norowzian v Arks*.[198]

---

[195] Factors in favour of the use being 'fair' were that the defendant's use was considered *transformative* in nature and the thumbnail images were unlikely to affect the market for the plaintiff's full sized images. Although the defendant copied the entire image, this was said to be reasonable in the circumstances and the creative nature of the copyright work did not tip the balance against a finding of 'fair' use. See *Kelly v Arriba Soft Corp* 280 F 3d 934 (9th Cir, 2002), 1119–21.

[196] *Kelly v Arriba Soft Corp* 336 F 3d 811 (9th Cir, 2003), 818–22.

[197] WR Cornish, *Intellectual Property: Omnipresent, Distracting Irrelevant?* (OUP, Oxford, 2004), 65. On the question of whether the UK should adopt a 'fair use' scheme see R Burrell, 'Reining in Copyright Law: Is Fair Use the Answer?' [2001] *IPQ* 361. In Australia, the CLRC has recommended that the fair dealing exceptions (which mirror those in the UK), be replaced by a US-style 'fair use' defence: see SR:1, paras 6.10, 6.29, 6.35, 6.44. On whether Australia should adopt a 'fair use' defence see S Ricketson, 'Simplifying Copyright Law: Proposals from Down Under' [1999b] *EIPR* 537.

[198] Discussed above pp 77–80, 110–12.

Where the multimedia work is classified as a film, the playing or showing of the work in public similarly may not amount to infringement. The *audience* viewing the performance of a dramatic work, or the showing of a film, must consist of teachers and pupils at an educational establishment. This would seem to include university lecturers and postgraduate students,[199] as well as high school teachers and students. If, for example, a university lecturer was showing a particular multimedia work to a postgraduate computer science class, in order to demonstrate how the work operated, or particular aspects of its design features, this would be for the purposes of instruction. Further, a music high school teacher, in teaching about the history of music, may wish to demonstrate to the class a multimedia work that deals with music history. This would also seem to be for the purpose of instruction. But the exception would not cover making available multimedia video games on the school computing network for student use, because this would be for entertainment, as opposed to educational, purposes and also because it would involve the act of making available, which is not covered by section 34.

(c) Incidental Inclusion

Section 31 of the CDPA stipulates that the incidental inclusion of a copyright work in an artistic work, sound recording, film or broadcast will not constitute an infringement. For multimedia works that are protected as *films*,[200] the question arises whether inclusion of various copyright works within a multimedia work would fall within this exception. If so, this has the potential to reduce drastically the number of copyright permissions to be obtained by a creator or producer of a multimedia work.

A key question is what is meant by *incidental* inclusion. This term has been interpreted by the Court of Appeal in *Football Association Premier League Ltd v Panini UK Ltd*.[201] In this case, the defendant, Panini, distributed for sale within the UK collectible stickers of famous football players, together with an album into which the stickers could be placed. The stickers and album in dispute in this case was 'Panini's Football 2003 Sticker Collection'. Each sticker in the collection depicted a photographic image of a player typically in their club 'strip', but occasionally in their international 'strip', and in total 396 football players were included. On the footballer's strip the individual club badge and the premier league emblem were depicted. The defendant's album collection was marketed as unofficial. Whereas the 'official' collection was marketed by a company, Topps Europe Ltd, that had been licensed by the first claimant, Football Association

---

[199] Laddie, *et al* (2000) para 20.30.
[200] See above ch 3 at pp 73–77.
[201] *Football Association Premier League Ltd v Panini UK Ltd* [2004] FSR 1 (CA) ('*Panini*').

Premier League Ltd (FAPL), to use and reproduce official team crests and logos in the production of stickers and albums. FAPL, together with Topps and fourteen of the twenty clubs that are members of the premier league, brought proceedings against Panini for infringement of copyright in the club badges and emblems (as artistic works). Panini argued in its defence that its reproduction of the claimant's copyright works in its stickers and albums was an incidental inclusion within the meaning of section 31 of the CDPA. This defence was rejected by Mr Justice Peter Smith[202] at first instance and also by the Court of Appeal, on appeal.[203]

The Court of Appeal identified the relevant issue as whether the making of the image as it appears on the sticker (ie, an artistic work) or in the album (ie, compilation) was, by virtue of section 31(1), not itself an infringement of copyright in the emblem or badge. The Court emphasised that 'incidental' is an ordinary English word that was purposely left undefined by Parliament.[204] From the plain reading of section 31, it was clear that 'incidental' was not confined to unintentional, or non-deliberate, inclusion[205] and that there was 'no necessary dichotomy between "integral" and "incidental" '.[206] The key question is why, having regard to the circumstances in which the copyright work 'A' is created (in this case, the relevant artistic work was the sticker and not the photograph),[207] was copyright work 'B' (in this case the artistic works of the badges and emblems) included in work 'A'? In answering this question, consideration may be had to commercial, as well as aesthetic reasons, for including work 'B' in work 'A'.[208] Further, this entails an objective assessment of the circumstances in which work 'A' was created, as opposed to looking at the subjective intent of the person creating the work.[209] Thus, in this case, one had to consider the circumstances in which the image of the player as it appears on the sticker or in the album was created. The objective of creating the images on the sticker or in the album was to produce something attractive to the collector and, in order to be attractive, it was important that the player featured should be in appropriate and authentic football 'strip'. This in turn

---

[202] *Football Association Premier League Ltd v Panini UK Ltd* [2003] FSR 698, 703: 'To my mind, [the inclusion of the badge] is self-evidently not incidental. It is an integral part of the artistic work comprised of the photograph of the professional footballer in his present-day kit. That is the intent behind the reproduction of the photograph.'

[203] For discussion see K Garnett, 'Incidental Inclusion under Section 31' [2003] *EIPR* 579.

[204] *Panini*, 11 Chadwick LJ (Brooke LJ in agreement), and 15 Mummery LJ.

[205] *Panini*, 11 Chadwick LJ (Brooke LJ in agreement).

[206] *Panini*, 12 Chadwick LJ (Brooke LJ in agreement).

[207] Although query how the sticker could be treated as an artistic work, given that it was directly copied from the photograph of the footballer onto an adhesive material and thus arguably would not be an *original* work: see *Interlego v Tyco* [1989] 1 AC 217; *Bridgeman Art Library Ltd v Corel Corp* 25 F Supp 2d 421; 36 F Supp 2d 191 (1998). If the relevant artistic work had been characterised as the photograph, arguably the defence of incidental inclusion may have succeeded according to an objective test, but not according to a subjective test: see *Football Association Premier League Ltd v Panini UK Ltd* [2003] FSR 698 (ChD) (Peter Smith J); [2004] FSR 1 (CA).

[208] *Panini*, 12 Chadwick LJ (Brooke LJ in agreement).

[209] *Panini*, 12 Chadwick LJ (Brooke LJ in agreement), and at 15 Mummery LJ.

meant that the individual club badge and FAPL should be included. As such, it was impossible to say that the inclusion was incidental.[210]

In the light of the *Panini* decision, it is unlikely that works included within a multimedia work will be able to benefit from section 31 of the CDPA. First, this defence would be applicable only to those multimedia works that were classified as a *film*, as opposed to those classified as a compilation or database (since the defence does not apply to the inclusion of copyright material in literary works).[211] Second, even if the multimedia work is protected as a film, the inclusion of most copyright material within the work is unlikely to be incidental. This is because copyright material frequently will be included in order to make the multimedia work more comprehensive and thus more commercially valuable or attractive. Or it will be included to make the user interface of the multimedia work more aesthetically attractive, which may also have a commercial value. Thus, there is likely to be limited scope for reliance on this defence in the context of creating multimedia works.

Conclusion

This chapter has examined the exceptions relevant to multimedia works that are protected under copyright law as computer programs, databases, dramatic works and films. It has also considered the exceptions relevant to multimedia works that are protected as *sui generis* databases. For users of multimedia works, the most comprehensive set of copyright exceptions concerns the underlying software, since the user is able to reverse engineer and decompile the program, make a back up copy of the program and do certain acts necessary for the lawful use of the program. Where the multimedia work qualifies as a copyright database, the user may do certain acts necessary for lawful use of the database. The user may also rely on the exception of fair dealing for the purpose of research or private study, however, this will be limited to acts which are non-commercial in nature and which relate to the selection or arrangement of the contents, as opposed to the contents themselves. This may be contrasted with where the multimedia work is protected as a *sui generis* database, since fair dealing for the purpose of non-commercial research or study may relate to acts dealing with the contents of the work, and not merely its structure. For multimedia works that are protected as films, fair dealing for research or private study does not apply, but will be relevant where the work is

---

[210] *Panini*, 12–13 Chadwick LJ (Brooke LJ in agreement), and at 15 Mummery LJ.

[211] Indeed, this point was emphasised in *Panini*, 13–14 Mummery LJ who commented obiter that inclusion of the claimant's artistic works in the album could not be excused under s 31(1), CDPA since the album collection was a literary work in the form of a 'compilation'.

characterised as a dramatic work. The role that this exception has to play, however, is again limited by the fact that the acts of research or study must be non-commercial. Also relevant to where the multimedia work is characterised as either a dramatic work or film is the exception relating to performance of the dramatic work or playing/showing the film before an audience at an educational establishment.

In summary, classification of a multimedia work as a computer program will offer the greatest range of permissible exceptions to the user, whereas classification as a copyright database or *sui generis* database will offer a more restricted range of permissible uses. There are situations in which a user may wish to rely on exceptions available for both computer programs and databases (copyright and *sui generis*). For example, a user who decompiles the underlying software of a multimedia work may incidentally reproduce the contents of the work. Unless these contents can be classified as part of the computer program, this type of reproduction will not be excused by the decompilation exception in section 50BA of the CDA. Instead, the decompiler would have to rely on the lawful use exception for copyright databases in section 50D. Alternatively, they might rely upon fair dealing for the purpose of non-commercial research or study (for copyright databases) or extraction for non-commercial research purposes (for *sui generis* databases). This will not be realistic, however, where the decompiler is seeking to produce a competing, or commercial program or multimedia work. A further example is where a user wishes to study the operation of a multimedia work, in order to appreciate its scope, design and functional features and contents. In this situation they would be unable to rely upon the reverse engineering exception in section 50BA of the CDPA, since this only relates to the underlying computer program. Whilst the user could seek to rely on the fair dealing exceptions for databases, these are limited where the user has a non-commercial purpose.

The scope of protection for multimedia works has been thoroughly examined, according to whether such works are protected as computer programs, copyright databases, compilations, dramatic works, films and *sui generis* databases. Thus, we are now in a position to consider the sorts of reform that should be made to UK copyright law. It is to this issue that we now turn.

6

Reform Proposals

Introduction

Chapters 3 to 5 have comprehensively analysed the scope of protection available for entire multimedia works under UK copyright law, according to whether they are classified as a literary work (in the form of a compilation or database), dramatic work, film, or *sui generis* database. This final chapter will do several things. First, it will summarise the conclusions reached in chapters 3 to 5. Second, it will consider reforms to existing UK copyright law that may result in better protection of multimedia works. Third, it will consider the possibility of having a non-exhaustive or 'open' list of subject matter in the CDPA. Fourth, it will examine the desirability and feasibility of introducing a new copyright category of multimedia work. Finally, it will assess the need for, and practicability of, a *sui generis* right for multimedia works. This chapter concludes that while some reforms to UK copyright law are desirable, extensive reform is unwarranted. A shift to an 'open list' of subject matter is premature and neither a multimedia category nor a *sui generis* multimedia right should be introduced.

Summary of Existing Protection for Multimedia Works

The analysis so far has shown that characterising a multimedia work as a particular copyright work, or classifying it as a *sui generis* database, will protect different aspects of a multimedia work.

The weakest protection for multimedia works arises when they are characterised as computer programs (ie, literary works). The programmer typically will be the author of the work and protection will extend to prohibiting the copying of the program code, along with certain non-literal elements, such as the structure of the program code. However, neither the user interface, nor the interactive and navigational capabilities of multimedia works will be protected. Exceptions for black-box reverse engineering and decompilation also serve to reinforce the fact that interactive and user interface features may be imitated, provided the under-lying program code is not copied or adapted in a new program. Probably the biggest drawback of protection as a computer program is that the multiple inputs comprising a multimedia work and the way in which those inputs are grouped together are not protected.

Protection of multimedia works as a compilation or copyright database is also weak. Authorship of such works generally will be restricted to the designer of the multimedia work. The advantage of protection as a compilation or database is that the way in which multiple inputs are drawn together within a multimedia work, namely their selection or arrangement, can be protected. However, in the case of compilations there are limits upon the *type* of inputs which may be combined (ie, not musical and dramatic works). This is not a problem where a multimedia work is classified as a copyright database. However, multimedia works that utilise a dynamic user interface will have difficulty in satisfying the requirements of 'inde-pendent works' or 'individual accessibility' in the definition of database. The major disadvantage of protection as a compilation or database is that the scope of protection will be limited to the original *selection* of contents within the multi-media work. This is because the physical arrangement of contents tends to be determined by the exigencies of the software and the logical arrangement by either the user or the exigencies of the software. Thus, it is only the *selection* of contents that can be protected and *not the contents themselves*. However, a certain degree of rearrangement of databases may be prohibited by relying upon the right of adaptation.

A stronger form of protection for multimedia works occurs when they are classified as film works. Authorship of such works usually will reside in the designer and possibly also the project manager. The advantage of protection as a film work is that the way in which multiple digital contents are combined in a multimedia work, along with the aggregate of those digital contents, can be protected. However, this is the case only for those multimedia works that employ a moving user interface, with minimal use of static images. Reference type multimedia works or works that adopt a static user interface will not qualify as film works. The major disadvantage of classification as a film work is that the scope of protection is limited to the actual moving images and their embodiment: creating a similar sequence of images is not prohibited. Thus, a competitor could legitimately imitate the user interface and interactive elements of a multimedia work without infring-ing film copyright. This situation may be avoided if the multimedia work qualifies for protection as a dramatic work, a possibility which arises following the Court of Appeal decision in *Norowzian v Arks (No 2)*('*Arks (No 2)*').[1] However, as argued later in this chapter, the Court of Appeal's interpretation of 'dramatic work' should not be followed. Rather, the category of film work should be reformed.

---

[1] *Norowzian v Arks (No 2)* [2000] FSR 363 ('*Arks (No 2)*').

The strongest form of protection available to multimedia works arises via the database right regime. Protection as a *sui generis* database is limited by the definition of 'database', so that only reference type multimedia works or works that have a static user interface appear capable of satisfying the requirements that works, data or other materials be 'independent' and 'individually accessible'. Protection is linked to the investment applied in obtaining, verifying or presenting the contents of the work, however, investment in *creation* of materials will be excluded from consideration. Ownership of the work may extend to several multimedia contributors, rather than being limited to the designer of the work. The key advantage of protection as a *sui generis* database is clearly the scope of protection, which extends to extraction or re-utilisation of a substantial part of the *contents* of the work and, in some instances, an insubstantial part of the contents. The recent ECJ rulings have clarified the scope of protection under the database right. A substantial part of the contents will be determined by whether that part reflects substantial investment. Repeated and systematic extraction or re-utilisation of insubstantial parts of the contents will infringe where this effectively circumvents the prohibition on substantial taking. It seems that database right, rather than copyright, provides the best overall protection for multimedia works.

Neither copyright nor database right perfectly protects *all* types of multimedia works. Therefore, the following section considers the feasibility of reforms to copyright law which could result in improved protection for multimedia works.

Reforms to Existing Copyright Categories

1. Replacing Film Works with an Audiovisual Work Category

Protecting multimedia works as audiovisual works is not a new suggestion.[2] However, it has not been explored in detail.[3] This section considers the feasibility

---

[2] A Firth, 'Film, Ciné and Audio-visual Works: Questions of Definition' in E Barendt and A Firth (eds), *Yearbook of Copyright and Media Law* (OUP, Oxford, 2000) 221, 232; A Latreille, 'The Legal Classification of Multimedia Creations in French Copyright Law' in I Stamatoudi and P Torremans (eds), *Copyright in the New Digital Environment* (Sweet & Maxwell, London, 2000) 45–74; P Leonard, 'Beyond the Future—Multimedia and the Law' (1994) 7 *Australian Intellectual Property Law Bulletin* 105, 111; J Lahore and F Phillips, 'The Notion of an Audiovisual Work: International and Comparative Law' [1996] 7 *AIPJ* 208, 218–19; M Salokannel, *Ownership of Rights in Audiovisual Productions: A Comparative Study* (Kluwer, London, 1997) 314–19; Aust Copyright Law Review Committee, *Final Report on Computer Software Protection* (AGD, Canberra, 1995) ('Software Report'), paras 14.84–14.87; Aust Copyright Law Review Committee, *Simplification of the Copyright Act 1968: Part 2: Categorisation of Subject Matter and Exclusive Rights, and Other Issues* (AGD, Canberra, 1999) ('SR:2'), paras 7.15–7.16.

[3] Although see I Stamatoudi, *Copyright and Multimedia Works: A Comparative Analysis* (CUP, Cambridge, 2002) ch 8.

of replacing the category of film work in the Copyright Designs and Patents Act 1988 ('CDPA') with a category of audiovisual work.

Since there is no well defined concept of 'audiovisual work' in international copyright law,[4] US copyright law will be considered as a potential model for reform. Under US copyright law, protection extends to 'original works of authorship fixed in any tangible medium of expression', including 'motion pictures and audiovisual works'.[5] 'Motion pictures' are defined in section 101 of the US Copyright Act 1976 as:

> audiovisual works consisting of a *series of related images* which, when shown in succession, *impart an impression of motion*, together with accompanying sounds, if any. (Emphasis supplied)

However, 'audiovisual works' do not require an impression of motion. This is apparent from the definition in section 101 of the US Copyright Act 1976 which defines 'audiovisual works' as:

> works that consist of a *series of related images* which are intrinsically intended to be shown by the use of machines or devices such as projectors, viewers, or electronic equipment, together with accompanying sounds, if any, regardless of the nature of the material objects, such as films or tapes, in which the works are embodied. (Emphasis supplied)

Numerous US cases have considered the protection of video games (a type of multimedia work) as audiovisual works.[6] While the early cases usually focussed on whether video games were copyrightable subject matter, in the form of audiovisual works,[7] later cases have been more concerned with questions of infringement. In terms of copyrightability of video games as audiovisual works, two main issues arose. First, whether video games satisfied the definition of 'audiovisual work',

---

[4] Lahore and Phillips (1996) p 218. On different approaches to the definition of filmic works see Firth (2000) pp 227–29.

[5] US Copyright Act 1976, s 102(a)(6).

[6] For example: *Atari, Inc v Amusement World, Inc*, 547 F Supp 222 (D C Md, 1981); *Midway Mfg Co v Dirkschneider*, 543 F Supp 466 (D C Neb, 1981); *Williams Electronics v Artic International*, 685 F 2d 870 (3rd Cir, 1982); *Atari, Inc v North American Philips Consumer Electronics Corp*, 672 F 2d 607 (7th Cir, 1982); *Stern Electronics v Kaufman*, 669 F 2d 852(2nd Cir, 1982); *Midway Manufacturing Co v Artic International Inc*, 704 F 2d 1009 (7th Cir, 1983); *Midway Manufacturing Co v Strohon*, 564 F Supp 741 (ND Ill, 1983); *M Kramer Manufacturing Co Inc v Andrews*, 783 F 2d 421 (4th Cir, 1986); *Data East v Epyx*, 862 F 2d 204 (9th Cir, 1988); *Atari Games Corporation v Oman*, 888 F 2d 878 (DC Cir, 1989); *Interactive Network, Inc v NTN Communications*, Inc, 875 F Supp 1398 (ND Cal, 1995). For a pithy overview of the key decisions see S Lai, *The Copyright Protection of Computer Software in the United Kingdom* (Hart Publishing, Oxford, 2000) ch 5. On how screen displays of video games can be protected as audiovisual works under French law see P Kamina, *Film Copyright in the European Union* (CUP, Cambridge, 2002) 79–80; and Stamatoudi (2002) pp 173–74; and under German law see Stamatoudi (2002) pp 175, 177–78.

[7] Although a video game could be protected as a computer program under US copyright law, the scope of protection did not prevent competitors from producing a similar video game where different program code had been used. Thus, plaintiffs sought protection under the audiovisual work category in order to prevent 'knock-off' video games from being produced: see *Stern Electronics v Kaufman*, 669 F 2d 852 (2nd Cir, 1982) 855.

in particular, 'series of related images'. Second, whether video games could be considered as 'fixed in any tangible medium of expression'.[8]

The Court of Appeals for the Seventh Circuit in *Midway Manufacturing Co v Artic International Inc*[9] ('*Midway Manufacturing*') considered, *inter alia,* whether the video games 'Galaxian'[10] and 'Pac Man'[11] qualified for protection as audio-visual works. In so doing, the Court explored the meaning of the phrase 'series of related images' in the definition of 'audiovisual work'. The Court acknowledged that the phrase could be interpreted narrowly to 'refer only to a set of images displayed in a fixed sequence'.[12] Such an interpretation would preclude computer video games from protection as audiovisual works since 'each time a video game is played, a different sequence of images appears on the screen of the video game machine-assuming the game is not played exactly the same way each time.'[13] However, the Court preferred a broader interpretation of the phrase 'series of related images', in which it might be 'construed more broadly to refer to *any set of images displayed as some kind of unit*' (emphasis supplied).[14] Adopting the broader

---

[8] S 101 US Copyright Act 1976 states that a work is 'fixed' when its, 'embodiment in a copy or phonorecord, by or under the authority of the author, is sufficiently permanent or stable to permit it to be perceived, reproduced, or otherwise communicated for a period of more than transitory duration.'

[9] *Midway Manufacturing Co v Artic International Inc,* 704 F 2d 1009 (7th Cir, 1983) ('*Midway Manufacturing*').

[10] Described pithily in *Midway Mfg Co v Dirkschneider,* 543 F Supp 466 (D Neb, 1981) 473–74:

> The elements of the Galaxian video game appear on a background star pattern consisting of twinkling colored lights that roll from the top of the screen to the bottom. The game involves a missile-firing rocket ship operated by the player, plus a formation of enemy aliens. The aliens are arranged in a convoy of five horizontal rows. There are four denominations or ranks of aliens, with the highest ranking nearest the player's ship. Each rank has a distinguishing color. The highest ranking alien is shaped like a rocket ship, but the other ranks have flapping wings. Individual aliens unpredictably invert and swoop down to bomb the player's ship. Sometimes the alien attach consists of mini-formations involving the alien flagship or chief, as well as flying alien escorts. Whenever a ship is destroyed, a bright explosion appears on the screen, with appropriate sound effects. The player's score is measured by the number and rank of aliens destroyed.

[11] Described pithily in *Midway Mfg Co v Dirkschneider,* 543 F Supp 466 (D Neb, 1981) 474:

> The Pac-Man video game centers on a maze which covers the entire screen. The player guides the Pac-Man character through the maze. Points are scored when the Pack-Man eats dots in his path. Four ghost monsters, Inky, Blinky, Pinky and Clyde, chase after the Pac-Man, trying to capture and deflate him. The Pac-Man can counterattack by eating a big power capsule that enables him to overpower the monsters for additional scores. After all the dots are gobbled up, the screen is cleared, and the Pac-Man game continues for another round. Each round or rack features a special fruit target in the maze, which, if eaten, earns bonus points. Audio and musical effects accompany the play of the game.

For a detailed description of Pac-Man see *Atari, Inc v North American Philips Consumer Electronics Corp* 672 F 2d 607 (7th Cir, 1982) 610–11.

[12] *Midway Manufacturing,* 1011.

[13] Above.

[14] Above.

interpretation meant that the video games in question were copyrightable as audiovisual works.[15]

Whether video games were too changeable to satisfy the *fixation* requirement was considered in *Stern Electronics v Kaufman* ('*Kaufman*').[16] The case concerned the video game 'Scramble',[17] in which the plaintiff alleged, *inter alia*, that the defendants infringed copyright by producing and marketing a game virtually identical in both sight and sound. The defendants argued that the plaintiff was not entitled to copyright in the video game as an audiovisual work because, *inter alia*, it was too changeable properly to be considered 'fixed in any tangible medium of expression'.[18] This was because the sequence of images appearing on the screen

---

[15] Numerous cases have held that video games are copyrightable as audiovisual works: see, for example, *Atari, Inc v Amusement World, Inc*, 547 F Supp 222 (D Md 1981) 226; *Midway Mfg Co v Dirkschneider*, 543 F Supp 466 (D Neb, 1981) 479–80; *Williams Electronics v Artic International*, 685 F 2d 870 (3rd Cir, 1982) 874; *Stern Electronics v Kaufman*, 669 F 2d 852 (2nd Cir, 1982) 855–56; *Midway Manufacturing Co v Strohon*, 564 F Supp 741 (ND Ill, 1983) 746; *M Kramer Manufacturing Co, Inc v Andrews*, 783 F 2d 421 (4th Cir, 1986) 436; *Atari Games Corporation v Oman*, 888 F 2d 878 (DC Cir, 1989) 882.

[16] *Stern Electronics v Kaufman*, 669 F 2d 852(2nd Cir, 1982) ('*Kaufman*'). Note that memory devices, such as printed circuit boards and PROMs, can constitute a copy in which the audiovisual work is 'fixed': see *Midway Mfg Co v Dirkschneider*, 543 F Supp 466 (D Neb, 1981) 480; *Atari, Inc v Amusement World, Inc*, 547 F Supp 222 (D Md, 1981) 226 (printed circuit boards); and *Kaufman*, 855–56 (PROMs).

[17] Described in *Kaufman*, 853:

. . . the video screen displays a spaceship moving horizontally through six different scenes in which obstacles are encountered. With each scene the player faces increasing difficulty in traversing the course and scoring points. The first scene depicts mountainous terrain, missile bases, and fuel depots. The player controls the altitude and speed of the spaceship, decides when to release the ship's supply of bombs, and fires lasers that can destroy attacking missiles and aircraft. He attempts to bomb the missile bases (scoring points for success), bomb the fuel depots (increasing his own diminishing fuel supply with each hit), avoid the missiles being fired from the ground, and avoid crashing his ship into the mountains. And that is only scene one. In subsequent scenes the hazards include missile-firing enemy aircraft and tunnel-like airspaces. The scenes are in color, and the action is accompanied by battlefield sounds.

[18] *Kaufman*, 855. The defendant also argued that the video game lacked originality, which contention was rejected by the Court of Appeals: see *Kaufman*, 856–57. Whether a video game was an original work of authorship, in the form of an audiovisual work, was also raised in *Atari Games Corporation v Oman*, 888 F 2d 878 (DC Cir, 1989); and 979 F 2d 242 (DC Cir, 1992). The case concerned the video game, BREAKOUT, which was described as follows:

BREAKOUT is a relatively early video game of comparative simplicity. The sound accompaniment is four basic tones. The screen shows the two players' scores at the top. The players move a 'paddle' to hit a 'ball' against a 'wall.' The wall is built of eight rows of rectangles arranged in four monochromatic stripes (red, amber, green, yellow). When the square blue ball hits a rectangle, the rectangle vanishes. When the ball breaks through the wall of rectangles to the empty space beyond, it ricochets at greatly increased speed until it reemerges. Both the ball's speed and the size of the rectangular paddle change during play. The ball's movement does not follow the laws of physics; instead, the angle of the ball's rebound depends solely on where it impacts the paddle.

See *Atari Games Corporation v Oman*, 979 F 2d 242 (DC Cir, 1992) 243. The Court of Appeals for the DC Circuit held that the video game in issue was an original work of authorship, according to both pre and post-*Feist* tests of originality.

during each play of the game varied depending on the actions taken by the player.[19] The Court of Appeals for the Second Circuit stated that the audiovisual display would be protected, in addition to the underlying written computer program, in the absence of the player's participation in the game.[20] The Court went on to hold that the player's participation did not affect the eligibility of the video game for copyright protection as an audiovisual work because during each play of the game, 'many aspects of the sights and the sequence of their appearance' remained constant.[21] Thus, the repetitive sequence of a substantial portion of the sights and sounds of the game qualified for copyright protection as an audiovisual work.[22]

Would a US style audiovisual work category encompass a wider range of multimedia works than is the case under the UK notion of film works?[23] As was argued in chapter 3, the definition of 'film' in section 5B of the CDPA is presently capable of embracing multimedia video games. Therefore, apparently little would be gained in this respect by introducing a US category of audiovisual work. However, the definition of 'film' in section 5B of the CDPA is unlikely to protect those multimedia works that include a substantial quantity of *static* (as opposed to moving) inputs, such as reference type multimedia works. Would this type of multimedia work fare better under the US definition of 'audiovisual work', given that it does not require an impression of motion? In addition, would multimedia works with *non-linear* interactivity, which feature numerous permutations of how the set of images is displayed, satisfy the criteria of 'series of related images' and 'fixation'?

The phrase 'series of related images' could arguably embrace a set of images appearing *in any order* provided a logical relationship or connection between the images being displayed is demonstrated. Such an interpretation would enable

---

[19] *Kaufman*, 855.

[20] Above.

[21] *Kaufman*, 856: 'These include the appearance (shape, color, and size) of the player's spaceship, the enemy craft, the ground missile bases and fuel depots and the terrain over which (and beneath which) the player's ship flies, as well as the sequence in which the missile bases, fuel depots, and terrain appears. Also constant are the sounds heard whenever the player successfully destroys an enemy craft or installation or fails to avoid an enemy missile or laser.'

[22] *Kaufman*, 856. See also *Williams Electronics v Artic International* 685 F 2d 870 (3rd Cir, 1982) 874 where the US Court of Appeals for the Third Circuit rejected the arguments that the appearance of different images in the video game, along with player interaction, meant that the video game lacked fixation such that it could not qualify as an audiovisual work. Following *Kaufman*, the Court of Appeals for the Third Circuit held at 874 that: 'Although there is player interaction with the machine during the play mode which causes the audiovisual presentation to change in some respects from one game to the next in response to the player's varying participation, there is always a repetitive sequence of a substantial portion of the sights and sounds of the game, and many aspects of the display remain constant from game to game regardless of how the player operates the controls.'

[23] NJ Dasios, 'Virtual Environments: Protecting Virtual Works under Copyright' (1995) 9 *IPJ* 105, 121–24 argues that the US category of 'audiovisual work' would better encompass works of virtual reality than the cinematograph category under the Canadian Copyright Act 1985.

non-linear, reference type multimedia works to qualify as audiovisual works.[24] For example, displaying a multimedia database would produce a succession of images (from a set of images) and the relationship or connection between these images could be subject matter, author, genre, or year of publication. However, there are some obvious difficulties with this broad interpretation. First, it is probably inconsistent with *Midway Manufacturing*. Although the Court broadly interpreted the phrase 'series of related images' to include 'any set of images displayed as some kind of unit', it is arguable that this does not extend to a set of images appearing in any order. On the facts of *Midway Manufacturing* the images were displayed as part of an overall *sequence* of images that would emerge if the player successfully overcame the obstacles presented to him. In other words, the images were 'displayed as some kind of unit' because there was a *reasonably consistent sequence of images*. The same cannot be said for multimedia works with a high degree of interactivity. Second, even if highly interactive multimedia works are considered a 'series of related images', they may not satisfy the fixation requirement. *Kaufman* considered the video game 'Scramble' to be 'fixed' because a substantial portion of the sights and sounds of the game were constant. However, with a reference type multimedia work, a similar sequence of images, text or sound is unlikely to unfold because the user interactivity is much greater than player participation in a video game.[25] Finally, such a broad interpretation would substantially erode the difference between the categories of compilation or database and audiovisual work.[26] This would create an unacceptable overlap in that two or more categories would be protecting the same or similar creative effort in a similar manner.[27]

A clear advantage of a US audiovisual work category, however, is that the scope of protection would embrace non-exact reproduction. Audiovisual works attract a right of non-exact reproduction under US copyright law, so that a substantial similarity between audiovisual works amounts to infringement.[28] In assessing infringement of video games, US courts have tended to focus 'on only visual

---

[24] For support see Salokannel (1997) p 91: 'The use of the term "series" does not entail that the images would have to appear in a chronological or otherwise linear order, but that they may also be accessed individually and in random order.'

[25] See T Aplin, 'Not in our Galaxy: Why "Film" Won't Rescue Multimedia' (1999) 12 *EIPR* 633, 639:
Multimedia works (other than multimedia video games) do not work on the premise that some sort of overall sequence or narrative will emerge if the player or user enters all the correct inputs. Rather, multimedia products, in particular database-type works, aim for as much random access as possible for the user, so that the user can gain the most flexible and individualised access to the information within. This fact may thwart the ability of multimedia screen displays to obtain a sufficient amount of repetition to qualify as 'substantial' and therefore 'fixable' (footnote omitted).

[26] See also Lahore and Phillips (1996) p 219 who argue that close consideration should be given to how broadly 'audiovisual works' are defined.

[27] *Electronic Techniques (Anglia) Ltd v Critchley Components Ltd* [1997] FSR 401, 412–13 (Laddie J), although doubted in *Sandman v Panasonic UK Ltd* [1998] FSR 651, 658 (Pumfrey J).

[28] MB Nimmer and D Nimmer, *Nimmer on Copyright* (Matthew Bender, New York, 1998) at 2.18, [H][3][b].

videographical similarities and differences between video games in their substantial similarity analyses'.[29] Thus, for multimedia works qualifying as audiovisual works, protection would extend to prohibiting substantially similar visual user interfaces. This would provide significant protection to the interactive aspects of a multimedia work and to the combination of digital media inputs comprising the work. However, US courts, in applying the substantial similarity principle to computer video games, have tended to ignore similarities in 'game play'.[30] This has been criticised by McKnight,[31] who argues that:

> If courts analyze video games as they do movies to determine substantial similarity, then they could grant video game plaintiffs protection against defendants who disguise copied video game expressions with cosmetic differences.[32]
>
> Thus, a substantial similarity inquiry should search for similarities between two games in both perceivable videographical characteristics and game play. The concept of game play in a video game is analogous to the concept of mood or tone in a movie or story.[33]

If UK courts decided to follow the approach of the US courts, a right of non-exact reproduction would have limited usefulness in protecting the interactive elements of a multimedia work, *unless* these elements were reflected in the visual user interface.

A US-style definition of 'audiovisual works' would not lead to significantly more multimedia works being protected than is the case under the UK film work category. However, a benefit of an audiovisual work definition is that the language is more 'neutral'.[34] Further, introduction of an audiovisual work category would involve the right of non-exact reproduction. Certainly, there is a strong case for introducing a right of non-exact reproduction for film works, which is discussed in the following section.

2. Right of Non-literal Reproduction

An obvious reform to UK copyright law is to introduce a right of non-literal reproduction in respect of film works. This would protect films to a similar level as literary, dramatic, artistic and musical works. Further, it would provide enhanced

---

[29] SG McKnight, 'Substantial Similarity between Video Games: An Old Copyright Problem in a New Medium' (1983) 36 *Vanderbilt Law Review* 1277, 1312. See also TMS Hemnes, 'The Adaptation of Copyright Law to Video Games' (1982) 131 *University of Pennsylvania Law Review* 171 for a discussion of the difficulties that emerged in protecting video games as 'audiovisual works'.

[30] Examples of where elements of 'game play' were disregarded are *Atari Inc v North American Philips Consumer Electronics Corp*, 672 F2d 607 (7th Cir, 1982); and *Data East v Epyx*, 862 F 2d 204 (9th Cir, 1998).

[31] McKnight (1983).

[32] Above, at 1307.

[33] Above, at 1310.

[34] SR:2, paras 6.08–6.11 (dissenting view).

protection for multimedia works that qualify as films. To justify the greater protection of film works, the standard of originality that is applied to literary, dramatic, musical and artistic works should also apply to films. There is no originality standard for film works in the UK, but there is the basic requirement that copyright may not subsist in a film to the extent that it has been copied from a previous film.[35] Laddie explains the reason for such a minimal requirement, as opposed to an originality requirement:

> This requirement [originality] is unnecessary in the case of films because what is protected is the actual images themselves, and not the skill and labour expended in creating the subject matter save insofar as this is unavoidably exploited by lifting the images. That being so, the only task remaining to the legislature was to prevent film copyright being extended indefinitely by the making of successive copies, and to prevent a third party who recorded the images from himself acquiring a copyright in the taken material.[36]

If greater protection of film is to occur, beyond the actual images themselves to the way these images are combined, it seems necessary that films meet a standard of originality.[37] In addition, the full gamut of exceptions for fair dealing ought to apply to films that have this increased protection. In particular, fair dealing for the purpose of non-commercial research or private study should be extended to film works. This is critical to maintaining balance between incentives to create such works and the public use of these works.

Reforming the category of film works to include non-literal reproduction as an economic right is complicated by the fact that, post *Arks (No 2)*, films may also qualify as *original dramatic works* and thereby attract the right of non-literal reproduction.[38] Thus, the question arises whether it is necessary or desirable to amend the scope of protection available for film works under the CDPA. It is argued that it is preferable to amend the 'film' category, rather than rely upon protection as a 'dramatic work', for two main reasons.

First, it makes sense comprehensively to deal with protection of cinematographic works under the one category of 'film', rather than splitting protection between two categories. Article 2(1) of the Berne Convention[39] makes a clear distinction between works comprising 'dramatic or dramatico-musical works, choreographic works and entertainments in dumb show' and those works which are 'cinematographic works to which are assimilated works expressed by a process analogous to cinematography'. The separation of dramatic works from films in section 1(1) of the CDPA is consistent with this distinction, but the decision to

---

[35] See s 5B(4), CDPA.

[36] H Laddie, *et al*, *The Modern Law of Copyright and Designs*, 3rd edn, (Butterworths, London, 2000) para 7.29.

[37] See SR:2, para 5.74 (majority view) for support.

[38] See ch 3 and 4 above at pp 77–80 and pp 111–12.

[39] Berne Convention for the Protection of Literary and Artistic Works 1886 ('Berne Convention').

treat films *per se* as capable of being dramatic works under the CDPA serves only to confuse it. For example, following *Arks (No 2)*, it is not entirely clear who would be classed as the author of a film that is protected as a dramatic work. The author of a dramatic work is defined as the person who creates it,[40] yet any or all of several contributors, including the director, producer, screenwriter, musical composer, author of the dialogue, editor and director of photography, might be regarded as the author or co-author of the work.[41] Similarly, it is unclear who would be the author of the film as dramatic work for the purposes of moral rights protection. By contrast, for works protected as 'films' under section 5B of the CDPA, it is clear that the principal director and producer are considered as joint authors for the purposes of copyright[42] and the director of the film is considered as the author for the purposes of moral rights.[43] Thus, classifying a film as *both* a film work under section 5B of the CDPA and dramatic work under section 3 of the CDPA could result in the vesting of economic and moral rights in different persons.[44]

Difficulties regarding the duration of copyright in films also arise because of uncertainties concerning who may be classified as an author of a film protected as a *dramatic work*. According to Article 2(2) of the Term Directive,[45] cinematographic or audiovisual works shall be protected for 70 years after the death of the last of the following persons to survive (whether or not they are classified as co-authors): the principal director, the author of the dialogue; the author of the screenplay and the composer of music specially created for use in the cinematographic or audiovisual work. Article 2(2) has been implemented in section 13B of the CDPA in respect of films.[46] However, if films are protected as dramatic works, in an attempt to protect the cinematic content rather than just the recording,[47] the length of protection will be calculated from 70 years after the death of the author or last co-author to die. Yet there is no way of guaranteeing that the four persons listed in section 13B of the CDPA will be characterised as the co-authors of the film protected as a dramatic work. Consequently, there is the potential for UK copyright law on duration of protection of film (cinematographic) works to operate inconsistently with Article 2(2) of the Term Directive.

---

[40] S 9(1), CDPA.

[41] Kamina (2002) pp 144–53.

[42] Ss 9(2)(ab) and 10(1A), CDPA.

[43] Ss 77(1), 80(1), 84(1), CDPA.

[44] I Stamatoudi, '"Joy" for the Claimant: Can a Film Also Be Protected as a Dramatic Work?' [2000] *IPQ* 117, 124–25.

[45] Directive 93/83/EEC of 29 October 1993 harmonising the term of protection of copyright and related rights OJ L 290, 24/11/1993, pp 9–13 ('Term Directive').

[46] Thus, even though the producer and principal director are treated as joint authors of a film (see s 10(1A)), s 13B states that duration of copyright in a film will end 70 years after the death of the last of the following persons to die: the principal director, the author of the screenplay, the author of the dialogue or the composer of music specially created for and used in films.

[47] R Arnold, '*Joy*: A Reply' [2001] *IPQ* 10, 17–19.

The second reason to amend the film category to provide more comprehensive protection for cinematographic works, rather than simply relying on *Arks (No 2)*, is that the decision strains the notion of what is a 'dramatic work'.[48] Previous cases on dramatic works indicate that they are essentially concerned with works that are *performed* in a theatrical sense, that is, acted[49] and not merely *shown* to an audience, which is what occurs in the case of film. The Court of Appeal seemed to equate these two activities, with Buxton LJ stating that 'a cinematographic work. . . will usually be a dramatic work . . . it being capable of being performed before an audience by the showing of the film.'[50] Of course, films may constitute a recording of a dramatic work,[51] but it seems a rather large leap to suggest that films, in themselves, can comprise a dramatic work. The view of Rattee J, at first instance, that 'the dramatic work is something that exists apart from the film, even if the film is the only form in which it is recorded'[52] is preferable.

Thus, it is argued that reform of protection for film works should occur through legislative changes to the CDPA, rather than via the judicial innovation reflected in *Arks (No 2)*. Straightforward amendments would be to subject film works to an originality requirement and to grant them the exclusive right of non-exact reproduction. Ideally, however, legislative reform should go further and *distinguish* between the fixation of a film (ie, recording) and the cinematic content of a film (ie, cinematographic work),[53] in order to give effect to EC law in the form of the Rental Right and Term Directives.[54]

The Rental Right Directive[55] states that Member States shall grant the exclusive right of rental and lending to, *inter alia*, the author in respect of the original and copies of his work and to the producer of the first fixation of a film in respect of the original and copies of his film.[56] The principal director of a cinematographic or audiovisual work shall be considered as its author or one its co-authors.[57] In addition, Article 4 provides that: 'Where an author . . . has transferred or assigned

---

[48] See *Norowzian v Arks Ltd (No 2)* [1999] FSR 79, 88 (Rattee J). See also Stamatoudi (2000) pp 122–23. *Cf* Arnold (2001) p 14.

[49] *Chatterton v Cave* [1878] 3 App Cas 483; *Tate v Fullbrook* [1908] 1 KB 821; *Jennings v Stephens* [1936] Ch 469; *Green v Broadcasting Corp of New Zealand* [1989] RPC 700 (sufficient unity to be capable of performance). See also J Pila and A Christie, 'The Literary Work within Copyright Law: an Analysis of its Present and Future Status' (1999) 13 *IPJ* 133, 142–43; and T Rivers, '*Norowzian* Revisited' [2000] *EIPR* 389, 391.

[50] *Arks (No 2)*, 369.

[51] See *Arks (No 2)*, although in this case the film was held not to be a recording of a dramatic work.

[52] *Norowzian v Arks Ltd (No 2)* [1999] FSR 79, 87 (Rattee J).

[53] Doubting the necessity of double protection for audiovisual works see Kamina (2002) pp 85–87.

[54] Kamina (2002) pp 63–65.

[55] Directive 92/100/EEC of 19 November 1992 on rental and lending right and on certain rights related to copyright in the field of intellectual property OJ L 346, 27/11/1992, pp 61–66 ('Rental Right Directive').

[56] Art 2(1) Rental Right Directive. This provision also states that the term 'film' designates a cinematographic or audiovisual work or moving images, whether or not accompanied by sound.

[57] Art 2(2), Rental Right Directive.

his rental right concerning . . . an original or copy of a film to a . . . film producer, that author . . . shall retain the right to obtain an equitable remuneration for the rental.' Further, Article 9 stipulates that producers of the first fixations of films shall have a distribution right in respect of the original and copies of their films. In other words, the Rental Right Directive makes a distinction between the rights of authors in the cinematographic work and the rights of producers in the first fixation of a film.

The Term Directive also adopts this distinction. In addition to stipulating the length of protection for cinematographic works, Article 3(3) of the Term Directive states that the rights of producers of the first fixation of a film shall expire 50 years after when the fixation is made or 50 years from the date of the first lawful publication or lawful communication to the public, whichever is the earlier. Thus, the Term Directive draws a clear distinction between the film as a *recording* and the film as a *cinematographic work* which UK copyright law does not do.[58] Instead, the producer of a film (as a joint owner of the film) will have exclusive rights in the recording of a film for 70 years after the death of the last of the persons listed in section 13B. Further, the producer might qualify as a co-author of the film as a dramatic work[59] and thus obtain protection for the cinematographic work for 70 years *post mortem auctoris*. Both of these outcomes appear to be contrary to Article 3(3) of the Term Directive.[60]

Reform to film works should be based on the distinction made in EC law, namely, the cinematographic work versus the fixation of the film. Economic and moral rights in the former should inhere initially in the author of the *original* cinematographic work (ie, the principal director) and include the right of non-exact reproduction (thus prohibiting the reproduction in the form of a similar sequence of images). The length of protection for cinematographic works should be measured according to Article 2(2) of the Term Directive. By contrast, rights in the fixation of the film should inhere initially in the producer and the length of protection should be determined according to Article 3 of the Term Directive.

3. Computer Program

In order to improve protection of multimedia works, two changes could be made to protection of computer programs. First, digital data could be included within the notion of computer program.[61] Second, the non-literal features of programs could be protected beyond the structure or architecture of the program. Neither option, however, is particularly feasible.

---

[58] Although Arnold (2001) p 21 argues that the Court of Appeal's decision in *Arks (No 2)* results in UK copyright law more nearly giving effect to the Rental Right Directive and Term Directive.

[59] Kamina (2002) pp 144–46.

[60] Kamina (2002) pp 122–24.

[61] See J Douglas, 'Too Hot to Handle? Copyright Protection of Multimedia' (1997) 8 *AIPJ* 96, 105.

There is a significant obstacle to implementing the first option based on the principle that protection must apply to the *expression,* and not the idea, of a computer program. The principle that only expression must be protected has been iterated in Article 1(2) of the EC Software Directive, which states:

> Protection in accordance with this Directive shall apply to the expression in any form of a computer program. Ideas and principles which underlie any element of a computer program, including those which underlie its interfaces, are not protected under this Directive.

In a similar vein, Article 2 of the WIPO Copyright Treaty 1996 ('WCT') provides that in general:

> Copyright protection extends to expressions and not to ideas, procedures, methods of operation or mathematical concepts as such.

The data upon which a program acts arguably is not part of the expression of the program. Most commentators agree that, at the very least, expression in relation to software relates to the coded instructions that implement the underlying algorithm.[62] Controversy exists, however, regarding whether levels of abstraction higher than the program code should be regarded as expression.[63] But these higher levels of abstraction are usually concerned with user interfaces, non-user interfaces or the functional design of a program,[64] as opposed to the digital information manipulated or processed by the program.

The feasibility of the second option is also questionable, in the light of the present legal trends in copyright protection of software. The high watermark of protection for non-literal elements of software seems to have been reached and the trend is towards a more tightly defined notion of non-literal protection. In the UK, the approach to non-literal infringement appears to be the US *Altai* test.[65] This is a strict test[66] that counters the previously wide approach reflected in *Whelan v Jaslow.*[67] Indeed, in applying the *Altai* test in *John Richardson Computers Ltd v Flanders* ('*Flanders*'),[68] few non-visual user interface features were held to be

---

[62] A Christie, 'Designing Appropriate Protection for Computer Programs' (1994) 11 *EIPR* 486, 491–92; S Gordon, 'The Very Idea!: Why Copyright Law is an Inappropriate way to Protect Computer Programs' [1998] *EIPR* 10, who argues that protection of computer programs should be restricted to object and source code expression.

[63] See eg, Gordon (1998).

[64] See Christie (1994) p 493; J Drexl, *What is Protected in a Computer Program? Copyright Protection in the United States and Europe* (Max Planck Institute, Munich, 1994) 18–32.

[65] *Computer Associates International Inc v Altai Inc* (1992) 23 USPQ 2d 1241. Discussed above in ch 4 at p 116. Although, see the recent decision in *Navitaire Inc v Easyjet Airline Co* [2005] ECDR 17.

[66] See A Fitzgerald, 'Square Pegs and Round Holes: Recent US Developments in Copyright Protection for Computer Software' (1993) 4 *Journal of Law & Information Science* 142, 143, 147.

[67] *Whelan v Jaslow,* 797 F 2d 1222 (3rd Cir, 1986). The approach was to nominate the purpose or function of a program as its idea, while everything that was not necessary to that purpose of function was the expression of the idea.

[68] *John Richardson Computers Ltd v Flanders* [1993] FSR 497 ('*Flanders*').

infringing.[69] The future is unlikely to see a shift away from this tightly defined notion of non-literal infringement for two reasons. First, anything but carefully limited non-literal protection risks undermining the fundamental principle that copyright law protects expression of ideas and not the ideas themselves. If protection of software appears to distort this principle, the claims of those who believe copyright is an inappropriate vehicle by which to protect software will be strengthened.[70] Second, the eligibility of software related inventions for patent protection in the UK is now firmly established[71] and this relieves some of the pressure on copyright law to protect the functionality of software.

4. Compilation/Database

A minimal reform would be to ensure that compilations could comprise any type of work.[72] The problem remains, however, that protection extends only to the original selection, and sometimes arrangement, of constituent works.

One possibility is to protect the aggregate of contents reflected in a compilation[73] or database. The problem with this approach is that it would necessitate recourse to an originality criterion which is focussed on labour. This is because if protection of the aggregate contents is to be justified, there must be significant effort applied to collecting and producing the aggregate work. In other words, copying the aggregate contents or part thereof is seen as an appropriation of the earlier effort.[74] Utilising this standard of originality for databases conflicts with the express statement in section 3A of the CDPA that the selection or arrangement of database contents must be an 'author's own intellectual creation'. Although section 3A does not expressly apply to compilations, it is arguable that an originality test centred on labour would be inconsistent with the Database Directive.

---

[69] *Flanders*, 558–59.

[70] P Samuelson, *et al*, 'A Manifesto Concerning the Legal Protection of Computer Programs' (1994) 94 *Columbia Law Rev* 2308; IR Gross, 'A New Framework for Software Protection: Distinguishing between Interactive and Non-Interactive aspects of Computer Programs' (1994) 20 *Rutgers Computers & Technology L J* 107; Gordon (1998); Christie (1994).

[71] *Merrill Lynch's Application* [1989] RPC 561; *Gale's Application* [1991] RPC 305; *Wang Laboratories Inc's Application* [1991] RPC 463; *Fujitsu Limited's Application* [1997] RPC 608. As well as at the European level: see *Vicom/Computer-Related Inventions* [1987] 2 EPOR 74; T110/90 *IBM/Editable Document Form* [1995] EPOR 185; T935/97 *IBM/Computer Programs* [1999] EPOR 301; T1173/97 *IBM/Computer Programs* [2000] EPOR 219.

[72] Supported by A Monotti, 'Works Stored in Computer Memory: Databases and the CLRC Draft Report' (1993b) 4 *Journal of Law & Information Science* 265; T Dreier, 'Adjustment of Copyright Law to the Requirements of the Information Society' (1998) 29 *IIC* 623.

[73] See JB Hicks, 'Copyright and Computer Databases: Is Traditional Compilation Law Adequate?' (1990) 37 *Copyright L Symp* 85, 120–22.

[74] Hicks (1990) p 101; J Ginsburg, 'Creation and Commercial Value: Copyright Protection of Works of Information in the United States' in EJ Dommering and PB Hugenholtz, (eds), *Protecting Works of Fact* (Kluwer, Deventer, 1991) 41, 52–53.

A New Copyright Category

Some commentators have advocated the introduction of a new copyright category of 'multimedia work'.[75] Three main arguments have been made in support of this reform. First, that a new category would prevent corruption of existing categories, which risk being distorted if they are interpreted to accommodate multimedia works.[76] Second, because existing categories are not directly applicable there is a gap in protection which threatens the creation of multimedia works.[77] Finally, a new category would allow protection of multimedia works to be shaped to its unique qualities.[78] The following section will examine the above arguments and conclude that none are particularly convincing.

1. Distortion of Existing Categories

Interpreting existing categories of copyright works to accommodate multimedia works may stretch those categories to an unacceptable degree. This is not a new argument. For example, it has been made before in relation to software.[79] Some commentators have argued that computer programs are inappropriately charac-terised as 'literary works' because the value of computer programs lies in how they behave or function as opposed to their expression.[80] Source code is close enough

---

[75] In a European and UK context see Stamatoudi (2002) pp 206–10 and ch 10. In a US context, see JD Choe, 'Interactive Multimedia: a New Technology Tests the Limits of Copyright Law' (1994) 46 *Rutgers Law Rev* 929, 995–96. In an Australian context, see Douglas (1997) p 105; MJ O'Connor, 'Squeezing into Traditional Frames: Intellectual Property Law in the Shadow of the Information Society' (1998) 12 *IPJ* 285, 311. See generally G Wei, 'Multimedia and Intellectual and Industrial Property Rights in Singapore' (1995) 3 *Intl J of L & Information Technology* 214, 244–245.

[76] Douglas (1997) p 105; O'Connor (1998) p 311; and Wei (1995) pp 244–45.

[77] Stamatoudi (2002); Choe (1994) pp 993–96.

[78] Douglas (1997) p 105; Stamatoudi (2002); Wei (1995) pp 244–45.

[79] It has also been made in relation to semiconductor chips: eg, see J McKeough, 'Semi Conductor Chip Protection: Copyright or *Sui Generis*?' (1986) 9 *U New South Wales L J* 101, 107–14.

[80] P Samuelson, *et al*, 'A Manifesto Concerning the Legal Protection of Computer Programs' (1994) 94 *Columbia L Rev* 2308, 2315–20 and at 2319: 'Programs have almost no value to users as texts. Rather their value lies in their behaviour.' Gordon (1998) p 11: '. . . despite a very superficial resemblance to literary works, computer programs are more analogous to cogs in a machine.' Stamatoudi (2002) pp 45–46 argues that the inclusion of computer programs within the notion of literary works is a 'depurification' of copyright and that the step was taken for pragmatic reasons, rather than because computer programs were analogous to literary works. See also Christie (1994) p 488. *Cf* KW Dam, 'Some Economic Considerations in the Intellectual Property Protection of Software' (1995) 24 *J Legal Studies* 321, 323–26; J Ginsburg, 'Four Reasons and a Paradox: the Manifest Superiority of Copyright over *Sui Generis* Protection of Computer Software' (1994) 94 *Columbia L Rev* 2559, 2566–68 who argues that copyright protects a wide variety of works that 'behave' and that 'functionality' is not a gen-eral bar to copyright protection; and JM Griem, 'Against a *Sui Generis* System of Intellectual Property for Computer Software' (1993) 22 *Hofstra L Rev* 145, 152–53.

to natural language to qualify as a literary work, in that it conveys information, instruction or pleasure in the form of literary enjoyment.[81] However, the same cannot necessarily be said for the object code version of a computer program (which is the version responsible for implementing the program instructions).[82] A further objection to treating a computer program as a literary work is that it is said to lead to either under-protection or over-protection,[83] neither of which is desirable. Despite these objections it has been recognised at a national, European and an international level that computer programs, in both source and object code, are eligible for protection as literary works.[84]

The argument that new technological works distort existing categories has also been made in relation to multimedia video games, in the context of Australian copyright law. O'Connor[85] argues that multimedia video games were unjustifiably 'squeezed' within the notion of 'cinematograph film' in *Galaxy Electronics Pty Ltd v Sega Enterprises Ltd* ('*Galaxy Electronics*').[86] The case concerned Sega video games, 'Virtua Cop' and 'Daytona USA Twin',[87] and whether they were protected as 'cinematograph films' under the Australian Copyright Act 1968 (Cth). Section 10(1) of the Copyright Act 1968 (Cth) defines 'cinematograph film' as:

---

[81] This test derives from *Hollinrake v Truswell* [1894] 3 Ch 420, 428 (Davey LJ), as followed in *Exxon Corpn v Exxon Insurance Ltd* [1982] 1 Ch 119, 142–43 (Stephenson LJ), and 144 (Oliver LJ). In favour of source code satisfying this test see Gordon (1998) p 10; and Christie (1994) p 488. See also *Computer Edge Pty Ltd v Apple Computer Inc* (1986) 161 CLR 171, 182–83 (Gibbs CJ), 193 (Mason and Wilson JJ), and 201 (Brennan J).

[82] *Computer Edge Pty Ltd v Apple Computer Inc* (1986) 161 CLR 171, 183–84 (Gibbs CJ): 'It seems to me a complete distortion of meaning to describe electrical impulses in a silicon chip, which cannot be perceived by the senses and are not intended to convey any message to a human being and which do not represent words, letters, figures or symbols, as a literary work', and at 203 (Brennan J), and at 215 (Deane J). See also Gordon (1998) p 10; and B Napier, 'The Future of Information Technology Law' (1992) 51 *Cambridge L J* 46, 56–57.

[83] This criticism has been made especially in relation to US law: see Samuelson, *et al*,(1994) pp 2356–61; Christie (1994) pp 488–89; Gordon (1998) pp 12–13; and JC Phillips, 'Sui Generis Intellectual Property Protection for Computer Software' (1992) 60 *George Washington L Rev* 997, 1026. *Cf* Ginsburg (1994) pp 2569–72.

[84] At an international level see Art 4 WIPO Copyright Treaty 1996 ('WCT'); and Art 10 Agreement on Trade Related Aspects of Intellectual Property Rights 1994 ('TRIPs Agreement'). At a European level see Art 1, Directive 91/250/EEC on the legal protection of computer programs OJ L122 17/5/91, pp 42–46 ('Software Directive'). In the UK, see s 3, CDPA. In Germany, see Art 69a, German Law on Copyright and Neighbouring Rights 1965 ('German Law'). In France, see *The Pachot Decision* (1986) 129 RIDA 130. In Australia, see s 10(1) Copyright Act 1968 (Cth); and *Autodesk v Dyason (No 1)* (1993) 173 CLR 330, 347–48 (Dawson J delivering the main judgment of the High Court of Australia).

[85] O'Connor (1998) pp 314–16.

[86] *Galaxy Electronics Pty Ltd v Sega Enterprises Ltd* (1997) 37 IPR 462 (FFCA) ('*Galaxy Electronics*'). Proceedings seeking special leave to appeal from the Full Federal Court of Australia to the High Court of Australia were discontinued on 19 May 1998. See High Court of Australia Bulletin no 5, 1998. See Aplin (1999) for a detailed discussion of the case.

[87] The video games are described by Burchett J at first instance: *Sega Enterprises Ltd v Galaxy Electronics Pty Ltd* (1996) 35 IPR 161 ('*Sega Enterprises*') 162–63.

the aggregate of the visual images *embodied* in an article or thing so as to be capable by the use of that article or thing:

(a) of being shown as a moving picture; or

(b) of being *embodied* in another article or thing by the use of which it can be so shown;

and includes the aggregate of the sounds embodied in a sound track associated with such visual images. (Emphasis supplied)

At first instance, Burchett J held that the video games were protected as cinematograph films and that Galaxy had infringed Sega's copyright by parallel importation of the games. A critical issue was whether the video games represented 'visual images *embodied* in an article or thing'. There was no question that what the viewer saw was 'shown as a moving picture'.[88] Galaxy argued that the visual images were not 'embodied' because a two dimensional image of what appeared on the screen did not exist in the computer. The images on the screen were said to result from the three-dimensional vertices of a polygon model and computer calculations on that model. This argument turned on how 'embodied' was understood. Burchett J referred to section 24 of the Copyright Act 1968 (Cth), which states:

For the purposes of this Act, sounds or visual images shall be taken to have been embodied in an article or thing if the article or thing has been so treated in relation to those sounds or visual images that those sounds or visual images are capable, with or without the aid of some other device, of being reproduced from the article or thing.

Burchett J disagreed that the interpretation of the definition of 'cinematograph film' should be confined to two-dimensional images. Rather, the definition should be interpreted to cover new technologies because it is expressed 'in terms of the result achieved rather than of the means employed'.[89] Section 24 was said to strengthen this view.

The Full Federal Court affirmed the decision of Burchett J. The Court held that 'embodied' refers to the 'giving of a material or discernible form to an abstract principle or concept'.[90] The abstraction had to pre-exist the material manifestation. The visual images in the video games were held to exist before the game was played because they 'existed in the minds of their creators and the drawings and models they made'.[91] As to the form given to the visual images, this was the computer program and, by the use of that program, the visual images could be shown as a moving picture. The form of the embodiment, whether a two dimensional image or three-dimensional vertices of a polygon model (calculated by the computer program), was irrelevant since the definition did not require a technology specific form of embodiment.[92] Since the video games fell directly within the

---

[88] Above, at 164–65.

[89] Above, at 167.

[90] *Galaxy Electronics*, 470 (Wilcox J).

[91] Above. But compare the observation of Lindgren J at 475.

[92] *Galaxy Electronics*, 470 (Wilcox J).

definition of 'cinematograph film', there was no need to resort to section 24. Nevertheless, section 24 was considered to put the matter beyond doubt.[93]

O'Connor argues that the Full Federal Court misunderstood the nature of Galaxy's argument which was that 'only a *model* was stored from which possible images could be calculated, not retrieved.'[94] O'Connor explains that only a model for producing images, and not the images themselves, were embodied in the circuit boards. While graphic designers had created the fundamental images for the game, the remainder of the images were created by the sophisticated calculations of the model. He argues that the definition of 'cinematograph film' is technology neutral regarding how the images are stored. However, it still requires that images be retrieved, ie, that they should pre-exist.[95] O'Connor concludes that:

> What was protected in *Sega* was essentially *algorithms* for the construction of images from player input and data. This leads to the general objection that the interpretation given to 'embodied' was altogether too broad.[96]

Yet the courts have also resisted attempts to interpret the definition of 'cinematograph film' in an overly broad fashion. This is illustrated by the decision in *Aristocrat Leisure Industries Pty Ltd v Pacific Gaming Pty Ltd* (*'Aristocrat'*).[97] In this case the applicant sought to protect electronic gaming machines[98] as, *inter alia,* cinematograph films. Tamberlin J in the Federal Court distinguished the decision in *Galaxy Electronics* on the basis that it concerned video games which presented a series of images resembling a traditional movie film. By contrast, the sequences and types of visual images under consideration in *Aristocrat* were 'simply moving pictures of static symbols which simulate the spinning of the reels.'[99] Tamberlin J further commented:

> It is literally true that the specific symbols appear to rotate on the reels but *there is no element of progression or movement in the symbols themselves as there is in a traditional movie film*, which is comprised of a series of marginally different pictures, which when repeated quickly, *give the impression of motion.* I appreciate that the language is not to be restricted by any static view anchored to previous technology but there is real difficulty in accepting that the aggregate of the symbol images in the present case constitutes a moving picture.[100] (Emphasis supplied)

---

[93] Above, at 472 (Wilcox J).

[94] O'Connor (1997) p 314.

[95] Above, at 316.

[96] Above, at 315.

[97] *Aristocrat Leisure Industries Pty Ltd v Pacific Gaming Pty Ltd* (2000) 105 FCR 153 (Tamberlin J) (*'Aristocrat'*).

[98] See *Aristocrat*, 157–60 for a detailed description of the gaming machines.

[99] *Aristocrat*, 168.

[100] *Aristocrat*, 168.

Tamberlin J held that the images of simulated spinning did not amount to a 'cinematograph film'. In other words, his honour was unwilling to interpret overly broadly the phrase 'moving picture' in the definition of 'cinematograph film'.

The 'distortion' arguments discussed above reflect two types of concerns. The first is that the new subject matter is inappropriate to copyright law, but is nevertheless protected because it bears a superficial resemblance to existing copyright subject matter. In other words, the underlying argument is about whether or not copyright or another intellectual property regime (such as patent law or a *sui generis* regime) should apply. The second type of concern is not about the appropriateness of the copyright protection, but whether new subject matter can fit within the existing list of categories and, if not, whether a new category of work should be added. This concern arises in the context of 'closed list' copyright systems (such as the UK and Australia), where eligible subject matter is defined *exhaustively*, as opposed to 'open list' systems (as in France, Germany and the United States) where subject matter is defined non-exhaustively. In the latter systems, it is not necessary to show that the new subject matter fits within an existing category in order for copyright to subsist. Rather, it is only necessary to show that this new subject matter is an 'original work of authorship'[101] (in the case of the US), a 'personal intellectual creation'[102] (in the case of Germany) or a 'work of the mind'[103] (in the case of France). The objection to copyright protection of computer programs appears to be the first type (ie, copyright is the inappropriate regime),[104] whereas O'Connor's objection to protecting video games as cinematograph films is of the latter type (ie, film is an inappropriate category—video games do not fit within that notion).

In the case of multimedia works, the objection is of the second type.[105] But is it valid to claim that multimedia works fit inappropriately within existing categories? Chapters 3 to 5 comprehensively examined how existing UK copyright categories can accommodate multimedia works. The analysis was conducted from first principles because there are no reported UK cases in which multimedia works

---

[101] S 102(a) US Copyright Act 1976.

[102] Art 2(2), German Law.

[103] Art L111–1, French Intellectual Property Code 1992 ('French Code').

[104] S Ricketson, 'New Wine into Old Bottles: Technological Change and Intellectual Property Rights' (1992) 10 *Prometheus* 53 at 73:

> The pressure from the advocates of increased protection is commonly towards the expansion of existing regimes. The latter are usually well understood and it is generally easier from a legislative point of view to add something to an existing system than to create something entirely new. Nonetheless, however malleable these systems may be, a breaking point must come at some stage. In the case of copyright, this is to be seen in the blanket protection of computer programs that occurred under the 1984 amendments to the *Copyright Act 1968*. Generous as the broad church of copyright has always been, the inclusion of software seems quite out of character with the traditional categories of literary and artistic works protected under that head.

[105] It is not of the first type, for the reasons discussed at length in ch 2.

have been sought to be included within the existing categories. As there are no relevant decisions, it is impossible to claim that courts have stretched legal doctrine to accommodate multimedia works. However, it is possible to form a view about whether such categories would be unjustifiably stretched. Chapter 3 examined how the existing categories could be interpreted to embrace multimedia works. It is submitted that if these interpretations are followed the existing copyright categories will not be distorted.

Chapter 3 also concluded that no single category is able successfully to accommodate all multimedia works. Certain reforms to the existing categories have therefore been considered in this chapter. The conclusion reached was that a US style definition of 'audiovisual work' would be useful. However, to interpret the phrase 'series of related images' to include *any series of related images* would distort that definition. Therefore, this very broad interpretation should not be adopted. Further, interpreting 'computer program' to include the data upon which the program operates or certain non-literal elements of the program would unreasonably stretch that category. Thus, this was also considered an unfeasible reform.

2. Gaps in Protection

Stamatoudi argues that 'although [second generation] multimedia products cut across many categories of works, still there is no perfect match with any of them. We are presented with a *vide juridique* (ie, a complete absence of directly applicable legal rules).'[106] Thus, according to her, the preferable solution is to introduce a new category of multimedia works along with a *sui generis* right 'relating to the investment put into the contents of the multimedia work and perhaps to the way its interactivity is presented on screen.'[107] Stamatoudi proposes this reform in relation to both 'closed list' and 'open list' copyright traditions. Thus, her reforms would apply to the UK (a 'closed list' tradition), along with France and Germany (both 'open list' traditions). In the case of the UK, problems for multimedia works arise because as a prerequisite to protection they first have to be classified according to the existing eight categories. Classification of multimedia works may not be straightforward. Even if they can be classified as an existing work, the protection provided by that category may be partial.[108] In France and Germany (and other 'open list' traditions), difficulties arise because classification occurs in order to determine the applicability of special rules (such as those concerning authorship and ownership).[109] If multimedia works do not fit within certain categories for the

---

[106] Stamatoudi (2002) p 206.
[107] Above at 210 and 270–76.
[108] Above at 192–93.
[109] Above at 191–92.

purpose of applying special rules they fall to be protected according to the general copyright regime 'which coincides with that of traditional literary works.'[110] However, Stamatoudi argues that protection as a traditional literary work is wholly inappropriate and inadequate for multimedia works.[111]

This book argues that a new category of multimedia works should *not* be introduced into UK copyright law.[112] From the analysis conducted thus far, it can be concluded that neither copyright nor database right protects *all* types of multimedia works. However, database right offers robust protection for reference type and searchable multimedia works. Further, if copyright law is reformed in the manner argued for above (ie, the introduction of an audiovisual work category), multimedia video games, and other types of multimedia works that employ a moving visual user interface, will obtain strong protection. Stamatoudi argues that 'primitive' or 'first generation' multimedia products will often qualify as audiovisual works or databases but that 'advanced' or 'second generation multimedia' products will not.[113] However, the few examples of 'second generation' multimedia that she cites[114] are works that would be capable of protection by database right.[115]

For those multimedia works which do not qualify as audiovisual works or *sui generis* databases sufficient protection may occur through two avenues. The first is to claim protection of *part* of the multimedia work. The second is to utilise *technological protection measures* whose circumvention is prohibited under EC and UK law. It is argued that using either or both of these mechanisms will significantly reduce any remaining 'gaps' in protection.

---

[110] Above at 192.

[111] Above at 64–70. 192.

[112] See also Lahore and Phillips (1996) p 219 who argue that 'one should not be overzealous in introducing a new category of multimedia work into copyright law'; and Salokannel (1997) pp 89–90.

[113] Stamatoudi (2002) pp 204–6. For an explanation of the difference between first and second generation multimedia products see ch 1 above at pp 10–11.

[114] See Stamatoudi (2002) pp 205–6, n 54 where she discusses a hypothetical Beethoven multimedia work and also the *Moorditj* multimedia CD.

[115] See ch 3, n 107 where it is argued that *Moorditj* would satisfy the definition of 'database'. Stamatoudi (2002) pp 205–6, n 54 describes the hypothetical Beethoven multimedia work as follows:

> An example [of an advanced multimedia product] would be a multimedia product on Beethoven's life which contains pictures of his life as well as a database of all the musical works he composed. It might also contain clips with electronically re-enacted scenes, which can be manipulated by the user. The user would be able to interfere substantially with the contents of the multimedia product by including or excluding instruments, changing bits of the orchestration and the melody, blurring the pictures and so on.

It is submitted that this hypothetical example would also satisfy the definition of 'database'. The fact that a user can create new material from the existing content of the multimedia work does not change this fact.

(a) Protection of Part of a Multimedia Work

For multimedia works that cannot be brought within the notion of audiovisual works or which do not qualify for database right, protection will still be available for parts of the multimedia work. In particular, the computer program in a multimedia work could be relied upon to protect the creators' interests. Indeed, it would make sense to rely on this element because the computer program underpins the multimedia work and has a direct bearing on how the work is presented. Stamatoudi rejects this as an option for protecting *all* multimedia works, on the basis that it is impractical from the point of view of effective exploitation of the work.[116] However, what is advocated here is reliance on protection of the computer program for a narrow range of multimedia works, ie, those works that *are not otherwise protected* in their entirety by copyright or database right. The argument is that some protection for this range of multimedia works will provide sufficient incentives to create them and thus it is unnecessary to introduce a new category of multimedia.[117] Where the only available protection relates to the underlying computer program this will be effective against wholesale copying of the multimedia work. It will be less effective where contents of the multimedia work are copied. In this situation, it is recommended that technological protection measures be used to minimise the risk of market failure.

(b) Use of TPMs

The use of TPMs in relation to multimedia works will also minimise the risks of market failure. Chapter 2 discussed the use of TPMs when looking at whether or not copyright protection of multimedia works could be justified according to an economic analysis. It was argued that producers of multimedia works could not rely exclusively on TPMs to protect their investment, since the efficacy of TPMs cannot be guaranteed.[118] Thus, the availability of TPMs did not undermine the claim that multimedia works should be accorded copyright protection. However, it is submitted that for those multimedia works which attract partial copyright protection, the use of TPMs *in addition* to copyright will reduce the risk of market failure.[119]

---

[116] Stamatoudi (2002) p 193.

[117] Stamatoudi (2002) p 195 recognises this possibility in the following statement: 'If under the current copyright regimes of protection a class of works is found which can even partly accommodate multimedia products, then the remaining elements of these products, which are not protected under this class of works, could arguably still be satisfactorily protected by the operation of the market.'

[118] See ch 2 above at p 21.

[119] This argument has been made by J Ginsburg, 'US Initiatives to Protect Works of Low Authorship' in R Dreyfuss, DL Zimmerman and H First, (eds), *Expanding the Boundaries of Intellectual Property: Innovation Policy for the Knowledge Society* (OUP, Oxford, 2001) 55–77 in relation to databases. Ginsburg at 63 argues that a database producer could combine public domain information with minimal amounts of copyrightable matter, so that the database qualified as a copyrighted work for the purpose of s 1201(a) of the US Copyright Act 1976 which prohibits circumvention of technological

TPMs will operate as a *practical* obstacle to unauthorised copying and their success in doing so will depend on the robustness of the particular technology used. The range of TPMs is varied and includes encryption, digital watermarks, invisible messages and passwords.[120] In addition, TPMs will operate as a *legal* obstacle because their circumvention is regulated by Article 7 of the Software Directive and Article 6 of the Information Society Directive.[121] These provisions, and their implementation into UK law, will be examined below.

(i) Article 7(1)(c) Software Directive

Article 7(1)(c) of the Software Directive obligates Member States to provide appropriate remedies against a person committing:

> any act of putting into circulation, or the possession for commercial purposes of, any means the sole intended purpose of which is to facilitate the unauthorised removal or circumvention of any technical device which may have been applied to protect a computer program.

This provision does not prohibit circumvention *per se*, but rather commercially dealing in circumvention means.[122]

In order to implement the above provision into UK law, section 296 of the CDPA was amended to extend the category of persons against whom remedies could be sought under that section.[123] After 31 October 2003, ie, the date when the Copyright Regulations became operative, section 296 was revised to take into account implementation of Article 6 of the Information Society Directive. The following sections discuss both the 'old' section 296 (pre- 31 October 2003) and the 'revised' section 296 (post-31 October 2003) of the CDPA.

(ii) Pre-31 October 2003

Section 296 applied where copies of a copyright work were issued to the public, by or with the licence of the copyright owner, in an electronic form which was copy-protected.[124] Copy-protection was defined to include 'any device or means

---

measures used to control access to the work. See also L Bently and R Burrell, 'Copyright and the Information Society in Europe: A Matter of Timing as well as Content' (1997) 34 *Common Market L Rev* 1197 at 1209–10 who argue that extension of copyright protection in response to digitization is premature, especially in view of the fact that copyright owners can use technological measures to help prevent or control unauthorised copying of their works.

[120] See Dam (2001) pp 106–110; S Dusollier, 'Electrifying the Fence: The Legal Protection of Technological Measures for Protecting Copyright' [1999] *EIPR* 285, 285–86; C Sellars, 'Digital Rights Management Systems: Recent European Issues' (2003) 14 *Entertainment L Rev* 5, 5–6.

[121] Directive 2001/29/EC on the harmonisation of certain aspects of copyright and related rights in the information society OJ L167 22/6/2001, pp 10–19 ('Information Society Directive').

[122] *Cf* Art 6 of the Information Society Directive discussed below.

[123] See Copyright (Computer Programs) Regulations 1992, SI 1992/3233 ('Software Regulations') which came into effect on 1 January 1993, regulation 10 inserting para 2A into section 296 of the CDPA.

[124] S 296(1), CDPA.

intended to prevent or restrict *copying* of a work or to impair the quality of copies made.'[125] The reference to 'copying' in the definition of 'copy-protection' meant section 296 was narrower than Article 7(1)(c) of the Software Directive because it only protected against infringement of the reproduction right (and not infringement of all exclusive rights).[126] The person issuing copies of the work (including a computer program) to the public had the same rights as the copyright owner against a person who commercially dealt[127] with 'any device or means specifically designed or adapted to circumvent the form of copy-protection employed'[128] or who published information intended to enable or assist persons to circumvent that form of copy-protection, where the person knew or had reason to believe that it would be used to make infringing copies.[129]

An action based on section 296 was brought in *Sony Computer Entertainment v Owen* ('*Owen*').[130] The claimant, Sony, made and sold the Playstation 2 console. It built three different versions of its Playstation 2 console for different world regions. These regions are Japan, US and Europe (and other PAL countries). The games available (on CD or DVD-Rom) were encoded with a special code which the Playstation 2 console sought when the game was loaded. The purpose of the codes was to prevent pirated Sony games and also other games (including legitimate Sony games from other world regions) from being played on the console. The defendant, Owen, imported the 'Messiah chip' into the UK. The Messiah chip could be inserted into the Playstation 2 console, enabling the authorisation process to be bypassed. The defendant wanted to sell the chips in the UK but the claimant objected under section 296 of the CDPA and applied for summary judgment.

Jacob J held that the defendant was liable under section 296 and granted summary judgment. The special codes used by Sony on games qualified as 'copy protection' within the meaning of section 296(4). This was because the codes were a device or means intended to prevent copying of the work, ie, loading of the game into the console and causing temporary copying in the RAM chip.[131] The defend-

---

[125] S 296(4), CDPA. Emphasis supplied. Laddie, *et al*, (2000) para 35.22 comment that the copy-protection does not have to be particularly efficacious: '. . . provided the person issuing the work in this form genuinely intends that the technology employed shall to some degree reduce the quality of unauthorised copies it would appear that his copies count as "copy-protected" even if there is no discernible degradation.'

[126] L Bently and B Sherman, *Intellectual Property Law*, 2nd edn, (OUP, Oxford, 2004) 311, n 136; Lai (2000) p 158.

[127] This is a shorthand description of the activities listed in ss 296(2) and (2A), CDPA, which are 'makes, imports, sells or lets for hire, offers or exposes for sale or hire, or advertises for sale or hire and possesses in the course of a business.'

[128] According to Lai (2000) p 158 this language arguably implemented the 'sole intended purpose' test in Art 7(1)(c) of the Software Directive.

[129] S 296(2), CDPA.

[130] *Sony Computer Entertainment v Owen* [2002] ECDR 27 (Jacob J) ('*Owen*').

[131] *Owen*, 301. *Cf* the position in Australia, in *Kabushiki Kaisha Sony Computer Entertainment v Stevens* (2003) 57 IPR 161, 208–9 (Lindgren J in obiter) in relation to section 116A of the Copyright Act 1968 (Cth).

ant argued that the chip would not involve infringement because it enabled independent software and/or Sony games from other world regions to be played on the console. Jacob J held that the fact that the Messiah chip could enable some lawful use was immaterial. He stated:

> The language of the section is, 'any device or means specifically designed or adapted to circumvent the form of copy-protection'. That is just what the Messiah does. It does not matter that once circumvented, the machine may read non-infringing material. Once it is conceded—as I think it must be—that the special codes which Sony put in are a device intended to prevent or restrict copying of a work within the meaning of subsection (4), it follows that the Messiah is a device designed to circumvent that.[132]

Mr Justice Jacob's reasoning seems inconsistent with the language of section 296. Section 296(2) refers to a person knowing or having reason to believe that the device or means specifically designed or adapted (in this case the Messiah chip) to circumvent the form of copy protection (in this case the special codes) *will be used to make infringing copies.* Thus, Sony should have had to show that the Messiah chip circumvented the code authorisation process *and* that circumvention would result in infringing copies. On the facts, however, it was possible to point to circumvention of the copy-protection resulting in infringing copies. To the extent that the Messiah chip enabled pirated games to be played, the temporary reproduction of the game in the console would amount to an infringing copy. In terms of allowing Sony games from other regions to be played, the Messiah chip would also enable temporary copying of these games to occur. This would amount to infringement because the licence to use the games is restricted to a particular territorial region.[133] The fact that the Messiah chip enabled some independent software to be played on the Sony console would not negate the fact that the defendant knew or had reason to believe that the chip would be used to make infringing copies.

Support for the above criticism of Jacob J's approach to section 296 may be drawn from the decision in *Kabushiki Kaisha Sony Computer Entertainment Inc v Ball* (*'Ball'*).[134] This case also concerned the Sony Playstation 2 consoles. As explained above, authentic Sony games are embedded with a special code which is read by the console. The defendants were involved in the design, manufacture, sale and installation of an electronic chip called Messiah 2. This chip could be fitted into a Playstation 2 console, enabling the authorisation process to be bypassed. Using this chip, legitimate Sony games designed for different world regions, along with unauthorised copies of Sony games, could be played on the Playstation 2

---

[132] *Owen*, 302.

[133] *Owen*, 303: 'The games are sold, as appears to be common ground, abroad with, for example, "For Japan only". I see no reason from that to suppose that there is a licence for use outside Japan. In the end, it is for a licensee to prove his licence and I do not think any such licence is proved.'

[134] *Kabushiki Kaisha Sony Computer Entertainment Inc v Ball* [2004] ECDR 33 (*'Ball'*).

console. Sony brought an action claiming, *inter alia*, that the first defendant infringed section 296 of the CDPA prior to and after 31 October 2003. They brought an application for summary judgment before Laddie J.

The first defendant argued, *inter alia*, that since a large quantity of Messiah2 chips were exported for foreign customers they would not result in the creation of infringing copies. This is because there would be no infringement of UK copyright[135] and none of the consoles which were fitted with exported Messiah2 chips would be imported back into the UK.[136] Sony argued that the legislative intent behind section 296(2) was to catch those persons who had actual or constructive knowledge that the equipment in which they are trading is to be used to overcome copy-protection and it was irrelevant whether the equipment caused infringement of copyright. Laddie J rejected this construction of section 296, on the basis that it 'would amount to ignoring the words "will be used to make infringing copies" ' in subsection (2). He stated that '[h]ad the legislature wished to prohibit trade in devices which overcome copy-protection without regard to whether that assisted copyright infringement, it could easily have done so. In this section of the Act it did not.'[137] Sony argued that its construction of section 296 found support in Article 7(1)(c) of the Software Directive. Laddie J did not find this argument persuasive given that the 1988 Act was passed before the Software Directive and did not purport to give effect to it.[138] Insofar as the Messiah2 chips were sold *in the UK*, Laddie J found that the defendant was infringing section 296 because he knew or had reason to believe that they would be used to make infringing copies (ie, temporary copies of the program in the RAM chip).[139] But in respect of the rest of his stock and other commercial activities it was unclear whether he had the requisite knowledge. The defendant's liability would depend on the particular facts of each type of commercial activity which was not a matter that could be resolved on a summary judgment application.[140]

The meaning of 'infringing copies' was also considered in *Ball*. The first defendant argued that he did not have actual or constructive knowledge that the Messiah2 chip would be used to make 'infringing copies'. Sony argued that an infringing copy resulted when the game was inserted into the console because an unauthorised temporary copy of the program was made in the RAM. However, the defendant argued that 'infringing copy' as defined in section 27 of the CDPA refers to an 'article' and RAM copies did not constitute an article. Laddie J rejected this argument, finding that a silicon RAM chip was an article and that it was an infring-

---

[135] Thus, no infringement under s 27(2), CDPA.

[136] Thus, no infringement under s 27(3), CDPA.

[137] *Ball*, 331.

[138] Above, at 331: 'It seems to me that it is not permissible to stretch the meaning of the Act so as to accord with what [the claimant] says is the intended scope of the 1991 Directive.'

[139] Above, at 329.

[140] Above, at 331.

ing article when it contained the copy data.[141] It did not matter that it was an infringing article only for a short time. This view was also consistent with section 17(6) of the CDPA.[142]

(iii) Post-31 October 2003

Section 296 was amended as a result of the Copyright Regulations. The new section 296 deals with technical devices applied to computer programs. Section 296A *et seq* regulates the circumvention of technological protection measures applied to copyright works other than computer programs. These provisions will be discussed later.

The new section 296 provides:

(1) This section applies where—

    (a) a technical device has been applied to a computer program; and

    (b) a person . . . knowing or having reason to believe that it will be used to make infringing copies—

        (i) manufactures for sale or hire, imports, distributes, sells or lets for hire, offers or exposes for sale or hire, advertises for sale or hire or has in his possession for commercial purposes any means the sole intended purpose of which is to facilitate the unauthorised removal or circumvention of the technical device; or

        (ii) publishes information intended to enable or assist persons to remove or circumvent the technical device . . .

(6) In this section references to a technical device in relation to a computer program are to any device intended to prevent or restrict acts that are not authorised by the copyright owner of that computer program and are restricted by copyright.

This provision is broader than the old section 296 in that it covers technical devices which would prevent *any act* which would infringe copyright and not just devices intended to prevent or restrict *copying* of a work.[143] Previously, only the person issuing copies of the work to the public in an electronic, copy-protected form could sue for infringement of section 296. By contrast, revised section 296(2) gives standing to sue to three types of persons. There is the person issuing to the public copies of or communicating to the public the computer program to which the technical device has been applied. There is also the copyright owner or his exclusive licensee. Finally, there is the owner or exclusive licensee of any intellectual property right in the technical device applied to the computer program. Another

---

[141] Above, at 329.

[142] Above, at 329–30: 'Just as a transient act of copying amounts to infringement, so an article which transiently contains a copy is an infringing copy for the purpose of this legislation . . . It would produce an unwarranted inconsistency in the Act were that material form not to be considered an article for the purpose of s 27.'

[143] Although it no longer encompasses any device or means intended to impair the quality of copies made.

difference is that section 296(1)(b)(i) now refers to 'any means the *sole intended purpose* of which is to facilitate the unauthorised removal or circumvention of the technical device' (emphasis supplied), whereas the previous version referred to 'any device or means specifically designed or adapted to circumvent the form of copy-protection employed.' As a result, the language of section 296(1)(b)(i) is now closer to that of Article 7(1)(c) of the Software Directive.[144]

The meaning of 'sole intended purpose' was considered in *Ball*. The first defendant (Ball) argued that it was not the sole intended purpose of the Messiah2 chip to facilitate unauthorised removal or circumvention of the technical device. This was because the chip was designed to enable any necessary back-up of the original games to be played and to enable playing of UK (PAL) games on non-European (non-PAL) Playstation 2 consoles imported into the UK. This argument was rejected by Laddie J on the basis that neither of these activities was authorised by Sony. Laddie J held that purchasers of Sony games were not entitled to make and play back-up copies of the games. Purchasers could not rely on section 50A of the CDPA to justify making a back-up copy because there was no necessity to make a back up.[145] Playing a back-up copy would be unauthorised and the resultant transient copy of the program in the RAM would be unauthorised. Laddie J concluded that the purpose of the chip to enable back up copies to be played amounted to an unauthorised circumvention of the Sony copy-protection system.[146] As regards the purpose of the Messiah2 chip being to enable playing Sony games from different regions, Laddie J held that purchasers of a Sony game for the PAL region were 'told in clear language that it is not designed to be played on a non-PAL machine.'[147] Thus, there was no licence or authorisation to play a non-PAL game on a PAL console. Laddie J concluded that '[i]n this respect as well the Messiah2chip is designed to facilitate unauthorised removal or circumvention of the copy protection system.'[148]

Section 296 (pre and post 31 October 2003) could prove useful to producers of multimedia works insofar as such works feature an underlying computer program. A multimedia producer could apply a copy-protection or technical device to the underlying computer program, in order to prevent or restrict unauthorised copying or exclusive acts in respect of the program. However, the technical device could also operate as an obstacle to accessing and using the multimedia work. This is because in order to use the multimedia work it will be necessary to load (or download) the work into a computer RAM and, in so doing, this will cause a temporary copy of the computer program to occur. As the *Sony* cases illustrate,

---

[144] Bently and Sherman (2004) p 312, n 138 point out the difference between the language will be important if there is a second purpose.
[145] *Ball*, 333–34.
[146] Above, at 334.
[147] Above.
[148] Above.

such temporary copying amounts to an exclusive act which the copyright owner can authorise and a copy-protection or technical device can be applied in order to restrict or prevent that act. Although circumvention *per se* is not prohibited, commercially dealing in circumvention devices or services *is* prohibited. Thus, both a practical and legal obstacle to using the multimedia work can be created *via* applying a copy-protection or technical device to the underlying computer program. Alternatively, based on Article 6 of the Information Society Directive, TPMs may be applied to individual copyright works (other than a computer program) within a multimedia work.[149]

(iv) Article 6 of the Information Society Directive

Article 6 was a fiercely debated provision of the Information Society Directive, as shown by the way in which it evolved from the Proposal[150] to the Amended Proposal[151] to the Common Position[152] to its current form. This provision seeks to implement obligations under Article 11 of WCT and Article 18 of WIPO Performances and Phonograms Treaty 1996 ('WPPT').[153] Article 11 of the WCT provides:

> Contracting Parties shall provide adequate legal protection and effective legal remedies against the circumvention of effective technological measures that are used by authors in connection with the exercise of their rights under this Treaty or the Berne Convention and that restrict acts, in respect of their works, which are not authorized by the authors concerned or permitted by law.

Article 18 of WPPT is in almost identical terms, except that instead of referring to 'authors' and 'works', it refers to performers and their performances and phonogram producers and their phonograms. The language of Article 11 of the WCT and Article 18 of WPPT is broad, thus permitting signatories a wide discretion as to how to implement their obligations.[154] As a consequence, countries have implemented these obligations in divergent ways.[155]

---

[149] They may also be applied to multimedia works protected as a film, copyright database or *sui generis* database, thereby bolstering the protection available under copyright and database right.

[150] See Proposal for a European Parliament and Council Directive on the harmonization of certain aspects of copyright and related rights in the Information Society OJ C108/6 7/4/98.

[151] Amended Proposal for a European Parliament and Council Directive on the harmonization of certain aspects of copyright and related rights in the Information Society OJ C180/6 25/6/1999.

[152] Common Position (EC) No 48/2000 OJ C344/1 1/12/2000.

[153] Recital 15, Information Society Directive.

[154] For a discussion of the scope of Art 11 of WCT see M Ficsor, *The Law of Copyright and the Internet: the 1996 WIPO Treaties, their Interpretation and Implementation* (OUP, Oxford, 2002) 544–49.

[155] For a brief discussion of implementation in different countries see Ficsor (2002) pp 550–63. For a comparison between the US and EU see N Braun, 'The Interface between the Protection of Technological Measures and the Exercise of Exceptions to Copyright and Related Rights: Comparing the Situation in the United States and the European Community' [2003] *EIPR* 496; and T Foged, 'US v EU Anti Circumvention Legislation: Preserving the Public's Privileges in the Digital Age' (2002) 24

Article 6(1) and (2) of the Information Society Directive obliges Member States to provide adequate legal protection against circumvention of any effective technological measure and 'trafficking' in circumvention devices or services. Article 6(3) defines 'technological measure' to mean:

> any technology, device or component that, in the normal course of its operation, is designed to prevent or restrict acts, in respect of works or other subject-matter, which are not authorised by the rightholder of any copyright or any right related to copyright as provided for by law or the *sui generis* right provided for in Chapter III of Directive 96/9/EC.

Article 6(3) goes on to state that technological measures shall be deemed 'effective':

> where the use of a protected work or other subject-matter is controlled by the rightholders through application of an access control or protection process, such as encryption, scrambling or other transformation of the work or other subject-matter or a copy control mechanism, which achieves the protection objective.

A 'technological measure' appears to include access control *and* copy-protection technology.[156] This is implicit in Article 6(3)[157] which refers to 'any technology . . . designed to *prevent* or *restrict* acts, in respect of works or other subject matter'.[158] Further, in defining 'effective', Article 6(3) explicitly refers to an access control process and copy control mechanism.[159] It may be queried whether a password system, where a user has to enter a password in order to access a work, can be classified as an access control process. This is because a password is not an 'encryption, scrambling or other transformation of the work or other subject matter'. However, a password system probably qualifies as a copy control mechanism, on the basis that it operates to prevent the temporary copying of a work in the RAM of a computer.

Where a technological measure is capable of circumvention it has been argued that it is 'ineffective' and outside Article 6.[160] The difficulty with this interpretation is that it would render Article 6 redundant since most TPMs are, to some extent,

---

EIPR 525. For a discussion of the Australian position see T Aplin, 'Contemplating Australia's Digital Future: the Copyright Amendment (Digital Agenda) Act 2000' [2001] *EIPR* 565, 574–75. For a comparison of the US, EU and New Zealand positions see J Smillie, 'Digital Copyright Reform in New Zealand' [2004] *EIPR* 302, 306–10.

[156] Foged (2002) pp 529–30 expresses the view that the WIPO provisions probably cover both copy control and access control measures.

[157] Cf s 1201(a) and (b), US Copyright Act 1976 introduced by the Digital Millennium Copyright Act 1998, which makes the distinction explicit.

[158] Emphasis supplied. See also J Perritt, 'Protecting Technology over Copyright: a Step Too Far' (2003) 14 *Entertainment L Rev* 1, 2.

[159] Braun (2003) pp 498–99; Foged (2002) p 535.

[160] Perritt (2003) p 2.

fallible.[161] Indeed, the objective of the provision is to protect effective technological measures against acts of circumvention, which assumes that such measures can and will be circumvented.[162] Further, Article 6(3) states that a technological measure is to be assessed, 'in the normal course of its operation'.[163] Thus, the better view is that a technological measure is not ineffective simply because it can be circumvented.[164] However, it seems possible for a rightholder to apply a weak (or easily circumvented) technological measure and for it to be still characterised as 'effective'. This is because a technological measure is 'effective' if the access control or protection process or copy control mechanism achieves its *protection objective*. If the protection objective is simply to provide low-level protection against access or copying by ordinary users, the fact that the technological measure may be easily circumvented by a more sophisticated user should not preclude it from being 'effective'.[165] On the other hand, if the protection objective is to prevent all users from making copies of the work and an unreliable form of access or copy control technology is utilised, then the technological measure may not in fact achieve its protection objective.

Article 6(1) obligates Member States to 'provide adequate legal protection against the circumvention of any effective technological measures' in situations where the person carries out the circumvention with actual or constructive knowledge that he or she is pursuing that objective. It is clear that circumvention of both access control and copy control measures is prohibited.[166]

Article 6(2) stipulates:

> Member States shall provide adequate legal protection against the manufacture, import, distribution, sale, rental, advertisement for sale or rental, or possession for commercial purposes of devices, products or components or the provision of services which:
>
> (a) are promoted, advertised or marketed for the purpose of circumvention of, or
> (b) have only a limited commercially significant purpose or use other than to circumvent, or

---

[161] Braun (2003) p 499. Perritt (2003) p 3 argues that 'while lack of effectiveness is an appealing argument for those opposed to the Directive it seems unfair in practice. It is hard to believe that there are many TPMs which would withstand the attention of a dedicated hacker, but that doesn't mean these should be afforded less protection.'

[162] Ficsor (2002) p 545.

[163] Ficsor (2002) p 546.

[164] As Ficsor (2002) p 546 acknowledges, this means that the word 'effective' adds little to 'technological measure' in Art 11, WCT.

[165] In support see T Cook and L Brazell, *The Copyright Directive: UK Implementation* (Jordans, Bristol, 2004) 45.

[166] *Cf* the position in the US where s 1201(a) of the Copyright Act 1976 only prohibits the circumvention of *access* control measures. The lack of prohibition on circumvention of *copy* control measures is supposed to facilitate the exercise of fair use rights: see Ficsor (2002), 551. However, Smillie (2004) p 307 describes this concession as 'largely illusory since those rights can be exercised only if there is no *access* control on a work, and even then the sweeping ban on trafficking denies fair users the technological means to circumvent a "stand alone" control on *copying*.' For a similar criticism see Braun (2003) p 497.

(c) are primarily designed, produced, adapted or performed for the purpose of enabling or facilitating the circumvention of,

any effective technological measures.

Unlike the prohibition against circumvention *per se* the above prohibition against 'trafficking' in circumvention devices or services does not contain a knowledge requirement. Article 6(2) also targets those devices or services which have circumvention as their primary or commercial purpose (as opposed to sole intended purpose).[167]

Article 6(1) and (2) applies to copyright works, *other than computer programs*,[168] and to *sui generis* databases. This creates a disparity in regulation of TPMs as applied to computer programs and to other copyright works. This is because Article 7(1)(c) of the Software Directive does not prohibit circumvention *per se* and prohibits commercially dealing in circumvention devices or services whose *sole intended purpose* is to facilitate circumvention and where there is actual or constructive knowledge. This inconsistency at a European level has been criticised by commentators.[169] The Commission, however, has no intention of amending Article 7 of the Software Directive 'until more experience has been gained from the application of Article 6 of the Information Society Directive.'[170]

A concern that arises is whether Article 6(1) and (2) of the Information Society Directive continue to apply once copyright (or database right) has expired. These provisions relate to circumvention of, and trafficking in devices or services primarily designed to circumvent, effective technological measures. Thus, the issue is whether a technological measure is still effective if it is applied to a work in the public domain. Article 6(3) stipulates that a technological measure is 'effective' where 'the use of *a protected work* or other subject-matter is controlled by the rightholders through application of an access control or protection process . . . or a copy control mechanism' (Emphasis supplied). Where a work (or *sui generis* database) is no longer protected because copyright (or database right) has expired, it is submitted that the technological measure would no longer be 'effective' and Article 6(1) and (2) would be rendered inapplicable. However, if the technological measure is applied to a combination of protected and non-protected works, then it is submitted the measure would still be 'effective' and Article 6(1) and (2) would remain applicable. This means that Article 6 has the potential severely to circumscribe the ability of the public to access and use works in which protection has expired or does not exist.

---

[167] The US anti-trafficking provisions, contained in ss 1201(a)(2) and 1201(b)(1) are similar to Art 6(2) of the Information Society Directive.

[168] That Art 6 is without prejudice to Art 7(1)(c) of the Software Directive is made clear from Art 1(2) and recital 50 of the Information Society Directive.

[169] Eg, see Bently and Sherman (2004) pp 311–12; Cook and Brazell (2004) p 27.

[170] *Commission Staff Working Paper on the review of the EC legal framework in the field of copyright and related rights* Brussels, 19 July 2004 SEC (2004) 995 ('Working Paper') para 2.2.1.4.

A major concern is the extent to which TPMs override users' ability to rely on copyright exceptions.[171] Article 6(3) defines 'technological measure' to include any technology, device or component that is designed to prevent or restrict acts which are *not authorised by the rightholder*.[172] Thus, a technology, device or component will constitute a 'technological measure', whose circumvention is prohibited, even where it prevents or restricts acts that would *not* constitute an infringement of copyright or database right because a relevant exception is applicable.[173] Further, Article 6 does not create any exceptions to the prohibition on circumvention of technological measures or the trafficking in circumvention devices or services.[174] The only safeguard for the interests of beneficiaries of exceptions is Article 6(4).[175] Article 6(4) provides:

4. Notwithstanding the legal protection provided for in *paragraph 1, in the absence of voluntary measures taken by rightholders, including agreements* between rightholders and other parties concerned, Member States *shall take appropriate measures* to ensure that rightholders make available to the beneficiary of an exception or limitation provided for in national law in accordance with *Article 5(2)(a), (2)(c), (2)(d), (2)(e), (3)(a), (3)(b) or (3)(e) the means of benefiting from that exception or limitation*, to the extent necessary to benefit from that exception or limitation and *where that beneficiary has legal access* to the protected work or subject-matter concerned.

A Member State *may* also take such measures in respect of a beneficiary of an exception or limitation provided for in accordance with *Article 5(2)(b)*, unless reproduction for private use has already been made possible by rightholders to the extent necessary to benefit from the exception or limitation concerned and in accordance with the provisions of Article 5(2)(b) and (5), without preventing rightholders from adopting adequate measures regarding the number of reproductions in accordance with these provisions.

The technological measures applied voluntarily by rightholders, including those applied in implementation of voluntary agreements, and technological measures applied in implementation of the measures taken by Member States, shall enjoy the legal protection provided for in paragraph 1.

[171] Cook and Brazell (2004) pp 27–28 describe how the major controversy with respect to Art 6 was the relationship between protection of technological measures and copyright exceptions and limitations and how this issue almost brought the entire Directive to a halt.

[172] As explained in the Statement of the Council's Reasons, para 43, these terms 'make it clear that Article 6(1) protects against circumvention of all technological measures designed to prevent or restrict acts not authorised by the rightholder, regardless of whether the person performing the circumvention is a beneficiary of one of the exceptions provided for in Article 5.'

[173] *Cf* this with the Proposal where Art 6(2) provided that 'technological measures' meant 'any device, product or component incorporated into a process, device or product *designed to prevent or inhibit the infringement of any copyright* or [related rights] or [the database right].' Emphasis supplied. See also Art 6(3) in the Amended Proposal which referred to 'any technology, device or component that, in the normal course of its operation, is designed to prevent or inhibit the infringement of any copyright [or related right or database right]'.

[174] *Cf* the position under ss 1201(e) and 1201(d)–(j) of the US Copyright Act 1976.

[175] This paragraph was added by the Council: see Common Position OJ C 344/1 1/12/2000, Statement of Reasons, para 44.

The provisions of the first and second subparagraphs shall not apply to works or other subject-matter made available to the public on agreed contractual terms in such a way that members of the public may access them from a place and at a time individually chosen by them.

When this Article is applied in the context of Directives 92/100/EEC and 96/9/EC, this paragraph shall apply mutatis mutandis. (Emphasis supplied)

Article 6(4) does not create exceptions which an alleged infringer can rely upon to exclude liability for circumvention of technological measures. Instead, it introduces 'a unique legislative mechanism which foresees an ultimate responsibility on the rightholders to accommodate certain exceptions to copyright or related rights'.[176] As subparagraph (5) makes clear, Article 6(4) applies also to *sui generis* databases. The provision has been criticised for its complex and opaque nature.[177] The following discussion will highlight the validity of this criticism.

Subparagraph (1) of Article 6(4) imposes a mandatory obligation on Member States. However, this is only in relation to persons seeking to circumvent technological measures and *not* in relation to persons trafficking in circumvention devices or services.[178] Further, the obligation arises only in the *absence of voluntary measures* taken by rightholders. Article 6(4) and recital 51 indicate that voluntary measures include 'agreements' between rightholders and other parties concerned. Apart from agreements, however, it is unclear what else might constitute a 'voluntary measure'. Recital 51 also indicates that Member States do not have an obligation to adopt appropriate measures *unless* a rightholder has failed to take voluntary measures within a 'reasonable period' of time. What constitutes a 'reasonable period' is also unclear.

The obligation on Member States imposed by subparagraph 1 of Article 6(4) only relates to *specific* exceptions listed in Article 5(2) and (3) (assuming they exist in the law of the respective Member State) and not to all exceptions. These exceptions are: reproductions on paper and any similar medium (Article 5(2)(a));

---

[176] Braun (2003) p 499.

[177] Braun (2003) p 499: 'The provision is complicated and although some guidance can be found in Recitals 51, 52 and 53, it seems difficult to draw a clear picture of its scope, and Member States seem to have struggled to establish legal mechanisms that ensure a workable application of this provision in practice.' Bently and Sherman (2004) p 310: 'Article 6(4) of the Information Society Directive provides for a strange, barely comprehensible, compromise.' M Hart, 'The Copyright in the Information Society Directive: an Overview' [2002] *EIPR* 58, 63 comments: 'What is clear is that Article 6.4 is a highly unusual and unclear provision and very much the creature of political compromise.' Perritt (2003) p 3: 'Article 6(4) . . . is one of the most complex and most criticised areas of the Directive. Even with the help of the recitals the exceptions are still difficult to fathom'.

[178] Cook and Brazell (2004) p 29 comment that '[t]his produces a bizarre result: where a rightholder has protected copyright works by means of a technological measure, although circumvention may be exempted under Article 6(4), the means by which the exempted use is facilitated remains outlawed by virtue of Article 6(2).' Braun (2003) p 499 argues that since Art 6(2) is not mentioned in Art 6(4) subpara 1, 'it could be concluded that Article 6(2) establishes strict liability and that Member States are not entitled to introduce any exceptions to the provisions of Article 6(2) in their national laws.'

specific acts of reproduction by libraries, educational establishments, museums or archives (Article 5(2)(b)); ephemeral recording by broadcasting organizations (Article 5(2)(c)); reproduction of broadcasts made by certain social institutions (Article 5(2)(e)); use for illustration for teaching or scientific research (Article 5(3)(a)); use for the benefit of people with disability (Article 5(3)(b)); use for the purposes of public security or for administrative, parliamentary or judicial proceedings (Article 5(3)(e)). The basis upon which these exceptions have been singled out as important matters of public policy has not been made clear.[179] This is particularly a concern since Member States are not under any obligation to ensure beneficiaries of the remaining exceptions or limitations can benefit from them. In fact, Foged argues that a natural reading of Article 6(4) is that Member States would not be permitted to assist beneficiaries in respect of the exceptions not listed in subparagraphs (1) and (2).[180]

Article 6(4), subparagraph 1 obligates Member States to *take appropriate measures* to ensure that rightholders make available to the beneficiary of the listed specific exception or limitation, the *means* of benefiting from it. The Information Society Directive is not particularly helpful about what will constitute an 'appropriate measure' and 'means'. Sellars suggests that an 'appropriate measure' could include, 'an escrow system for encryption keys for permitted users, providing unprotected copies on request to permitted users, or obliging content providers to deposit not technologically protected copies in designated places where permitted users can make fair use copies.'[181] Recital 51 indicates that 'means' could include modifying an implemented technological measure. In implementing Article 6(4), the legislation of Member States has left undefined what may constitute 'means' of benefiting from an exception. Braun suggests that 'means' would *not* include handing over to users the 'key' to circumvent the technological measure, since this would threaten the system of technological measures. Further, it is clear from Article 6(4) subparagraph (1) that it would not include allowing beneficiaries themselves to circumvent a technological measure.[182]

Finally, subparagraph (1) of Article 6(4) emphasises that the beneficiary of a specific exception or limitation must have *legal access* to the protected work or subject matter. This requirement indicates that the obligation on a Member State to take appropriate measures exists only in relation to *copy control* measures and not access control measures.[183] As Foged comments: '[t]his certainly diminishes the value of Article 6(4) to beneficiaries in circumstances where lack of access stands as an obstacle to the beneficiary's exercise of the fair dealing rights conferred under Article 5.'[184]

---

[179] Ficsor (2002) p 561.
[180] Foged (2002) p 537.
[181] Sellars (2003) p 8.
[182] Braun (2003) p 502.
[183] Foged (2002) p 537; Smillie (2004) p 307.
[184] Foged (2002) p 537.

Article 6(4), subparagraph (2) provides that Member States *may* intervene to assist a beneficiary of an exception or limitation provided for in accordance with Article 5(2)(b). Article 5(2)(b) relates to non-commercial reproductions on any medium made by a natural person for private use, on condition that rightholders receive fair compensation. Recital 52 of the Information Society Directive makes clear that Member States should 'promote the use of voluntary measures to accommodate achieving the objectives of such exception or limitation'. Where, within a reasonable period of time, no such voluntary measures have been taken, Member States *may* take measures to enable beneficiaries of the exception or limitation to benefit from it. As discussed above, it is uncertain what constitutes 'voluntary measures' by rightholders (aside from such as agreements between rightholders and other concerned parties) and what 'measures' may be taken by a Member States. Further, rightholders are not precluded from using technological measures which are consistent with the private use exception, in particular the condition of fair compensation.[185]

Article 6(4), subparagraph (4) considerably narrows the scheme set out above.[186] This is because it stipulates that the obligation under subparagraph (1) and the discretion under subparagraph (2) shall not apply 'to works or other subject-matter made available to the public on *agreed contractual terms* in such a way that members of the public may access them from a place and at a time individually chosen by them.' (Emphasis supplied) Recital 53 indicates that the exclusion relates to where interactive on-demand services are governed by contractual arrangements. Thus, the assistance created by Article 6(4), subparagraphs (1) and (2) can be potentially overridden by the use of click-wrap and browse-through licences.[187]

(v) UK Implementation of Article 6

The Copyright Regulations inserted new sections 296ZA–296ZF into the CDPA in order to implement Article 6 of the Information Society Directive.[188]

Section 296ZF defines 'technological measures' in terms very similar to Article 6(3) of the Information Society Directive.[189] Technological measures are any technology, device or component which is designed, in the normal course of its operation, to protect a work other than a computer program.[190] Protection of a work refers to the 'prevention or restriction of acts that are not authorised by the copyright owner of that work and are restricted by copyright'.[191] A technological

---

[185] Art 6(4), subpara (2) and recital 53, Information Society Directive.

[186] Braun (2003) p 501.

[187] Ficsor (2002) p 561; Foged (2002) p 537.

[188] See The Copyright and Related Rights Regulations 2003 SI 2498 ('Copyright Regulations'), which came into force on 31 October 2003, reg 24.

[189] Cook and Brazell (2004) p 45.

[190] S 296ZF(1), CDPA.

[191] S 296ZF(3)(a), CDPA.

measure will be 'effective' if the copyright owner controls use of the work through an access control or protection process (such as encryption, scrambling or other transformation of the work) or a copy control mechanism, which achieves the intended protection.[192]

Pursuant to section 296ZA, a civil right of action is created where a person does anything which circumvents an effective technological measure applied to a copyright work (other than a computer program)[193] with actual or constructive knowledge that they are pursuing that objective.[194] Two categories of persons may bring this civil right of action (and these rights are concurrent).[195] First, a person issuing to the public copies of the work, or communicating to the public the work, to which the effective technological measure has been applied. Second, the copyright owner or his exclusive licensee. Section 296ZA, paragraph (2) explicitly states that the prohibition does not apply to a person who does anything which circumvents an effective technological measures *for the purposes of research into cryptography*. This is provided the person does not prejudicially affect the right of the copyright owner by circumventing the measure or issuing information derived from that research. This exception gives effect to recital 48 of the Information Society Directive.

Cook and Brazell argue that circumvention of technological measures does not become permissible once a copyright work ceases to be protected and thus the owner's monopoly right may be extended indefinitely.[196] This is because there is no express provision governing this situation. Further, section 296ZF applies 'where effective technological measures *have been* applied to a copyright work' and not 'where a work *is* protected by effective technological measures.' (Emphasis supplied) It is submitted that the better view is that where copyright in a work has expired, there is no longer an effective technological measure because the definitions of both 'technological measure' and 'effective' refer to a *copyright work*.[197] This view is consistent with Article 6 of the Information Society Directive.

Section 296ZD also creates a civil right of action where a person makes or commercially deals in circumvention devices or services. This right arises where effective technological measures have been applied to a copyright work (other than a computer program),[198] and a person makes or commercially deals[199] in any device, product or component, or provides services which:

[192] S 296ZF(2), CDPA.

[193] S 296ZA(6), CDPA makes clear that prohibition applies to rights in performances, the publication right and the database right.

[194] S 296ZA(1), CDPA.

[195] S 296ZA(3), CDPA.

[196] Cook and Brazell (2004) p 50.

[197] Cook and Brazell (2004) pp 50–51 describe this argument as 'somewhat strained'.

[198] S 296ZD(8), CDPA makes clear that this provision applies *mutatis mutandis* to effective technological measures used in relation to performances, the publication right and database right.

[199] S 296ZD(1)(b), CDPA applies to a person who 'manufactures, imports, distributes, sells or lets for hire, offers or exposes for sale or hire, advertises for sale or hire, or has in his possession for commercial purposes . . .' circumvention devices.

(i)   are promoted, advertised or marketed for the purpose of the circumvention; or

(ii)   have only a limited commercially significant purpose or use other than to circumvent; or

(iii)   are primarily designed, produced, adapted or performed for the purpose of enabling or facilitating the circumvention of, those measures.

Three categories of persons may bring this civil right of action.[200] First, a person issuing to the public copies of the work, or communicating to the public the work, to which the effective technological measure has been applied. Second, the copyright owner or his exclusive licensee. Third, the owner or exclusive licensee of any intellectual property right in the effective technological measure applied to the work. There is no defence of lack of knowledge. However, a person will not be liable for damages where he did not know or have reason to believe that his acts enabled or facilitated infringement of copyright.[201]

Section 296ZB creates two criminal offences in relation to devices and services designed to circumvent effective technological measures.[202] First, it is an offence to make for sale or hire, or import otherwise than for private and domestic use, or commercially deal[203] in the course of business, or distribute to such an extent as to affect prejudicially the copyright owner, any device, product or component which is 'primarily designed, produced, or adapted for the purpose of enabling or facilitating the circumvention of effective technological measures.'[204] Second, it is an offence to provide, promote, advertise or market in the course of business, or to such an extent as to affect prejudicially the copyright owner, a service 'the purpose of which is to enable or facilitate the circumvention of effective technological measures.'[205] However, anything done by or on behalf of law enforcement or intelligence services in the interests of national security for the purpose of prevention or detection of crime, or the investigation of an offence or the conduct of a prosecution is not unlawful.[206] Further, the accused will have a defence if he can prove that he did not know and had no reasonable grounds for believing that the device, product or component, or the service, enabled or facilitated the circumvention of effective technological measures.[207] The penalty for summary conviction is imprisonment for up to three months or a fine not exceeding the statutory

---

[200] S 296ZD(2), CDPA.

[201] S 296ZD(7), CDPA.

[202] Bently and Sherman (2004) p 307 comment that '[t]he addition of criminal liability reflects the fact that these acts are regarded as the ones which seriously threaten the copyright-holder's interests.'

[203] Ie, sell or let for hire, or offer or expose for sale or hire, or advertise for sale or hire, or possess or distribute: see s 296ZB(1)(c), CDPA.

[204] S 296ZB(1), CDPA.

[205] S 296ZB(2), CDPA.

[206] S 296ZB(3), CDPA.

[207] S 296ZB(5), CDPA.

maximum or both. For conviction on indictment it is a fine or imprisonment for up to two years or both.[208]

Article 6(4) of the Information Society Directive has been implemented via section 296ZE and schedule 5A of the CDPA. Where the application of any effective technological measure to a copyright work prevents a person from carrying out a permitted act then that person, or a person representative of a class of persons prevented from carrying out a permitted act, may issue a notice of complaint to the Secretary of State.[209] A 'permitted act' is an act which may be done in relation to copyright works by virtue of a provision in the CDPA listed in Part 1 of Schedule 5A.[210] Upon receiving a notice of complaint, the Secretary of State *may* give relevant directions to the copyright owner, for the purpose of establishing whether any voluntary measure or agreement subsists in relation to the copyright work under complaint.[211] Where it is established that there is no subsisting voluntary measure or agreement, the Secretary of State *may* give relevant directions ensuring that the copyright owner or exclusive licensee makes available to the complainant the means of carrying out the permitted act to the extent necessary to so benefit from it.[212] The Secretary of State may also give directions as to the form and manner in which the notice of complaint, or evidence of any voluntary measure, may be delivered to him, and generally as to the procedure to be followed in relation to a complaint made under this section.[213] Directions given by the Secretary of State under this provision must be in writing and may be varied or revoked by a subsequent direction under this provision.[214]

Section 296ZE does not apply to copyright works 'made available to the public on agreed contractual terms in such a way that members of the public may access them from a place and at a time individually chosen by them.'[215] Further, the section only applies where a complainant has lawful access to the protected copyright work or if the person is representative of a class of persons, where the class of persons have lawful access to the work.[216]

Producers of multimedia works will find sections 296ZA–ZE highly useful in protecting their investment. So long as there is a copyright work within the multimedia work (which should not be difficult to satisfy), a multimedia producer can apply a technological measure to the entire multimedia work, to control access or

---

[208] S 296ZB(4), CDPA.

[209] S 296ZE(2), CDPA.

[210] S 296ZE(1), CDPA. In relation to performances, it is Part 2 of Schedule 5A and in relation to the database right, Part 3 of Schedule 5A (which refers to regulation 20 and Schedule 1 of the Databases Regulations): see s 296ZE(11), CDPA.

[211] S 296ZE(3)(a), CDPA.

[212] S 296ZE(3)(b), CDPA.

[213] S 296ZE(4), CDPA.

[214] S 296ZE(7), (8), CDPA.

[215] S 296ZE(9), CDPA.

[216] S 296ZE(10), CDPA.

copying of the individual copyright work, and claim protection under sections 296ZA–ZE. Circumvention of the technological measure will be unlawful, as will making or commercially dealing in circumvention devices or provision of circumvention services. Further, it will not be permissible for a user of a multimedia work to circumvent the technological measure on the basis that he was seeking to rely on a copyright exception. At the most, the user could complain to the Secretary of State who may take action requiring the copyright owner to make the means of benefiting from a permitted act available to the user. However, even this limited remedy is strictly circumscribed. This is because the user must have lawful access to the copyright work. Further, the copyright work must not have been made available to the user on agreed contractual terms via an interactive on-demand service.

Thus, it is argued that for multimedia works that fail to qualify for protection as film works or *sui generis* databases, there are no 'gaps' in protection requiring a new multimedia category. This is because the underlying computer program will attract protection as a copyright work and provide some protection for the overall multimedia work. More significantly, producers of multimedia works will be able to protect their investment by relying upon TPMs. To the extent that a TPM is applied in relation to the underlying computer program, section 296 of the CDPA will govern. To the extent that a TPM is used in relation to an individual copyright work (other than a computer program) within a multimedia work, sections 296ZA–ZE will be applicable.

3. Better Tailored Protection

Some commentators favour the introduction of a new category of multimedia work because it 'would enable the clear definition of multimedia and specific rights tailored to suit its unique nature.'[217] Stamatoudi has suggested the most detailed proposal for a multimedia copyright category. She describes this as 'an amalgamation of the regime of protection for audiovisual works and that for databases.'[218] The details of her proposed multimedia category will be briefly described here.

Stamatoudi proposes to define the subject matter of a new multimedia category as follows: 'works which combine (on a single medium) more than one different kind of expression in an integrated digital format, and which allow their users to manipulate their contents with a *substantial degree of interactivity*'[219] (emphasis

---

[217] Douglas (1997) p 105. Douglas makes this suggestion in respect of the Australian Copyright Act 1968 (Cth). See also Wei (1995) pp 244–45 who recommends a new category of multimedia databases where protection inheres in the multimedia database producer in selecting the material for compilation into the multimedia application.

[218] Stamatoudi (2002) p 211.

[219] Above.

supplied). The emphasis on *substantial* interactivity is said to ensure that there is no overlap between the existing categories (of database and film/audiovisual work) and the proposed new category.[220] Stamatoudi proposes that multimedia works satisfy an originality requirement of 'author's own intellectual creation'.[221] This test would be directed at the 'contents of the work as a merged entity' as opposed to the 'selection or arrangement of the various contributions'.[222] Her reasons for adopting this approach to originality are expressed in the following statement:

> originality should be assessed in relation to the contents of the multimedia work rather than the selection and arrangement of its contents. The selection and arrangement of the contents of a multimedia work are important only at a pre-production stage, when the work is conceived and the ingredients are assembled in order to make up the final image. Nothing of this selection and arrangement is retained in the final production stage of the multimedia work. Everything appears as one coherent entity which is capable of being viewed in parts (in a format other than that in which the various works have been initially entered) through the operation of interactivity. Any originality in relation to the initial selection and/or arrangement of the materials of the multimedia product would disregard their subsequent transformation through a sewing and a merging process. The birth of a totally new and separable work which constitutes the added value of the multimedia product would be disregarded. Apart from that, the existence of creative interactivity alone, enabling morphing, blurring and transformation (though not permanent) of the original contents of the multimedia work, discredits any notion of selection and arrangement. Even if contents, after their use, return to their original status, they still represent no more than a selection and arrangement along the lines of works in a literary work or melodies in a musical work.[223]

Stamatoudi proposes that authorship, and thus first ownership, would be attributed to the editor of a multimedia work. According to her, the editor is the person who:

> gives the final form and creates the product. He puts the various elements together, in the same sense as the compiler of a collection of works or the director of a film. The difference with these authors though is that the editor of the multimedia product goes one step further. He integrates the various materials to such a degree that on most occasions the final outcome does not resemble in any sense the individual contributions that have been incorporated in it.[224]

Granting authorship to the editor of the multimedia work appears to be largely pragmatic. Stamatoudi argues that it is not viable to recognise all creative contributors as authors since they are too numerous.[225] However, the editor has a

---

[220] Above, at 212–13.
[221] Above, at 213–14.
[222] Above, at 215.
[223] Above.
[224] Above, at 222.
[225] Above, at 222–23.

prominently creative role in relation to the multimedia work and from the point of view of effective exploitation of the work it is better to nominate a single author.[226] The first owner of copyright in the multimedia work would be the author (ie, the editor). However, where the author is an employee Stamatoudi favours vesting ownership in the employer.[227] This is a rule which she believes should be harmonised at a European level.[228]

Stamatoudi proposes that the full range of exclusive (economic) rights vest in the editor of the multimedia work and that the full range of exceptions be applicable.[229] The duration of protection would be the standard term of 70 years *post mortem auctoris*, even though Stamatoudi doubts whether this length of time is necessary given the short commercial life of most multimedia products.[230] She also favours the applicability of moral rights, in particular the right of divulgation, the right of attribution and the right of integrity.[231] These moral rights would be subject to a narrowly construed concept of waiver and a balancing exercise would be preferable in assessing whether the right of integrity was infringed or not. Finally, where technological protection measures are used in relation to multimedia works Stamatoudi argues that attempts to circumvent them should be regulated.[232]

Is Stamatoudi's proposed multimedia category better suited to the qualities of multimedia than the existing copyright categories? Apart from the definition of subject matter, and the rules on originality and authorship, the features of the proposed category appear to be highly similar to the existing categories under UK copyright law. Can it be said that the definition of subject matter, the test of originality and the designation of authorship deal with unique aspects of a multimedia work?

In terms of authorship, the editor of a multimedia work can be accommodated under present authorship rules. As discussed in chapter 3, the designer of a multimedia work (which coincides with Stamatoudi's notion of editor) can qualify as the author of a copyright database, or as the principal director of a film, or as the database maker (under the database right). Under current authorship rules there is unlikely to be a proliferation of joint authors in respect of multimedia works.

---

[226] Above, at 223–25. At 225 Stamatoudi argues:

> In an era when use, clearance of rights and further exploitation of a work have to take place easily, quickly and with a great degree of certainty, the option of one author can only offer greater efficiency without at the same time taking any well-deserved rights from other contributors. These contributors still have rights in their separate contributions and can use them as long as they do not compete with, or cause harm to, the initial multimedia project.

[227] Above, at 225–26.
[228] Above.
[229] Above, at 216–21.
[230] Above, at 248–49.
[231] Above, at 230–40.
[232] Above, at 244.

Further, vesting of initial ownership in the employer is made possible by the general rule contained in section 11(2) of the CDPA. Thus, it is argued that a new multimedia category would not result in better crafted rules on authorship and ownership of multimedia works.

It is also submitted that Stamatoudi's definition of multimedia work, insofar as it refers to 'substantial interactivity', is undesirable. As argued in chapter 1, there is a lack of support in the literature for restricting multimedia works to those which are substantially interactive. Further, it is unclear how to distinguish substantially interactive multimedia works from those which are not. Therefore, to introduce a category of multimedia works according to a definition which requires 'substantial interactivity' will produce uncertainty and the potential for overlap with the categories of literary work (ie, database) and film (or audiovisual) work.

Under Stamatoudi's proposal the originality of multimedia works will be judged according to their 'contents' rather than the selection or arrangement of materials. This is because the materials in a multimedia work are melded together and it becomes impossible to identify the relevant selection or arrangement. Stamatoudi refers to everything appearing as 'one coherent entity which is capable of being viewed in parts . . . through the operation of interactivity.'[233] However, it is unclear how to judge whether or not the contents reflect an 'intellectual creation'. One possibility is to consider the aggregate digital contents as original if they are displayed in a creative sequence. This, of course, resembles the sort of originality test that would be applied to audiovisual works (ie, is the series of related images original?). Another possibility is to judge creativity according to how the user *interacts* with the digital contents. If this is the case both visual user interface features, such as the screen display or the sequence of screen displays, and non-visual user interface features, such as functions that may be performed by the user in relation to the digital contents, must be examined. However, creativity in deriving the visual user interface might be regarded as similar to the assessment that is made for audiovisual works (in terms of the sequence of screen displays). In terms of the creativity applied in respect of non-visual user interface features this overlaps with the creativity applied to the software. Thus, it is seems as if the originality test for a separate multimedia category would target creativity that is already considered under categories of 'literary work' and 'audiovisual work'.

A related question is how does the scope of protection, especially under the economic rights, relate to the contents of a multimedia work? If there is an original combination of digital contents in terms of the sequence in which they appear, then that particular sequence should be protected from exact and non-exact reproduction. This would prevent others from creating a similar sequence of digital media. Yet this protection mirrors the type of protection that is available for films or audiovisual works. If creativity has been applied to the interactive aspects

---

[233] Above, at 215.

of the work then the right of reproduction should theoretically prohibit the use of similar user interfaces and also prevent similar functionality in a competing multimedia work. The problem with this approach is that it would protect features that stem from the underlying software. Yet copyright protection of computer programs is limited and is unclear why protection should be more extensive under a different category.

In theory, a separate category of multimedia work promises greater specificity and tailoring of protection to these works. However, from the above discussion, it is apparent that the features of Stamatoudi's new multimedia category would in fact closely resemble the features of existing copyright works. Therefore, it seems unnecessary to introduce a separate multimedia category.

It is also undesirable to introduce a new category. This is because it would create a real risk of confusion and overlap between categories. Further, introducing a specific category of multimedia work runs the risk of obsolescence. Thus, it is better to continue relying on the existing categories, subject to the film category being replaced with that of audiovisual work.

Abolishing the 'Closed List' Approach to Copyright Works

Christie has proposed replacing the 'closed list' approach to copyright works in the CDPA with an 'open list'.[234] This suggestion is part of a wider set of proposed reforms which aim to simplify UK copyright law. Christie's simplification proposal for the UK is an adapted version of the one developed by the Copyright Law Review Committee (CLRC) in respect of Australian copyright law.[235]

Christie puts forward three main reasons for reforming UK copyright along the lines of the CLRC proposal. First, the CDPA is structurally complex. Second, categorisation of copyright works under a 'closed list' creates 'gaps' in protection and 'some of these gaps constitute unjustifiable discrimination.'[236] Finally, a 'closed list' approach to subject matter results in technological specificity, which in turn creates uncertainty with the emergence of new technological subject matter such as multimedia works.[237]

---

[234] A Christie, 'A Proposal for Simplifying United Kingdom Copyright Law' [2001] *EIPR* 26.

[235] See generally SR:2. The CLRC (majority view) in SR:2, paras 5.05–5.08 voiced several concerns regarding the closed list approach in the Australian Copyright Act 1968 (Cth). First, the unnecessary legislative complexity and repetition caused by dividing up copyright material into Parts III and IV of the Act. Second, the fact that there are different levels of protection for different categories of copyright material within the same part of the Act. Finally, the technological specificity of the copyright categories, which makes them unable to cope properly with new sorts of creative products, such as multimedia works.

[236] Christie (2001) p 28.

[237] Above, at 30.

There is a degree of structural complexity to the CDPA.[238] However, as Christie acknowledges, 'an argument for reform of the Act's structure cannot be based on the fact of complexity *per se*' but rather on the fact the complexity is unwarranted.[239] As Christie points out, the purpose of categorisation of copyright subject matter is to allow the differential treatment of various subject matters (both in terms of subsistence and the applicable exclusive rights) under the legislation.[240] He argues that a 'fundamental consequence of categorisation of protected subject-matters and exclusive rights is that there are "gaps" in the legislative framework of protection'.[241] He cites *Creation Records v News Group Newspapers*[242] as an example of an unjustifiable gap in protection. In this case, an ensemble of objects was arranged by Noel Gallagher for the purposes of a 'photo-shoot', the results of which would be used for the front sleeve of the Oasis album 'Be Here Now'. The defendant newspaper engaged a freelance photographer to take an unauthorised photograph of the scene,[243] which it subsequently published and offered for sale. In an action for an interlocutory injunction restraining further publication of the photograph, Lloyd J held that no copyright subsisted in the 'photo-shoot' scene since the scene itself could not be categorised as a dramatic work or as an artistic work, in the form of a sculpture, collage or work of artistic craftsmanship.[244] Christie argues that this outcome offends against policy since the intellectual and manual effort applied to creating the photo-shoot scene reflected significant creativity and was more deserving of protection than a photograph of the scene.[245]

A further reason why Christie believes the UK should adopt an 'open list' is because the CDPA's categorisation of subject matter and exclusive rights leads to

---

[238] Although it is not as structurally complex as the Australian Copyright Act 1968 (Cth).

[239] Christie (2001) p 27.

[240] Above, at 27–28.

[241] Above, at 28.

[242] *Creation Records v News Group Newspapers* [1997] EMLR 444.

[243] The scene is described by Lloyd J in *Creation Records v News Group Newspapers* [1997] EMLR 444 at 447:

> [there is a] swimming pool in the foreground with the Rolls Royce seemingly emerging from the water towards the camera. The hotel is beyond and to the right. In the far distance is a wooded area with a partly clouded sky above. The five members of the group are posed round the pool, one on a scooter, one climbing out of the pool and others with or near other objects seemingly unrelated to each other.

[244] *Creation Records v News Group Newspapers* [1997] EMLR 444, 448–50. The scene was not a dramatic work because it was 'inherently static, having no movement, story or action' (at 448). The scene was not a sculpture because 'no element in the composition has been carved, modelled or made in any of the other ways in which sculpture is made' (449), and it was not a work of artistic craftsmanship because the scene did not seem to result from the exercise of any craftsmanship, but was merely an assembly of objects (449). The scene was not a collage because it did not involve 'the sticking of two or more things together . . . [but were] random, unrelated and unfixed elements' and the 'composition was intrinsically ephemeral' (450). However, the claimants were successful in obtaining an injunction on the basis of breach of confidence: see Lloyd J at 455.

[245] Christie (2001) p 29.

a degree of technological specificity.[246] As a result, it is unclear whether new types of works, such as multimedia, can be brought within the existing categories.[247]

Christie thus proposes that the CDPA use broad and inclusive definitions of protected subject matter. This is an approach found in Article 2 of the Berne Convention and in civil law countries, such as France.[248] He proposes that copyright material be divided into two categories, based on the degree of originality. Creative (ie, original) material would be protected to a high level and productive (ie, non-original) material would be protected to a lower level.[249] There would be no requirement of fixation.[250] Thus, protected subject matter would be divided into 'Creations' and 'Productions' according to their 'innovation threshold'. A Creation would be 'defined as a tangible or non-tangible embodiment of subject-matter in the literary and artistic domain, which is the result of intellectual effort by the person who undertakes its creation.'[251] A Production would be 'defined as a tangible or non-tangible embodiment, other than a creation, of subject matter in the literary and artistic domain, which is the result of the application of labour and/or resources by the person who undertakes its product.'[252] According to this model, Christie argues that the 'gaps' in protection will be eliminated since works that fall outside the existing categories will be protected provided they meet the innovation threshold of either a Creation or Production.[253] For example, the CLRC considered multimedia works could be protected as either a Creation or Production and that a separate category of multimedia work was therefore unnecessary.[254] The exclusive rights would be generalised to the right of reproduction and the right of dissemination to the public.[255] These rights would apply to both Creations and Productions, with modifications in certain instances. For example, Creations would attract the right of non-literal reproduction, whereas Productions would be limited to the right of literal reproduction.[256] The right of dissemination to the public would apply to all subject matter with the

---

[246] Above, at 30.

[247] Above, at 30.

[248] Above, at 32.

[249] Above, at 33, 34–36.

[250] Above, at 33–34.

[251] Above, at 34. Christie also states that a specific provision would have to be included whereby creation is defined to include a computer program. This is because the Software Directive, along with Art 10(1) TRIPs Agreement and Art 4 WCT require computer programs to be protected as literary works within the meaning of Art 2 of the Berne Convention.

[252] Christie (2001) p 34. Christie also suggests that a production be defined to include and a creation defined to exclude broadcasts, cable programmes (which no longer exists as a category in the CDPA) and published editions.

[253] Christie (2001), p 33.

[254] SR:2, paras 7.15–7.16.

[255] Christie (2001) pp 37–38.

[256] Above, at 37–38.

exclusion of published editions.[257] The moral rights of attribution and integrity would only apply to Creations.[258]

Several counter-arguments to Christie's proposal may be raised. First, the 'gap' in protection said to be exemplified by *Creation Records* is arguably not a consequence of having a 'closed list' approach to subject matter. Rather, as Barron argues, the case is typical of the 'materialist' approach of the courts to defining an 'artistic work'.[259] This approach is:

> to focus on the physical embodiments through which visual representations of that type are 'normally' made manifest, and upon the technical processes which 'normally' (ie, as a matter of ordinary common sense) yield physical items corresponding to the entities mentioned in section 4 [of the CDPA]. In other words, their judgements have proceeded from the aesthetically neutral features of entities assigned by ordinary language use to the classifications within the category, with no reference to whether these entities can claim the status of 'art'.[260]

Barron explains that the courts are driven towards this approach 'as a by-product of copyright law's pursuit of certainty, objectivity and closure'.[261] In other words, it is the courts desire to *avoid* making subjective, aesthetic judgments about what constitutes an 'artistic' work that leads them to define artistic works in technical or materialist terms. A consequence of this approach, however, is that large swathes of contemporary art will be excluded from the definition of 'artistic work'.[262]

A second counter-argument is that although the existing categories are 'closed', they can operate in an 'open-ended' manner. This is probably best illustrated by absorption of computer programs into the category of 'literary works'. Replacing the film category with that of audiovisual works would further facilitate the absorption of multimedia works into existing categories.[263]

A third counter-argument is that it is not clear that adopting an 'open list' approach to copyright subject matter will avoid issues of classification. The US has an 'open list' approach whereby it protects 'original works of authorship' and provides a non-exhaustive list of protectible subject matter.[264] Yet new works, in the form of video games, were fitted within the non-exhaustive list of subject matter

---

[257] Above, at 38.

[258] Above, at 39.

[259] A Barron, 'Copyright Law and the Claims of Art' [2002] *IPQ* 368, 384.

[260] Above, at 373–74.

[261] Above, at 381. Barron explains that 'in order to position an intangible entity as an object of property, the law must be able to see it as identifiable and self-sufficient, attributable to some determinate author, and perceptible to the senses through the physical medium in which it is recorded or embodied.' She also argues that that this way of thinking about artistic works has striking parallels in art theory, in particular Modernist art theory.

[262] Above, at 372, 374, 380–81, 397.

[263] See also SR:2 (dissenting view), paras 6.08–6.13.

[264] S 102(a) Copyright Act 1976.

(specifically the categories of literary work and audiovisual work), as opposed to being protected simply on the basis that they were original works of authorship. This could have been because creators of video games desired the specific form of protection available for literary works and audiovisual works. Or it could be that drawing analogies with well-recognised forms of subject matter adds to the legitimacy of a claim that new subject matter is an 'original work of authorship'. France also follows an 'open list' approach. Yet there has been disagreement over whether a multimedia work should be classified as composite, collective or collaborative work.[265] These classifications relate to the type of co-operation of the contributors to the work,[266] as opposed to the nature of the subject matter.[267] Classification along these lines affects who is considered as the author/s and owner/s of the work[268] and the way in which the exclusive rights may be exercised.[269] Thus, where a second tier of categorisation occurs, in order to provide differential treatment, the pressure to classify new subject matter will remain.

A *Sui Generis* Regime for Multimedia Works

Stamatoudi has proposed a *sui generis* regime for multimedia works.[270] This regime would apply only to those multimedia works that did not attract copyright protection under the proposed new category of multimedia works (discussed above). According to Stamatoudi, the regimes of protection would be mutually

---

[265] See P-Y Gautier, '"Multimedia" Works in French Law' (1994) 160 *RIDA* 90, (who favours classification as a collective work); Latreille (2000) pp 45–74 (who favours classification as a collaborative work); and Stamatoudi (2002) pp 196–203 (who favours classification as a collective work). Disagreement has also arisen about whether an audiovisual work should be classed as a collective or collaborative work: for a detailed discussion see F Pollaud-Dulian, 'The Authors of Audiovisual Works' (1996) 169 *RIDA* 51.

[266] Art L113–2 of the French Code defines a 'work of collaboration' to mean 'a work in the creation of which more than one natural person has participated.' It defines a 'composite work' to mean 'a new work in which a pre-existing work is incorporated without the collaboration of the author of the latter work.' It also defines 'collective work' to mean 'a work created at the initiative of a natural or legal person who edits it, publishes it, and discloses it under his direction and name and in which the personal contributions of the various authors who participated in its production are merged in the overall work for which they were conceived, without it being possible to attribute to each author a separate right the work as created.'

[267] Stamatoudi (2002) pp 196–97, 203–6.

[268] For example, classification as a 'collective work' will enable the exclusive rights in the work to vest in a legal person: see Art L113–5 French Code.

[269] For example, classification as a 'collaborative work' means that the work is the joint property of the authors and exercise of their exclusive rights in the work must be by common accord: Art L113–3 French Code.

[270] Stamatoudi (2002) pp 253–56.

exclusive in order to avoid an unacceptable overlap between copyright and *sui generis* protection of multimedia works. This is because the proposed new copyright category and the proposed *sui generis* right would both protect the contents of the multimedia work.[271]

Stamatoudi's *sui generis* regime for multimedia is 'heavily inspired by the *sui generis* protection for databases'.[272] She outlines the basic features of the proposed regime.[273] The multimedia right would be granted to the *producer* of the multimedia product where there has been *substantial investment* (of a quantitative or qualitative kind) in 'the bringing together of the various components, combining, integrating and making them interactive'.[274] The right would enable the producer to prevent extraction or re-utilisation of the whole or a substantial part of the *content* of the multimedia product and 'substantiality' would be evaluated qualitatively and/or quantitatively. There would be no exception for private copying and the right would last for five years measured from the date of completion of the multimedia product, with no prospect of renewal of term. Stamatoudi justifies the short term of protection on the basis that most multimedia works will be outdated within five years and also because of the need to facilitate public access to information and the creation of derivative works.

Stamatoudi justifies the new multimedia right on the following basis:

> Non-original multimedia products are, after all, extremely similar to databases. It would therefore be unfair to deny *sui generis* protection to these multimedia products that are not copyrightable, but that share with databases the very reasons for which a *sui generis* right for databases was created. *In practice these multimedia products form a small niche group that falls outside the scope of copyrightable multimedia products, whilst nevertheless not being relegated entirely to the database category.*[275] (Emphasis supplied)

It is submitted that Stamatoudi's proposed *sui generis* right for multimedia works is unnecessary. It is difficult to imagine multimedia works failing to surmount an originality hurdle of 'intellectual creation'. For those few multimedia works that cannot satisfy this criterion, the database right probably would apply, assuming the multimedia work was a reference type or of a searchable nature. Thus, as Stamatoudi recognises, her proposed multimedia right would apply to an extremely narrow range of multimedia works.

---

[271] This differs from situation with respect to databases where copyright and database right are not mutually exclusive. Unacceptable overlap is avoided because copyright protects the selection or arrangement of the contents of the database, whereas the database right protects the extraction or re-utilisation of a substantial part of the contents of a database. See Stamatoudi (2002) pp 251–53.

[272] Above, at 253.

[273] See above, at 253–56.

[274] Above, at 253.

[275] Stamatoudi (2002) p 256.

It is also submitted that the proposed regime is undesirable. First, it would involve significant implementation costs for the benefit of only a narrow range of works. Second, the regime would create uncertainty around whether the database right or the multimedia right (or both) were applicable to non-original multimedia works. Finally, it is unclear whether *sui generis* legislation will be useful in relation to an industry that is subject to swift technological change.[276] Thus, it is argued that Stamatoudi's proposed *sui generis* regime should not be adopted.

Conclusion

This chapter considered whether it is necessary or desirable to reform UK copyright law in order to better protect multimedia works. A range of reforms was examined: amending the categories of film work and literary work; creating an 'open list' of subject matter; adding a new multimedia category; and introducing a *sui generis* multimedia right.

It was argued that it is not desirable to amend the category of literary work, except in relation to compilations. A minor amendment should be introduced so that compilations may comprise a selection or arrangement of any type of work. The film work category, however, should be significantly reformed. This reform would lead to better protection for multimedia works, and also for films generally. Further, it would bring UK law into line with its international and EC obligations concerning cinematographic works. The category of film works should be renamed 'audiovisual works' and a definition similar to that used in US copyright law should be adopted. Although the present definition of 'film' in the CDPA is broad, the proposed definition of 'audiovisual work' reflects more neutral language that would clearly embrace multimedia video games. The scope of protection for audiovisual works should extend to non-literal reproduction. Even if the film work category is not replaced by an audiovisual work category, it is imperative that the CDPA is amended to grant films a right of non-literal reproduction. This avoids the fiction of protecting films as dramatic works, as occurred in *Arks (No 2)*. Reliance on the category of dramatic works to protect films is unappealing. This is because it causes confusion in respect of ownership and duration of protection and creates the potential for UK copyright law to operate inconsistently with EC Directives. Ideally, UK copyright law should be amended so that it

---

[276] Dam (1995) pp 374–75 makes this point in relation to whether *sui generis* legislation for software is desirable. He cites the Semiconductor Chip Act 1984 (US) as an example of *sui generis* legislation with severe shortcomings which stemmed from the rapid technological changes in the semiconductor chip industry.

distinguishes between protection of the content of an audiovisual work and its fixation.

This chapter also considered whether it is desirable to abolish the 'closed list' approach to subject matter in the CDPA and replace it with a non-exhaustive approach. It was argued that the existing categories in the CDPA operate in a sufficiently flexible and 'open-ended' manner, as evidenced by the absorption of computer programs into the category of literary works. To the extent that they do not (eg, in relation to artistic works), this is not necessarily a consequence of a 'closed list' approach. For example, in relation to artistic works it is arguably the court's 'materialist' approach to defining subject matter. Finally, an 'open list' approach does not avoid difficulties concerning classification, since these still arise in relation to authorship, ownership and the scope of protection.

Whether a new category of multimedia work is necessary and feasible was examined at length. It was argued that the existing categories of film and literary works are appropriate vehicles for protecting multimedia works and these categories would not be distorted. It was also argued that, to the extent that multimedia works are not protected as film (or audiovisual) works or *sui generis* databases, sufficient protection can be obtained by relying on the underlying software and via the use of TPMs. Protection of the underlying software may prevent wholesale copying of the multimedia work. Technical devices may be used in conjunction with the computer program to prevent or restrict acts which are unauthorised by the copyright owner of the computer program and are restricted by copyright. Although circumvention *per se* is not prohibited, it is unlawful commercially to deal in means the sole intended purpose of which is to facilitate unauthorised circumvention or to publish information intended to facilitate persons circumventing such devices. Alternatively, a multimedia producer may apply a technological measure to a copyright work (other than a computer program) contained within a multimedia work. This may be either an access control or copy control measure. Circumvention of an effective technological measure is prohibited, along with commercially dealing in circumvention devices or services. There is also very limited scope for a person to circumvent an effective technological measure on the basis that he wishes to rely on a copyright exception. Thus, a multimedia producer can digitally 'lock up' a multimedia work quite successfully. As such, this should adequately protect the producer's investment in creating a multimedia work. However, commentators such as Stamatoudi argue that a separate category would tailor copyright protection to the specific nature of multimedia works. Stamatoudi's proposal was considered in detail. It was argued that the features of her proposed category are contained within existing copyright works. Thus, there is little to be gained—apart from the risk of confusion and overlap— by introducing a separate category of multimedia work.

Linked to Stamatoudi's proposal for a new multimedia category is the introduction of a multimedia right for those works that are not protected by copyright.

It was argued that a *sui generis* right is unnecessary in the light of protection under the copyright *and* database right regimes. A multimedia right would benefit a very narrow range of works. In addition, it would create confusion and overlap with the existing forms of protection.

Bibliography

Books and Book Chapters

D Bainbridge, *Software Copyright Law*, 4th edn, (Butterworths, London, 1999).

D Bainbridge, *Intellectual Property*, 5th edn, (Longman Harlow, 2002).

L Bently and B Sherman, *Intellectual Property Law*, 2nd edn, (OUP, Oxford, 2004).

S Biegel, *Beyond Our Control? Confronting the Limits of Our Legal System in the Age of Cyberspace* (MIT Press, Cambridge, MA, 2003).

JD Bolter, 'Virtual Reality and the Redefinition of Self' in L Strate, RL Jacobson and S Gibson, (eds), *Communication and Cyberspace*, 2nd edn, (Hampton Press, NJ, 2003) 123.

V Bouganim, *The Legal Protection of Databases: from Copyright to Dataright* (UL unpublished PhD thesis, 1999).

K Bowrey, 'Ethical Boundaries and Internet Cultures' in L Bentley and S Maniatis, (eds), *Ethical Issues in Intellectual Property* (Sweet & Maxwell, London, 1998) 3.

J Boyle, *Shamans, Software and Spleens: Law and the Construction of the Information Society* (Harvard University Press, Cambridge, MA, 1996).

D Brennan, 'Simplification, Circumvention, Fair Dealing and Australian Copyright Reform' in A Fitzgerald, *et al*, (eds), *Going Digital 2000: Legal Issues for E-Commerce, Software and the Internet*, 2nd edn, (Prospect Media, NSW, 2000) 105.

R Burrell, 'The Future of the Copyright Exceptions' in D Maclean and K Schubert, (eds), *Dear Images: Art, Copyright and Culture* (Ridinghouse, London, 2002) 455.

N Chapman and J Chapman, *Digital Multimedia* (Wiley, Chicester, 2000).

A Christie and S Gare, (eds), *Blackstone's Statutes on Intellectual Property*, 7th edn, (OUP, Oxford, 2004).

A Christie, 'Copyright Protection for Web Sites' in A Fitzgerald, *et al*, (eds), *Going Digital 2000: Legal Issues for E-Commerce, Software and the Internet*, 2nd edn, (Prospect Media, NSW, 2000) 1.

H Cohen Jehoram, P Keuchenius and J Seignette, (eds), *Audiovisual Media and Copyright in Europe* (Kluwer Deventer, 1994).

DE Comer, *Internetworking with TCP/IP—Volume 1: Principles Protocols and Architecture*, 3rd edn, (Prentice Hall, NJ, 1995).

T Cook and L Brazell, *The Copyright Directive: UK Implementation* (Jordans, Bristol, 2004).

R Coombe, 'Author/izing the Celebrity: Publicity Rights, Postmodern Politics, and Unauthorized Genders' in M Woodmansee and P Jaszi, (eds), *The Construction of Authorship: Textual Appropriation in Law and Literature* (Duke University Press, Durham, NC, 1994) 101.

WR Cornish, 'Protection of and vis-à-vis Databases' in M Dellebeke, (ed), *Copyright in Cyberspace: Copyright and the Global Information Infrastructure* (Otto Cramwinckel, Amsterdam, 1997) 435.

WR Cornish, *Intellectual Property: Patents, Copyright, Trade Marks and Allied Rights*, 4th edn, (Sweet & Maxwell, London, 1999).

WR Cornish and D Llewelyn, *Intellectual Property: Patents, Copyright, Trade Marks and Allied Rights*, 5th edn, (Sweet & Maxwell, London, 2003).

WR Cornish, *Intellectual Property: Omnipresent, Distracting, Irrelevant?* (OUP, Oxford, 2004).

S Cotter, (ed), *International Information Technology Law* (Wiley, Chicester, 1997).

B Cotton & R Oliver, Richard, *Understanding Hypermedia: from multimedia to virtual reality* (Phaidon, London, 1992).

KD Crews, 'Copyright and Distance Education: Displays, Performances, and the Limitations of Current Law' in LN Gasaway, (ed), *Growing Pains: Adapting Copyright for Libraries, Education and Society* (Colorado Rothmans, 1997) 377.

B Czarnota and R Hart, *Legal Protection of Computer Programs in Europe: A Guide to the EC Directive* (Butterworths, London, 1991).

K Dam, 'Self Help in the Digital Jungle' in R Dreyfuss, DL Zimmerman and H First, (eds), *Expanding the Boundaries of Intellectual Property: Innovation Policy for the Knowledge Society* (OUP, Oxford, 2001) 103.

A D'Amato and DE Long, (eds), *International Intellectual Property Law* (Kluwer, London, 1997).

G Davies, *Copyright and the Public Interest* (Sweet & Maxwell, London, 2002).

MJ Davison, *The Legal Protection of Databases* (CUP, Cambridge, 2003).

M Dellebeke, (ed), *Copyright in Cyberspace: Copyright and the Global Information Infrastructure* (Otto Cramwinckel, Amsterdam, 1997).

F Dessemontet, 'Copyright and Human Rights' in J Kabel and G Mom, (eds), *Intellectual Property and Information Law: Essays in Honour of Herman Cohen Jehoram* (Kluwer, The Hague, 1998) 113.

A Dietz, A, 'Authenticity of Authorship and Work' in M Dellebeke, (ed), *Copyright in Cyberspace: Copyright and the Global Information Infrastructure* (Otto Cramwinckel, Amsterdam, 1997) 165.

EJ Dommering and PB Hugenholtz, (eds), *Protecting Works of Fact* (Kluwer Deventer, 1991).

EJ Dommering, 'Copyright Being Washed Away through the Electronic Sieve: Some Thoughts on the Impending Copyright Crisis' in PB Hugenholtz, (ed), *The Future of Copyright in a Digital Environment* (Kluwer, The Hague, 1996) 1.

P Drahos, *A Philosophy of Intellectual Property* (Aldershot, Dartmouth, 1997).

T Dreier, 'Copyright in Audiovisual Works vis à vis Digital Technology and Databases' in H Cohen Jehoram, P Keuchenius and J Seignette, (eds), *Audiovisual Media and Copyright in Europe* (Kluwer, Deventer, 1994) 53.

T Dreier, 'The Cable and Satellite Analogy' in PB Hugenholtz, (ed), *The Future of Copyright in a Digital Environment* (Kluwer, The Hague, 1996) 57.

J Drexl, *What Is Protected in a Computer Program? Copyright Protection in the United States and Europe* (Max Planck Institute, Munich, 1994).

G Dworkin, 'Understanding the New Copyright Environment: an Assessment of the state of Copyright Law—from Whitford to Multimedia' in E Barendt, (ed), *Yearbook of Media and Entertainment Law* 1995, (Clarendon Press, Oxford 1995) 161.

RA Earnshaw and JA Vince, (eds), *Multimedia Systems and Applications* (Academic Press, London, 1995).

N Fawcett, *Multimedia* (Hodder Stoughton, Berkshire, 1994).

J Feather, 'From Rights in Copies to Copyright: the Recognition of Authors' Rights in English Law and Practice in the Sixteenth and Seventeenth Centuries' in M Woodmansee and P Jaszi, (eds), *The Construction of Authorship: Textual Appropriation in Law and Literature* (Duke University Press, Durham, NC, 1994) 191.

M Ficsor, 'Towards a Global Solution: the Digital Agenda of the Berne Protocol and the New Instrument' in PB Hugenholtz, (ed), *The Future of Copyright in a Digital Environment* (Kluwer, The Hague, 1996) 111.

M Ficsor, *The Law of Copyright and the Internet: the 1996 WIPO Treaties, their Interpretation and Implementation* (OUP, Oxford, 2002).

A Firth, 'Film, Ciné and Audio-visual Works: Questions of Definition' in E Barendt and A Firth, (eds), *Yearbook of Copyright and Media Law* (OUP, Oxford, 2000) 221.

A Fitzgerald, *et al*, (eds), *Going Digital 2000: Legal Issues for E-Commerce, Software and the Internet*, 2nd edn, (Prospect Media, NSW, 2000).

A Fitzgerald and C Cifuentes, 'Copyright Protection for Digital Multimedia Works' in A Fitzgerald, *et al*, (eds), *Going Digital 2000: Legal Issues for E-Commerce, Software and the Internet*, 2nd edn, (Prospect Media, NSW, 2000) 13.

A Fitzgerald and C Cifuentes, 'Pegging Out the Boundaries of Computer Software Copyright: the Computer Programs Act and Digital Agenda Bill' in A Fitzgerald, *et al*, (eds), *Going Digital 2000: Legal Issues for E-Commerce, Software and the Internet*, 2nd edn, (Prospect Media, NSW, 2000) 37.

F Fluckiger, *Understanding Networked Multimedia: Applications and Technology* (Prentice Hall, London, 1995).

M Foucault, 'What is an Author?' in P Rainbow, (ed), *The Foucault Reader* (Penguin Books, 1984) 101.

K Garnett, JR James and G Davies, (eds), *Copinger and Skone James on Copyright*, 14th edn, (Sweet & Maxwell, London, 1999) vol 1.

LN Gasaway, (ed), *Growing Pains: Adapting Copyright for Libraries, Education and Society* (Rothmans, 1997).

LN Gasaway, 'Library Reserve Collections: From Paper to Electronic Collections' in LN Gasaway, (ed), *Growing Pains: Adapting Copyright for Libraries, Education and Society* (Rothmans, 1997b) 125.

Y Gaubiac, 'Remarks about the Internet in International Copyright Conventions' in F Pollaud-Dulian, (ed), *The Internet and Authors' Rights* (Sweet & Maxwell, London, 1999) 107.

P Geller, 'Must Copyright Be Forever Caught between Marketplace and Authorship Norms?' in B Sherman and A Strowel, (eds), *Of Authors and Origins* (Clarendon Press, Oxford, 1994) 159.

Y Gendreau, 'Intention and Copyright Law' in F Pollaud-Dulian, (ed), *The Internet and Authors' Rights* (Sweet & Maxwell, London, 1999) 1.

Y Gendreau, 'A Technologically Neutral Solution for the Internet: Is It Wishful Thinking?' in I Stamatoudi and P Torremans, (eds), *Copyright in the New Digital Environment* (Sweet & Maxwell, London, 2000) 3.

J Ginsburg, 'Creation and Commercial Value: Copyright Protection of Works of Information in the United States' in EJ Dommering and PB Hugenholtz, (eds), *Protecting Works of Fact* (Kluwer, Deventer, 1991) 41.

J Ginsburg, 'A Tale of Two Copyrights: Literary Property in Revolutionary France and America' in B Sherman and A Strowel, (eds), *Of Authors and Origins* (Clarendon Press, Oxford, 1994) 131.

J Ginsburg, 'Putting Cars on the "Information Superhighway": Authors, Exploiters and Copyright in Cyberspace' in PB Hugenholtz, (ed), *The Future of Copyright in a Digital Environment* (Kluwer, The Hague, 1996) 189.

J Ginsburg and Y Gaubiac, 'Private Copyright in the Digital Environment' in J Kabel and G Mom, (eds), *Intellectual Property and Information Law: Essays in Honour of Herman Cohen Jehoram* (Kluwer, The Hague, 1998) 149.

J Ginsburg, 'US Initiatives to Protect Works of Low Authorship' in R Dreyfuss, DL Zimmerman and H First, (eds), *Expanding the Boundaries of Intellectual Property: Innovation Policy for the Knowledge Society* (OUP, Oxford, 2001) 55.

P Goldstein, *Copyright's Highway: From Gutenberg to the Celestial Jukebox*, Revised edn, (Stanford Law and Politics, Stanford, 2003).

P Goldstein, *International Copyright: Principles, Law and Practice* (OUP, Oxford, 2001).

C Gringas, *The Laws of the Internet* (Butterworths, London, 1997).

FW Grosheide, 'Copyright and Publishers' Rights: Exploitation of Information by a Proprietary Right' in Altes, *et al*, (eds), *Information Towards the 21st Century* (Kluwer, 1992) 295.

L Guibault, *Copyright Limitations and Contracts* (Kluwer, The Hague, 2002).

AS Gutterman and BJ Anderson, *Intellectual Property in Global Markets: A Guide for Foreign Lawyers and Managers* (Kluwer, London, 1997).

DJ Halbert, *Intellectual Property in the Information Age: the Politics of Expanding Ownership Rights* (Quorum Books, Westport, Conneticut, 1999).

S Heath, *Multimedia and Communications Technology*, 2nd edn, (Focal Press, Oxford, 1999).

G Hegel, TM Knox, (tr), *Philosophy of Right* (OUP, Oxford, 1967).

JS Heller, 'The Impact of Recent Litigation on Interlibrary Loan and Document Delivery' in LN Gasaway, (ed), *Growing Pains: Adapting Copyright for Libraries, Education and Society* (Rothmans, 1997) 189.

M Henry, *Publishing and Multimedia Law* (Butterworths, London, 1994).

PB Hugenholtz, 'Protection of Compilations of Facts in Germany and the Netherlands' in EJ Dommering and PB Hugenholtz, (eds), *Protecting Works of Fact* (Kluwer, Deventer, 1991) 59.

PB Hugenholtz, (ed), *The Future of Copyright in a Digital Environment* (Kluwer, The Hague, 1996).

PB Hugenholtz, 'Adapting Copyright to the Information Superhighway' in PB Hugenholtz, (ed), *The Future of Copyright in a Digital Environment* (Kluwer, The Hague, 1996) 81.

PB Hugenholtz, 'Copyright and Freedom of Expression' in R Dreyfuss, DL Zimmerman and H First, (eds), *Expanding the Boundaries of Intellectual Property: Innovation Policy for the Knowledge Society* (OUP, Oxford, 2001) 343.

P Jaszi, 'On the Author Effect: Contemporary Copyright and Collective Creativity' in M Woodmansee and P Jaszi, (eds), *The Construction of Authorship: Textual Appropriation in Law and Literature* (Duke University Press, Durham, NC, 1994) 29.

J Jonkers and W Wanrooij, 'Music, Copyright and New Techniques Seen From the Perspective of Collecting Societies' in W Roos J and Seignette, (eds), *Multimedia Deals in the Music Industry* (Apeldoorn: MAKLU, 1996), 131.

P Kamina, *Film Copyright in the European Union* (CUP, Cambridge, 2002).

B Kaplan, *An Unhurried View of Copyright* (Columbia University Press, New York, 1966).

GWG Karnell, 'The Nordic Catalogue Rule' in E Dommering and PB Hugenholtz, (eds), *Protecting Works of Fact* (Kluwer, The Hague, 1991) 67.

GWG Karnell, 'European Originality: A Copyright Chimera' in J Kabel and G Mom, (eds), *Intellectual Property and Information Law: Essays in Honour of Herman Cohen Jehoram* (Kluwer, The Hague, 1998) 201.

E Katsh, *Law in a Digital World* (OUP, New York, 1995).

T Koopmans, 'Information Monopolies in European Community Law' in E Dommering and PB Hugenholtz, (eds), *Protecting Works of Fact* (Kluwer, The Hague, 1991) 83.

H Laddie, P Prescott and M Vitoria, *The Modern Law of Copyright and Designs*, 2nd edn, (Butterworths, London, 1995) vol 1.

H Laddie, *et al*, *The Modern Law of Copyright and Designs*, 3rd edn, (Butterworths, London, 2000) volumes 1 and 2.

J Lahore, *Copyright and Designs*, 3rd edn, (Butterworths, Sydney, 1996) vol 1.

S Lai, *The Copyright Protection of Computer Software in the United Kingdom* (Hart Publishing, Oxford, 2000).

A Latreille, 'The Legal Classification of Multimedia Creations in French Copyright Law' in I Stamatoudi and P Torremans, (eds), *Copyright in the New Digital Environment* (Sweet & Maxwell, London, 2000) 45.

L Lessig, *Code and other Laws of Cyberspace* (Basic Books, New York, 1999).

L Lessig, *The Future of Ideas: The Fate of the Commons in a Connected World* (Random House, New York, 2001).

L Lessig, *Free Culture: How Big Media Uses Technology and the Law to Lock Down Culture and Control Creativity* (Penguin, New York, 2004).

J Litman, *Digital Copyright* (Prometheus, New York, 2001).

J Litman, 'New Copyright Paradigms' in LN Gasaway, (ed), *Growing Pains: Adapting Copyright for Libraries, Education and Society* (Rothmans, 1997) 63.

J Locke, P Laslett, (ed), *Two Treatises of Government* (CUP, Cambridge, 1988).

L Longdin, 'Copyright Infringement and the On-line Service Provider: Shooting the Messenger Now and Then' in CEF Rickett and GW Austin, (eds), *International Intellectual Property and the Common Law World* (Hart Publishing, Oxford, 2000) 63.

E Mackaay, 'The Economics of Emergent Property Rights on the Internet' in PB Hugenholtz, (ed), *The Future of Copyright in a Digital Environment* (Kluwer, The Hague, 1996) 13.

D Maclean and K Schubert, (eds), *Dear Images: Art, Copyright and Culture* (Ridinghouse, London, 2002).

PF Macmillan, 'Towards a Reconciliation of Free Speech and Copyright' in Barendt, (ed), *Yearbook of Media and Entertainment Law* (Clarendon Press, Oxford, 1996) 201.

PF Macmillan, 'Legal Policy and the Limits of Literary Copyright' in P Parrinder and WL Chernaik, (eds), *Textual Monopolies: Literary Copyright and the Public Domain* (King College Office for Humanities Communication, London, 1997) 113.

HL MacQueen, 'Copyright and the Internet' in L Edwards and C Waelde, (eds), *Law and the Internet: a Framework for Electronic Commerce* (Hart Publishing, Oxford, 2000) 181.

LW McClure, 'Interlibrary Loan in the Electronic World' in LN Gasaway, (ed), *Growing Pains: Adapting Copyright for Libraries, Education and Society* (Rothmans, 1997) 173.

J McKeough and A Stewart, *Intellectual Property in Australia,* 2nd edn, (Butterworths, Sydney, 1997).

M Makeen, *Copyright in a Global Information Society: the Scope of Copyright Protection Under International, US, UK and French Law* (Kluwer, London, 2000).

Murray, 'Entering into Contracts Electronically: the Real WWW' in Edwards and Waelde, (eds), *Law and the Internet: A Framework for Electronic Commerce* (Hart Publishing, Oxford, 2000) 17.

J Monaco, *How to Read a Film: Movies, Media Multimedia,* 3rd edn, (OUP, Oxford, 2000).

J Naughton, *A Brief History of the Future: the Origins of the Internet* (Phoenix, London, 2000).

N Negroponte, *Being Digital* (Hodder Stoughton, London, 1995).

J Nielsen, *Hypertext and Hypermedia* (Academic Press, Cambridge, MA, 1993).

J Nielsen *Multimedia and Hypertext, the Internet and Beyond* (AP Professional, Boston, 1995).

MB Nimmer and D Nimmer, *Nimmer on Copyright* (Matthew Bender, New York, 1998).

D Nimmer and P Geller, (eds), *Intl Copyright Law and Practice* (Looseleaf, Matther Bender, New York).

RL Oakley, 'Preservation and Copyright' in LN Gasaway, (ed), *Growing Pains: Adapting Copyright for Libraries, Education and Society* (Rothmans, 1997) 111.

C Oppenheim, 'Copyright in the Electronic Age' in H Cohen Jehoram, P Keuchenius and J Seignette, (eds), *Audiovisual Media and Copyright in Europe* (Kluwer Deventer, 1994) 97.

A Oram, (ed), *Peer-to-Peer: Harnessing the Benefits of a Disruptive Technology* (O'Reilly, Sebastopol, 2001).

JR Pardo, *Copyright and Multimedia* (Kluwer, The Hague, 2003).

P Parrinder and WL Chernaik, (eds), *Textual Monopolies: Literary Copyright and the Public Domain* (King's College Office for Humanities Communication, London, 1997).

J Passa, 'The Protection of Copyright on the Internet under French Law' in F Pollaud-Dulian, (ed), *The Internet and Authors' Rights* (Sweet & Maxwell, London, 1999) 25.

LR Patterson, *Copyright in Historical Perspective* (Vanderbilt University Press, Nashville, 1968).

LR Patterson, 'Fair Use for Teaching and Research: the Folly of Kinko's and Texaco' in LN Gasaway, (ed), *Growing Pains: Adapting Copyright for Libraries, Education and Society* (Rothmans, 1997) 351.

DD Peck, *Pocket Guide to Multimedia* (Delmar Publishers, New York, 1999).

K Pimental, *Virtual Reality: Through the New Looking Glass* (Windcrest/McGraw-Hill, New York, 1993).

F Pollaud-Dulian, (ed), *The Internet and Authors' Rights* (Sweet & Maxwell, London, 1999).

ME Price and M Pollack, 'The Author in Copyright: Notes for the Literary Critic' in M Woodmansee and P Jaszi, Peter, (eds), *The Construction of Authorship: Textual Appropriation in Law and Literature* (Duke University Press, Durham, NC, 1994) 439.

M Radcliffe, 'Legal Issues in New Media: Multimedia for Publishers' in D Campbell and S Cotter, (eds), *International Intellectual Property Law: New Developments* (Wiley, Chicester, 1995) 181.

C Reed, *Internet Law: Text and Materials* (Butterworths, London, 2000).

C Rees and S Chalton, (eds), *Database Law* (Jordans, Bristol, 1998).

J Reinbothe and S von Lewinski, *The WIPO Treaties 1996* (Butterworths, London, 2002).

S Ricketson, *The Berne Convention for the Protection of Literary and Artistic Works: 1886–1986* (Kluwer, London, 1987).

S Ricketson, 'Copyright and Databases' in G Hughes, (ed), *Essays on Computer Law* (Longman Professional, Melbourne, 1990) 67.

S Ricketson, 'New Wine into Old Bottles: Technological Change and Intellectual Property Rights' (1992) 10(1) *Prometheus* 53, reproduced in P Drahos, (ed), *Intellectual Property* (Aldershot Dartmouth Ashgate, 1999) 387.

W Roos and J Seignette, (eds), *Multimedia Deals in the Music Industry* (MAKLU, Apeldoorn, 1996).

M Rose, *Authors and Owners: The Invention of Copyright* (Harvard, Cambridge, 1993).

W Rumphorst, 'The EC Directive on Satellite Broadcasting and Cable Retransmission' in H Cohen Jehoram, P Keuchenius and J Seignette, (eds), *Audiovisual Media and Copyright in Europe* (Kluwer, Deventer, 1994) 17.

M Salokannel, 'Film Authorship in the Changing Audio-Visual Environment' in B Sherman and A Strowel, (eds), *Of Authors and Origins* (Clarendon Press, Oxford, 1994) 57.

M Salokannel, *Ownership of Rights in Audiovisual Productions: a Comparative Study* (Kluwer, London, 1997).

P Samuelson, 'Copyright, Digital Data and Fair Use in Digital Networked Environments' in E Mackaay, D Poulin and P Trudel, (eds), *The Electronic Superhighway: the Shape of Technology and Law to Come* (Kluwer, 1995) 117.

D Saunders, *Authorship and Copyright* (Routledge, London, 1992).

J Seignette, *Challenges to the Creator Doctrine: Authorship, Copyright Ownership and the Exploitation of Creative Works in the Netherlands, Germany and the United States* (Kluwer, 1994).

M Senftleben, *Copyright, Limitations and the Three-Step Test* (Kluwer, The Hague, 2004).

AL Shapiro, *The Control Revolution: How the Internet is Putting Individuals in Charge and Changing the World that We Know* (Century Foundation, New York, 1999).

B Sherman and L Bently, *The Making of Modern Intellectual Property Law* (CUP, Cambridge, 1999).

B Sherman and A Strowel, (eds), *Of Authors and Origins: Essays on Copyright Law* (Clarendon Press, Oxford, 1994).

M Sherwood-Edwards and J Dickens, 'Legal Developments in Multimedia in 1994' in E Barendt, (ed), *Yearbook of Media and Entertainment Law 1995* (Clarendon Press, Oxford, 1995) 457.

BJ Sheu and M Ismail, *Multimedia Technology for Applications* (IEEE Press, NJ, 1998).

GJH Smith, (ed), *Internet Law and Regulation*, 2nd edn, (FT Law & Tax, London, 1997).

GJH Smith, (ed), *Internet Law and Regulation*, 3rd edn, (Sweet & Maxwell, London, 2002).

M Spence, 'Justifying Copyright' in McClean and Schubert, (eds), *Dear Images: Art, Copyright and Culture* (Ridinghouse, Manchester, 2002) 389.

JH Spoor, 'The Copyright Approach to Copying on the Internet: (Over)Stretching the Reproduction Right?' in PB Hugenholtz, (ed), *The Future of Copyright in a Digital Environment* (Kluwer, The Hague, 1996) 67.

JH Spoor, 'The Economic Rights Involved: General Report' in M Dellebeke, *Copyright in Cyberspace: Copyright and the Global Information Infrastructure* (Otto Cramwinckel, Amsterdam, 1997) 41.

I Stamatoudi, *Copyright and Multimedia Works: A Comparative Analysis* (CUP, Cambridge, 2002).

I Stamatoudi, 'To what extent are Multimedia Products Databases?' in I Stamatoudi and P Torremans, (eds), *Copyright in the New Digital Environment* (Sweet & Maxwell, London, 2000) 17.

JAL Sterling, *World Copyright Law*, 2nd edn, (Sweet & Maxwell, London, 2003).

R Steinmetz and K Nahrstedt, *Multimedia: Computing, Communications and Applications* (Prentice Hall, Upper Saddle River, NJ, 1995).

S Stokes, *Digital Copyright: Law and Practice* (Butterworths, 2002).

SE Strasser, *Digital Technologies and Law: Linking and Framing on the World Wide Web* (unpublished D Phil thesis, Bodlean Law Library, Oxford, 2002).

T Streeter, 'Broadcast Copyright and the Bureaucratization of Property' in M Woodmansee and P Jaszi, (eds), *The Construction of Authorship: Textual Appropriation in Law and Literature* (Duke University Press, Durham, NC, 1994) 303.

A Strowel, 'Droit d'auteur and Copyright: between History and Nature' in B Sherman and A Strowel, (eds), *Of Authors and Origins* (Clarendon Press, Oxford, 1994) 235.

C Tapper, *Computer Law*, 4th edn, (Longman, London, 1989).

Terrett and Monaghan, 'The Internet—An Introduction for Lawyers' in L Edwards and C Waelde, (eds), *Law and the Internet: a Framework for Electronic Commerce* (Hart Publishing, Oxford, 2000) 1.

J Tranter, *Linux Multimedia Guide* (O'Reilly, Sebastopol, CA, 1996).

G Tritton, *Intellectual Property in Europe*, 2nd edn, (Sweet & Maxwell, London, 2002).

S Vaidhyanathan, *Copyrights and Copywrongs: the Rise of Intellectual Property and How it Threatens Creativity* (NYU Press, New York, 2001).

DJG Visser, 'Copyright Exemptions Old and New: Learning from Old Media Experiences' in PB Hugenholtz, (ed), *The Future of Copyright in a Digital Environment* (Kluwer, The Hague, 1996).

WIPO, *WIPO Worldwide Symposium on the Impact of Digital Technology On Copyright And Neighboring Rights*, (Harvard University, Cambridge, MA, US, 31 March to 2 April 1993).

EK Wesel, *Wireless Multimedia Communications: Networking Video, Voice and Data* (Massachusetts Addison Wesley Longman, 1998).

SK Wiant, 'Users' Rights to Photocopy: the Impact of Texaco and Michigan Document Services' in LN Gasaway, (ed), *Growing Pains: Adapting Copyright for Libraries, Education and Society* (Rothmans, 1997) 315.

M Woodmansee, 'On the Author Effect: Recovering Collectivity' in M Woodmansee and P Jaszi, (eds), *The Construction of Authorship: Textual Appropriation in Law and Literature* (Duke University Press, Durham, NC, 1994) 15.

B Woolley, *Virtual Worlds* (Blackwell, Oxford, 1992).

C-H Wu and JD Irwin, *Emerging Multimedia Computer Communication Technologies* (Prentice Hall, NJ, 1998).

AC Yen, 'The Interdisciplinary Future of Copyright Theory' in M Woodmansee and P Jaszi, (eds), *The Construction of Authorship: Textual Appropriation in Law and Literature* (Duke University Press, Durham, NC, 1994) 159.

Dictionaries

F Botto, *Dictionary of Multimedia and Internet Applications: A Guide for Developers and Users* (Wiley, Chicester, 1999).

B Cotton & R Oliver, *The Cyberspace Lexicon: An Illustrated Dictionary of Terms from Multimedia to Virtual Reality* (Phaidon, London, 1994).

B Hansen, *The Dictionary of Multimedia: Terms and Acronyms* (Fitzroy Dearborn, Chicago, 1999).

J Schofield, *The Hutchinson Dictionary of Computing, Multimedia and the Internet*, 3rd edn, (Helicon, Oxford, 1999).

The Shorter Oxford English Dictionary on Historical Principles, 3rd edn, (Clarendon Press, Oxford, 1991) vols 1 and 2.

Refereed Articles, Notes and Opinions

JN Adams, 'The Reporting Exception: Does it Still Exist?' [1999] *EIPR* 383.

J Adams and V Marsland, 'Choice of the Legal Regime' [1995] 54 *Copyright World* 33.

E Adeney, 'The Moral Right of Integrity of Authorship: A Comparative View of Australia's Proposals to Date' [1998] 9 *AIPJ* 179.

E Adeney, 'Moral Rights/Statutory Licence: the notion of Debasement in Australian Copyright Law' [1998] 9 *AIPJ* 21.

A Adrian, 'Who Owns the Copyright in Multi Author Interactive Works' (2003) 14 *Entertainment L Rev* 35.

P Akester, 'Survey of Technological Measures for Protection of Copyright' (2001) 12 *Entertainment L Rev* 36.

N Aldous and G Defries, 'Potential Pitfalls in the New Digital Television Age' (1998) May/June' *Copyright World* 35.

Anonymous, 'The Criminalization of Copyright Infringement in the Digital Era' (1999) 112 *Harvard L Rev* 1705.

Anonymous, 'Developments—the Law of Cyberspace' (1999) 112 *Harvard L Rev* 1574.

K Aoki, 'Adrift in the Intertext: Authorship and Audience "Recoding" Rights' (1993) 68 *Chi-Kent L Rev* 805.

K Aoki, '(Intellectual) Property and Sovereignty: Notes Toward a Cultural Geography of Authorship' (1996) 48 *Stanford L Rev* 1293.

T Aplin, 'Copyright Protection of Multimedia' (1997) 22 *Alternative L J* 118.

T Aplin, 'Not in our Galaxy: Why "Film" Won't Rescue Multimedia' (1999) 12 *EIPR* 633.

T Aplin, 'When are Compilations Original? *Telstra Corporation v Desktop Marketing Systems Pty Ltd*' [2001] *EIPR* 543.

T Aplin, 'Contemplating Australia's Digital Future: the Copyright Amendment (Digital Agenda) Act 2000' [2001] *EIPR* 565.

T Aplin, 'The Copyright Dangers of Music on Hold: *Telstra Corporation Ltd v Australasian Performing Right Association Ltd*' [1997] 4 (3) *E Law* at http://www.murdoch.edu.au/elaw/issues/v4n3/apli43.html.

R Arnold, '*Joy*: A Reply' [2001] *IPQ* 10.

WL Austin, 'A Thoughtful and Practical Analysis of Database Protection under Copyright Law and a Critique of Sui Generis Protection' [1997] 3 *Journal of Technology, Law & Policy* at http://journal.law.ufl.edu/~techlaw/3–1/austin.html.

D Balaban, 'The Battle of the Music Industry: the Distribution of Audio and Video Works via the Internet, Music and More' (2001) 12 *Fordham Intellectual Property, Media & Entertainment L J* 235.

C Barlas, 'Approaches to the problems of multimedia: an author's perspective' [1995] 8 *Entertainment L Rev* 303.

A Barron, 'Copyright Law and the Claims of Art' [2002] *IPQ* 368.

MJ Bastian, 'Protection of "Noncreative" Databases: Harmonization of United States, Foreign and International Law' (1999) 22 *B C Intl & Comp L Rev* 425.

U Bath, 'Access to Information v Intellectual Property Rights' [2002] *EIPR* 138.

CCM Beams, 'The Copyright Dilemma Involving Online Service Providers: Problem Solved...for Now' (1999) 51 *Fed Comm L J* 823.

S Bechtold, 'Multimedia and Urheberrecht' [1998] 1 *GRUR* 18.

C Benson, 'Fair Dealing in the United Kingdom' [1995] *EIPR* 304.

JR Benson, 'Copyright Protection for Computer Screen Displays' (1988) 72 *Minnesota L Rev* 1123.

L Bently, 'European Developments in Copyright' unpublished paper delivered for the *Irish Centre for European Law* (copy held on file with the author).

L Bently and R Burrell, 'Copyright and the Information Society in Europe: a Matter of Timing as well as Content' (1997) 34 *Common Market L Rev* 1197.

K Beresford, 'Software Protection in Europe and the UK: Patenting v Copyright' (1997) 70 *Copyright World* 31.

J Berkvens and G Alkemade, 'Software Protection: Life after the Directive' [1991] *EIPR* 476.

J Berkvens, 'Data Regulation in Copyright Law: Will the Problem of Software Ever Be Solved?' [1993] *EIPR* 79.

S Beutler, 'The Protection of Multimedia Products through the European Community's Directive on the Legal Protection of Databases' [1996] 8 *Entertainment L Rev* 317.

MD Birnhack, 'Acknowledging the Conflict between Copyright Law and Freedom of Expression Under the Human Rights Act' (2003) 14 *Entertainment L Rev* 24.

M Blakeney and F Macmillan, 'Bringing Australian Copyright Law into the Global Age' (1998) 5(1) *E Law* at http://www.murdoch.edu.au/elaw/issues/v5n1/blake51.html.

K Bowrey, 'Who's Writing Copyright History' [1996] 6 *EIPR* 322.

J Boyle, 'The Second Enclosure Movement and the Construction of the Public Domain' (2003) 66 *L & Contemporary Problems* 33.

J Boyle, 'Cruel, Mean, or Lavish? Economic Analysis, Price Discrimination and Digital Intellectual Property' (2000) 53 *Vand L Rev* 2007.

D Bradshaw, 'Fair Dealing and the Clockwork Orange Case: "A Thieves Charter"?' [1994] 5 *Entertainment L Rev* 6.

D Bradshaw, '"Fair Dealing" as a Defence to Copyright Infringement in UK Law: An Historical Excursion from 1802 to the Clockwork Orange Case 1993' [1995] *Denning L J* 67.

D Bradshaw, 'Copyright, Fair Dealing and the *Mandy Allwood* Case: the Court of Appeal gets the Max out of Multiple Pregnancy Opportunity?' [1999] *Entertainment L Rev* 125.

WJ Braithwaite, 'Derivative Works in Canadian Copyright Law' (1982) 20 *Osgoode Hall L J* 191.

N Braun, 'The Interface between the Protection of Technological Measures and the Exercise of Exceptions to Copyright and Related Rights: Comparing the Situation in the United States and the European Community' [2003] *EIPR* 496.

D Brennan, 'Locksmiths and Safecrackers in Cyberspace' (2000b) 2(1) *Digital Technology L J* at: http://wwwlaw.murdoch.edu.au/dtlj/articles/vol2_1/brennanDTLJ2_1.htm.

T Brennan, 'Copyright, Property, and the Right to Deny' (1993) 69 *Chicago-Kent L Rev* 677.

D Brenner, 'In Search of the Multimedia Grail' (1994) 47 *Federal Communications L J* 197.

S Breyer, 'The Uneasy Case for Copyright: A Study of Copyright in Books, Photocopies and Computer Programs' (1970) 84 *Harvard L Rev* 281.

RA Browes, 'Copyright: Court of Appeal Considers Fair Dealing Defence and Rejects Common Law Defence of Public Interest' [2000] *EIPR* 289.

M Brown, 'The UK Protection of Films: Issues Raised by the Case of *Norowzian v Arks*' [1998] *Entertainment L Rev* 323.

P Brudenall, 'Fair Dealing in Australian Copyright Law: Rights of Access Under the "Microscope"' (1997) 20 *U New South Wales L J* 443.

P Brudenall, 'The Future of Fair Dealing in Australian Copyright Law' (1997b) 1 *J of Information, L & Technology* at http://elj.warwick.ac.uk/jilt/copright/97_1brud/.

DL Burk, 'Proprietary Rights in Hypertext Linkages' [1998] 2 *J of Information, L & Technology* at http://elj.warwick.ac.uk/jilt/intprop/98_2burk/.

J Burnside, 'The *Powerflex* Case: Legal and Industry Implications' (1998) 16(1) *Copy Rep* 31.

R Burrell, 'Defending the Public Interest' [2000] *EIPR* 394.

R Burrell, 'Reining in Copyright Law: Is Fair Use the Answer?' [2001] *IPQ* 361.

J Cameron, 'Approaches to the Problems of Multimedia' [1996] *EIPR* 115.

Z Chafee, 'Reflections on the Law of Copyright: I' (1945) 45 *Columbia L Rev* 503.

Z Chafee, 'Reflections on the Law of Copyright: II' (1945) 45 *Columbia L Rev* 719.

S Chalton, 'The Amended Database Directive Proposal: A Commentary and Synopsis' [1994] 3 *EIPR* 94.

S Chalton, 'The Effect of the EC Database Directive on UK Copyright Law in Relation to Databases: A Comparison of Features' [1997] *EIPR* 278.

S Chalton, 'The Copyright and Rights in Databases Regulations 1997: Some Outstanding Issues On Implementation of the Database Directive' [1998] *EIPR* 178.

S Chalton, 'Implementation of the Software Directive in the United Kingdom: the Effects of the Copyright (Computer Programs) Regulations 1992' [1993] *EIPR* 138.

R Chavil, R, 'Software Patents: Has Fujitsu Taken Us any Further Forward?' (1997) *Patent World* 15.

J Choe, 'Interactive Multimedia: A New Technology Tests the Limits of Copyright Law' (1994) 46 *Rutgers L Rev* 929.

M Chon, 'Postmodern Progress: Reconsidering Copyright and Patent Power' (1991) 43 *DePaul L Rev* 97.

A Christie, 'Re-writing the Rules on the Form of Protection for Computer Software' (1993) 4 *Journal of Law & Information Science* 224.

A Christie, 'Designing Appropriate Protection for Computer Programs' (1994) 11 *EIPR* 486.

A Christie, 'Reconceptualising Copyright in the Digital Era' (1995) 11 *EIPR* 522.

A Christie, 'A Proposal for Simplifying United Kingdom Copyright Law' [2001] *EIPR* 26.

A Christie and K Fong 'Copyright Protection for Non-Code Elements of Software' (1996) 7 *Journal of Law & Information Science* 149.

A Christie and S Syme, 'Patents for Algorithms in Australia' (1998) 20 *Sydney Law Review* 517.

AL Clapes, P Lynch and MR Steinberg, 'Silicon Epics And Binary Bards: Determining the Proper Scope of Copyright Protection For Computer Programs' (1987) 34 *UCLA L Rev* 1493.

JE Cohen, 'WIPO Copyright Treaty Implementation in the United States: Will Fair Use Survive?' [1999] *EIPR* 236.

H Cohen Jehoram, 'Copyright and Freedom of Expression, Abuse of Rights and Standard Chicanery: American and Dutch Approaches' [2004] *EIPR* 275.

M Colombe and C Meyer, 'Interoperability still Threatened by EC Software Directive: A Status Report' [1990] *EIPR* 325.

C Colston, 'Fair Dealing: What is Fair?' [1995] *Denning L J* 91.

WJ Cook, 'Why Internet Service Providers Should be Copyright Guardians' (1996) 60 *Copyright World* 18.

T Cooke, 'Implementation of the Database Directive in the UK' (1998) 78 *Copyright World* 35.

R Coombe, 'Objects of Property and Subjects of Politics: Intellectual Property Laws and Democratic Dialogue' (1991) 69 *Tex L Rev* 1853.

R Coombe, 'Authorial Cartographies: Mapping Proprietary Borders in a Less-Than-Brave-New World' (1996) 48 *Stanford L Rev* 1357.

JM Conley and K Bemelmans, 'Intellectual Property Implications of Multimedia Products: A Case Study' [1997] 6 (1) *Information & Communications Technology L* 3.

JP Connolly and S Cameron, 'Fair Dealing in Webbed Links of Shetland Yarns' [1998] 2 *J of Information, L & Technology* at http://elj.warwick.ac.uk/jilt/copright/98_2conn/.

WR Cornish, 'Authors in Law' (1995) 58 *Mod L Rev* 1.

WR Cornish, 'Copyright Across the Quarter-Century' (1995) 26 *IIC* 801.

KW Dam, 'Some Economic Considerations in the Intellectual Property Protection of Software' (1995) 24 *J Legal Stud* 321.

NJ Dasios, 'Virtual Environments: Protecting Virtual Works under Copyright' (1995) 9 *IPJ* 105.

F Daun, 'The Content Shop: Toward an Economic Legal Structure For Clearing And Licensing Multimedia Content' (1996) 30 *Loyola of Los Angeles L Rev* 215.

J Davies, 'The Developing Law of Multimedia' (1994) 10(1) *Computer L & Practice* 6.

MJ Davison, '*Sui Generis* or Too Generous: Legislative Protection of Databases, Its Implications For Australia And Some Suggestions For Reform' (1998) 21(3) *U New South Wales LJ* 729.

MJ Davison, 'Proposed US Database Legislation: A Comparison with the UK Database Regulations' [1999] *EIPR* 279.

R Denicola, 'Copyright in Collections of Facts: A Theory for the Protection of Nonfiction Literary Works' (1981) 81 *Col LR* 576.

RC Denicola, 'Mostly Dead? Copyright Law in the New Millennium' (2000) 47 *J of Copyright Society of USA* 193.

E Derclaye, 'Software Copyright Protection: Can Europe Learn From American Case Law? Part I' (2000) 22 *EIPR* 7.

E Derclaye, 'Software Copyright Protection: Can Europe Learn From American Case Law? Part 2' (2000) 22 *EIPR* 56.

E Derclaye, 'Do Sections 3 and 3A of the CDPA Violate the Database Directive? A Closer Look at the Definition of a Database in the UK and its Compatibility with European Law' [2002] *EIPR* 466.

E Derclaye, 'What is a Database? A Critical Analysis of the Definition of a Database in the European Database Directive and Suggestions for an International Definition' (2002b) 5 *J of World Intellectual Property* 981.

E Derclaye, 'The Copyright Directive: How will the Statutory and Case Law of England and Wales be Affected?' [2001] *Copyright World* 19.

E Derclaye, 'Databases *Sui Generis* Right: Should We Adopt the Spin Off Theory?' (2004) 26 *EIPR* 402.

A Dietz, 'The Protection of Intellectual Property in the Information Age—The Draft EU Copyright Directive of November 1997' [1998] *IPQ* 335.

A Dixon and LC Self, 'Copyright Protection for the Information Superhighway' (1994) 11 *EIPR* 465.

A Dixon and MF Hansen, 'The Berne Convention Enters the Digital Age' (1996) 11 *EIPR* 604.

M Doherty and I Griffiths, 'The Harmonisation of European Union Copyright Law for the Digital Age' [2000] *EIPR* 17.

J Douglas, 'Too Hot to Handle? Copyright Protection of Multimedia' [1997] 8 *AIPJ* 96.

J Dowell, 'Bytes and Pieces: Fragmented Copies, Licensing, and Fair Use in a Digital World' (1998) 86 *Cal L Rev* 843.

P Drahos, 'Indigenous Knowledge and the Duties of Intellectual Property Owners' (1997) 11 *IPJ* 179.

T Dreier, 'Copyright in the Age of Digital Technology' (1993) 24 *IIC* 481.

T Dreier, 'Adjustment of Copyright Law to the Requirements of the Information Society' (1998) 29 *IIC* 623.

T Dreier, 'The Council Directive of 14 May 1991 on the Legal Protection of Computer Programs' [1991] *EIPR* 319.

T Dreier, 'Authorship and New Technologies from the Viewpoint of Civil Law Tradition' (1995) 26 *IIC* 989.

A Duigan, 'Why the Copyright of "Look and Feel" is Not Applicable to Australian Law' (1994) 5 *Journal of Law & Information Science* 78.

S Dusollier, 'Electrifying the Fence: The Legal Protection of Technological Measures for Protecting Copyright' [1999] *EIPR* 285.

WA Effross, 'Withdrawal of the Reference: Rights, Rules, and Remedies for Unwelcomed Web-Linking' (1998) 49 *South Carolina L Rev* 651.

N Elkin-Koren, 'Copyright Law and Social Dialogue on the Information Superhighway: The Case Against Copyright Liability of Bulletin Board Operators' (1995) 13 *Cardozo Arts & Ent L J* 345.

N Elkin-Koren, 'Copyright Policy and the Limits of Freedom of Contract' (1997) 12(1) *Berkeley Technology L J* at http://www.law.berkeley.edu/journals/btlj/articles/vol12.html.

D Engel, 'ISPs Cannot Turn a Blind Eye to Material on their Systems' [1999] *Entertainment L Rev* 184.

J Enser, 'Legal Developments in Multimedia' in E Barendt, (ed), *The Yearbook of Media and Entertainment Law 1997/98* (Clarendon Press, Oxford, 1997) 463.

D Fewer, 'A *Sui Generis* Right to Data? A Canadian Position' (1998) 30 *Can Bus LJ* 165.

WW Fisher, 'Reconstructing the Fair Use Doctrine' (1988) 101 *Harvard L Rev* 1661.

A Fitzgerald, 'Square Pegs and Round Holes: Recent US Developments in Copyright Protection for Computer Software' (1993) 4 *Journal of Law & Information Science* 142.

A Fitzgerald and C Cifuentes, 'Copyright Protection for Digital Multimedia Works' [1999] *Entertainment L Rev* 23.

B Fitzgerald, 'Theoretical Underpinning of Intellectual Property: "I am a Pragmatist But Theory is my Rhetoric"' (2003) 16 *Canadian J of L & Jurisprudence* 179.

J Fitzgerald, 'Licensing Content for Multimedia' [1998] *Copyright World* 23.

T Foged, 'US v EU Anti Circumvention Legislation: Preserving the Public's Privileges in the Digital Age' (2002) 24 *EIPR* 525.

M Fraser, 'Fair is Foul and Foul is Fair: from Analogue to Digital Fair Dealing' (1998) 9 *Journal of Law & Information Science* 93.

S Fraser, 'The Copyright Battle: Emerging International Rules and Roadblocks on the Global Information Infrastructure' (1997) 15 *John Marshall J of Computer & Information L* 759.

CD Freedman, 'Should Canada Enact a New *Sui Generis* Database Right?' (2002) 13 *Fordham Intellectual Property Media & Entertainment L J* 35.

J Frow, 'Public Domain and Collective Rights Culture' (1998) 13 *IPJ* 39.

G Fulton, 'A New Transmission Right for Australia?' (1997) 15 *Copy Rep* 64.

K Garnett, 'Incidental Inclusion under Section 31' [2003] *EIPR* 579.

C Garrigues, 'Databases: A Subject Matter for Copyright or for a Neighbouring Rights Regime?' [1997] 1 *EIPR* 3.

IJ Garrote, 'Linking and Framing: A Comparative Law Approach' [2002] *EIPR* 184.

LN Gasaway, 'Fair Use for Faculty-Created Multimedia' (1997c) 6 *Information & Communications Technology Law* 153.

J Gaster, 'The New EU Directive Concerning the Legal Protection of Databases' (1997) 20 *Fordham Intl L J* 1129.

P-Y Gautier, '"Multimedia" Works in French Law' (1994) 160 *RIDA* 90.

PE Geller, 'Copyright History and the Future: What's Culture Got to Do With It?' (2000) 47 *J Copyright Society of USA* 209.

Y Gendreau, 'Digital Technology and Copyright: Can Moral Rights Survive the Disappearance of the Hard Copy?' [1995] 6 *Entertainment L Rev* 214.

D Gervais, '*Feist* Goes Global: A Comparative Analysis of the Notion of Originality in Copyright Law' (2002) 49 *J Copyright Soc'y USA* 949.

D Gervais, 'The Compatibility of the Skill and Labour Originality Standard with the Berne Convention and the TRIPS Agreement' [2004] *EIPR* 75.

M Gilligan, 'The Multimedia Maze—an Illustration of the Legal Rights in Multimedia Products' (1997) 2 *Communications Law* 49.

J Ginsburg, 'Creation and Commercial Value: Copyright Protection of Works of Information' (1990) 90 *Columbia L Rev* 1865.

J Ginsburg, 'No "Sweat"? Copyright and other Protection of Works of Information after *Feist v Rural Telephone*' (1992) 92 *Columbia L Rev* 338.

J Ginsburg, 'Copyright without Walls? Speculations on Literary Property in the Library of the Future' (1993) 42 *Representations* 53.

J Ginsburg, 'Four Reasons and a Paradox: The Manifest Superiority of Copyright over *Sui Generis* Protection of Computer Software' (1994) 94 *Columbia L Rev* 2559.

JC Ginsburg, 'Domestic and International Copyright issues Implicated in the Compilation of a Multimedia Product' (1995) 25 *Seton Hall L Rev* 1397.

JC Ginsburg, 'Berne without Borders: Geographic Indiscretion and Digital Communications' [2002] *IPQ* 111.

JC Ginsburg, 'International Copyright: from a "Bundle" of National Copyright Laws to a Supranational Code?' (2000) 47 *J of the Copyright Society of the USA* 265.

J Ginsburg, 'The Concept of Authorship in Comparative Copyright Law' (2003) 52 *DePaul L Rev* 1063.

L Goebel, 'The Role of History in Copyright Dilemmas' (1998) 9 *Journal of Law & Information Science* 22.

J Goldberg, 'Now that the Future has Arrived, Maybe the Law Should Take a Look: Multimedia Technology and its Interaction with the Fair Use Doctrine' (1995) 44 *American U L Rev* 919.

P Goldstein, 'Comments on A Manifesto Concerning the Legal Protection of Computer Programs' (1994) 94 *Columbia L Rev* 2573.

P Goldstein, 'Derivative Rights and Derivative Works in Copyright' (1983) 30 *J of the Copyright Society of the USA* 209.

MJ Gordon, 'Derivative Work Protection for Computer Software Conversion' (1985) 7 *Communications and the Law* 3.

ML Gordon, 'Copying to Compete: the Tension between Copyright Protection and Antitrust Policy in Recent Non-literal Computer Program Copyright Infringement Cases' (1996) 25 *John Marshall Journal of Computer & Information L* 171.

S Gordon, 'The Very Idea! Why Copyright Law is an Inappropriate Way to Protect Computer Programs' [1998] *EIPR* 10.

WJ Gordon, 'Fair Use as Market Failure: A Structural and Economic Analysis of the *Betamax* Case and its Predecessors' (1982) 82 *Columbia L Rev* 1600.

WJ Gordon, 'An Inquiry into the Merits of Copyright: The Challenges of Consistency, Consent and Encouragement Theory' (1989) 41 *Stanford L Rev* 1343.

WJ Gordon, 'A Property Right in Self-Expression: Equality and Individualism in the Natural Law of Intellectual Property' (1993) 102 *Yale L J* 1533.

WJ Gordon, 'On the Economics of Copyright, Restitution, and "Fair Use": Systematic Versus Case-by-Case Responses to Market Failure' (1997) 8 *Journal of Law & Information Science* 7.

G Greenleaf, 'Intellectual Property and Data Protection' (1988) 62 *ALJ* 630.

JM Griem, 'Against a *Sui Generis* System of Intellectual Property for Computer Software' (1993) 22 *Hofstra L Rev* 145.

J Griffiths, 'Preserving Judicial Freedom of Movement—Interpreting Fair Dealing in Copyright Law' [2000] *IPQ* 164.

J Griffiths, 'Copyright Law after *Ashdown*—Time to Deal Fairly with the Public' [2002] *IPQ* 240.

FW Grosheide, 'Database Protection—the European Way' (2002) 8 *Wash. U J L & Pol'y* 39.

IR Gross, 'A New Framework for Software Protection: Distinguishing between Interactive and Non-Interactive aspects of Computer Programs' (1994) 20 *Rutgers Computers & Technology L J* 107.

M Grotticelli, 'The DTV Consumer' in ch 7: Delivery & Duplication in *The Guide to Digital Television* at http://www.digitaltelevision.com/dtvbook/ch7.shtml.

GK Hadfield, 'The Economics of Copyright: an Historical Perspective' (1995) 38 *Copyright L Symp* 1.

M Haftke, 'Net Liability: Is an Exemption from Liability for On-Line Service Providers Required' [1996] 2 *Entertainment L Rev* 47.

M Haftke, '*Pro Sieben Media AG v Carlton UK Television Ltd and Twenty-Twenty Vision Ltd*' [1999] *Entertainment L Rev* 118.

E Hagen, 'On-Line Service Provider Liability: the Latest US Copyright Conundrum' [1996] 7 *Entertainment L Rev* 274.

CW Hager, 'Apples & Oranges: Reverse Engineering as a Fair Use after *Atari v Nintendo* and *Sega v Accolade*' (1994) 20 *Rutgers Computer & Technology L J* 259.

RL Hails, 'Liability of On-line Service Providers Resulting from Copyright Infringement Performed by their Subscribers' [1996] 5 *EIPR* 304.

M Hart, 'The Future of Copyright Protection in the Digital Networked Age' (1999/2000) *Copyright World* 17.

M Hart, 'The Copyright in the Information Society Directive: an Overview' [2002] *EIPR* 58.

M Hart and S Holmes, 'Implementation of the Copyright Directive in the United Kingdom' (2004) 26 *EIPR* 254.

R Hart, 'Interfaces, Interoperability and Maintenance' [1991] *EIPR* 111.

C Hawkins, 'Technological Measures: Saviour or Saboteur of the Public Domain?' (1998) 9 *Journal of Law & Information Science* 45.

DL Hayes, 'Advanced Copyright Issues on the Internet' (1998) 7 *Texas Intellectual Property L J* 1.

W Hayhurst, 'Creativity as an Aspect of Originality: Copyright in Works that are Included in Other works' [2003] *EIPR* 326.

C Heath, 'Multimedia and Urheberrecht in Japan' [1995] *GRUR* Int 843.

T Heide, 'Reinterpreting the Right of Integrity under Article 6bis of the Berne Convention' (1997) 31 *Copyright Bull* 5.

T Heide, 'The Berne Three-Step Test and the Proposed Copyright Directive' [1999] 3 *EIPR* 105.

T Heide, 'The Approach to Innovation under the Proposed Copyright Directive: Time for Mandatory Exceptions?' [2000] *IPQ* 215.

TMS Hemnes, 'The Adaptation of Copyright Law to Video Games' (1982) 131 *University of Pennsylvania Law Review* 171.

J Hennigan, 'Copyright—Just what is the meaning of Incidental?' [2003] *Entertainment L Rev* 215.

M Henry, 'Multimedia: Mythology, Metaphor and Reality' [1995] 3 *Entertainment L Rev* 79.

EC Hettinger, 'Justifying Intellectual Property' (1989) 18 *Philosophy & Public Affairs* 31.

JB Hicks, 'Copyright and Computer Databases: Is Traditional Compilation Law Adequate?' (1990) 37 *Copyright L Symp* 85.

N Higham, 'The New Challenges of Digitisation' (1993) 15 *EIPR* 355.

T Hoeren, 'The Answer to the Machine is in the Machine: Technical Devices for Copyright Management in the Digital Arena' (1995) 4 *Law Computer & Artificial Intelligence* 175.

T Hoeren, 'UCC Article 2B and the Impact on Copyright Licensing—A European Perspective' (1998/1999) 2 *Intl J of Communications L & Policy* at http://www.digital-law.net/IJCLP/index.html.

M Holderness, 'Moral Rights and Authors' Rights: the Keys to the Information Age' (1998) *J of Information, L & Technology* at http://elj.warwick.ac.uk/jilt/infosoc/98_1hold/.

D Horowitz, 'Film Creators and Producers vis-à-vis the New Media: Reflections on the State of Authors' Rights in Audio Visual Works' (1989) 13 *Columbia-VLA J L & Arts* 157.

PB Hugenholtz, 'Caching and Copyright: The Right of Temporary Copying' [2000] *EIPR* 482.

PB Hugenholtz, 'Why the Copyright Directive is Unimportant, and Possibly Invalid' [2000] *EIPR* 499.

PB Hugenholtz, 'The New Database Right: Early Case Law from Europe' paper presented at *Ninth Annual Conference on Intl IP Law & Policy*, Fordham University School of Law, New York, 19–20 April 2001, available at www.ivir.nl.

PB Hugenholtz, 'The Database Right File' available at www.ivir.nl.

PB Hugenholtz, 'Program Schedules, Event Data and Telephone Subscriber Listings under the Database Directive' Paper presented at Fordham University School of Law *11th Annual Conference on Intl IP Law & Policy*, 14–25 April 2003 available at www.ivir.nl.

J Hughes and M Parry, 'An Unsettling Feeling: A Second View of the *Norowzian* Decision' [2000] *Entertainment L Rev* 56.

J Hughes, 'The Philosophy of Intellectual Property' (1988) 77 *Georgetown L J* 287.

GM Hunsucker, 'The European Database Directive: Regional Stepping Stone to an International Model?' (1997) 7 *Fordham Intellectual Property Media & Entertainment L J* 697.

D Hunter, '"Look and Feel" Computer Copyright in the United States and Australia' [1992] 3 *AIPJ* 63.

D Hunter, 'Recent US Computer Copyright Cases and the Australian Law: The Fourth International Conference on Artificial Intelligence and Law' (1994) 5 *Journal of Law & Information Science* 114.

M Jackson, 'Linking Copyright to Homepages' (1997) 49 *Federal Communications L J* 731.

M James, 'Some Joy at Last for Cinematographers' [2000] *EIPR* 131.

S John, 'What Rights do Record Companies have on the Information Superhighway' [1996] 2 *EIPR* 74.

P Johnson, 'One Small Step or One Giant Leap?' [2004] *EIPR* 265.

L Jones, 'An Artist's Entry into Cyberspace: Intellectual Property on the Internet' [2000] *EIPR* 79.

R Jones, 'Legal Pluralism and the Adjudication of Internet Disputes' (1999) 13 *Intl Rev of L, Computers and Technology* 49.

S Jones, 'Multimedia and the Superhighway: Exploring the Rights Minefield' (1996) 1 *Communications Law* 28.

R Julia-Barcelo, 'Liability for On-Line Intermediaries: A European Perspective' [1998] *EIPR* 453.

DS Karjala, 'The Relative Roles of Patent and Copyright in the Protection of Computer Programs' (1998) 27 *John Marshall J of Computer & Information L* 41.

P Karlen, 'Time and Copyright' [1997] *Copyright World* 16.

GWG Karnell, 'The European Sui Generis Protection of Databases: Nordic and UK Law Approaching the Court of the European Communities—Some Comparative Reflections' (2002) 49 *J Copyright Soc'y USA* 983.

L Kaye, 'The Proposed EU Directive For the Legal Protection of Databases: A Cornerstone of the Information Society' [1995] *EIPR* 583.

G Kennedy, 'Copyright in the Information Society: A World of More Copies and Rights?' (1999) 93 *Copyright World* 15.

P Kern, 'The EC "Common Position" on Copyright Applicable to Satellite Broadcasting and Cable Retransmission' [1993] 8 *EIPR* 276.

C Kervégant, 'Are Copyright and Droit d'Auteur Viable in the Light of Information Technology?' [1996] 10(1) *Intl Rev of L, Comp & Tech* 55.

Z Kitagawa, 'Comment on *A Manifesto Concerning the Legal Protection of Computer Programs*' (1994) 94 *Columbia L Rev* 2610.

E W Kitch, 'Elementary and Persistent Errors in the Economic Analysis of Intellectual Property' (2000) 53 *Vand L Rev* 1727.

P Knight, 'The impact of Copyright Law on the Use of New Multimedia Technology' (1994) 2(5) *Intl Computer Lawyer* 2.

C Koboldt, 'The EU Directive on the Legal Protection of Databases and the Incentives to Update: an Economic Analysis' (1997) 17 *Intl Rev L & Econ* 127.

F Koch, 'Software—Urhebrrechtsschutz für Multimedia—Anwendungen' [1995] *GRUR* 459.

R Kreile and J Becker, 'Multimedia und die Praxis der Lizenzierung von Urheberrechten' [1996] *Gewerblicher Rechtsschutz und Urheberrecht Internationaler Teil* 677.

R Kreile and D Westphal, 'Multimedia und das Filmbearbeitungsrecht' [1996] *GRUR* 254.

B Kremer, 'Copyright and Computer Programs: *Data Access v Powerflex* before the High Court' (1998) 20 *Sydney L Rev* 296.

B Kremer, 'Copyright Protection of Computer Programs: *Data Access v Powerflex*' [2000] *EIPR* 292.

M Kretschmer, 'Digital Copyright: the End of an Era' (2003) 25 *EIPR* 333.

E R Kroker, 'The Computer Directive and the Balance of Rights' [1997] *EIPR* 247.

LJ Lacey, 'Of Bread and Roses and Copyright' [1989] *Duke L J* 1532.

D Ladd, 'Securing the Future of Copyright: A Humanist Endeavor' (1985) 16 *IIC* 76.

H Laddie, 'Copyright: Over-Strength, Over-Regulated, Over-Rated?' [1996] 5 *EIPR* 253.

J Lahore and F Phillips, 'The Notion of an Audiovisual Work: International and Comparative Law' [1996] 7 *AIPJ* 208.

S Lai, 'Database Protection in the United Kingdom: the New Deal and its Effects on Software Protection' [1998] 1 *EIPR* 32.

S Lai, 'The Impact of the Recent WIPO Copyright Treaty and Other Initiatives on Software Copyright in the United Kingdom' [1998b] *IPQ* 35.

S Lai, 'Recent Developments in Copyright, Database Protection and (On-line) Licensing' (1999) 7 *Intl J of L & Information Technology* 73.

S Lai, 'Substantive Issues of Copyright Protection in a Networked Environment' (1999b) 8 *Information & Communications Technology Law* 127.

S Lai, 'Digital Copyright and Watermarking' [1999c]' *EIPR* 171.

J Lambrick, 'Hyperlinking, Framing and Copyright—Waiting for the Dust to Settle' (1998) 37 *Computers & Law* 11.

J Lambrick, 'Protecting Content in an On-Line Environment' (1999) 1(2) *Digital Technology L J* at http://wwwlaw.murdoch.edu.au/dtlj/.

WM Landes and RA Posner, 'An Economic Analysis of Copyright Law' (1989) 28 *J Legal Stud* 325.

LM Lavenue, 'Database Rights and Technical Data Rights: the Expansion of Intellectual Property for the Protection of Databases' (1998) 38 *Santa Clara L Rev. 1.*

M Lehmann, 'The European Database Directive and Its Implementation into German Law' (1998) 29 *IIC* 776.

J Leland, 'Internet Video: Broadcasting Bandwidth Converges On the Web's Interactivity' ch 7: Delivery & Duplication in *The Guide to Digital Television* at http://www.digitaltelevision.com/dtvbook/ch7.shtml.

P Leonard, 'Beyond the Future—Multimedia and the Law' (1994) 7 *Australian Intellectual Property L Bulletin* 105.

PN Leval, 'Toward a Fair Use Standard' (1990) 103 *Harvard L Rev* 1105.

K Liebman, 'Opinion: Untying the Knot—Copyright Law and the New Technologies' (1993) 1 *Intl J of L & Information Technology* 225.

YF Lim, 'Multimedia: Authorisers of Copyright Infringement?' (1994) 5 *Journal of Law & Information Science* 306.

D Lindsay, 'Copyright Protection of Electronic Databases' (1993) 4 *Journal of Law & Information Science* 287.

J Lipton, 'A Revised "Property" Concept for the New Millennium?' (1999) 7 *Intl J of L & Information Technology* 171.

J Lipton, 'Databases as Intellectual Property: New Legal Approaches' [2003] *EIPR* 139.

J Lipton, 'Balancing Private Rights and Public Policies: Reconceptualizing Property in Databases' (2003b) *Berkeley Technology L J* 773.

J Litman, 'The Public Domain' (1990) 39 *Em L J* 965.

J Litman, 'The Exclusive Right to Read' (1994) 13 *Cardozo Arts & Ent L J* 29.

G Llewelyn, 'Does Copyright Law Recognise a Right to Repair' (1999) 21 *EIPR* 596.

I Lloyd, 'Software Patents After Fujitsu: New Directions or (another) Missed Opportunity?' [1997] 2 *J of Information, L & Technology* at http://elj.warwick.ac.uk/jilt/cases/97_2fuji/.

U Loewenheim, 'Multimedia and the European Copyright Law' (1996) 27 *IIC* 41.

DE Long, 'The Protection of Information Technology in a Culturally Diverse Marketplace' (1996) 25 *John Marshall J of Computer & Information L* 129.

L Longdin, 'Copyright Protection for Computerized Compilations: A Cautionary Tale From New Zealand' (1997) 5 *Intl J of L & Information Technology* 249.

P Loughlan, 'Music on Hold: The Case of Copyright and the Telephone: *Telstra Corporation Ltd v Australasian Performing Rights Association Ltd*' (1996) 18 *Sydney L Rev* 342.

P Loughlan, 'Patents: Breaking into the Loop' (1998) 20 *Sydney L Rev* 553.

S Loughnan, 'Service Provider Liability for User Copyright Infringement on the Internet' [1997] 8 *AIPJ* 18.

D Loundy, 'Revising the Copyright Law for Electronic Publishing' (1995) 14 *John Marshall J of Computer & Information L* 1.

R Lubens, 'Survey of Developments in European Database Protection' (2003) 18 *Berkeley Technology L J* 447.

A Lucas, 'Intellectual Property and Global Information Infrastructure' (1998) 32 *Copyright Bull* 3.

A Macandrew, 'Managing Rights in the Interactive Age' (1995) 52 *Managing Intellectual Property* 10.

E Mackaay, 'Legal Hybrids: Beyond Property and Monopoly' (1994) 94 *Columbia L Rev* 2630.

F Macmillan and M Blakeney, 'The Copyright Liability of Communications Carriers' [1997] 3 *J of Information, L & Technology* at http://elj.warwick.ac.uk/jilt/commsreg/97_3macm/.

F Macmillan and M Blakeney, 'Internet and Communication Carriers' Copyright Liability' [1998] 2 *EIPR* 52.

F Macmillan, 'Striking the Copyright Balance in the Digital Environment' [1999] 12 ICCLR 350.

F Macmillan, 'Adapting the Copyright Exceptions to the Digital Environment' [1999b] Digital Technology L J at http://wwwlaw.murdoch.edu.au/dtlj/.

MJ Madison, 'Legal-ware: Contract and Copyright in the Digital Age' (1998) 67 *Ford L Rev* 1025.

JV Mahon, 'A Commentary on Proposals for Copyright Protection on the National Information Infrastructure' (1996) 22 *Rutgers Computer & Technology L J* 233.

AM Major, 'Copyright Law Tackles Yet Another Challenge: The Electronic Frontier of the World Wide Web' (1998) 24 *Rutgers Computer & Technology L J* 75.

P Mallam, 'Copyright and the Information Superhighway: Some Future Challenges' [1995] 6 *Entertainment L Rev* 234.

JJ Marcellino and M Blakeslee, 'Fair Use in the Context of a Global Computer Network—Is a Copyright Grab Really Going On?' [1997] 6 *Information & Communications Technology Law* 137.

A Mason, 'The Users' Perspective on Issues Arising in Proposals for the Reform of the Law of Copyright' (1997) 19 *Sydney L Rev* 65.

A Mason, 'Public-Interest Objectives and the Law of Copyright' (1998) 9 *Journal of Law & Information Science* 7.

V McEvedy, 'The DMCA and the E-Commerce Directive' [2002] EIPR 65.

J McKeough, 'Semi Conductor Chip Protection: Copyright or *Sui Generis?*' (1986) 9 *University of New South Wales Law Journal* 101.

SG McKnight, 'Substantial Similarity between Video Games: An Old Copyright Problem in a New Medium' (1983) 36 *Vand L Review* 1277.

HJ Meeker, 'Multimedia and Copyright' (1994) 20 *Rutgers Computer & Technology L J* 375.

P Menell, 'The Challenges of Reforming Intellectual Property Protection for Computer Software' (1994) 94 *Columbia L Rev* 2644.

RP Merges, 'The End of Friction? Property Rights and Contract in the "Newtonian" World of On-Line Commerce' (1997) 12(1) *Berkeley Technology L J* at http://www.law.berkeley.edu/journals/btlj/articles/vol12.html.

G Middleton, 'Australia—Copyright in Telephone Directories' [2002] 24(10) *EIPR* 161–64.

C Mileson, 'The Multimedia Challenge' (1995) 69 *Law Inst J* 127.

A Millé, 'Copyright in the Cyberspace Era' (1997) 10 *EIPR* 570.

ML Mills, 'New Technology and the Limitations of Copyright law: An Argument for Finding Alternatives to Copyright Legislation in an Era of Rapid Technological Change' (1989) 65 *Chi-Kent L Rev* 307.

A Monotti, 'Copyright Protection of Computerised Databases' [1992] 3 *AIPJ* 135.

A Monotti, 'The Extent of Copyright Protection for Compilations of Artistic Works' [1993] 5 *EIPR* 156.

A Monotti, 'Works Stored in Computer Memory: Databases and the CLRC Draft Report' (1993b) 4 *Journal of Law & Information Science* 265.

A Monotti, 'University Copyright in the Digital Age: Balancing and Exploiting Rights in Computer Programs, Web-Based Materials, Databases and Multimedia in Australian Universities' [2002] *EIPR* 251.

AD Moore, 'Intellectual Property: Theory, Privilege, and Pragmatism' (2003) 16 *Canadian J of L & Jurisprudence* 191.

L Moran, 'Distance Education, Copyright and Communication in the Information Society' (1999) 33 *Copyright Bull* 3.

A Morrison, 'Hijack on the Road to Xanadu: The Infringement of Copyright in HTML Documents via Networked Computers and the Legitimacy of Browsing Hypermedia Documents' [1999] 1 *J of Information, L & Technology* at http://elj.warwick.ac.uk/jilt/99–1/morrison.html.

N Muenchinger, 'French Law and Practice Concerning Multimedia and Telecommunications' [1996] 4 *EIPR* 186.

K Murray, 'The Draft Directive on the Harmonisation of Certain Aspects of Copyright' [1998] *Entertainment L Rev* 190.

B Napier, 'The Future of Information Technology Law' (1992) 51 *Cambridge L J* 46.

S Norman, 'The Electronic Environment: the Librarian's View' [1996] *EIPR* 71.

MJ O'Connor, 'Squeezing into Traditional Frames: Intellectual Property Law in the Shadow of the Information Society' (1998) 12 *IPJ* 285.

S Olswang, 'Accessright: an Evolutionary Path for Copyright into the Digital Era?' [1995] 5 *EIPR* 215.

MA O'Rourke, 'Copyright Preemption After the *ProCD* Case: A Market-Based Approach' (1997) 12(1) *Berkeley Technology L J* at http://www.law.berkeley.edu/journals/btlj/articles/vol12.html.

D Panethiere, 'The Basis for Copyright Infringement Liability: The Law in Common Law Jurisdictions' (1997) 13 *EIPR* 13.

LR Patterson, 'Free Speech, Copyright, and Fair Use' (1987) 40 *Vand L Rev* 1.

H Paynter and R Foreman, 'Liability of Internet Service Providers for Copyright Infringement' (1998) 21 (2) *U New South Wales L J* 578.

G Pedde, 'Multimedia Works under Italian Copyright Law and Contractual Practice' [1988] 2 *Ent LR* 39.

S Pep, 'Multimedia Computing: Copyright Law's "Last Stand"' (1995) 12 *Touro L Rev* 143.

J Perritt, 'Protecting Technology Over Copyright: A Step Too Far' (2003) 14 *Entertainment L Rev* 1.

J Phillips and L Bently, 'Copyright Issues: The Mysteries of Section 18' [1999] 3 *EIPR* 133.

J Phillips, 'Fair Stealing and the Teddy Bears' Picnic' [1999] *Entertainment L Rev* 57.

JC Phillips, '*Sui Generis* Intellectual Property Protection for Computer Software' (1992) 60 *George Washington L Rev* 997.

JH Pilarski, 'User Interfaces and the Idea—Expression Dichotomy, or Are the Copyright Law Users Friendly?' (1990) 37 *Copyright L Symp* 45.

J Pila and A Christie, 'The Literary Work Within Copyright Law: An Analysis of its Present and Future Status' (1999) 13 *IPJ* 133.

F Pollaud-Dulian, 'The Authors of Audiovisual Works' (1996) 169 *RIDA* 51.

SK Pomeroy, 'Promoting the Progress of Science and the Useful Arts in the Digital Domain: Copyright, Computer Bulletin Board, and Liability for Infringement by Others' (1996) 45 *Em L J* 1035.

H Porter, 'A "Dramatic Work" Includes…a Film' [2000] *Entertainment L Rev* 50.

M Powell, 'The European Union's Database Directive: an International Antidote to the Side Effects of *Feist*?' (1997) 20 *Fordham Intl L J* 1215.

MJ Radin, 'Property and Personhood' (1982) 34 *Stanford L Rev* 957.

M Radcliffe, 'The Technical Provisions of the DMCA' [1999] *Copyright World* 25.

JH Reichman, 'Legal Hybrids between the Patent and Copyright Paradigms' (1994) 94 *Columbia L Rev* 2432.

JH Reichman and P Samuelson, 'Intellectual Property Rights in Data?' (1997) 50 *Vand L Rev* 51.

M Rennie, 'EU Copyright Directive: May 1999 Amendments to Appease Some Industry Sectors' (1999) 5(5) *CTLR* 123.

PL Rich, 'When Technology and the Law Collide—Look and Feel Copyright Evolves' (1988) 16 *Western State U L Rev* 183.

M Richardson, '*Sui Generis* Intellectual Property Law Reform: Issues for Australia' (2001) 32 *VUWLR* 19.

S Ricketson, 'Moral Rights and the *Droit de Suite*: International Conditions and Australian Obligations' [1990] 3 *Entertainment L Rev* 78.

S Ricketson, 'The Boundaries of Copyright: Its Proper Limitations and Exceptions: International Conventions and Treaties' [1999] *IPQ* 56.

S Ricketson, 'Simplifying Copyright Law: Proposals from Down Under' [1999b] *EIPR* 537.

T Rivers, 'Norowzian Revisited' [2000] *EIPR* 389.

SJ Rizzi, 'The Digital Millennium Copyright Act: Y2K Compliant or Bugged?' [1998] *Copyright World* 18.

H Rosenblatt, 'Protocol to the Berne Convention: The WIPO Diplomatic Conference—the Birth of Two New Treaties' (1997) 13 *CL&SR* 307.

A Ross, 'The Future of EU Copyright Law: The Amended Proposal for a Directive on Copyright and related Rights in the Information Society' (1999) 4 *Communications Law* 128.

A Ross, 'Implementation of the Copyright Harmonisation Directive in the United Kingdom' (2004) 15 *Entertainment L Rev* 47.

W Rothnie, 'Idea and Expression in a Digital World' [1998] 9 *Journal of Law & Information Science* 59.

RH Rotsein, 'Beyond Metaphor: Copyright Infringement and the Fiction of the Work' (1993) 68 *Chi-Kent L Rev* 725.

W Rumphorst, 'Fine Tuning Copyright for the Information Society' [1996] *EIPR* 79.

M Sableman, 'Link Law: the Emerging Law of Internet Hyperlinks' (1999) 4 *Communication Law & Policy* 557.

C Saez, 'Enforcing Copyright in the Age of Multimedia' (1995) 21 *Rutgers Computer & Technology L J* 351.

H Sakkers, 'Licensing and Exploiting Rights in Multimedia Products' (1995) 11 *CL&SR* 244.

P Samuelson, 'The Copyright Grab' Issue 4.01 *Wired Magazine* January 1996.

P Samuelson, 'Digital Media and the Changing Face of Intellectual Property' (1990) 16 *Rutgers Computer & Technology L J* 323.

P Samuelson, *et al*, 'A Manifesto Concerning the Legal Protection of Computer Programs' (1994) 94 *Columbia L Rev* 2308.

P Samuelson, 'Authors' Rights in Cyberspace: Are New International Rules Needed?' (1996) 30 *Copyright Bull* 3.

P Samuelson, 'The Quest for Enabling Metaphors for Law and Lawyering in the Information Age' (1996b) 94 *Mich L Rev* 2029.

P Samuelson, 'The US Digital Agenda at WIPO' (1997) 37 *Virginia J Intl L* 369.

P Samuelson, 'Challenges for the World Intellectual Property Organization and the Trade-Related Aspects of Intellectual Property Rights Council in Regulating Intellectual Property Rights in the Information Age' [1999] *EIPR* 578.

S Saxby, 'A Jurisprudence for Information Technology Law' (1994) 2 *Intl J of L & Information Technology* 1.

C Schaal, 'The Copyright Exceptions of Art 5(2)(a) and (b) of the EU Directive 2001/29' (2003) 14 *Entertainment L Rev* 117.

E Schlachter, 'Cyberspace, the Free Market and the Free Marketplace of Ideas: Recognising Legal Differences in Computer Bulletin Board Functions' (1993) 16 *Hastings Comm & Ent L J* 89.

E Schlachter, 'The Intellectual Property Renaissance in Cyberspace: Why Copyright Law Could be Unimportant on the Internet' (1997) 12(1) *Berkeley Technology L J* at http://www.law.berkeley.edu/journals/btlj/articles/vol12.html.

M Scott and S Talbott, 'Interactive Multimedia: What is it, Why is it Important and What does One Need to Know About It?' [1993] 8 *EIPR* 284.

C Sellars, 'Digital Rights Management Systems: Recent European Issues' (2003) 14 *Entertainment L Rev* 5.

D Self, 'Copyright Protection for the Information Superhighway' (1994) 11 *EIPR* 465.

M Sherwood-Edwards, 'The Redundancy of Originality' (1994) 25 *IIC* 658.

M Sherwood-Edwards, 'It's Cruel to be Clear: Clearing Rights in a Multimedia World' [1995] 6 *Entertainment L Rev* 3.

A D Shuz, 'An Overview of the Berne Convention—Generally and in Relation to Computer Programs and Semiconductor Chips' (1993) 9 *Computer Law & Practice* 115.

K Siver, 'Good Samaritans in Cyberspace' (1997) 23 *Rutgers Computer & Technology L J* 1.

J Smillie, 'Digital Copyright Reform in New Zealand' [2004] *EIPR* 302.

G Smirnoff III, 'Copyright on the Internet: A Critique of the White Paper's Recommendation for updating the Copyright Act and How the Courts are Already Filling in its Most Important Shortcoming, On-Line Service Provider Liability' (1996) 44 *Clev State L Rev* 197.

S Smith, 'Legal Protection of Factual Compilations and Databases in England—How Will the Database Directive Change the Law In This Area' [1997] *IPQ* 450.

H M Spector, 'An Outline of a Theory Justifying Intellectual and Industrial Property Rights' (1989) 11 *EIPR* 270.

RD Sprague, 'Multimedia: the Convergence of New Technologies and Traditional Copyright Issues' (1994) 71 *Denv U L Rev* 635.

I Stamatoudi, '"Joy" for the Claimant: Can a Film Also Be Protected as a Dramatic Work?' [2000] *IPQ* 117.

M Stefik, 'Shifting the Possible: How Trusted Systems and Digital Property Rights Challenge us to Rethink Digital Publishing' (1997) 12 *Berkeley Technology L J* at http://www.law.berkeley.edu/journals/btlj/articles/vol12.html.

S Stokes, 'The UK Implementation of the Information Society Copyright Directive: Current Issues and Some Guidance for Business' (2004) 10 *CTLR* 5.

S Strasser, 'Industrious Effort is Enough' [2002] *EIPR* 599.

S Strömholm, 'Droit Moral—the International and Comparative Scene from a Scandinavian Viewpoint' (1983) 14 *IIC* 1.

J Swinson, 'Software Patents in the United States' (1993) 4 *Journal of Law & Information Science* 116.

DP Tackaberry, 'Canada: Copyright—Originality—Communication to Public By Telecommunication' (2003) 14(3) *Entertainment L Rev* N17–18.

S Talbott, 'Content and Licensing issues in Multimedia Agreements' (1995) 11 *CL&SR* 250.

V Testa, 'DVD: Risk and Benefits for the European Audiovisual Market' [1999] *Entertainment L Rev* 71.

N Thakur, 'Database Protection in the European Union and the United States: the European Database Directive as an Optimum Global Model?' [2001] *IPQ* 100.

D Thi Phan, 'Will Fair Use Function on the Internet?' (1998) 98 *Columbia L Rev* 169.

A Thomas, 'MP3—Devil or Angel: an Analysis of Compression' [1999] *Entertainment L Rev* 202.

J Thomas, 'Copyright in Australia's "New Communications Environment": Convergence, Transmission Rights and the Internet' (1995) 6 *Journal of Law & Information Science* 3.

C Thorne, 'Copyright and Multimedia Products—Fitting a Round Peg in a Square Hole' (1995) issue 49 *Copyright World* 18.

C Thorne, 'EC Green Paper on Copyright and Related Rights in the Information Society' (1995b) issue 54 *Copyright World* 14.

P Treyde, 'Simplification of the Exceptions to the Exclusive Rights Comprising Copyright' (1998) 9 *Journal of Law & Information Science* 77.

I Trotter Hardy, 'The Proper Legal Regime for "Cyberspace"' (1994) 55 *U of Pitt L Rev* 993.

I Trotter Hardy, 'Contracts, Copyright and Preemption in a Digital World' (1995) 1 *Richmond J of L & Technology* at http://www.richmond.edu/jolt/v1i1/hardy.html.

J Tunbridge, 'Canada Defines "Originality" and Specifies the Limits of "Fair Dealing"' [2004] *EIPR* 318.

M Turner, 'Do the Old Legal Categories Fit the New Multimedia Products? A Multimedia CD-Rom as a Film' [1995] *EIPR* 107.

V Vanovermeire, 'The Concept of the Lawful User in the Database Directive' (2000) 31 *IIC* 63.

WA Van Caenegam, 'Copyright, Communications and New Technologies' (1995) 23 *Federal L Rev* 322.

W Van Caenegam, 'Communication Issues in Copyright Reform' (1995b) 13 *Copy Rep* 72.

J-P Vanden Dorpe, 'Incidental Reproduction: The Implications of the Draft Copyright Directive' [1999] *Entertainment L Rev* 234.

D Van der Merwe, 'The Dematerialization of Print and the Fate of Copyright' (1999) 13(3) *Intl Rev of L, Comp & Tech* 303.

R Versteeg, 'Sparks in the Tinderbox: *Feist*, "Creativity" and the Legislative History of the 1976 Copyright Act' (1995) 56 *U of Pittsburgh L Rev* 549.

TC Vinje, 'The New WIPO Copyright Treaty: A Happy Result in Geneva' [1997] 5 *EIPR* 230.

S Von Lewinski, 'A Successful Step towards Copyright and Related Rights in the Information Age: The New EC Proposal for a Harmonisation Directive' [1998] *EIPR* 135.

AB Wagner, 'Patenting Computer Science: Are Computer Instruction Writings Patentable?' (1998) 27 *John Marshall J of Computer & Information L* 5.

J Wald, 'Legislating the Golden Rule: Achieving Comparable Protection Under the European Union Database Directive' (2002) *25 Fordham Intl LJ* 987.

J Waldron, 'From Authors to Copiers: Individual Rights and Social Values in Intellectual Property' (1993) 68 *Chicago-Kent L Rev* 841.

B Wassom, 'Copyright Implications of "Unconventional Linking" on the World Wide Web: Framing, Deep Linking and Inlining' (1998) 49 *Case Western Reserve L Rev* 181.

K Weatherall, 'An End to Private Communications in Copyright? the Expansion of Rights to Communicate Works to the Public' [1999] *EIPR* 342; [1999] *EIPR* 398.

D Webber, 'Software Patents: A New Era in Australia and the United States?' [1993] 5 *EIPR* 181.

G Wei, 'Multimedia and Intellectual and Industrial Property Rights in Singapore' (1995) 3 *Intl J of L & Information Technology* 214.

G Wei, 'Telephone Directories and Databases: The Policy at the Helm of Copyright Law and a Tale of Two Cities' [2004] *IPQ* 316.

L Weinreb, 'Fair's Fair: A Comment on the Fair Use Doctrine' (1990) 103 *Harvard L Rev* 1137.

G Westkamp, 'Balancing Database *Sui Generis* Right Protection with European Monopoly Control under Article 82 EC' [2001] *ECLR* 13.

G Westkamp, 'Protecting Databases Under US and European Law—Methodical Approaches to the Protection of Investments between Unfair Competition and Intellectual Property Concepts' (2003) 34 *IIC* 772.

S Whalley, 'The Internet: A Threat to Copyright?' (1997/1998) issue 76 *Copyright World* 29.

M Wyburn, 'Copyright, Databases and Misuse of Market Power' (1997) 15 *Copy Rep* 46.

N Yastreboff, 'Copyright for Online Databases on the Internet' (1996) 9 *Australian Intellectual Property L Bulletin* 33.

Reports and Working papers

Australia Copyright Law Review Committee, *Report on Reprographic Reproduction* (1976).

Australia Copyright Convergence Group, *Highways to Change: Copyright in the New Communications Environment* (AGPS, Canberra, 1994).

Australia Copyright Law Review Committee, *Report on Journalists' Copyright* (AGD, Canberra, 1994).

Australia Copyright Law Review Committee, *Final Report on Computer Software Protection* (AGD, Canberra, 1995).

Australia Attorney-General's Department and Department of Communication and the Arts, *Copyright Reform and the Digital Agenda* (AGPS, Canberra, 1997).

Australia Copyright Law Review Committee, *Simplification of the Copyright Act 1968, Part 1: Exceptions to the Exclusive Rights of Copyright Owners* (AGD, Canberra, 1998).

Australia Copyright Law Review Committee, *Simplification of the Copyright Act 1968: Part 2: Categorisation of Subject Matter and Exclusive Rights and Other Issues* (AGD, Canberra, 1999).

Australia House of Representatives Standing Committee on Legal and Constitutional Affairs, *Advisory Report on the Copyright Amendment (Digital Agenda) Bill 1999* (Canberra: Commonwealth Parliament, November 1999), available at http://www.aph.gov.au/house/committee/laca/digitalagenda/contents.htm.

Australia Intellectual Property and Competition Review Committee, *Review of Intellectual Property Legislation under the Competition Principles Agreement* (Canberra, 2000).

Business Software Alliance, *First Annual BSA and IDC Global Software Piracy Study* (July 2004) available at http://www.bsa.org/globalstudy/.

Business Software Alliance, *The Thriving European Software Industry*, available at http://global.bsa.org/usa/policyres/admin/2002–04–17.108.pdf.

EC, *Green Paper on Copyright and Related Rights in the Information Society* Brussels, 19 July 1995 COM (95) 382 final.

EC, *Follow-up to the Green Paper on Copyright and Related Rights in the Information Society*, Brussels, 20 November 1996 COM (96) 586 final.

EC, *Report from the Commission to the Council, the European Parliament and the Economic and Social Committee on the implementation and effects of Directive 91/250/EEC on the Legal Protection of Computer Programs*, Brussels 10 April 2000 COM (2000) 199 Final, p 12.

EC, *First Report on the application of Directive 2000/31/EC of the European Parliament and of the Council of 8 June 2000 on certain aspects of the information society, in particular electronic commerce in the Internal Market*, Brussels 21 November 2003 COM (2003) 702 Final.

EC, *Commission Staff Working Paper on the review of the EC Legal Framework in the Field of Copyright and Related Rights*, Brussels, 19 July 2004 SEC (2004) 995.

H Hoegh Guldberg, for Copyright Agency Ltd, *The Economics of Copyright and the Digital Agenda* (November 1999), available at http://www.copyright.com.au/reports.htm.

Institute for Information Law, *Contracts and Copyright Exemptions* (Amsterdam, 1997).

Institute for Information Law, *Rights, Limitations and Exceptions: Striking a Proper Balance* (Amsterdam, 1997).

Institute for Information Law, *Liability for On-line Intermediaries* (Amsterdam, 1997).

Institute for Information Law, *The Law and Practice of Digital Encryption* (Amsterdam, 1998).

Institute for Information Law, *Watermarking Technology for Copyright Protection: General Requirements and Interoperability* (Amsterdam, 1998).

Institute for Information Law, *Privacy, Data Protection and Copyright: Their Interaction in the Context of Electronic Copyright Management Systems* (Amsterdam, 1998).

Institute for Information Law, *Formation and Validity of On-Line Contracts* (Amsterdam, 1998).

K Koelman and PB Hugenholtz, *Online Service Provider Liability for Copyright Infringement for WIPO Workshop on Service Provider Liability* (Geneva, 1999).

Publishers Association and Joint Information Systems Committee, *Guidelines for Fair Dealing in an Electronic Environment* (1998), available at http://www.publishers.org.uk and http://www.jisc.ac.uk.

UK Commission on Intellectual Property Rights, *Integrating Intellectual Property Rights and Development Policy* (2002).

UK, *Consultation on UK Implementation of Directive 2001/29/EC on Copyright and Related Rights in the Information Society: Analysis of Reponses and Government Conclusions* available at http://www.patent.gov.uk/about/consultations/responses/copydirect/index.htm.

DTI, *From Exuberant Youth to Sustainable Maturity: Competitiveness Analysis of the UK Games Software Sector* (2002) available at: www.dti.gov.uk/cii/services/contentindustry/computer_games_leisure_software.shtml.

US Information Infrastructure Task Force, *Intellectual Property and the National Information Infrastructure: the Report of the Working Group on Intellectual Property Rights* (Washington DC, 1997).

US Copyright Office, *Report on Legal Protection of Databases* (1997) at http://www.loc.gov/copyright/reports/.

INDEX